WOMEN'S STUDIES QUARTERLY
VOLUME 50   NUMBERS 1 & 2   SPRING/SUMMER 2022

An educational project of the Feminist Press at the City University of New York, the College of Staten Island, City University of New York, Kingsborough Community College, City University of New York, and Borough of Manhattan Community College, City University of New York, with support from the Center for the Study of Women and Society and the Center for the Humanities at the Graduate Center, City University of New York

EDITORS
Red Washburn, Kingsborough Community College
Brianne Waychoff, Borough of Manhattan Community College

GUEST EDITORS
Mary Frances Phillips, Lehman College, City University of New York
Rashida L. Harrison, Michigan State University
Nicole M. Jackson, Bowling Green State University

POETRY EDITORS
Julie R. Enszer, Cheryl Clarke, and JP Howard

PROSE EDITORS
Marci Blackman, Keisha-Gaye Anderson, and Nicole Shawan Junior

VISUAL ARTS EDITOR
Mel Michelle Lewis

EDITORIAL ASSISTANTS
Kayla Reece
Googie Karrass

EDITORS EMERITAE
Natalie Havlin 2017–2020 ▪ Jillian M. Báez 2017–2020 ▪ Matt Brim 2014–2017
Cynthia Chris 2014–2017 ▪ Amy Herzog 2011–2014 ▪ Joe Rollins 2011–2014
Victoria Pitts-Taylor 2008–2011 ▪ Talia Schaffer 2008–2011 ▪ Cindi Katz 2004–2008
Nancy K. Miller 2004–2008 ▪ Diane Hope 2000–2004 ▪ Janet Zandy 1995–2000
Nancy Porter 1982–1992 ▪ Florence Howe 1972–1982; 1993–1994

The Feminist Press at the City University of New York

EXECUTIVE DIRECTOR & PUBLISHER
Margot Atwell

ART DIRECTOR
Drew Stevens

SENIOR EDITOR
Lauren Rosemary Hook

SENIOR SALES & MARKETING MANAGER
Jisu Kim

ASSISTANT EDITOR
Nick Whitney

WSQ: Women's Studies Quarterly, a peer-reviewed, theme-based journal, is published by the Feminist Press at the City University of New York.

COVER ART
Be Still My Heart by Lennox Commissiong

WEBSITE
feministpress.org/wsq

EDITORIAL CORRESPONDENCE
WSQ: Women's Studies Quarterly, The Feminist Press at the City University of New York, The Graduate Center, 365 Fifth Avenue, Suite 5406, New York, NY 10016; wsqeditorial@gmail.com.

PRINT SUBSCRIPTIONS
Subscribers in the United States: Individuals—$60 for 1 year; $150 for 3 years. Institutions—$85 for 1 year; $225 for 3 years. Subscribers outside the United States: Add $40 per year for delivery. To subscribe or change an address, contact *WSQ* Customer Service, The Feminist Press at the City University of New York, The Graduate Center, 365 Fifth Avenue, Suite 5406, New York, NY 10016; 212-817-7915; info@feministpress.org.

FORTHCOMING ISSUES
50!, Heather Rellihan, Anne Arundel Community College, Jennifer C. Nash,
    Duke University, and Charlene A. Carruthers, Northwestern University
State/Power, Christina B. Hanhardt, University of Maryland, and Dayo F. Gore,
    Georgetown University

RIGHTS & PERMISSIONS
Fred Courtright, The Permissions Company, 570-839-7477; permdude@eclipse.net.

SUBMISSION INFORMATION
For the most up-to-date guidelines, calls for papers, and information concerning forthcoming issues, write to wsqeditors@gmail.com or visit feministpress.org/wsq.

ADVERTISING
For information on display-ad sizes, rates, exchanges, and schedules, please write to *WSQ* Marketing, The Feminist Press at the City University of New York, The Graduate Center, 365 Fifth Avenue, Suite 5406, New York, NY 10016; 212-817-7918; sales@feministpress.org.

ELECTRONIC ACCESS AND SUBSCRIPTIONS
Access to electronic databases containing backlist issues of *WSQ* may be purchased through JSTOR at www.jstor.org. Access to electronic databases containing current issues of *WSQ* may be purchased through Project MUSE at muse.jhu.edu, muse@muse.jhu.edu; and ProQuest at www.il.proquest.com, info@il.proquest.com. Individual electronic subscriptions for *WSQ* may also be purchased through Project MUSE.

ISSN: 0732-1562   ISBN: 978-1-55861-292-1 $25.00

Carolina Rupprecht, The Graduate Center, CUNY
L. Ayu Saraswati, University of Hawai'i
Gunja SenGupta, Brooklyn College
Barbara Shaw, Allegheny College
Lili Shi, Kingsborough Community College
Robyn Spencer, Lehman College
Saadia Toor, College of Staten Island
Laura Westengard, New York City College of Technology, CUNY
Kimberly Williams, Mount Royal University
Kimberly Williams Brown, Vassar College
Karen Winkler, Psychotherapist

This special issue on Black Love
is dedicated to the life, legacy,
and love of bell hooks.

Contents

Editors' Note

Red Washburn and Brianne Waychoff

bell hooks states, "Love is an action, never simply a feeling." This issue, *Black Love*, arrives during a critical moment in the ongoing struggle for racial justice. With the political urgency of the Movement for Black Lives, prison abolition, cops out of Pride, decolonize the curriculum, and bell hooks joining the ancestors, we remember love is a verb. We use this vision to help us imagine a better life in which love transcends rigid concepts of romantic coupledom under capitalism, and instead, expands the thought and practice of love as a community project of mutual aid, trust, care, kindness, compassion, respect, and solidarity across the spectrum of difference. The politics of love holds much promise for honoring self-care, educating for critical consciousness, and promoting social change. Love allows us to hold space for Black people to heal under white supremacy, cisheteropatriarchy, and capitalism, as well as move toward a collective social responsibility to build a better world where we all are free. The guest editors, writers, and artists who contributed to this issue explore the knowledge/power of Black love from different angles of vision that enrich this interdisciplinary area of study in exciting ways. We are indebted to the guest editors Mary Frances Phillips, Rashida L. Harrison, and Nicole M. Jackson for convening this issue. We are delighted to feature work on Black love, nationally and transnationally, ranging from the United States to Nigeria, as well as Trinidad and Tobago. We commend the stellar academic essays on social movements, self-care, and cultural productions, especially centering the writings of Toni Morrison and Audre Lorde. We celebrate the stunning creative writing and visual art by Arisa White, Roya Marsh, and Mel Michelle Lewis, among other notable contributors. We are grateful for this scholarship and activism.

We want to thank *WSQ*, including the editorial board; poetry, prose, and

WSQ: Women's Studies Quarterly 50: 1 & 2 (Spring/Summer 2022) © 2022 by Red Washburn and Brianne Waychoff. All rights reserved.

art editors; and editorial assistants. In particular, we want to extend a tremendous thank-you, thank-you, thank-you to the editorial assistants, Amy Iafrate, Alex Johnson, Joe Goodale, Ivy Bryan, Googie Karrass, and Kayla Reece, all of whom worked tirelessly on communicating with the scholars, writers, and artists to make this issue happen. In addition, we want to extend a very generous thank-you to Dána-Ain Davis, Director of the Center for the Study of Women in Society, and administrative staff Eileen Liang and Jennifer Bae for providing *WSQ* with internships in feminist publishing for graduate students in women's and gender studies at the City University of New York. Our partnership has significantly enriched the quality of the journal for our feminist communities across CUNY and beyond. We are greatly indebted to the Feminist Press for all its help with scheduling, copyediting, and distributing our issues, especially to Interim Executive Director Lauren Rosemary Hook and Assistant Editor Nick Whitney. We cannot thank you enough for your help and support. We also wish to thank Associate Director of the Center for the Humanities Kendra Sullivan, as well as Jordan Lord and Sampson Starkweather for collaborating with us and building a new vision for the journal, including aiding with publicity and administrative matters. We acknowledge the support we have received from President Kaye Wise Whitehead and Former Interim Executive Director Jen Ash of the National Women's Studies Association, as well as the Community of Literary Magazines and Presses (CLMP). Lastly, we want to thank each other as general editors of *WSQ* for continuing this work during a global pandemic with much loss and grief. We are looking forward to celebrating fifty years of *WSQ* and the future of this important feminist journal.

Red Washburn
Kingsborough
    Community College
Director of Women's and
    Gender Studies
Associate Professor of English
City University of New York

Brianne Waychoff
Borough of Manhattan
    Community College
Associate Professor of Speech
    Communications and
    Theatre Arts, Gender and
    Women's Studies Program
City University of New York

Works Cited

hooks, bell. 2001. *All About Love: New Visions.* New York: William Murrow.

Introduction: Love Is Solidarity in Action

Rashida L. Harrison, Mary Frances Phillips,
and Nicole M. Jackson

On November 24, 2021, we watched as a white southern judge reported
the verdicts determined by a marjority white jury; they convicted two white
men of murdering Ahmaud Arbery, a Black man, while a third, received
guilty verdicts for his actions as an accomplice. Arbery, a twenty-five-year-
old Black man, was out jogging in a white neighborhood when he was
violently pursued by a retired police officer and his son. They claimed Arbery
was responsible for several thefts in the predominantly white neighborhood. Many of us were holding our breaths and exhaling a little more with
each guilty count. The week prior, however, we experienced a collective
anger as a seventeen-year-old white teenager was acquitted for several counts
of homicide, even as he purportedly left his home with a loaded assault rifle
and drove roughly thirty minutes away to "help protect private property
and serve as a medic" at a Black Lives Matter demonstration. Protestors of
all backgrounds were out in support of an unarmed Black man, Jacob Blake,
who was shot by a white police officer seven times in Kenosha, Wisconsin.
Even as the two men killed were white, they supported Black lives, and their
lives were rendered inconsequential. The white teenager who was acquitted was rewarded for his loyalty to white supremacy as sanctioned by the
state.

As has been required in countless instances surrounding the extralegal
lynching of Black bodies, the survival of Black people over those two weeks
has been preserved because love imbues us with hope and the energy to
continue the fight for justice. We began our coediting journey thinking
about freedom and justice. As our conversations evolved, we often came
back to the question of what motivates and sustains Black communities.
We came back to love and care as core to our foundation.

WSQ: Women's Studies Quarterly 50: 1 & 2 **(Spring/Summer 2022)** © 2022 by Rashida L. Harrison, Mary Frances
Phillips, and Nicole M. Jackson. All rights reserved.

In our early discussions, we realized the necessity for ongoing attention to a canon of Black love, particularly within Black feminist traditions. We had several discussions among ourselves about the meaning of love, the historical approach to uncovering Black love, and the barriers to teasing out moments of love in a past too often shaped by violence. We realized that Black love is not always an explicit theme in the writings of Black scholars, but it can function as the prevailing framework in which we research. This realization offered a myriad of possibilities, most importantly, the notion that a conceptualization of love is intertwined with a pursuit of justice. It is from here that we began to reinvision both the intentional and unintentional acts of justice that amount to a particular expression of Black love. We turn to two less obvious examples of public acts of love and the gendered nature of enacting love and care for people of color.

Even as they occur in the U.S., they illustrate transnational solidarities. The example of activist and immigrant from the Democratic Republic of Congo Therese Patricia Okoumou opened conversations about how we "do love." Okoumou climbed the Statue of Liberty on July 4, 2018, in protest of the federal government's policy separating immigrant children from their parents at the U.S. border. After being found guilty by the state of New York, she defined her political action as centered in empathy and care for dispossessed people. Okoumou's protest to climb the Statue of Liberty highlighted that instead of welcoming them "what we showed them is cages. So, if I go in a cage with them, I am on the right side of history." Her activism is firmly rooted in empathy, offering the potential for radical solidarity based on love.

During the summer of 2018, another event held the attention of Black and brown communities during an Atlanta Braves baseball game. Players, Curacaoan, Ozzie Albies and Venezuelan-born Ronald Acuna Jr. shared an intimate embrace in the dugout. There were varied responses to this public display, which ultimately denied these men the space to show affection, demonstrating the depths of toxic masculinity and the feminization of emotion. But, as one person commented on Twitter, "Men of color loving themselves and one another is truly a revolutionary act!" Sara Ahmed reflects that the ways in which people are allowed to express emotion is "characteristic of some bodies and not others" (2014, 5). Thus, the response to Albies and Acuna's embrace illustrates that societal expectations for emotional displays of care and love are gendered and raced.

Several questions were derived from these examples, including: What does it mean to lead with care in everyday actions? What does it mean to jeopardize one's freedom for one's community? How have expressions and practices of Black love changed across locales and periods? What does it mean to transgress boundaries of affect? How do gender roles shape political engagement? How do we reconcile loving harmful Black folks as they are violent toward us? Scholars, creative writers, and artists explored these questions in nuanced ways, allowing for a more robust discussion on the currency of Black love. We engaged in the contemplation bell hooks underwent at the end of the twentieth century (2001, xxix). We wanted to understand the practice of love in everyday life; how Black people continued to create spaces of love in a western world framed by lovelessness. Ultimately, we knew that the understanding would come in the community.

The centrality of love in Black life is akin to bell hooks's concept of "love ethic" (hooks 2001, xxiv). That ethic is mirrored in the work of many Black authors interested in what sustains, motivates, and frames Black life and liberation. Robin D. G. Kelley asserts that "once we strip radical social movements down to their bare essence and understand the collective desires of people in motion, freedom and love lay at the very heart of the matter" (2002, 12). For Kelley, much like hooks, love is not only what we ought to consciously invoke, but it is always already there. It is the essence of Black initiated movements past and present. Even as it is present, what hooks and many of the authors in this issue offer us, is the practice of love.

In the practice of love, we begin the issue with a love letter tribute by Kevin Powell. The poem entitled "letter to bell hooks" charts Powell's introduction to bell as a "man-child and angry 'momma's boy,'" into her son. He reminisces on critical lessons he learned from her, like "when it came to understanding that women folks ain't just 'spose to be your momma or your mattress, or your mule to punch and kick—" His tribute reflects the deep love that hooks both embodied and imbued in the people around her. His poem is love enacted through grief. And he ends with an important reminder and understanding in Black diasporic traditions, the freedom that exists in the realm of the ancestors.

In 2000, hooks published the first of her love series, *All About Love: New Visions*. Throughout the text, the author justifies her decision to write about something she believes many readers will see as frivolous. In this text and the ones that follow (*Salvation: Black People and Love*; *Communion: The Female Search for Love*; and *The Will to Change: Men, Masculinity, and Love*), hooks argues for seating love right at the center of cultural criticism, movements for justice, and individual and communal projects for justice and change. But in truth, hooks had been writing about love right from the beginning of her career. In her earliest published essays, she wrote about her intimate partners and her search for companionship, she deconstructed images of Black women's self-love and romantic and sexual relationships in film, and she considered the ways in which love (or ideas about love) had shaped the lives of her family members and her own life and intellectual development. The body of hooks's work, in fact, is a long rumination of the centrality of love in Black life, Black art, and Black movements for justice. At the heart of her work is a strong desire to consider affect and emotion as integral to Black feminist thought, an aspect of Black feminism that is just as important as anger or rage, protests, or artistic expression, because it could be found in all these places.

In this issue, we reaffirm the importance of love in Black pasts, presents, and futures, and the articles in the section, "Feminist Affective Love," remind us of the ways in which love as affect can be a powerfully generative force on its own. Most directly, in "Phantom Love: Affective Politics of Love in Toni Morrison's Love," Peace Kiguwa analyzes Toni Morrison's novel, which focuses not on love but its absence, and how that affects two young Black girls' expressions of rage and resentment. But love, Morrison and Kiguwa assert, can be a site of possibility, which Ololade Faniyi and Sharon Omotoso demonstrate. In "Young Feminists Redefining Principles of Care in Nigeria," the authors uncover feminist collectives that center care as a necessary feminist ethic of community-building, which allow young women to navigate state repression and various health crises to provide for one another.

In another vein, Bimbola Akinbola considers the works of experimental filmmaker and photographer Zina Saro-Wiwa to dissect affective expression as markers of belonging for African Diasporic peoples. "In African Intimacy and Love with No Pretense," the author considers depictions of intimacy and pleasure in Saro-Wiwa's work as spaces to reject the stigmatization of sensuality and sexuality within African diasporic communities. Like Akinbola, Ana Quiring's "Going with the Gut" is interested in the erotic as politics. Using Audre Lorde's 1978 essay "The Uses of the Erotic," Quiring analyzes Zadie Smith's novel, *On Beauty*, to consider how the author positions the fat body as a site of erotic knowledge, which can provide a pathway toward aesthetic liberation from thinness and racialized and racist beauty politics.

It is easy to limit discussions of love to the realm of affect only. But in hooks's work on Black people and love, she repeatedly returns to the idea that love ought to be expressed interpersonally, in politics, and in movements for justice (2001, 13). For Black people, love is not just about what we do but what we work to undo, thus the articles in this section see affect as a point of communal and analytical origin, not its end.

In the section "Black Power Love," the authors explore the diverse experiences and images that work to facilitate Black love. Authors in this section attend to the era, culture, and iconography of Black Power, while also illustrating the potency of Black love's radical potential for liberation. Central to Kimberly Lamm's essay, "Dear Angela, *a/k/a Mrs. George Gilbert*: Coco Fusco's Love Letter to an Icon," is the examination of the surveillance of Black activist Angela Davis, and the ways in which images created an icon in the American imagination—one that is often used to serve others needs while dismissing the subjective singularity of Davis, and Black women more largely. Additionally, she explores the state's illegal seizures of letters between Soledad Brother George Jackson and Angela Davis, and the lack of privacy granted to Black people with the production of an icon. Lamm, however, offers an example of the power to reenvision Black affect through the publicizing of their intimate connections. She argues that Davis's work advocating for the Soledad brothers, shows that "love is the affective ground and virtual glue of radical solidarity." Such a claim speaks to the requisite nature of love as the source to resist constructs of white supremacy.

Emanuel H. Brown and Michelle Phillips reflect on the loving results of radical solidarity. In this prose, the authors recall the coming together of Black participants from the U.S., Canada, and the Caribbean at the first "Black Love Convergence" in April 2018 in Raleigh, NC. The gathering was imagined after the devastating results of the 2016 U.S. elections, and heeded bell hooks's 1992 call to "'reclaim Black life,' heal internalized oppression, and live into freedom."[1] The authors explore the rebirth experienced from a space of collective healing, political, spiritual, and sexual awakening. They declare, while ruminating on a love experience in which they were fully seen, "I had been to the consummate place where my free Black love was born." Their words reflect the power of Black love and its liberatory effects.

Keisha V. Thompson and Liseli A. Fitzpatrick offer diasporic histories and perspectives on the revolutionary nature of Black Power Love. In "Living with Their Consciousness: Black Women in Trinidad and Tobago Black Power," Thompson focuses on the impact of women's resistance in the Black Power Revolution in Trinidad and Tobago in the late 1960s and 1970s. She offers a historical sketch of the movement through personal interviews and archival analyses of materials from Black nationalist organizations. Thompson reconstructs the mainstream narrative of the movement to center women, illustrating how they were critical to the frame of collective love through their consciousness-raising, educational praxis, and direct confrontation tactics. The women she writes about are from a privileged class, and she sees their political motivations as stemming from a distinct consciousness of love for the larger community that is still felt in contemporary society through the arts. Fitzpatrick's poem, "revolutionary love," reinforces the emancipatory nature of the interconnections of mind, body, and soul; that is the heart of Black Power Love.

Building on that power, our third section upholds a critical force in Black life, mothers. The ability to enact mother love is not merely for those who give birth or are even gendered as women. Black mother love is a praxis that comes with responsibility and an ethic of community care that consists of operating as doula in life and death to Black communities. The selections in "Mother Love" look in practice and wrestle with societal violence and oppression impacting mothers while reinforcing the critical meaning occurring in Black mothers' grief. In addition, the authors deconstruct a distinct lens to uncover the nuances of love. Teigha Mae VanHester's poem, "Love in Till's Casket," references the experience of Mamie Till, mother of Emmett Till. She reflects on the audacious capacity of Black women to mother in the face of their children's death at the hands of white violence. She writes on the way grieving mother love looks in all its inconsolability. Black mother love sustains families and communities as they transcend. That love is a catalyst for change and provides an unyielding devotion to the quest for freedom.

Wendy M. Thompson in "Black Women Watchers" beautifully illustrates the role that Black mothering encompasses as watchers of the community. She opens with a focus on Black women nurses and medical staff as a call to Kiese Laymon's inquiry of the care work of Black nurses. She expands that act of watching and intervening to the larger task of Black mothers in communities and families. She also inserts her own birthing and aging experience, to explore her path in becoming a watcher; she writes, it is a "a role that so many other Black women, othermothers, and ancestors freely took on . . . an intentional looking out for Black children, an affirming of Black young adults, an advocacy for the safety and bare minimum rights . . . the greeting and listening to our elders." Taiwo's essay is critical to framing Mae's and Ajani's lamentations on the distinct manifestations Black love in the midst of suffering. Watchers are critical to Black care and healing.

Ashia Ajani's poem "deep sea diving" presents a spiritually charged reflection on the depths of our love. Grounded in the ecological, she uses fish as a metaphor to reinforce that there is spirit in every being, alluding to the ocean's capacity to hold ancestral wisdom. She emphasizes the role mothers have in translating that knowledge. The poem speaks to liberation, regeneration, and movement. Ajani illustrates the practice of love by the kinship of the spiritual and political.

In "Communal Love," the authors write in the spirit of hooks's ethic, illustrating Kelley's radical love potential, and exhibiting Lorde's assertion of Black creations as not being a luxury. The love that is both cultivated and enacted in Black communities, even when they are shaped by white systems of violence, and a global health pandemic, is the necessary intervention for healing and growing. Desireé R. Melonas reminds us of the importance of loving intention in "Cultivating Habits of Assembly: Black Womxn's Communal Writing as a Gathering Practice and a Love Letter to InForUs." Here she reminisces on the formation of a Black womxn's writing group, "InForUs," a quartet of Black academic womxn formed in 2020, during the initial global lockdown of the COVID-19 health pandemic. She illustrates how collective writing spaces for Black womxn operate as a site for strength, trust, support, and love to construct a "standard for an ethics of care" that is lacking in the larger academic sphere. In fact, the communal practice is contrary to the commonly taught notion that "real scholars labor in solitude." Black women's communal writing, however, makes space for "vessel work," attending to the mind, body, and spirit as necessary to the emotional, physical, and mental well-being of these scholars.

In "BIPOC Solidarities, Decolonization, and Otherwise Kinship through Black Feminist Love," the authors Sewsen Igbu, Shanna Peltier, Ashley Caranto Morford, and Kaitlin Rizarri, similar to Melonas, center Black feminist practices of love when building community, particularly in the white academy. These four women of color, a diaspora Eritrean settler, an Anishinaabe Kwe, a diaspora Filipina-British settler, and a mixed Filipina settler, created and cofacilitated "an online reading, writing, and dreaming group on BIPOC solidarities" framed by Black feminist love. They actively decenter and deny the reliance of white supremacist spaces as inextricable to their coming together, but rather note "our kinship connections and desires to be in community" come from a desire to be in "these relationships forever." They grapple with the tensions cultivated by larger white society, while remaining firm on a love ethic, and a resistance to enact violence "against one another." They employ Lorde's concept of difference as a critical reflection of how they build coalitions while attending to the risks of difference, including the potential for anti-Blackness. The BIPOC Solidarities Project illustrates Black love's eclipse of majority Black communities and its potential to build multiracial coalitions as liberatory spaces.

monét cooper's "no" reflects on the pain of collective memory and trauma of Black communities, when they are invaded by state actors. She invokes the collective anger and sadness of Black mothers as well as the determination to cultivate and sustain life. Similarly, Roya Marsh highlights the collective power of "Blk Anger," and the ways we use our love ethic to cultivate Black joy. That joy is not merely about the ephemeral but also a joy that shapes political action, often in gendered ways. Marsh embodies Lorde's uses of anger in her reflection of her response to racism. She writes: "You think me being angry is the problem?" and goes on to suggest the answer, "Black joy." Black joy is Black Power as we grapple with inter- and intracommunal violence resulting from the project of white supremacy. She emphasizes self-definition and ends with a call for reparations.

"The Years They've Taken: Systemic Oppression, Black Bodies, and the Materiality of Grief" provides a glimpse into the meaning-making process Black love undergoes when communities are inundated with grief, surviving under brute force by the state, and navigating human life processes of birth and death. The transcribed, intimate, yet public conversation between comrades and artists M. Carmen Lane and Sondra Perry in October of 2020, comes after witnessing familial and Black death in part due to COVID-19, political violence, and old age. Their reflection invokes the spiritual and makes clear their art rises above the material.

Lane thoughtfully exclaims, "I collaborate with my ancestors. They're with me right now in this conversation with you." Perry in her response understands and contemplates the uses of this knowledge when she says, "I'm thinking about all the work that the dead are asked to do." She is alluding to the loving work expected of the ancestral realm. These two artists share the loving process of Black art that is not confined to a cis-het male frame of Blackness. Their conversation points out Black love's ability to disrupt notions of space and time, marrying birth and death as important institutions and making space for the myriad of possibilities in the face of pain, rage, and grief.

The section on "Recollecting Love" underscores the significance of memorializing Black experiences. The intent is often driven by a need to cultivate belonging within spaces that actively worked to keep Black people invisible even as we play major parts in its existence. Loren S. Cahill's "Memoirs of the Colored Girls Museum: For Blackgirls Everywhere to Remember That Our Love Is Enuf" captures the loving intent and result of a creation process. Her essay focuses on the "imaginative resilience" of the Colored Girls Museum in the Germantown neighborhood of Philadelphia, and its role in cultivating a loving space. She argues that the museum as an important site for inquiry "serves as proof that cultural memory work allows Black communities to remember, preserve, celebrate and affirm Blackgirls' freedom dreams."

keisha bruce's "'Everyone Has a Pic Like This in the Album!': Digital Diasporic Intimacy and the Instagram Archive" interrogates how Black people utilize technology to find belonging in digital spaces. She gives us the term "digital diasporic intimacy" to describe the ways Black people in the diaspora use social media, to make meaning across space and time. She does this by deconstructing photos on the @BlackArchives.co Instagram account and engaging in "speculative remembering," a love practice that highlights the ways that "digital diasporic intimacy is created through acknowledgments of time, memory, and affect." Jameka Hartley, in her poem "May I," engages in the speculative to emphasize the love and care that comes with consent. With remnants of a love letter, she uses sexual innuendos to establish the agency garnered when consent is employed. Such an agency reverberates in the recollecting process of care, validation, and belonging.

The articles in the "Love Culture" section ask readers to think about sites where a love culture can, and has already, emerged. hooks tells us that love shouldn't just change the individual; it can and should change the worlds in which we live. "Profound changes in the way we think, and act must take place if we are to create a loving culture" (hooks 1999, xxiv). The authors in this section attend to what it means to create and live in a loving culture, what we owe to the spaces we inhabit, and how we may transform what already exists into spaces that can nurture our new loving culture.

Myles W. Mason's beautiful dissection of Lizzo's 2019 NPR Tiny Desk performance argues that the artist repurposes a small space that is ill-fitting for her body into a space for love and pleasure. Mason points out the many ways Lizzo joyfully stretches a physical space that wants to contain her and her music. In remaking the Tiny Desk concert stage to fit her big body, voice, and band, Lizzo centers self-love and joy in her popular performance. Additionally, Mason is interested in Lizzo's communicative technique of call-and-response to "trace the constitution of a choric self-love" she establishes with her audience. Similarly, coeditor Rashida L. Harrison's interview with Lennox Commissiong, surfaces the artist's desire to reject and recover narratives of Black love in his work to center community-defined and affirming images. Like the artist Lizzo, Commissiong imbues his audience with agency, accepting his role as translator, and delivering the message with love.

Taylor Leigh Tate in "Contemporary Love Stories: Love in the Trap, Hookup, and Consumer Culture" deftly demonstrates the need for a new generation of critical thought, where love and survival are messy, nonlinear, and iterative. In her words, contemporary traditions of Black love, including the everyday actions of surviving and thriving, "have the capacity to be spiritually enriching." Tate illustrates that the resurgence of spirit work, ancestral healing, and changing are related to loving practices found in trap culture, consumer culture, and hookup culture. She urges us to attend to changing social mores; to look forward, not just in congruence with the past.

However, Black feminist's foundations of a loving praxis cannot be adequately attended to without engaging Audre Lorde. For our Classics Revisited, we chose her 1978 essay "Scratching the Surface: Some Notes on Barriers to Women and Loving" because it provides a foundation to intersectional analyses of the structures that confine Black love's liberatory potential. The essay emphasizes Black women's allegiance to one another, and the ways in which those bonds champion solidarity across sexuality. Additionally, she calls for the end of the proverbial "oppression wars" that continue to exist within Black communities. She warns us of the false notion that there is a limited amount of freedom, and that Black women's fight is tied to Black men's. In the contemporary, as the binary of gender and sexuality is contested, rightly so, "Scratching the Surface" reminds us that we have the right to define and love without fear. Arisa White exemplifies that courage in her poem, "There are parts in me without place"; her account is possible because of Lorde's call to break down the barriers. In her provocative account of queer Black love, she grapples with belonging, self-doubt, the impact of trauma, all in the context of an intimate, sexual moment. She begins and ends understanding that the fullness of Black queer bodies have yet to be uncovered.

One of the tasks of this issue is to shed light on the contemporary work about and shaped by Black love. Many of the pieces are in conversation with recent book publications that interrogate, utilize, and expand on Black love as a praxis. The books we chose for review provide various lenses in which to consider Black love. They illustrate examples of queerness, activism, wellness and spiritual practices, sex and sensuality, trauma and anger, peace, and hope, all in the context of Black love. The texts are inquiries into how we love, why love in a given moment, and engagement in the practice of imagining Black love's possibilities. The texts add to a canon of literature on "how do Black people get free." The scholars who review—Terrance Wooten, Mélena Laudig, Kimberly Akano, Leigh-Anne K. Goins, Brianna Eaton, and Eziaku A. Nwokocha—provide insightful explanations that will provoke further dialogue.

Our next section explicitly engages us in the labor of Black love. Here, we center the role of art as an expression of love for the self and the community. We worked with *WSQ*'s inaugural visual arts director, Mel Michelle Lewis, to curate "The Moment Love Moves: From Theory to [Art] Practice," which features the work of three artists, including OZ Sanders, Lewis herself, and Nina Q. Allen. Art illustrates the everyday practice of love. We often take love as a concept for granted; the artist translates what already exists in our community, as well as provokes us to imagine loving possibilities. Therefore, for Black people, art is a necessary practice. In the same way that Audre Lorde reminds us that poetry is not luxury, Black art is vital; "it forms the quality of the light within which we predicate our hopes and dreams toward survival and change" (Lorde 2007, 37). Similar to hooks and Kelley, Lorde is describing a love ethic that informs the creative. Black creativity offers us the ability to unpack our humanity to its full extent.

The art pieces address Black queerness, family life, the mundane, the ecological, and the spiritual components of who we are. Sanders's work directly speaks to the way she invokes the practice of love in family in her pieces, *All the Gifts You Gave Us* and *LOVE*. Her illustration of the Sankofa bird invokes the important adage of "know whence you came. If you know whence you came, there is really no limit to where you can go" (Baldwin, 1963, 22). This sentiment is also echoed in how Lewis conjures the past in *Crabbing Bayou Como, Royal Oaks Plantation*, and makes meaning of it by situating themselves as entwined in the ancestral lineage. The river in *Yellow Mary Artist Self-Portrait, Daughters of the Oaks* represents a nexus of Black experiences. And finally, Allen allows us to see the freedom of attending to the spiritual through the mundane with her photos of *A Sacred Night Bath in Maryland USA (One and Two)*. Allen grounds us in important African spiritual traditions that, reminding us of that water, an important life force, nourishes us both in the physical and divine.

The Alerts and Provocations close the issue with Namulundah Florence's "a bell tolls for bell hooks (1952–2021)." Florence offers a homage of hooks important love lessons while drawing on an important feminist trope of "the personal as political." She reminds us of the mainstream silence on love and its complexity, and the gift that bell offered to all of humanity. For Black people that gift of love is key to survival and eventual liberation.

This issue is an embodiment of our commitment to center Black love. The process was deeply compounded by the pandemic, and like many in our community, we felt it personally and professionally. We learned what Tiya Miles asserts, that the politics of Black love means "decentering the self for the good of another" (2021, 3). Our work is a creative victory that we struggled to keep in the forefront when there were moments of disagreement. It is a practice that, as Lorde reminds us, is necessary when we are involved in a craft of love (1978, 34).

Black Love would not be possible without the care and encouragement of friends and allies. The relevance and necessity of Black love as a scholarly interrogation with theoretical and practical applications, even in the era of Black Lives Matter, is questioned by gatekeepers of academia. "Black love" exists despite racism. The coeditors had a number of supporters of diverse backgrounds that championed the issue. We are grateful for the community's show of the politics of Black love. That politic involves taking risks, saying "yes!," and bearing witness to its glaring omission from our social conversations. It involves a fierceness, a relentless declaration of Black humanity in the face of hostility. The politics of Black love is community driven and solidarity in action.

Rashida L. Harrison is an assistant professor of social relations and policy at James Madison College at Michigan State University. Her research examines how Black women build coalitions across social identities, political realities, and national borders. Her most recent writing project is focused on Black women's health movements and their impact on renewed political action in Black communities. She can be reached at harri516@msu.edu.

Mary Frances Phillips is a proud native of Detroit, Michigan. She is an associate professor of Africana studies at Lehman College, City University of New York. She is currently working on her book manuscript, *Sister Love: Ericka Huggins, Spiritual Activism, and the Black Panther Party,* which is under contract with New York University Press. She can be reached at phill190@gmail.com.

Nicole M. Jackson is an associate professor of history at Bowling Green State University. Her areas of expertise include the twentieth century, African diaspora, Black British history, and Black social movements. She can be reached at nmjacks@bgsu.edu.

Notes

1. The language of "reclaim Black life" is taken directly from bell hooks, *Black Looks: Race and Representation* (Boston: South End Press, 1992), 2.

Works Cited

Ahmed, Sara. 2014. *The Cultural Politics of Emotion.* Edinburgh: Edinburgh University Press.

Baldwin, James. 1963. *The Fire Next Time.* New York: Dial Press.

hooks, bell. 1992. *Black Looks: Race and Representation.* Boston: South End Press.

———. 2000. *All About Love: New Vision.* New York: HarperCollins.

———. 2001. *Salvation: Black People and Love.* New York: HarperCollins.

———. 2002. *Communion: The Female Search for Love.* New York: HarperCollins.

———. 2004. *The Will to Change: Men, Masculinity, and Love.* New York: Washington Square Press.

Kelley, Robin D. G. 2002. *Freedom Dreams: The Black Radical Imagination.* Boston: Beacon Press.

Kennedy, Merit, and Jaclyn Diaz. 2021. "3 White Men Are Found Guilty of Murder in the Killing of Ahmaud Arbery." *NPR,* November 24, 2021. https://www.npr.org/2021/11/24/1058240388/ahmaud-arbery-murder-trial-verdict-travis-greg-mcmichael

Lorde, Audre. 1978. "Scratching the Surface: Some Notes on Barriers to Women and Loving." *The Black Scholar* 9, no. 7: 31–5.

———. 2007. "The Uses of Anger: Women Responding to Racism." In *Sister Outsider: Essays and Speeches.* Berkeley, CA: Crossing Press, 124–33.

Miles, Tiya. 2021. *All That She Carried: The Journey of Ashley's Sack, a Black Family Keepsake.* New York: Random House.

Romo, Vanessa, and Sharon Pruitt-Young. 2021. "What We Know about the 3 Men Who Were Shot by Kyle Rittenhouse." *NPR,* November 20, 2021. https://www.npr.org/2021/11/20/1057571558/what-we-know-3-men-kyle-rittenhouse-victims-rosenbaum-huber-grosskreutz.

letter to bell hooks

Kevin Powell

my dearest bell:

I was not only a man-child
teething fractured knuckles
when I met you—I was also
an angry and misplaced
momma's boy, and you crushed
the cold ice beneath my holey sneakers
so decidedly that first encounter
as words such as
sexism and misogyny and homophobia
hemmed me up at da Lawd's crossroads
I am ashamed I cannot recall
that first person's name
who airdropped a sojourner's truth
into my concrete knapsack
because she was among the many women
of Spelman College I knew
back in the day
like Miss Kupenda Auset
who goaded me to become
something more than a man
Ayy, ayy, yeah, I was gifted photocopies
of your feminist candied yams
the way my ma shoplifted
reparation pennies so we could eat
My ma and her four sisters
and my Grandma Lottie
hot-combed and curled story after story
about the ways of White folks

WSQ: Women's Studies Quarterly 50: 1 & 2 (Spring/Summer 2022)

about the ways of men folks
while I sat there and took it
yet I remained bone-thin
with bonier brain
when it came to understanding
that women folks ain't
just 'spose to be your momma
or your mattress or your
mule to punch and kick—

In the beginning
I was utterly frightened of your fearlessness:
Your Kentucky fried soul was un-digging
future and past generations
of women
long left for dead
Your Kentucky fried soul was un-dressing
future and past generations
of men
long left for dead
I was hunchbacked before you, and stark-naked
one of your books in my shaky hands
my unsalted ego crashing to the rug-less floor
like a beer pitcher full of lies
bell, I had already been
the devil's willing volcano
when I pushed a girlfriend
into a bathroom door
in July of 1991
that is why my body and mind
became a ferocious hurricane
when I first read you:
the ski mask was knifed from my face
the grime was sucked from my heart
the quicksand was scraped from my ankles
the clay was carved from my colon
a musty and sticky holy ghost triggered me
as my blood overflowed and retched

the absent father the single mother
the men on them liquor corners
the men in them barbershops
the men in them big positions
the communities the churches the chicken shacks
the reverends so-and-so the politicians no-and-no
the television shows the movies the sports the warts
the miseducation the ghetto plantation the prison cell
the swaying noose awaiting arrival of my neck—

bell, I remember we
sat down
greased elbow to greased elbow
a few years later
when I was writing for that magazine
I had never interviewed anyone
as brazenly free as you
one-woman emancipation proclamation
bold and snappy tongue
who painstakingly stiff-armed
capitalism and racism and toxic manhood
and politics and pop culture
like you were
the wind hurriedly washing away
the bulging whip marks of runaway slaves
I collapsed
in love with your genius
I dropped
my bags at your exposed feet
I stared
at myself with your x-ray eyeglasses
I shook and recoiled
whenever you scratched and peeled my history—

Oh, bell, you are gone,
and it is hella hard to write this
I jab these words with my half-crooked fingers:
I would not be the man I am without you

And you once said I was like a son to you
I am your son, bell, I am—

That is why
I am so terribly sorry I let you down
when I had to abandon
my trip to Berea, Kentucky
a couple of years ago because I had not
taken seriously what you
had sketched so many times about love
I was in a wretched place, bell,
my self-esteem
the bursting, rat-attacked garbage
in front of a Brooklyn bodega
But I still phoned you
every few months
simply to hear your voice
on your old-school answering machine
I was hurt and confused
as to why you never returned my calls
We had never gone that long
without talking in some form—

bell, I did not know you were dying—

Death embracing you like
a head-less family member
at an Appalachian train station
inside the home state you had fled in your youth
Only to return as an elder shero of the world
thirty-plus books in thirty-plus years
To die to sleep perhaps to dream
of a slow and methodical suicide
To die to sleep perhaps to dream
of a slow and methodical good-bye
to box and store
the great love-ship you never had
love hastily shedding pounds:

flesh draping your bones like a flimsy dress
love desperately crawling up stairs:
hands and knees like suction cups gripping a wall
I did not know bell I did not know—

I flew to Kentucky
through a diabolical tornado
I had no clue was happening
I was driven by Dr. DaMaris Hill
from Lexington to Berea to your house
on a block over yonder
I shall forget in a heap of tomorrows
I wandered anxiously around your 'hood
while you were prepared for the day's visitors
I was terrified of going inside
I was terrified of what I would see
I was terrified of what I would feel
At last, I was welcomed into your home
by one of your sisters and your literary executor
Original Black art over here
Buddhist symbols over here
Countless books like air tiles
to plug your home's lonesome spaces
You in a hospital bed in your living room
Tubes plunging from your nose
Cranky oxygen tank on the side next to your bed
Your hair totally gray, your body totally frail
I gasped and cried and cried and gasped
I was the only guest at that moment
bell, I got to sit with you for over an hour
I held and rubbed and squeezed your left hand
I held and rubbed and squeezed your left knee
I held and rubbed and squeezed your left toes
I gasped and cried and cried and gasped
I kept saying it was me
I finally made it to Berea, bell
You snored, you snored some more
When you did awake

you strained to unleash your eyes
I wondered if you knew it was me
You kept shouting "Let's go!"
as if you were ready to go somewhere
You kept saying "Yup"
whenever I asked you if you could hear me
That famously shrill voice as sassy as ever
I gasped and cried and cried and gasped
bell, I told you I loved you, several times
Then I did not know what else to say
As I arose to leave, I said a prayer
to the Goddess of wings and warriors
to safeguard your travel to the other side
I thanked you and I said good-bye quietly
I gasped and cried and cried and gasped
I knew I would never see you as flesh upon flesh again
And when I stepped out into the biting Kentucky air
I felt you strolling with me
bell, I hugged your spirit
Your spirit hugged me back
I gasped and cried and cried and gasped
And less than a week later, bell,
you had your freedom, at last—

Wednesday, December 15, 2021
9:25pm

Kevin Powell is a poet, journalist, civil and human rights activist, filmmaker, and author of fourteen books. His upcoming books include a new poetry collection and a biography of Tupac Shakur. He can be reached at kevin@kevinpowell.net.

PART I. **FEMINIST AFFECTIVE LOVE**

Phantom Love: Affective Politics of Love in Toni Morrison's *Love*

Peace Kiguwa

Abstract: Toni Morrison's novel *Love* invites us to consider structuring systems in how Black women embody and practice love for each other. What is the affective quality of healing love between Black women? What happens when the social and psychic structuring of this love are implicated in patriarchal, racializing, and classed systems of relating? The paper engages two primary concerns: (1) how the erasure and distortion of Black women's love is made possible when love's backdrop consists of anti-Black, capitalist, and racist systems and histories, and (2) why Black women's reclamation of love for each other is necessary to a project of healing and community building. **Keywords:** *Love*; Toni Morrison; Black women; affect; racism; community; healing

"Beauty, love . . . actually, I think, all the time that I write, I'm writing about love or its absence. Although I don't start out that way . . . But I think that I still write about the same thing, which is how people relate to one another and miss it or hang on to it . . . or are tenacious about love."
—Toni Morrison 1977, 40 ("The Seams Can't Show:
An Interview with Toni Morrison," Jane S. Bakerman)

*"Dear sisters in melanin,
we need each other."*
—Upile Chisala

Black Women in Rage/Enraged

Two Black women living together, bonded in their hate and rage against each other, different in their education and relationships to a man long dead and buried, these are the protagonists of Toni Morrison's novel *Love*. Their fights, we are told, are intensely physical, "bruising" even, with "hands, feet,

WSQ: Women's Studies Quarterly 50: 1 & 2 (Spring/Summer 2022) © 2022 by Peace Kiguwa. All rights reserved.

teeth, and soaring objects" (2003, 73). They nurture a hatred so fierce that it demands more than physical altercation to survive: "It wanted creativity and hard work to sustain itself" (74). And so, they cultivate silence full of rage and suspicion. The house they forcibly live in together marks this atmosphere of rage, resentment, and suspicion, their bodies pitted against the other so intensely and in equalizing and paralyzing ways. The novel tracks the two female protagonists' development from girlhood to womanhood. Morrison provides an insightful study into how loss and grief may structure and distort Black women's love for each other in the form of the novel's two female protagonists, Christine and Heed. And yet, it is *not* love that structures the narrative events in the novel but rather sorrow, rage, hate, and violence. It is therefore necessary to engage these juxtaposing affective registers of love's distortion and absence. Ranging in depth and form, melancholic rage, sorrow, indifference and hate cuts across the novel. *And yet*, the intensity of these affective forces almost erases the undercurrent of love between these two women.

The novel opens with the present-day musings of a nameless narrator—identified only by the initial "L"—who guides us through some of the key events and unfoldings in the book. We meet the two protagonists early, both single adult women living in the same dilapidated house. We do not know much about these women, only that there seems to exist (indeed, they do not seem to even *speak* directly to each other) a burning hatred and suspicion of the other. Even in their silent rage, they perform the mundane and necessary tasks that are a part of living together: for example, in our first introduction to their unusual domesticity, Christine prepares food for and serves Heed, who is paralyzed and so unable to perform this task for herself. Her gesture is neither kind nor loving but part of a long-standing game of comeuppance between the two and is met with irate rejection on Heed's part: "What she knows is, I don't eat shellfish" (28). It is only much later in the novel, in the fourth chapter, that we are made aware of their childhood friendship and attachment to each other. Through this circular narrative motif (friends-to-enemies/enemies-to-friends), Morrison aptly captures the enmeshment of love with hate that structures their relationship with each other. Together, they bury the patriarch that both binds them together and tears them apart, Bill Cosey—a husband to one and grandfather to the other. So intense is their simmering rage and hatred of the other that observers at the funeral fail to distinguish between them.

So why center rage, hate, and resentment in an article about love? A simple answer would be because *Love*'s (2003) dominant structuring narrative seems to center rage and hate. Indeed, love as a distinct object of interest is hardly foregrounded in the novel. What we have instead is a novel illustrating love's bankruptcy (Wardi 2005). In her reflection of the novel, Bennett (2014, 59) notes that "*Love*, therefore, is about the stuff we forget to mention when we use the word—when we simplify and romanticize it. It is about language and social arrangements." Morrison herself flags the complexity of reading the emotion of love in overly naive and romanticized ways that divorce it from its sociality, politics, and enmeshment with other affective registers that include hate and rage:

> It [love] is easily the most empty cliché, the most useless word, and at the same time the most powerful human emotion—because hatred is involved in it, too. I thought if I removed the word from nearly every other place in the manuscript, it could become an earned word. If I could give the word, in my very modest way, its girth and its meaning and its terrible price and its clarity at the moment when that is all there is time for, then the title does work for me. (Houston 2003)

And so, this article paradoxically examines Black women in rage, not love. And yet, *Love* (2003) is an insightful exploration of the nuances of healing love. The unfolding narrative of the novel is interesting in the way that rage and hate seem to center and guide the actions of its two female protagonists. In this sense then, in choosing to title her novel in the way that she does, Morrison invites us to consider registers of rage that attest to love's failures. Similarly, Judith Butler's observation that "speaking from rage does not always let us see how rage carries sorrow and covers it over" (2014) is a useful way to ponder Heed and Christine's rage toward each other. In the characters of Heed and Christine, Morrison offers us a reflection on the affective feeling of love between two Black women and its distortion through the register of rage. Feminists have explored rage in its myriad dimensions, highlighting its power and force for change (Chemaly 2020; Cooper 2018; Kaplan, Haley, and Mitra 2021). These scholars demonstrate that women in rage/enraged are an igniting force for asserting women's rights as humans worthy of dignity and respect. This scholarship also notes that rage may take on burdensome as well as liberating effects (Kaplan, Haley, and Mitra 2021).

Recently, Orem (2021) has taken up a different exploration of rage that fails to mobilize for change and justice as theorized by much feminist scholarship, what Sara Ahmed describes as "ambiguous anger" (2004, 171). This anger is slippery in its ambiguous target (who/what exactly is the source of the rage?), its temporal roots (when exactly was it birthed, how is it alive in the moment, and how/what will be its cause of departure?). It is also slippery in terms of its registers (when rage defies a neat labelling, when rage is interwoven with other affects of hate, fear, and resentment). As Butler reminds us, rage may sometimes seem to cover or hide other registers such as sorrow and grief. For Heed and Christine, it also seems to cover/hide love. It is these "knotty articulations of anger" that Orem draws our attention to (Orem 2021, 964). In this first section, I therefore foreground rage and anger as part of a project of untangling the failures of love (Bakerman 1981) as this unfolds in the novel. To do this, I draw on feminist scholarship on affect and emotions to illustrate Ratele's observation that explorations of Black interiority must contend with "how we felt, thought about, and 'did' intimacy in a white male-ruled world" (Ratele 2005, 558).

Phantom Love: *Love*'s Ghostly Hauntings

In this section, I turn to an affective politics of love that is implicated in other registers of affect. I choose to explore love's failure as it is depicted in the novel through the idea or quality of a phantom. In so doing, I want to connect the practice of love and its distortions between Black women more generally to a kind of ghostly haunting that may encapsulate both real and imagined relations between Black women. My premise is rooted in an affective reading of love that is entwined within historical, political, material, and social matrices of subjugation and privilege that render love as always encapsulated within a politics of "hauntology" (Gordon 1990, 2008). What ghosts haunt both these women and seems to shape their hatred and rage against the other? Real or imagined, what affective energies feed this haunting into the present?

The *Oxford English Dictionary* offers the following definition of *phantom*:

> phantom, *n.* and *adj.*
> 1. As a mass noun: illusion, unreality; emptiness, vanity; delusion, deception, falsity.
> 2. A thing (usually with human form) that appears to the sight or other sense, but has no material substance; an apparition, a specter, a ghost.
> 3. Originally: an ineffectual person or thing; *spec.* one that has merely

the title or outward appearance of power, authority, mastery, etc.; a cipher.
Now chiefly: a weak, attenuated, or practically non-existent version *of*
something.

4. A thing that merely resembles, in form or appearance some other
thing, *esp.* a mirage, reflection, or other optical image *of* something. Now
rare.

5. *Medicine.* A phantom limb, or other body part that is felt to be present
after amputation.

6. Something merely imagined; an image in a dream, vision, etc. Also:
a (usually delusory) notion or idea which plays on the mind or haunts the
imagination.

To theorize phantom love, I want to consider these layered readings of the
word—to simultaneously connote a sense of love that is nonexistent, illusory, and even empty and to speak of an empty love that signifies a lack of
substance to it. I argue that part of the task Morrison sets for herself is to
subvert our common understandings of empty love by presenting us ironically with a profound illustration of love (in the friendship of her two
protagonists) that is also simultaneously presented in the form of rage and
hate. Secondly, to play with the idea of a ghost in the full connotation of
the word, to speak about the dead. As Bennett (2014) points out, it is in
the figure of L, our trusted narrator, that this figure becomes relevant. The
novel's surprising narrative twist that reveals both L's ghostly status as well
as her full name ("Love"), invites us to consider love as dead and yet still
present and haunting. This evokes very strongly the nature of the circulating emotion between the two women. Phantom love may thus be seen as a
kind of ghostly haunting in which we have experienced loss of a loved object.
This reading of a haunting concerns itself with the absence of a real embodied other, whose loss we feel as amputation. This is another for whom we
may also have and demonstrate feelings of love. We may consider phantom
is in terms of its imaginative qualities. Here, we may speak of a desire and
perhaps fear of the Other that causes or inspires a sense of danger and inse-
curity in us. In this latter sense, we may thus project states of feeling and
intent onto another that is evocative of our own longings, desires, and/or
fears. Thus, our imagined sense of threat finds "proof" by virtue of the other's
mere existence. Desired attributes of the Other become distorted as ugly
and therefore undesirable.

Ahmed's (2014) work on affective economies demonstrates how
emotions, such as rage, grief, hate, and love, may function to bind

collective bodies together while simultaneously excluding others. Part of this politics of emotion involves the attachment of negative value to the embodied Other, what Ahmed refers to as a kind of "stickiness" (2014, 132). That is, specific bodies come to be associated with naturalized negative affects and meanings. Consider for example the racialized and gendered trope of the angry Black woman. Rage, in this instance as negative affect, is attached to the body of the Black woman in ways that both naturalize and pathologize anger when enacted by Black women. The function of this is to trivialize Black women's rage against social and political discrimination. This attachment of stickiness to the body of the pariah Other does the work of reproducing systems and relations of oppression.

In attending to the ghostly hauntings of love, I also consider a politics of gendered resentment as an organizing feature of this structuring of collective bodies that also ruptures the possibility of community and female bonding. The rage and anger that Heed and Christine embody is not the linear "againstness" that scholars such as Ahmed (2014), Lorde (1997), and others identify as necessary to raging against injustice. Heed and Christine's anger seems to encompass this linear direction (they do direct rage against each other), but it also seems to embody something more that remains unnameable—not because both women ignore it but because they do not read beyond their rage. They do not explore Ahmed's (2014, 171) suggestion to "read and interpret" ambiguous anger to discern its cause (Orem, 964). Their rage is both focused and unfocused, aimed to hurt the Other but also hurting of others and themselves.

In the fictive tale of a pure love between two Black girls that transitions into pure hate that is in turn enacted in rage, Morrison almost presents us a cautionary tale of love's fragility against a backdrop of racist, patriarchal, and capitalist structuring systems. As the story unfolds, we learn not only about the young girls' first coming together but also their ensuing bond. So bonded they are that they create their own language, *idagay*, through which they communicate with each other, that allows them to remain locked in their own world. We also learn that this sisterly bond is abruptly shattered when Heed, the financially destitute of the two, marries Bill Cosey, Christine's wealthy grandfather. Much later in the novel, we further learn the age disparity of the bride and groom—eleven years old to fifty-two. Feeling her childhood friend's sudden and confusing new role in her life as both a betrayal of their sister love and a theft of her grandfather's love, and with the enthusiastic encouragement of her mother, Christine reacts with rage hurt. In an especially poignant moment, when the girls gather in the kitchen with the other two women in the household, Heed offers her wedding ring to Christine, to connect once again with her lost childhood friend. Christine, after days of communication only in the form of insults and silent rage, reverts to their private language:

> Christine burst out crying and ran through the back door. From the rain barrel, Heed could hear her shouting: "Ou-yidagay a ave-slidagay! E-hidagay ought-bidagay ou-yidagay ith-widagay a ear's-yidagay ent-ridagay an-didagay a andy-cidagay ar-bidagay!" Heed examined the string beans as closely as she could while "Ave-slidagay! Ave-slidagay!" rang in her head. (Morrison 2003, 129)

These words will mean nothing to us until much later in the book, when after they have reconciled as old women, a dying Heed admonishes Christine: "That hurt, Christine. Calling me a slave. Hurt bad." Christine replies with: "It was meant to. I thought I would die" (188). This interaction haunts in its enactment of grief in rage. The melancholic loss that both girls suffer for each other in the face of this marriage has no other language with which to express itself other than through rage and hate.

So blinded are Christine and the other women in the novel by this child-bride and her groom that they do not register the patriarchal and abusive context of the union. That an eleven-year-old can be perceived to have seduced a fifty-two-year-old man into marriage is only criticized, ironically, by Sandler, the foreman who forms a friendship with Cosey, the groom and patriarch around whom the women (including Sandler's wife, Vida) in the novel seem to galvanize around. Sandler, unlike these women who idolize Cosey, recognizes the pariah scapegoating of the young child Heed for what it is. Reflecting on his own wife, Vida, and her dismissal of the child as morally suspect, Sandler questions the burden of morality placed on a young girl of eleven. Even L, our narrator, fails to name Cosey's behavior as pedophilic, preferring to skirt over this blemish of a benefactor (Ho 2006). May, Christine's mother, equally demonstrates hostility toward the young Heed for the presumed slight against her matriarch status in the household.

The seduction to read these women's rage and hate toward a child bride as nothing more than false consciousness might be limiting. Rather, it is more useful to attend to the ways that systems of domination that implicate gendered, raced, and classed intersections of power function to disrupt communities that are nurturing of marginalized peoples. These communities are often already marginalized and disempowered within society, and the destabilization of community exacerbates their marginalization.

Maintaining communities of support and nurture is thus fundamental to a feminist agenda of reclaiming our strengths and possibilities for justice. The Latina feminist decolonial scholars Maria Lugones and Pat Rosezelle have observed that "sisterhood and friendship have been proposed by feminists as *the* relationships that women need to foster or recognize among ourselves if our liberation from sexist oppression is to end" (1995, 135). For both Lugones and Rosezelle, pluralist friendship must be part of feminist ideals. Similarly, they argue that "sisterhood . . . is about egalitarian kinship bonding" (136), and it addresses egalitarian relations between women. Speaking as a Black feminist, Rosezelle argues that the term *sister* as used within many Black communities connotes more than a blood tie, as it also invokes histories, struggles, and resistance: "The slave experience is the beginning of *sister* and *brother*" (139). It is also about community, respect, and support among other modes of relating with each other. It is about "women trusting, celebrating, loving, and being bound to other women" (139). Then, in the women's turning on young Heed as pariah and seducer of a patriarchal figure, we witness instead a rupture of this vital bond that is necessary to sustain and nurture both the adult women and the young girls learning to become women. Bennett (2014) has pointed out that the young girls' loss also entails the loss (or rather absence) of maternal nurturing. Both girls have been failed by their maternal mothers and the other women that surround them in the absence of a female community that nurtures. This is part of their ghostly haunting—the loss of potentially nurturing women's community. Reflecting on the feminist movement and struggles, duCille laments that "in different ways and with different consequences, we all experience the pain and disappointment of failed community," which cuts deep in its reminder of our losses of each other (1996, 119). Part of the destabilization of Black women's communities of nurture involves a devaluation of the Black female body, a body that is not only devalued as unworthy but pitted against similar bodies, competing against these bodies for status, worth, and value. In the words of bell hooks:

> Our obsessions about love begin not with the first crush or the first fall. They begin with that first recognition that females matter less than males, that no matter how good we are, in the eyes of a patriarchal universe, we are never quite good enough. Femaleness in patriarchal culture marks us from the very beginning as unworthy or not as worthy. (2002, xi)

Another feature of love's ghostly haunting concerns the circulation and production of a gendered politics of resentment and shame. These affective registers are functional in silencing testimonies of sexual violence. Clara Fischer notes that "the significance of shame to feminists lies in the complex and often troubling implications it holds as a feeling that may be experienced differently by people of certain genders (and none), and in its relation to power" (2018, 371). The politics of shame is concerned with this differential experience of shame for the different genders and the emergence of shame within cultures that arrange hierarchies of gendered power. The circulation of shame in relation to women and women's bodies remains a powerful site for devaluing and silencing women's stories. The circulation of shame includes processes of self-surveillance that attribute guilt and responsibility to oneself. Shame here functions to detach the individual from the community and configures in individualizing ways. Reasons to be shameful (whether in terms of *feeling* shame or embodying a body that *induces* shame) are reposited as individual emotions that the individual must assume responsibility for. This function of shame is significant in its rupture of female bonds of friendship and solidarity that are necessary to healing and loving. Gendered shame stands as a barrier to speaking out against toxic cultures and practices that violate the bodily integrity of women in society. When the young Heed and Christine separately encounter sexual violation through Cosey—a sexual groping of one and a masturbatory act performed and witnessed in the other's bedroom window—they both internalize feelings of shame. This becomes the first instance of a rupture in their sisterly bond; they, who have no secrets between them, do not tell each other of these different encounters. They are children. While they can recognize the emotion of shame that they feel, they neither have the language and resources to recognize this shame as violating of their bodily integrity nor its circulation within a context of toxic patriarchal patronage and abuse:

> Even in idagay they had never been able to share a certain twin shame. Each one thought the rot was hers alone. (Morrison 2003, 190)

> It wasn't the arousals, not altogether unpleasant, that the girls could not talk about. It was the other thing. The thing that made each believe, without knowing why, that this particular shame was different and could not tolerate speech—not even in the language they had invented for secrets.
> Would the inside dirtiness leak?
> Now, exhausted, drifting toward a maybe permanent sleep, they don't speak of the birth of sin. Idagay can't help them with that. (192)

It is this lack of capacity to speak shame that marks the beginning of the end for the young girls and that entrenches them even further into silence and rage against each other and themselves. Fischer further notes that "work on shame can be challenging, not least because of the 'slipperiness' of shame, which makes identifying, defining, and analyzing this feeling a necessarily inexact science" (2018, 371). This slipperiness of shame, interwoven with a politics of resentment, may completely eradicate women's capacity to organize for personal and social change precisely at those moments when it matters most. In considering a politics of resentment, I am interested in the ways that resentment as emotion works in tandem with a gender-shaming culture to further silence women and render them voiceless. The gendered social order into which the young girls become introduced is a violent one, shattering their sense of selves and their bond of healing and love. L's musings toward the end of the novel about Heed and Christine's friendship recognize this influence of a social order that erases female bond and community.

In pitting Black women against each other, a capitalist, patriarchal, and racist culture nurtures resentment and shame in ways that feature in the interior and exterior lives of the women in the novel. For Wyatt (2017), Heed and Christine's loss is not only of each other but also of a past and history that could have been nurturing for them. This loss heralds a present-day disorientation with their immediate world that also does not recognize a meaningful future. Even when social organizing for social justice, in the Black civil rights group that the young woman Christine would become a part of, there is a failure to fully engage a politics of Black love among the group's members. When a young female comrade is raped by a male comrade, it is the women in the group who shame and silence their sister. Their response effectively sanctions the leaders' inactions against the sexual violence—they superficially support their sister while questioning her complicity in her own violation.

(Re)claiming Love: Naming Our Losses

In *Love*, Morrison traverses different terrains of Black love: communal love, familial love, revolutionary love, sexual and romantic love, self-love, and friendship. Across these terrains, she shows love's missed opportunities for nurturing connection when it fails to attend to its own fragility and melancholic underpinnings. David Eng and Shinhee Han's notion of a racial melancholia is a useful one to consider here (2000). Racial melancholia and how it may manifest in intergenerational sites of trauma flags the continued transmission of racialized trauma in the form of grief and loss within the community. The gendering of melancholia is also a critical site from which to think about unnameable loss and grief that pertain to gender (see Bell 1999; Butler 1995; Schiesari 2018). These melancholic underpinnings of loss and grief as well as the communal quality of love, then, must be part of the project of Black healing. Healing requires a readiness to name our losses (of self and of each other), as well as the sources of these losses. Audre Lorde (1984; 2017) and bell hooks (2002; 2004) have urged this practice of healing in their work. They attend not only to practices of healing for Black women but also more broadly communal healing and revival within the Black community. They do this via a centering of love as politics. Feminist scholarship on affect as politics of emotion offers us a methodology for engaging love as politics that includes a practice of self as well as a practice of community (hooks 2002, 2004; Lorde 1984; Nash 2013). What is at stake for us in reading interior lives in ways that center their affective dimensions? Lorde's work on rage between Black women invites us to consider this domain of affective arrangement as crucial to a politics of revolution and of healing (1984). In highlighting the importance of naming our losses and our grief, of (re)connecting with each other, Lorde foregrounds a politics of Black women's love as central to social justice. Similarly, the Black feminist poet and activist, June Jordan (1978) foregrounds love in her project of social justice. Indeed, Black feminism has centered love as essential to its revolution of social change (Nash 2013) and honoring the lived experiences of women. The affective turn in feminist theory in this sense is a recognition of the peril that underpins systemic and intersecting oppression in terms of its affective costs to healing. Amanda Holmes alerts us to the politics and practice of speaking shame as a means of rendering it powerless when she says:

> A politics of shame presents an interesting paradox: shame, in one of its most important senses, seems to dissipate when it is made public or when it is shared. That is, the negative and isolating qualities that are constitutive of the affect of shame are negated when it is confessed. To confess one's shame is to destroy it. (2015, 415)

It is in the last chapter, *Phantom*, that Heed and Christine return to language. They not only speak once again in their secret code, but also name and speak their shame to each other. Morrison's own adoption of a stylistic form that defies traditional speech conventions is an interesting one here, that evokes a return to prelanguage and symbolic rules. They name their losses—parental and communal—to each other and in naming are able to recognize the other's loss and grieving:

> You know May wasn't much of a mother to me.
> At least she didn't sell you.
> No, she gave me away. (184)

> It's like we started out being sold, got free of it, then sold ourselves
>   to the highest bidder.
> Who you mean "we"? Black people? Women? You mean me and you?
> I don't know what I mean. (185)

And when Heed repeats the shaming language that does not recognize her violation at the hands of her parents who sold her into marriage (two hundred to her father and a pocketbook to her mother) and at the hands of Cosey her suitor and eventual husband, it is Christine who speaks language that recovers her innocence. Christine for the first time is able to say, "No you didn't. You were too young to decide" (186) in response to Heed's self-naming as sexually immoral. And in so doing, they recover productive rage. Crucially, they are both able to name their idolization and desire for Cosey and what he represents as part of a symbolic ordering rooted in patriarchal fantasy and which demands women's complicity:

> We could have been living our lives hand in hand instead of looking for
>   Big Daddy everywhere.
> He was everywhere. And nowhere.
> We make him up?
> He made himself up.
> We must have helped. (189)

Notably, they can name their loss of each other and the theft of childhood. In the end, even *L*, acknowledges this theft of love between the two girls/women brought on by the misogynistic and punitive demands of patriarchal society within which they must grow up.

I quite like Daley's subversion of the coming-of-age narrative trope in fiction to rather underscore *coming-of-rage*: "I define lit as both the liminal space between Black girlhood and Black womanhood and the affective spectrum between Black-girl joy and Black-girl rage. As a result of these lit experiences, I assert that Black girls do not come of age. Rather, they come of (r)age" (2021, 1036). The unfolding of the gendered, classed, and racialized orders of power and violence that both girls are forcefully introduced to represent something akin to this sense of coming-of-rage. For there is no coming of age for Black girls due to the ways in which the historic traumas of slavery, civil rights, and racial formation have adulterated how their age, rates of physical maturation, and social development are constructed and perceived. In addition, coming of age is an insufficient categorization for the maturation processes of Black girls because they are not seen as innocent but rather as sassy, precocious, and smart-mouthed. (Daley 2021, 1036)

It is also in the final revelation of her name to us and in naming the authentic and healing love that exists between the young girls, that she (L) makes clear her sense of love's fragility and the penalties of its destructive fallout. L's role in the novel is an important one for us (Ho 2006). An ever-watchful arbiter to the different women in the Cosey household, we are never certain what to make of her existence: Is she living or dead? This motif is a deliberate one that Morrison adopts to be able to explore love in its multidimensional forms (Vega-Gonzalez 2005). As embodied love, she is our authoritative voice in the novel, providing a vantage view from which to reflect on love's failures and fallacies:

> People with no imagination feed it with sex—the clown of love. They don't know the real kinds, the better kinds, where losses are cut and everybody benefits. It takes a certain intelligence to love like that—softly, without props. (Morrison 2003, 63)

Alexandru (2008) emphasizes this reclamation of love in Morrison's work, showing that long-standing traditions of hatred of the Black subject necessitate such a politics of reclamation that centers love. Wardi (2005) in turn engages the materiality of love in the novel, arguing that Morrison presents us with love as more than a feeling. For Wardi, *Love* is also an intricate exploration of love as an action word, love not as noun but as verb. Wyatt (2017) similarly explores the subversion angle of the novel in her reminder that *Love* resists the taken-for-granted narrative frame that we have come to expect (love between a man and woman) and presents us with a same-gendered, coming-of-(r)age narrative unfolding instead.

Conclusion

This article has discussed affective economies of love between Black women through the work of Toni Morrison in her novel *Love*. While the novel attends to love in its myriad forms—sexual, romantic, familial, communal, and revolutionary love—it is more explicitly in the relationship between two vulnerable young girls who grow into adult-hating women that Morrison invites us to consider not only the failures of love but also its fragility. In asking what the affective quality of love can be between Black women and how such a love can become distorted, the article also asks us to consider love's possibilities outside of the confines of an anti-Black, patriarchal, and capitalist society. Morrison invites us to think anew the possibilities of/for Black women loving each other, even within these systems of oppression. The implications for feminist building of communities that nurture is at the heart of this invitation. In centering violence and rage, Morrison also draws our attention to the importance of engaging women's rage that fails to build community, that is unfocused, and, in the end, damaging to feminist ideals of sisterhood and friendship between women—the possibility of love to bond women together for change and healing that "is all part of Black community" (Lugones and Rosezelle 1995, 140). The possibilities are always present, but we must be vigilant in doing the work of naming, speaking, and (re)connecting so that, as Morrison argues, "love must earn its name, its place" (Houston 2003).

Acknowledgments
I thank the two anonymous reviewers for their critical insights on earlier drafts of this article. Their contributions were invaluable.

Peace Kiguwa is associate professor in psychology at the School of Human and Community Development, the University of the Witwatersrand, South Africa. Her research interests include critical social psychology, affective politics of gender and sexuality, racism and racialization, and the nuances of teaching and learning. She is the current chair of the Sexuality and Gender Division of the Psychology Society of South Africa and recent recipient of the Oppenheimer Memorial Trust Rising Star Fellowship at the University of the Witwatersrand. She can be reached at peace.kiguwa@wits.ac.za.

Works Cited
Ahmed, Sara. 2014. *Cultural Politics of Emotion*. Edinburgh University Press.
Alexandru, Maria-Sabina Draga. 2008. "Love as Reclamation in Toni Morrison's African American Rhetoric." *European Journal of American Culture* 27, no. 3: 191–205.
Bakerman, Jane. S. 1977. "The Seams Can't Show: An Interview with Toni Morrison." In *Conversations with Toni Morrison*, edited by D. Taylor-Guthrie. Jackson: University Press of Mississippi.

————. 1981. "Failures of Love: Female Initiation in the Novels of Toni Morrison." *American Literature* 52, no. 4: 541–63.

Bell, Vikki. 1999. "On Speech, Race and Melancholia: An Interview with Judith Butler." *Theory, Culture & Society* 16, no. 2: 163–74.

Bennett, Juda. 2014. *Toni Morrison and the Queer Pleasure of Ghosts*. Albany: SUNY Press.

Butler, Judith. 1995. "Melancholy Gender—Refused Identification." *Psychoanalytic Dialogues* 5, no. 2: 165–80.

Chisala, Upile. 2019. *Soft Magic*. Kansas City, MO: Andrews McMeel Publishing.

Daley, Lashon. 2021. "Coming of (R)age: A New Genre for Contemporary Narratives about Black Girlhood." *Signs: Journal of Women in Culture and Society* 46, no. 4: 1035–56.

duCille, Ann. 1996. *Skin Trade*. Cambridge: Harvard University Press.

Eng, David L., and Shinhee Han. 2000. "A Dialogue on Racial Melancholia." *Psychoanalytic Dialogues* 10, no. 4: 667–700.

Fischer, Clara. 2018. "Gender and the Politics of Shame: A Twenty-First-Century Feminist Shame Theory." *Hypatia* 33, no. 3: 371–383.

Gordon, Avery. 1990. "Feminism, Writing, and Ghosts." *Social Problems* 37, no. 4: 485–500.

————. 2008. *Ghostly Matters: Haunting and the Sociological Imagination*. Minneapolis: University of Minnesota Press.

Ho, Wen-ching. 2006. "'I'll Tell'—The Function and Meaning of L in Toni Morrison's *Love*." *EurAmerica* 36, no. 4: 651–75.

hooks, bell. 2000. *The Will to Change: Men, Masculinity, and Love*. New York: Atria Books.

————. 2002. *Communion: The Female Search for Love*. New York: William Morrow.

————. 2018. *All About Love: New Visions*. New York: William Morrow.

Holmes, Amanda. 2015. "That Which Cannot Be Shared: On the Politics of Shame." *The Journal of Speculative Philosophy* 29, no. 3: 415–23.

Houston, Pat. 2003. "The Truest Eye." *O, the Oprah Magazine* (online), November 2003. https://www.oprah.com/omagazine/toni-morrison-talks-love.

Jordan, June. 1978. "Where Is the Love?" Paper presented at the National Black Writers Conference, Howard University, Washington, DC, May 1978.

Kaplan, Carla, Sarah Haley, and Mitra Durba. 2021. "Outraged/Enraged: The Rage Special Issue." *Signs: Journal of Women in Culture and Society* 46, no. 4: 785–800.

LeighaCohen. 2014. "(2014) Judith Butler: Speaking of Rage and Grief." YouTube video. https://www.youtube.com/watch?v=ZxyabzopQi8.

Lorde, Audre. 1984. "Eye to Eye: Black Women, Hatred, and Anger." In *Sister Outsider: Essays and Speeches*, 145–75. California: Crossing Press.

———. 1997. "The Uses of Anger." *Women's Studies Quarterly* 25, no. 1/2: 278–85.

———. 2017. *A Burst of Light*. New York: Ixia Press.

Lugones, María C., and Pat Alaka Rosezelle. 1995. "Sisterhood and Friendship as Feminist Models." In *Feminism and Community*, edited by Penny A. Weiss and Marilyn Friedman, 406–12. Philadelphia: Temple University Press.

Morrison, Toni. 2003. *Love*. London: Vintage Press.

Nash, Jennifer C. 2013. "Practicing Love: Black Feminism, Love-Politics, and Post-Intersectionality." *Meridians* 11, no. 2: 1–24.

Orem, Sarah. 2021. "Tangles of Resentment." *Signs: Journal of Women in Culture and Society* 46, no. 4: 963–85.

Oxford English Dictionary. Oxford: Oxford University Press, 1989. https://0-www-oed-com.innopac.wits.ac.za/oed2/00177146.

Ratele, K. 2005. "The Interior Life of Mtutu: Psychological Fact or Fiction?" *South African Journal of Psychology* 35, no. 3: 555–73.

Schiesari, Juliana. 2018. *The Gendering of Melancholia: Feminism, Psychoanalysis, and the Symbolics of Loss in Renaissance Literature*. New York: Cornell University Press.

Vega González, Susana. 2005. "Toni Morrison's *Love* and the Trickster Paradigm." *Revista Alicantina de Estudios Ingleses* 18: 275–89.

Wardi, Anissa Janine. 2005. "A Laying on of Hands: Toni Morrison and the Materiality of *Love*." *Melus* 30, no. 3: 201–18.

Wyatt, Jean. 2017. *Love and Narrative Form in Toni Morrison's Later Novels*. Athens: University of Georgia Press.

Young Feminists Redefining Principles of Care in Nigeria

Ololade Faniyi and Sharon Omotoso

Abstract: Feminist and queer advocacies in Nigeria have resulted in a wave of radical care praxis due to backlash against members, sociopolitical upheaval, and burnout from ceaseless activist labor. This article discusses how conversations and cultures of radical care are transforming feminist and women's rights collectives and more heterogenous activist groups. It engages a critical synthesis of interviews and personal communications with ten Nigerian feminist and women's rights activists dedicated to various social issues. The findings from this article address undertheorized dynamics of Nigeria's young women and feminist labor, including their subversive reconstruction of radical care as a sustainable and political act, the limits to their feminist labor, and their challenges to the provision and reception of radical care. **Keywords:** radical care; Nigeria's activist communities; feminist labor; sustainability; funding

Introduction

Scholars have extensively debated *care* in global feminist discourse since the 1980s, with topics ranging from definition to adoption and implementation. In 1982, Gilligan sparked a notable debate by distinguishing the male and female conception of morality as ethics of justice and care, respectively (Gilligan 1982; Maihofer 2017). Situating her arguments in opposition to Kolberg's theory of moral development, she argues that the emphasis on ethics of justice was biased to women's moral reasoning, which often interprets situations through the lens of relationships, compassion, and responsibility to others. With histories of devaluing and relegation, feminist scholars like Fraser (2016) call for a need to ungender care to avoid

WSQ: Women's Studies Quarterly 50: 1 & 2 (Spring/Summer 2022) © 2022 by Ololade Faniyi and Sharon Omotoso. All rights reserved.

locking women in essentialist interpretations of femininity that compel women into caregiving roles. Lloro-Bidart and Semenko (2017) highlight the problematic way neoliberalism assigns women as the primary providers of care, with little regard for the impact of care work on their well-being. Situating her arguments in the context of Africa's new media misrepresentation of women, Omotoso (2018) also argues that ethics of care must be reconstructed as ethics of vigor, which takes risk, care, control, and justice into equal consideration.

With questions on how to sustain feminist communities, the idea of care began to shift from reductive connotations as feminists began to consider caring for self and others as an integral part of women's radical agency. Audre Lorde's affirmation thirty-three years ago in her book of essays, *A Burst of Light*, maps a significant point of reference in this chapter, especially as her reflections are cast against the threat of burnout within feminist communities and the precarious nature of organizing social movements (2017). Premiering the need for a feminist reconstruction of the concept of care as radical and political praxis, Lorde, writing after she was diagnosed with cancer for the second time in 1988, affirms, "Caring for myself is not self-indulgence, it is self-preservation, and that is an act of political warfare" (130). Lorde's famous quote on self-care as a political act of warfare conceptualized care in Black feminist thought as an act of generating and critiquing power and an act of love that shapes activism and definitions of freedom, set against a backdrop of the series of violence experienced in Black communities. Beyond the self, Black women in the Combahee River Collective brought to life notions of collective care by historically banding together at the kitchen table or standing side by side along picket lines (Sheeby and Nayak 2020, 235). Drawing strength from one another and organizing across their differences, healthy love of self, sisterhood, and community were the guiding principles of their politics against the political-economic system of capitalism, imperialism, and patriarchy. More recently, Angela Davis stated in an interview,

> I think our notions of what counts as radical have changed over time. Self-care and healing and attention to the body and the spiritual dimension—all of this is now a part of radical social justice struggles. That wasn't the case before. (Van Gelder 2016)

While care has since become a buzzword in global traditions (Chatzidakis et al. 2020, 1), the essence of community resounds in feminist reimaginations of the concept beyond popular self-care rituals. These reimaginations interpret well-being and safety as a shared responsibility rather than an individual task (Dockray 2019). With the threats of exhaustion, burnout, and disillusionment, the resulting praxis of collective care becomes crucial to activism, sparking recent conversations within academic settings and funding organizations.[1] In conceptualizing this continuity of care from self to the collective as radical care, Hobart and Knesse define these as "a set of vital but underappreciated strategies for enduring precarious worlds" (2020, 2). In the context of this paper, we establish that caring becomes radical in the face of threat and discrimination, especially in contexts where activists face violent backlash, harassment, criminal, and other state penalties for their work. An overarching question thus steers this article: How is radical care established in the work of young women's rights and feminist activists in Nigeria? The article proceeds with a reflection on radical care praxis within African feminist traditions and Nigerian activist settings that have core political, collective, and resistant undertones. Subsequently, we describe the methodology and analyze comments from semistructured interviews with young women's rights and feminist activists in Nigeria.

Conceptions of Radical Care in African Feminist Traditions

We may center African women's radical care praxis by looking to African community knowledge and literary traditions where women collectively worked to amplify agency and freedom. From the African feminist literary traditions of Buchi Emecheta and Sefi Atta, the concept of radical care manifests in the practice of communal banking. In Emecheta's *Joys of Motherhood* (1994), when Nnu Ego moves to Lagos, she borrows money from the Igbo women's society to start a business and support her family. In Atta's *Swallow* (2010), Tolani's mother, Arike, recounts her great aunt's group of women cloth dyers who were both an empowerment and vigilante collective. They teach other women the craft of adire (indigo-dyed cloth made by Yoruba women of Southwestern Nigeria), and they protect women from forced and abusive marriages by teaching erring men lessons about justice.

Moving beyond literary expressions to real-life traditions, Rebecca Lolosoli of Kenya founded Umoja village in 1990—a sanctuary for women who were survivors of rape perpetrated by local British soldiers (Bindel 2015). Lolosoli came up with the idea of a women-only community when she was in the hospital recovering from a beating by a group of men who targeted her for speaking about women's rights. Umoja started with fifteen other members, and as of 2015, its habitants had increased to forty-seven women and two hundred children. As Bindel (2015) describes, the village is sustainable, with the women earning a regular income from tourist visits and jewelry crafts. Women from this village also go out to surrounding Samburu villages to educate women and girls about female genital mutilation and disadvantages of early marriage. The consequent shifting positions in Samburu regarding female genital mutilation and the impact of informal learning have drawn research focus (Graamans et al. 2019; Nam 2018, 2021).

The actions of sjambok feminists in South Africa also help turn the conversation to contemporary practices of women creating communities to care for and protect themselves. In an interview with *Mail and Guardian* in 2020, Yvette Racheal, an HIV activist, described herself as a "professional protester, sjambok feminist, and hater of trash" (Patel 2020). Conversations unfolding from personal communication with Funzani Mtembu, a #feesmustfall activist and graduate student at the University of Witwatersrand (Wits), established that sjambok feminist signals a feminist activist who wields the sjambok, a long leather whip. Black feminists at Wits, Rhodes University, and University of Capetown have embraced this label in reaction to rape culture and gender-based violence in campus environments. South African feminist academic Simamkele Dlakavu tweeted a photo of a sjambok with the hashtag #1patriarch10sjamboks and captioned "Black Feminists at Wits gave me this as a birthday gift," two days after she divulged a harassment experience on campus.[2] More recently, with #feesmustfall advocacies to stop school fees increments and petitions to the government for increased university funding, feminists led protests carrying sjamboks to decry police brutality and internal cultures of homophobia and patriarchy within student activist movements where the activities of "womxn" bodies were ignored (Ndlovu 2017; TMG Digital 2016). At the core of their advocacies, Funzani highlighted that sjambok feminists protect women who were victims of abusive relationships and women who experienced harassment often asked to seek help from "feminists who sjambok" (Funzani Mtembu, pers. comm.). Decrying male activists' sexism toward women activists, sjambok feminists would stand up to the abusers and thrash them with a warning to never again lay hands on a woman, a practice reminiscent of the Gulabi gang, Indian stick-wielding women warriors who protect other women from abuse, rape, and other forms of gender-based violence (Desai 2014).

Drawing on radical care within traditional Yoruba communities, Faniyi (2013) centers her research on women from the Ogboni Lugiriso compound in the Esa-Oke town of Nigeria's Osun State who found community through musical performances. Women from this household performed "ere Obìn-rin-Ilé"[3] as an expression of communal joy and artistic freedom, a "testimony against artistic dominance of the male gender in the music performance domain," connected to the general perception of women as "eru" (slave) in that community (Faniyi 2013, 215). Initially performing "ere Obìnrin-Ilé" in the family courtyard using kitchen items like earthen calabashes and wares, Faniyi (2013) relays that this practice developed over the last hundred years from courtyard performances to a means of skill acquisition. Through funds realized from their performances at community day celebrations, child naming ceremonies, burial ceremonies, and more, these women had a pool of money, with which they empowered one another with soft loans for businesses and other needs. The group would settle internal rifts, pay visits to absent or sick members, and intervene when women were neglected or faced unfair divorce terms.

The work of Bisi Adeleye-Fayemi, Nigerian feminist activist, writer, and policy advocate, also highlights historical legacies of radical care within networks of African women while drawing connections to the degenerating effects of globalization on visions for care within African feminist movements of the 2000s. Arguing that African feminists were tired, depressed, burned out, and angry from the compounded effects of backlash against feminist organizing, media, cultural, and religious subjectivities, and pressures of balancing family and work life, Adeleye-Fayemi maintains that many feminists have inadvertently failed to reflect on how their radical agency should guide interpretations of responsibilities to self and others:

> We need to go back to the old feminist strategies of consciousness-raising and developing women's self-esteem. . . . Let us put the soul back into the movement. (Adeleye-Fayemi 2004, 52–53)

This idea of putting the soul back into the movement resonates with Hope Chigudu's concept of nurturing, called *organization with a soul*. The Ugandan organizational development expert has, through her work, called for activists to pay attention to the emotional dimension of feminist organizing and labor at both individual and organizational stages (Chigudu and Chigudu 2015; Horn 2020). Horn's (2019) centers on contemporary African feminist praxis of radical care within the collective model of HIV+

women's organizing. With the stigma affiliated with HIV+, support groups have had to establish cultures of care to respond to the practical and strategic needs of women living with this disease. Their radical care praxis extends to creating a political movement demanding policy reform as well as favorable state responses and social discourses. Framing their model as *positive living*, these support groups offered "emotional grounding and collective advice on how to eat well, live well, come to terms with being HIV+, and reclaim and live in your own power" (Horn 2019, para. 8). They also synthesize self-care and collective care by encouraging members to rest and eat well while setting up collective wellness spaces for conversations, advocacies, and experience sharing. These interventions connect with Musimbi Kanyoro's *Isirika*, a Maragoli word that means caring together for one another, or equal generosity. In Kanyoro's TED talk, she describes this concept as a "pragmatic way of life that embraces charity, services, and philanthropy all together. . . . Mutual responsibility for caring for one another" (Kanyoro 2017).

On Radical Care in Nigeria

In prior research and writing, scholars have used one or more of the terms *cooperativism, collective action,* and *solidarity* to describe practices of looking out for one another in discussions centered on corruption, insurgency, poverty, higher education, and social protection in Nigeria (Hoffmann and Patel 2017; Schaub 2014; Akanji 2020). Adeleye-Fayemi (2004) centers care to reconstruct African feminist concepts of women's agency and sustainability in feminist communities. Omotoso's (2020) work also highlights partnership and collaboration between rural and urban women to address intrafeminist concerns for social justice. While these works elucidate much about communal support, care as resistance, and Nigerian people's lives, particularly women's lives, this article fills a gap by focusing on the collective and radical dimensions of care within young women's rights and feminist activism in Nigeria, especially as their work[4] is caught in an upheaval of state policing, pandemic, backlash against women leading protest, harassment during protests, and other targeted violence against women activists.

The accomplishments of activist organizations like the Nigerian Initiative for Women's Rights (TIERS) have established radical cultures of solidarity and protection in a country where queerness is criminalized.[5]

Likewise, during the heat of the #ENDSARS crisis in Nigeria, the Feminist Coalition, in collaboration with the End SARS Response Unit, adopted radical acts of collective care, providing food and supplies, medical help-lines, free legal aid, mental health intervention lines, and more for protesters, in the face of severe government resistance and police force against these activists.[6] The feminist group, Wine and Whine Nigeria, also "fight the patri-archy" by whining (a Caribbean-inspired dance where dancers rhythmically thrust and rotate their pelvic girdle) and drinking wine.[7] The radical signif-icance of this practice lies in traditional prescriptions that frown against women's public bodily performances. Thus, by publicly sharing videos and pictures of their acts of joy and relaxation, they relay a radical performance of defiance and agency, resonating with global activist stories and strategies in Barry and Djordjevic's (2007) book *What's the Point of Revolution If We Can't Dance?* We argue that these are some of Nigeria's most visible and reactionary acts of radical care, which have leveraged social media and emerged from state and nonstate threats to members' safety and agency. Drawing on these works, the article considers cultures of radical care within young women's rights and feminist groups fighting for equality and justice in Nigeria outside major media spotlight.

Newer and more structured movements for radical care have been supported by funding organizations dedicated to young African feminist organizing, extending the conversations on care praxis to physical safety, financial security, healing, general well-being, and digital safety. The focus on digital safety resonates with Omotoso's argument on how new media technologies reinforce women's oppression thereby calling for renegotiation and reclaiming of digital spaces (Omotoso 2018). Conversations on reclaim-ing collaborative digital spaces highlight radical care enabling applications with end-to-end encryption serving community actions like WhatsApp and applications with two-step verification like Signal. Online manuals circulated by funding organizations like FRIDA, the Young Feminist Fund, detail holistic digital security for young women's rights and feminist activ-ists working in areas with high risks of judicial criminalization.[8] Other women's rights and feminist funding organizations, including African Women's Development Fund (AWID) and Urgent Action Fund-Africa, also draw attention to radical care by creating platforms, retreats, policy changes, and transnational conversations to generate knowledge on sustainable prac-tices in feminist organizing (Horn 2020).

These concerted efforts of drawing attention to care underscores that the task of addressing women's physical and emotional challenges within activist spaces has become a significant shortcoming of feminist work (Adeleye-Fayemi 2004, 52). Hence, sections in this article consider how years of upheaval and struggle have shaped cultures and conversations around radical care within grassroots young women's rights and feminist organizing in Nigeria. In navigating this, the article also explores the difficulties involved in receiving or providing radical care.

Methods and Materials

The first-named researcher conducted semistructured interviews with ten feminist and women activists from three cities in Nigeria: Lagos, Abuja, and Ibadan. We maintain that in-depth semistructured interviews aid self-reflection and open dialogue. Sampling was purposive, and the inclusion criteria were participants who were willing to participate and who belonged to varied feminist and women advocacy groups, including advocacy journalism, performance activism, children's welfare, legal activism, LGBT+ activism, wellness and feminist movements on sexual violence, domestic violence, and reproductive and abortion rights. Participant's contact information was identified through internet searches and personal social media networks. Participants were between the ages of nineteen and thirty-two years old.

Data was collected based on a single semistructured interview performed over phone calls or WhatsApp chats and voice notes. Each interaction took about sixty minutes. Before each interview, participants were told the purpose and intended use of the data derived from the project, and they gave oral or written consent to participate. Regarding participants' confidentiality, four asked for generic pseudonyms in place of their names and activist groups, while six participants permitted us to share their identities in the presentation of results.

Drawing on feminist methodologies of one-off interviews (Thwaites 2017), we maintain that the first-named author's personal experience with the research subject, as a feminist activist and advisor of a feminist funding organization, was beneficial to the interviews, as it created a rapport that helped establish shared viewpoints and reflective dialogue, and mitigate what Sobande, Fearfull, and Brownlie refer to as "exploitative research power dynamics" (2019, 9).

Interviews began by asking respondents to describe challenges faced in their work as activists, what they understood by radical care, their definitions of self-care and collective care, and which they thought was most effective in activist spaces. After that, they were asked to describe in their own words strategies of radical care adopted in spaces where they acted as leaders or members. Finally, participants were asked to reflect upon the significance of radical care in sustaining activist communities and the importance of funding radical care. Interview transcription and analysis involved an open-coding categorization of common expressions and sentiments. A thematic analysis of the main points of discussion revealed five interconnected themes.

Discussion of Findings

Through analysis of the interviews, five thematic categories were identified: (1) radical care as a political act key to sustaining feminist communities; (2) the mutual inclusivity of self-care and collective care; (3) exclusive self-care cannot solve systemic issues; (4) functioning in activist spaces without a soul is challenging; and (5) radical care deserves funding.

Radical Care as a Political Act Key to Sustaining Feminist Communities

The shared definitions of radical care expressed participants' understanding of the concept as a political act of resistance and solidarity, which they argue is underdiscussed and needs more attention. They maintained that internal cultures in more activist spaces needed to be turned toward radical care. Moyomade Aladesuyi, the cofounder of Walk Against Rape in Nigeria (WARN) and Pro-Choice Nigeria, explained:

> Radical care is a form of liberation because this world expects us to be so productive all the time. It's a radical thought because it proves we can exist, rest . . . and focus our energy on the things that matter . . . without having to pander to capitalism or any of these other systems that the world is built to work on. (Aladesuyi, WhatsApp interview, February 23, 2021)

Another participant, Ayo*, a member of a feminist wellness group, adds:

> If we don't care for ourselves in this Nigeria, we are leaving our sisters to deal with a society that wants us in pain, struggling to survive against

---

*Throughout this article, names with asterisks are generic pseudonyms adopted for participants' confidentiality.

heteropatriarchal traditions, fighting with each other and burnt out. See, we need to talk about it (radical care) more, especially for feminist groups. (Ayo, phone interview, January 20, 2021)

Sharing her thoughts, Halimah*, a joint coordinator of a group dedicated to feminist political education and participation, says:

With the amount of sexist jokes we encounter on our trips to offices of male political office holders and party leaders to inspire equality, I get so angry. You should see these men hugging us inappropriately and calling us their wives. That's why we take necessary time off to shake off their words and build resilience. I personally feel guilty for taking time off sometimes, but if we don't, we would literally explode and trend for slapping one of them someday. And that is not what we want to trend for. We want to trend for political numbers, female political office holders! (Halimah, phone interview, January 19, 2021)

Some online articles and book chapters have reflected on this frustration and sociopolitical backlash against women's rights and feminist activists: "Creating a New World with New Visions: African Feminism and Trends in the Global Women's Movement" by Adeleye-Fayemi (2004) and "On Africa's Feminist Frontlines, We Need Accessible Care Practices to Sustain Our Movements" by Horn (2019). Horn (2020) also elucidates the warning of Swazi feminist, Patrician McFadden over two decades ago in which she argues that women must understand the limits of their nurturing, especially as they shoulder increasing social and economic responsibilities that the state should otherwise bear:

Female nurturing can easily become a trap . . . we need to understand the limits of our nurturing, where we should draw the line in relation to the responsibilities which men must assume, and especially men who traffic in the state. (McFadden 1997, 25)

With two decades of reflection, African women's rights and feminist activists are coming to terms that they must see themselves as political beings who should balance the internal power relations of their activist groups and the burden of their feminist labor to achieve for themselves the freedom and equality they want for their communities. Sargsyan (2018) argues that this realization creates ripple effects necessary for the survival of feminist political work and visions of a feminist future. The radical possibilities of joy and sustainability emerging from care as a feminist political act can thus help to create what political anthropologist Deborah Thomas describes as "the most revolutionary transformations" arising from interior shifts in power, recognition and consciousness from all persons in activist spaces in "unexpected and necessarily non-linear ways" (Thomas 2015).

The Mutual Inclusivity of Self-Care and Collective Care

While there are recent definitions of self-care and collective care as two separate forms of empathy (Spicer 2019; Dockray 2019), respondents in this study addressed both as necessary and co-constitutive concepts. Karimot Odebode, ONE campaigner, a member of the Black Girls Dream Initiative, and an organizer of the Ibadan Walk Against Rape, highlights that if individual well-being is not ensured, then there will be no energy for collective care:

> I am looking out for all other sisters and then I'm also looking out for myself. It's a two-way thing and they can work together. And moving on in our work as a feminist collective, we are more active. (Odebode, WhatsApp interview, February 24, 2021)

Tosin Odukoya, the founder of Shoe a Child, a child welfare organization, also describes strategies of collective care adopted in her organization to pool funds for celebrating members' significant days, phoning team members and more: "The conditions of children we encounter on field trips is very distressing. I myself talk to a therapist on many occasions" (Odukoya, phone interview, February 19, 2021). Tosin maintains that she must maintain her well-being as her group's organizer to initiate collective care practices adequately. Karimot's and Tosin's remarks justify Lisa Chamberlain's arguments that activists who maintain self-care practices are more likely to be more innovative, productive, and collaborative (Chamberlain 2020, 218). Jane*, a feminist podcaster, protest organizer, and writer, also explained:

> I think of collective care as joint self-care. We take care of ourselves on individual basis and we bring the resources from our self-care practices into our collective space to take care of one another. (Jane, WhatsApp interview, March 2, 2021)

These comments link to Audre Lorde's radical care statement (Lorde 2017), in which her principle of self-care can also be interpreted as a reference to the intertwined nature of the two concepts: "If one Black woman I do not know gains hope and strength from my story, then it has been worth the difficulty of telling" (Lorde 2017, 90).

Exclusive Self-Care Cannot Solve Systemic Issues

With the mutual inclusivity of self-care and collective care established within these young women's rights and feminist activist traditions, respondents, however, attested that self-care has its limits in that it cannot solve systemic issues that require the intersectional praxis of collective care. Ayo* shared that she acknowledged her and her group's middle-class privileges as enabling them to coordinate feminine wellness practices like communal storytelling, Zoom meditation sessions, and more. She maintained that with the lower class, LGBT+, HIV+, and disabled women, who often have limited financial and emotional resources, the individualistic nature of self-care is inadequate for their experiences:

> We cannot ask these women to take care of themselves without assistance, so in that way, self-care is problematic and embraces neoliberal middle class-led narratives. We say there is no feminism without intersectionality and there should be no care without intersectionality too. (Ayo, phone interview, January 20, 2021)

Hobart and Kneese (2020) reflect on the one-dimensional model of self-care narratives, arguing that while it is a solution to the strains of activism, "it has become a symptom of late capitalism," pushing commoditized remedies like "specialized diets, therapies, gym memberships, and scheduled management" (2–3). Toyosi Morgan, a performance activist, also argued against the neoliberal culture of self-care:

> It is not sustainable for our under-funded and disregarded theatre for social change groups to push narratives of celebrity self-care. That's why I think of ways to have affordable and collective practices like being mindful of myself and my crew's nutrition. In many ways, it's a victory to even think of that as care, in the times of Hubert Ogunde, actors literally ran in various directions after a performance to avoid getting arrested. (Morgan, WhatsApp interview, February 18, 2021)

Chatzidakis et al. (2020) also present arguments on the implications of self-care narratives in which powerful business actors responsible for inequalities and ecological degradation push themselves as caring corporations by "promoting wellness products like sweet-smelling candles and fluffy towels" (3). These remarks and critical arguments suggest a need for activist spaces to comprehend identity markers including class, ability, sexuality, and more, in the conception of radical care. If they ignore the implications of a one-dimensional model of care within heterogeneous groups of activists, then radical care loses the necessary collective and resistant dynamics that establish it as a political act of liberation.

Functioning in Activist Spaces without Soul Is Challenging

Shade, a former intern with Sahara Reporters, a Nigerian journalistic advocacy newspaper founded by Omoyele Sowore, reflected that there was always stress and tensions of physical safety where she went for field events and reports (Shade, WhatsApp interview, February 19, 2021). Sowore is a Nigerian human-rights activist and former presidential candidate. He has been in state detention several times for his #RevolutionNow campaign, which the Nigerian State Security Service has described as "conspiracy to commit treason and insulting President Muhammadu Buhari" (Owolabi 2020). Shade, describing that her work made her a default member of Sowore's #RevolutionNow movement and presidential campaigns, stated:

> There was no training to prepare us; I faced the activist labor live and direct and had to absorb the challenges I met. I opted out when I realized it was too dangerous and I wasn't prepped for that. (Shade, WhatsApp interview, February 22, 2021)

Describing the internal culture of her group, Ebun Olaleye, a member of the International Federation of Women's Lawyers (FIDA), shared how the crisis of exclusion and injustice has resulted in feelings of resignation and discouragement:

> There is a lot of disillusionment within female legal spaces dedicated to advocacy beyond the courtroom. The corrupt and male-dominated justice system overtakes our efforts many times. And our chat spaces have mostly become a place of congratulating wins and appointments. We share that joy but the idea of radical care in real sense, no. (Olaleye, WhatsApp interview, February 22, 2021)

Chigudu and Chigudu (2020) discuss the essence of activist organizing with a soul as crucial to seeing activist collectives as made up of people defined by power relations that shape their work and the extent to which they find it liberating. Thus, they suggest that activist groups consider "not just the well-being of the entire organization but also the well-being of individual parts" (22–24). In response to activism without soul, participants like Shade and Ebun have underscored shortcomings and challenges in activist work that ignore radical care. Their comments point to how organizations must investigate their internal structures and amplify self-reflections from individual activists.

Radical Care Deserves Funding

Respondents collectively affirmed that radical care would define the future of relationships between activist groups, organizers, and grant funders. Arguing that radical care deserved attention and funding, Tosin Odukoya shared: "If we get funding, our team members can have group insurance for therapy" (Odukoya, phone interview, February 19, 2021). Sharing her reflections, Toyosi Morgan explained: "With funding, we can reestablish theatre community actions of double-casting for productive labor, so our actors do not feel the burden of performing even during difficult times" (Morgan, WhatsApp interview, February 19, 2021). Toyosi detailed challenges to this funding as performance donors are not often inclined to fund theatre for social change because "they want to fund comedy that will have a large audience wanting to pay gate fees. To go to them and say you want funds for collective care for activist theatre groups will most likely be doubly disregarded" (Morgan, WhatsApp interview, February 19, 2021). Ann*, the founder of an antisexual violence initiative, also noted: "If we gain collective care funding, then we can fund professional training and coaching for our members. Activists' professional development is also radical care" (Ann, phone interview, January 20, 2021).

Excerpts from these conversations turn the attention to funding organizations like the Human Rights Funders Network (HFRN), Urgent Action Fund-Africa, Open Global Rights, and FRIDA, the Young Feminist Fund, who are calling for activists to complete applications for funding care. In recent months and years, funding organizations seem to be obligated to support initiatives that institutionalize radical care. However, while this is a celebrated occurrence, this article is cautious about addressing these as a definite solution, especially as inaccessibility and lack of awareness of these organizations remain a problem for local activists in Nigeria. These grants also only cater to a limited number of groups who pass internal review processes, and respondents spotlight challenges with creative, literacy, and digital means to articulate their experiences. Therefore, future research avenues must continue to question how radical care funding can be comprehensive and explore the scope of funding organizations' models of care, especially within an intrusive setting of capitalist cultures and infrastructure.

Conclusion
Participants' conception of radical care had notable differences based on the scope of their work, individual interpretations, and the levels to which governments and law agencies policed their work. Common strategies of radical care include regular phone calls to fellow activists and activists collectively taking time off to rest. Others included attention to group nutrition, Zoom meditation sessions, and pooled funds for group needs. Funding was a common hindering factor to introducing more creative strategies of radical care. When there are threats to group objectives, radical care praxis embodied self-care and collective care traditions.

This article's focus on radical care contributes to knowledge highlighting undertheorized dynamics of young women's rights and feminist activism in Nigeria. In emphasizing the conceptualization of radical care, attention is drawn to the work of young feminists and women who often cannot afford not to challenge the powerful forces that enforce domination. Therefore, their present and future realities must be reimagined within radical care traditions that protect, energize, nurture, support, and sustain feminist communities.

Ololade Faniyi is a graduate student of American culture studies at Bowling Green State University, Ohio. She has worked with community-driven collectives on feminist politics and rape crisis. She is currently WESCA advisor of FRIDA, the Young Feminist Fund. She can be reached at ofaniyi@bgsu.edu.

Sharon Omotoso is a senior research fellow at the Institute of African Studies, University of Ibadan, and coordinator of Women's Research and Documentation Centre (WORDOC). She has created platforms for community education on applied ethics, African feminism, and political communication. She can be reached at sa.omotoso@ui.edu.ng.

Notes

1. See this funding road map on the Human Rights Funders network website: https://www.hrfn.org/community-voices/human-rights-funding-principles-offer-a-road-map-to-strengthen-philanthropy/.
2. See Simamkele Dlakavu's tweet here: https://twitter.com/simamkeleD/status/717085853353426944?s=20.
3. *Ere Obinrin-Ile* loosely translates to "a performance by women of the house." The women perform songs accompanied by Sekere (beaded gourd rattles) and an ensemble of agogos (metal gong).
4. The last five years had Nigerian women's rights and feminist activists involved in several protest movements, including anti-rape protests and the End SARS protests, Say Her Name Nigeria, Sex for Grades, MeToo Nigeria, ChurchToo, etc.
5. See pictures of House of Allure, a Nigerian queer safe house, shot by photographer Sabelo Mlangeni, on *Dazed Magazine* website, https://www.dazeddigital.com/art-photography/article/50535/1/sabelo-mlangeni-house-of-allure-photographs-life-inside-nigerian-queer-safehouse?amp=1
6. The collectives essentially adopted Twitter as a means of amplifying these radical care actions: https://mobile.twitter.com/fkabudu/status/1317403478516506625?s=21.
7. See Wine and Whine Nigeria's social media platform here: https://www.instagram.com/wineandwhineng/.
8. Watch a recap of the Principles Project Workshop on Collective Care jointly facilitated by FRIDA, HRFN, Astraea Lesbian Foundation for Justice and more here: https://drive.google.com/file/d/1WWp9Pcqiw1aVQV4x-E9bUoTWu8JYYLfMa/view, and browse through visual harvest here https://www.hrfn.org/wp-content/uploads/2016/11/Principles-Work-shop-5-Visual-Harvest.pdf Browse the digital safety resources curated by FRIDA, the Young Feminist Fund, https://youngfeministfund.org/solidarity-storms/security/.

Works Cited

Adeleye-Fayemi, Bisi. 2004. "Creating a New World with New Visions: African Feminism and Trends in the Global Women's Movement." In *The Future of Women's Rights: Global Visions and Strategies,* edited by Joanna Kerr, Ellen Sprenger, and Alison Symington, 38–55. 1st ed. London, UK: Zed Books.

Akanji, Ajibola Anthony. 2020. "The Poverty Challenge in Africa: Innovative Cooperativism through Political Incentives. A Case Study of Nigeria." *Cooperativismo & Desarrollo* 28, no. 116: 1.

Atta, Sefi. 2010. *Swallow*. Northampton, MA: Interlink Books.

Barry, Jane, and Jelena Djordjevic. 2007. *What's the Point of Revolution If We Can't Dance?* Alameda, CA: Urgent Action Fund for Women's Rights.

Bindel, Julie. 2015. "The Village Where Men Are Banned." *The Guardian*, August 16, 2015. https://www.theguardian.com/global-development/2015/aug/16/village-where-men-are-banned-womens-rights-kenya.

Chamberlain, Lisa. 2020. "From Self-Care to Collective Care." *Sur: International Journal on Human Rights* 17, no. 30: 215–25.

Chatzidakis, Andreas, Jamie Hakim, Jo Littler, Catherine Rottenberg, and Lynne Segal. 2020. "From Carewashing to Radical Care: The Discursive Explosions of Care during Covid-19." *Feminist Media Studies* 20, no. 6: 889–95.

Chigudu, Hope, and Rudo Chigudu. 2015. "Strategies for Building an Organisation with a Soul." *African Institute for Integrated Responses to VAWG & HIV/AIDS (AIR)*, August 2015. http://airforafrica.org/wp-content/uploads/2015/08/Strategies-for-Building-an-Organisation-with-Soul-WEB.pdf.

Desai, Shweta. 2014. "Gulabi Gang: India's Women Warriors." *Al Jazeera*, March 4, 2014. https://www.aljazeera.com/features/2014/3/4/gulabi-gang-indias-women-warriors.

Dockray, Heather. 2019. "Self-care Isn't Enough. We Need Community Care to Thrive." *Mashable*, May 24, 2019. https://mashable.com/article/community-care-versus-self-care/.

Emecheta, Buchi. 1994. *The Joys of Motherhood*. Portsmouth, NH: Heinemann.

Faniyi, Kehinde. 2013. "Ọbìnrin-Ilé Music in Esa-Oke Town of Osun State: A Female Dimension in Indigenous Musical Performance." *Journal of the Association of Nigerian Musicologists* 7: 213–26.

Fraser, Nancy. 2016. "Contradictions of Capital and Care." *New Left Review* 100: 99–117. https://newleftreview.org/issues/ii100/articles/nancy-fraser-contradictions-of-capital-and-care.

Gilligan, Carol, 1982. *In a Different Voice: Psychological Theory and Women's Development*. Cambridge, MA: Harvard University Press.

Graamans, Ernst, Peter Ofware, Peter Nguura, Eefje Smet, and Wouter T. Have. 2019. "Understanding Different Positions on Female Genital Cutting among Maasai and Samburu Communities in Kenya: A Cultural Psychological Perspective." *Culture, Health & Sexuality* 21, no. 1: 79–94.

Hobart, Hi'ilei J. K., and Tamara Kneese. 2020. "Radical Care: Survival Strategies for Uncertain Times." *Social Text* 38, no. 1: 1–16.

Hoffmann, Leena Koni, and Raj Navanit Patel. 2017. *Collective Action on Corruption in Nigeria: A Social Norms Approach to Connecting Society and Institutions*. London: Chatham House.

Horn, Jessica. 2019. "On Africa's Feminist Frontlines, We Need Accessible Care Practices to Sustain Our Movements." *Open Democracy*, July 2, 2019. https://www.opendemocracy.net/en/5050/on-africas-feminist-frontlines-we-need-accessible-care-practices-to-sustain-our-movements/

———. 2020. "Thoughts on Radical Care in African Feminist Praxis." *The Sociological Review*, March 18, 2020. https://www.thesociologicalreview.com/thoughts-on-radical-care-in-african-feminist-praxis/

Kanyoro, Musimbi. 2017. "To Solve the World's Biggest Problem, Invest in Women and Girls." Filmed November 2017 in New Orleans, LA. TED video, 01:27. https://www.ted.com/talks/musimbi_kanyoro_to_solve_the_world_s_biggest_problems_invest_in_women_and_girls?language=en.

Kohlberg, Lawrence. 1981. *Essays on Moral Development, Vol. I: The Philosophy of Moral Development*. San Francisco, CA: Harper and Row.

Lloro-Bidart, Teresa, and Keri Semenko. 2017. "Toward a Feminist Ethic of Self-Care for Environmental Educators." *The Journal of Environmental Education* 48, no. 1: 18–25.

Lorde, Audre. 2017. *A Burst of Light: And Other Essays*. New York: Courier Dover Publications.

Maihofer, Andrea. 2017. "Care." In *A Companion to Feminist Philosophy*, edited by Alison M. Jaggar and Iris Marion Young, 383–92. New Jersey: Blackwell Publishing Ltd.

McFadden, Patricia. 1997. "Challenges and Prospects for the African Women's Movement in the 21st Century." *Southern Africa Political & Economic Monthly* 10, no. 10: 25–8.

Nam, Young Eun. 2018. "The Power Structure in the Perpetuation of Female Genital Cutting in Kenya." *Asian Journal of Women's Studies* 24, no. 1: 128–39.

———. 2021. "Learning Through Social Interaction: Kenyan Women Against Female Genital Cutting in Kenya." *Culture, Health & Sexuality* 23, no. 6: 840–53.

Ndlovu, Hlengiwe. 2017. "Womxn's Bodies Reclaiming the Picket Line: The 'Nude' Protest During #FeesMustFall." *Agenda* 31, no. 3/4: 68–77.

Omotoso, S. Adetutu. 2018. "Communicating Feminist Ethics in the Age of New Media in Africa." In *Gendering Knowledge in African Diaspora*, edited by Toyin Falola and Olajumoke Yacob-Haliso, 64–84. London: Routledge.

———. 2020. "When the Hairy Suffer Baldness: Feminized Poverty and Social Exclusion as Problems of Social Justice in Africa." *Ethical Perspectives* 27, no. 1: 117–38.

Patel, Khadija. 2020. "Where the Governments See Statistics, I See the Faces of My Friends." *Mail and Guardian*, December 1, 2020. https://mg.co.za/

health/2020-12-01-where-the-governments-see-statistics-i-see-the-faces-
of-my-friends/.

Sargsyan, Nelli. 2018. "The Importance of Collective Care as a Feminist
(Prefigurative) Political Act." *Feminism and Gender Democracy*, March 9,
2020. https://feminism-boell.org/index.php/en/2018/03/09/
importance-collective-care-feminist-prefigurative-political-act

Schaub, Max. 2014. "Solidarity with a Sharp Edge: Communal Conflict and
Local Collective Action in Rural Nigeria." *Afrobarometer* 149: 1–33.

Sheeby, Chris, and Suryia Nayak. 2020. "Black Feminist Methods of Activism
Are the Tool for Global Social Justice and Peace." *Critical Social Policy* 40,
no. 2: 234–57.

Sobande, Francesca, Anne Fearfull, and Douglas Brownlie. 2019. "Resisting
Media Marginalisation: Black Women's Digital Content and Collectivity."
Consumption Markets & Culture 23, no. 5: 413–28.

Spicer, André. 2019. "'Self-Care': How a Radical Feminist Idea Was Stripped of
Politics for the Mass Market." *The Guardian*, August 21, 2019. https://www.
theguardian.com/commentisfree/2019/aug/21/self-care-radical-feminist-
idea-mass-market.

Thomas, Deborah. 2015. "On the Poetics and Politics of Redress." Paper
presented at the Symposium on What Are the Contemporary Debates
around Restitution, Redress, and Reclaiming Heritage, Research Center for
Material Culture, Leiden, Netherlands, November 2015. https://vimeo.
com/155410023.

TMG Digital. 2016. "Wits Encourages 'Women and Vulnerable Groups' to
Report Protest Violence." *Times Live*, April 7, 2016. https://www.timeslive.
co.za/news/south-africa/2016-04-07-wits-encourages-women-and-vulnerable-
groups-to-report-protest-violence/.

Thwaites, Rachel. 2017 "(Re) Examining the Feminist Interview: Rapport,
Gender 'Matching,' and Emotional Labour." *Frontiers in Sociology* 2: 18.

Van Gelder, Sarah. 2016. "The Radical Work of Healing: Fania and Angela Davis
on a New Kind of Civil Rights Activism." *Yes! Magazine*, February 19, 2016.

African Intimacy and Love with No Pretense: The Erotics of Diaspora in Zina Saro-Wiwa's *Eaten by the Heart*

Bimbola Akinbola

Abstract: This article examines Zina Saro-Wiwa's documentary project and video installation *Eaten by the Heart*, which explores intimacy, heartbreak, and love performances among Africans, both on the continent and in the diaspora. Considering the role of the erotic in how diasporic subjects conceptualize and negotiate their attachments to their homeland and host country, Akinbola argues that Saro-Wiwa marks the Black diasporic body as a site of erotic agency. In doing so, Saro-Wiwa simultaneously acknowledges and resists the burden of respectability and cultural norms that hide and dismiss the importance of emotional expression, intimacy, and vulnerability in the lives of African and African diasporic people. **Keywords:** African diaspora; performance art; Zina Saro-Wiwa; erotics; video art; Nigeria

In her exhibition *Did They Know We Taught Them How to Dance?* Zina Saro-Wiwa asserts: "Environment for me is not just about oil pollution. It is vital to consider emotional, social and spiritual ecosystems in order to transcend the status quo" (Saro-Wiwa 2015). Saro-Wiwa's work, which includes photography, documentary film, short film, and curatorial work, strives to reframe her migration story, as well as the stories of Africans across the continent, considering how geography maps itself onto bodies through feeling and gesture. In this article, I examine Saro-Wiwa's consideration of emotional ecosystems via her representations of love, intimacy, taboo, and pleasure, looking specifically to her 2012/2013 documentary project and video installation *Eaten by the Heart*, which explores intimacy, heartbreak, and love performances among Africans, both on the continent and in the diaspora. I consider the role of the erotic in how diasporic subjects conceptualize and negotiate their attachments to their homeland and host

WSQ: Women's Studies Quarterly **50**: 1 & 2 (Spring/Summer 2022) © 2022 by Bimbola Akinbola. All rights reserved.

country. I argue that Saro-Wiwa marks the Black diasporic body as a site of erotic agency and in doing so, simultaneously acknowledges and resists the burden of respectability and cultural norms and expectations that hide and dismiss the importance of emotional expression, intimacy, and vulnerability in the lives of African and African diasporic people. Audre Lorde defines the erotic as "an assertion of the life force of women; of that creative energy empowered, the knowledge and use of which we are now reclaiming in our language, our history, our dancing, our loving, our work, our lives" (Lorde 1981, 339). She argues that the erotic connection functions through the open and fearless underlining of one's capacity for joy and pleasure, contending that "when we begin to live from within outward, in touch with the power of the erotic within ourselves, and [allow] that power to inform and illuminate our actions upon the world around us, then we begin to be responsible to ourselves in the deepest sense" (Lorde 1981, 342). While Lorde speaks specifically of joy, I contend that the feeling and expression of joy and grief are so deeply intertwined that the two cannot be separated, something that Saro-Wiwa invites us to experience firsthand through *Eaten by the Heart*. Also embedded in our embrace of the erotic is the power gained from what Lorde describes as, "sharing deeply any pursuit with another person" (Lorde 1981, 341). I consider how Saro-Wiwa's work not only pushes the viewer beyond shame and repression but also how her embrace of the documentary-style moves *Eaten by the Heart* beyond the realm of the aesthetic into the creation of fleeting affective diasporic communities that converge in her video work.

Global historian Marc Epprecht contends that the study and corresponding stigmatization of African sexuality began with written accounts from Arab Muslim travelers during the ninth century. According to Epprecht, while scholar Akbar Muhammad found many of these observations to be "respectful meditations upon difference," the travel logs also included claims about the "immense potency and unbridled sexuality" of the Africans that they encountered (Epprecht 2010, 770). Historians speculate that these accounts had reached the Portuguese before they arrived on the African coast in the fifteenth century, and by the late eighteenth century, a number of European scholars were writing about African sexuality (Epprecht 2010, 770). Unsurprisingly, these accounts were bridled in racism, inaccurate translations, and exaggeration, and once African scholars began publishing in European languages, they prioritized contesting these accounts. This account is captured in the work of Jomo Kenyatta, the first known African to be trained as an anthropologist and former prime minister and president of Kenya, who wrote *Facing Mount Kenya* (1938), a monograph about his community, the Ginkuyu tribe. In the monograph, Kenyatta denies the existence of nonheterosexual intercourse within the Ginkuyu tribe, writing, "Any form of sexual intercourse other than the natural form, between men and women acting in a normal way, is out of the question. It is considered taboo even to have sexual intercourse with a woman in any position except the regular one, face to face" (Eppretch 2010, 773). His use of words like "natural," "normal," and "regular" embrace the European standard of asserting control via categorization, and his investments in depicting his tribe in such a way that would be legible to a European audience and appeal to their moral standards at that time.

By the 1940s, the study of African sexuality had been abandoned for what were seen as more pressing topics such as kinship networks and belief systems, and by the 1980s, the HIV/AIDS epidemic refocused the study of African sexuality altogether. Though in the past decade there has been an increase in the amount of scholarship on African sexuality, love, and pleasure, the same themes of sexual violence and disease have continued to define African sexuality (Diabate 2011, 8). Naminata Diabate argues that scholarship and cultural production about the sexuality of West African women disproportionately focuses on reproduction, female circumcision, and rarely, if ever, on pleasure. In her dissertation *Genital Power: Female Sexuality in West African Literature and Film,* she describes how upon entering her program in comparative literature at the University of Texas at Austin she became frustrated with how West African women were continuously depicted in her assigned readings:

> I was frustrated with my assigned readings and their images of West African women, continuously caught in the semiotic of cutting (clitoridectomy and infibulation), violation (corrective rape, rape as weapon of war, marital rape), pathology (HIV/AIDS), and over-reproduction, all practices I have come to call the pervasive picture of negative sexualities. To be more specific, an overwhelming number of pre-1990 fictional narratives from West Africa feature a wide spectrum of acts of violence against female bodies. In other words, these imaginings "restage" or "perform" the paradigm of victimization of women's lives. (Diabate 2011, 8)

Epprecht's historiography of the evolution of the study of African sexuality illustrates how contemporary African ideas about what constitutes

African morality (and perhaps the investment in morality at all) were formed in direct response to European misunderstandings, judgments, and exaggerations of precolonial African love, sex, and intimacy. Primarily invested in countering the inaccurate scholarship produced by European researchers, many Africans, a great number of whom had also converted to Christianity, sought to represent themselves as respectable, moral citizens in the eyes of the colonial elite. Today, the same colonial logics of respectability and morality have made public displays of affection a taboo act in many African communities. The ramifications can be especially dire for women who may be seen as "loose" or indecent by friends, families, and others in their community. This cultural opinion is reflected on the now defunct podcast from 2014, *Waza Africa,* which did an episode on the subject of public displays of affection (PDA) titled, "Public Display of Affection? Not in Africa." In the episode, one man says he frowns upon PDA, explaining, "We know that Africa is known for [having a] good moral standard. So, this issue of PDA in Africa is still seen as immorality" (Nalley 2014). In a 2020 article titled "6 Nigerian Women Talk About Overcoming Purity Culture," a twenty-three-year-old woman by the name of Yinka shares,

> A lot of the guilt and shame I felt around sex and decency came from following Christianity. I was taught that I needed to be "pure" until marriage. No sex, no masturbating, you have to "dress decently." So, abandoning Christianity has helped me abandon that conditioning. I learnt to understand that wanting sex is completely human and that it doesn't make me dirty or any less of a person. (Esekheigbe 2021)

For Yinka, the shame she experienced was directly tied to Christianity, and leaving the church was what allowed her to destigmatize her own relationship to not just sex but pleasure. Another woman, Mo, age twenty-two, explains how even once she believed she had stopped caring about purity culture, it was difficult for her to completely let go. In her words, "When I tried having sex for the first time, it was kind of in my head. I wanted to, but I couldn't. It just wasn't working" (Esekheigbe 2021). While the emphasis in both examples is on sex, the ambiguous use of "decency" can and often does include how one dresses, behaviors like cursing, and acts such as public kissing. In her article, "Nudity and Pleasure," Diabate argues that in recent years, there has been what she calls a "pleasure turn" on the African continent defined as:

The increasing visibility and availability in major African cities, and in their online spaces, of objects related to erotic pleasure; these include erotic, pornography, sex toys, fattening pills and butt enhancing underwear, chat rooms, aphrodisiacs, erotic dances, strip clubs, naked bodies, advertisements for surgical enhancements of male sexual parts, and sexy clothing. (Diabate 2020, 156)

Even as public opinions about heterosexual expressions of affection have perhaps begun to shift, Nigeria's 2014 anti-gay law threatens individuals with up to ten years in prison for public displays of affection with members of the same sex. In light of all of this, Saro-Wiwa's creation of *Eaten by the Heart* in 2012, which included both heterosexual and same sex couples, was a bold and necessary statement made in the midst of culture wars over what counts as decency and which relationships get surveilled and punished.

Saro-Wiwa's work is both political in its consideration of religion, cultural survival, and gender, and also concerned with what some may consider frivolous affective expressions, as well as experimentation within the video form more generally. By offering viewers the opportunity to hear African and African diasporic subjects, particularly women, speak frankly about love, intimacy, and heartbreak, and witness the intimate act of kissing, *Eaten by the Heart* serves as visual records of African diasporic vulnerability. The project takes private and taboo feelings, behaviors, and conversations and uses them as the basis for connection and community in an African diasporic context. In *Postnationalist African Cinemas,* Alexie Tcheuyap historicizes the emergence of African cinema, which he contends was introduced as a colonizing mechanism by Europeans. Tcheuyap writes that these early films were designed to "manufacture otherness, disseminate colonial propaganda, market the 'civilizing mission,' and convey ideologies of superiority" (2011, 3). Out of this mission emerged the Fédération Panafricanine des Cinéastes (FEPACI), an association of filmmakers from the African continent and the diaspora. Although the association began as a liberatory project, they quickly became prescriptive in their approach to film, defining African cinema as exclusively concerned with cultural struggles, education, information, and consciousness raising. According to Tcheuyap, until recently, these parameters worked to exclude certain forms from the category of African cinema, particularly explorations of allegedly frivolous topics such as laughter, joy, pleasure, sexuality, and experimentation. In the exhibition catalog for *Progress of Love,* Bisi Silva writes as follows:

An exhibition taking love as the thematic underpinning may seem unusual
in the context of presenting contemporary art from Africa. Most curatorial
endeavors over the past few decades have focused extensively on more pressing "grand" narratives such as history, colonialism, and the postcolonial as
well as new social-political conditions, new identities, and new subjectivities that epitomize societies in transition. . . . Consequently we are led to
think, "What's love got to do with it?" (Van Dyke and Silva 2012, 113)

Here Silva names the common misconception that matters of the heart are
not as worthy as sociopolitical concerns when it comes to telling African
stories. Saro-Wiwa's work shows us why love (as well as grief) has everything to do with it by pointing to the intricate ways history, colonialism,
and sociopolitical conditions intersect and collide with African diasporic
senses of self and community.

Zina Saro-Wiwa was born in Port Harcourt in the Niger Delta region of
Nigeria. At the age of one, she, along with her mother and two siblings,
moved to Sussex, England, only visiting Nigeria during school holidays.
Over time, mounting political tensions involving her father, writer, and environmental rights activist Ken Saro-Wiwa, made it increasingly dangerous
for the family to visit. Ken Saro-Wiwa, then president and spokesperson for
the Movement for the Survival of the Ogoni People, is most famous for
leading a nonviolent campaign against the pollution of the land and water
in Ogoniland by multinational oil companies, most notably Royal Dutch
Shell. He also spoke out against the military dictatorship led by Sani Abacha,
whom he criticized for failing to regulate foreign oil companies. In 1995,
when Zina Saro-Wiwa was nineteen, he was executed by the government
after being falsely accused of being involved in the murder of four Ogoni
leaders. Zina Saro-Wiwa did not visit Nigeria again until she was twenty-
four, when the government finally released his remains. She began connecting with her African heritage during a gap year in Brazil. Following her time
in Brazil, she returned to the UK to complete a degree in economics and
social history at Bristol University and worked for the BBC where one of
her projects included a two-part radio documentary about her time in the
Brazilian capital of Salvador da Bahia. Saro-Wiwa remained in broadcast
journalism for ten years before deciding to move to New York in 2009.
Saro-Wiwa's move to New York and away from broadcast journalism was
also the start of her career as an artist. While in New York, she directed and
produced *This Is My Africa* (2008), a film about Africans living in London,
which was picked up by HBO. She was also invited to curate a gallery show

at Location One gallery in Manhattan, which was titled "Sharon Stone in Abuja," after the 2003 Nollywood film. The show, which explored and reimagined the Nollywood film industry featured commissioned works from Wangechi Mutu, Andrew Esiebo, Pieter Hugo, and a collaboration between Mickalene Thomas and Saro-Wiwa who together created a Nollywood living room and two portraits. During this time, she traveled to Lagos to make her alt-Nollywood films *Phyllis* (2009a), *The Deliverance of Comfort* (2009b), and *Sarogua Mourning* (2011), which pulled heavily from Nigerian cultures of the everyday, and Nollywood aesthetics and themes, while telling subversive stories and questioning social norms. In 2013, Saro-Wiwa moved back to Port Harcourt and opened an art gallery, Boys Quarters Project Space, in her father's old office. She resides between the United States and Nigeria.

Part I: Interview Excerpts or How Do Africans Kiss?

Taking a documentary approach, *Eaten by the Heart* captures individuals reflecting on intimacy, love, and relationships. The series, which was commissioned by the Menil Collection in Houston and supported by the Houston Museum of African American Culture for the Menil's exhibition titled *The Progress of Love*, consists of a three-part video series, all shot interview style, *Eaten by the Heart: The Documentaries*, and *Eaten by the Heart: The Installation*. While Saro-Wiwa uses the language of documentary to describe the videos, the participants are not named, making them anonymous to the viewer.[1] Though Saro-Wiwa is not overt about who the participants are or where they come from, the varying amounts of familiarity from respondents gives the sense that they are a mix of strangers, friends, and acquaintances. In a call put out by the African Studies Program at the University of Wisconsin–Madison where Saro-Wiwa gave a video presentation about *Eaten by the Heart*, attendees were invited to be a part of the project. The call for participation reads:

> Video artist and documentary-maker Zina Saro-Wiwa is calling on Africans and African Diasporans aged eighteen to ninety to participate in a discussion and interview sessions discussing, love, kissing, heartbreak and intimacy from the African perspective. Zina is also looking for Africans or African diasporans prepared to kiss for the camera. (University of Wisconsin–Madison 2012)

In this article I focus on Part I of the documentaries and the installation.

Part I: Interview Excerpts or How Do Africans Kiss? begins with a single question, "How do Africans kiss?" The eleven-minute film captures interviews with several individuals from all over the African diaspora answering the deceivingly simple question (Saro-Wiwa 2012). At the beginning of the film, we see a young Black woman sitting in front of a white background with her hair in Bantu knots staring directly into the camera. We hear Saro-Wiwa who is off camera ask, "How do Africans kiss?" and the girl raises her eyebrows slightly as she repeats, "How do Africans kiss?" There is a quick cut to a young man in front of the white screen whose lips are in an exaggerated pucker, before the screen cuts back to the same young woman who hesitatingly answers with a smile, "I don't know. I don't really see Africans kiss." The answers offered at the beginning of the video repeat this sentiment: Africans do not kiss, Africans kiss badly, Africans kiss secretly. Kissing is not a part of African culture. An older woman in a deep-red headdress with what sounds like a Nigerian accent to my ears bluntly states, "I'm not comfortable seeing Africans kiss. I think that comes from the environment where I was raised," while a younger woman interviewee expresses that while she does not find Black people kissing strange, generally when she sees Nigerians kissing in Nollywood films, she experiences physical discomfort. Reflected in all of the responses is the feeling that for Africans, and especially Nigerians, the act of kissing is strange and troubling.

As the film progresses, the interviewees begin to consider why they might have these views on kissing. Two themes emerge: the difference between how kissing in Africa is perceived in rural areas versus in the city, and how *where* in the diaspora one is positioned determines their comfort with the act of kissing. To the first point, a couple that appears to be middle-aged explains, "I think it all depends on the exposure . . . outside exposure . . . where you live, how you were brought up and everything. In the rural areas, I didn't see any kissing going on . . . in the city parties and stuff like that, we see kissing . . . but in general we hold our emotions in. We don't express it as much as it needs to be expressed." In this reflection, exposure to certain public displays of affection becomes a marker of geography, with the countryside being more conservative than the city. The interviewee also speaks to a type of repression where she says, "we hold our emotions in. We don't express it as much as it needs to be expressed." By using the language of "need," she reveals that Africans are not naturally unexpressive, but that this holding back is an act of restraint and one that is detrimental.

The theme of geography comes up again when another interviewee explains that *where* in the diaspora one is positioned is also a key factor in whether and how Africans kiss:

> With the younger generations I think . . . um . . . there's definitely a little bit of spice when they kiss. Um . . . they're not shy about kissing anymore. They're a little bit expressive depending on what continent they're on. I think it's important to showcase that. I know I don't see that many couples in Nigeria of my generation kissing in public or whatever . . . it's just a kiss on the cheek but I do see couples here in the states who are a little bit more expressive. (Saro-Wiwa 2012)

Supporting her point, another interviewee shares that he did not become a good kisser until he came to the United States:

> I became a good kisser when I arrived here in America. I became a good kisser. My first time . . . it's almost like I have a tongue in my mouth . . . it's like a meat in my mouth . . . and after like two three times trying to educate myself . . . you know about tongue in my mouth . . . you know it's almost like you want to throw up . . . but today it's a pleasure but it takes time with mind and with body to accept. (Saro-Wiwa 2012)

For both of these interviewees, sexual intimacy and expression is something that happens in a more liberated fashion outside of the continent. This also helps us better understand Saro-Wiwa as the interviewer who speaks about how growing up in the West meant that she was used to seeing "certain types of white people kissing all of the time" (Saro-Wiwa 2020). Both the location of the interviews (in the United States) and Saro-Wiwa's hyperexposure to white people kissing in Western culture understandably make her more aware of her lack of exposure to Africans kissing. Moreover, in the later example, the interviewee expresses disgust as he describes feelings of wanting to throw up triggered by the experience of French kissing. Sianne Ngai writes in *Ugly Feelings*, "In its intense and unambivalent negativity, disgust thus seems to represent an outer limit or threshold of what I have called ugly feelings, preparing us for more instrumental or politically efficacious emotions" (Ngai 2009, 354). Ngai argues that disgust, contrary to other "weak" emotions such as envy, paranoia, and irritation, offers distinct possibilities. Building upon this, in her discussion of disgust and abjection in Julia Kristeva's *Powers of Horror*, Sara Ahmed writes, "Kristeva shows us that what threatens from the outside only threatens insofar as it is already within . . . It is not that the abject has got inside us; the abject turns us inside out, as well as outside in" (Ahmed 2015, 86). In his story about his earliest experiences kissing with tongue, the interviewee describes a process that requires him to push through his own disgust in order to find—to learn—pleasure. It is only through facing another person's tongue, and the disgust it evokes, that he crosses a physical threshold.

Saro-Wiwa then asks interviewees, "How do you like to be kissed?" The first person to answer is a middle-aged man who hesitatingly says, "Hmmm ummm . . . probably on my lips . . . probably on my cheek." The uncertainty communicated by his use of "ummm" and "probably" gestures at his own unpreparedness to answer that type of question and also seems reflective of how many African men, though often seen as the initiators of sex, are rarely put in a position where they are asked to articulate their desires, particularly around tender acts like kissing. After him, a young woman laughs and asks, "Are my parents going to see this video?" referencing the shadow of familial expectation and cultural burden African and African diasporic women in particular must consider. With this question, Saro-Wiwa pushes the interviewees to not only talk about "Africans kissing" as a reality, but also name and articulate their own sensual desires, acknowledging the erotic within themselves. In Lauren Berlant's *Desire/Love*, she argues, "Desire's formalism—its drive to be embodied and reiterated—opens it up to anxiety, fantasy, and discipline" (Berlant 2012, 20). That is to say, the naming and adoption of desire beyond just a fleeting affect is an action that makes one vulnerable. This is precisely what Saro-Wiwa asks her interviewees to do. In the final parts of the film, Saro-Wiwa asks, "When was your heart last broken?" The mood within the film shifts from playful to somber as we see a young man pause for several seconds, smiling uncomfortably, and then averting eye contact with the camera, as if to shield his actual emotions before saying, "I guess like . . . um . . . maybe nine months ago." He finishes the sentence and nods a few times as if relieved to have gotten the words out. We then hear Saro-Wiwa asking, "What happened?" from behind the camera. He pauses again and takes a breath, "Well . . . um," he shakes his head and smiles again, "I really don't want to talk about it."

"When did you last feel loved?" Saro-Wiwa asks. Again, he pauses, nervously licking his lips and averting his gaze, "The same time my heart was broken . . . nine months ago."

"Can you tell me about that?" She asks again. "Um no . . . I really don't want to talk about it."

The camera lingers on him while he struggles to stay composed and speak without breaking down, though his voice trembles. By asking him to elaborate, Saro-Wiwa pushes the interview to a place where he is forced to articulate that not only does he not want to share, but also that he cannot share his last heartbreak. This is the only moment in the film that we hear Saro-Wiwa speaking to the interviewee multiple times. She sits behind the camera as a woman asking him, an African man, to be vulnerable in front of her and does not "turn away" in the face of his tears. In doing so, she creates space for his vulnerability by normalizing his experience through her performance of a feminist ethics of care.

Still, his refusal to elaborate speaks to the limits of the format. It is a safe space, but not entirely safe. Immediately following his interview, we see the same older woman from earlier with the red headdress. Although the viewer does not hear Saro-Wiwa ask a question, we can gather that it is the same, "When was your heart last broken?" The woman speaks deliberately, "I can smile now when I tell you that it was when my kids were buried. But the reason why I smile is because I feel strengthened by the love my husband has for me and by my faith in God. So that was when my heart was last broken when I buried my children." She says it all very matter-of-factly with a neutral look on her face. It is clear to the viewer that she is well-practiced in sharing this difficult truth. After she speaks, we hear what sounds like a sob from behind the camera, presumably Saro-Wiwa. By editing the film in such a way where we see this woman share something so devastating without so much as a voice tremble, but hear Saro-Wiwa gasp, as if by affective transmission, Saro-Wiwa illuminates the interconnectedness, and at times shared grief, between the interviewees and herself—this too is the erotic Lorde speaks of. Saro-Wiwa also captures the often unseen and unacknowl- edged burdens African women carry and inherit, and the struggles African women in the diaspora experience as we reconcile our desire to be seen as whole, complex individuals and our desire to perform the roles that are expected of us and the roles that have been modeled by our mothers and grandmothers. Lorde writes, "The erotic is a measure between the begin- nings of our sense of self and the chaos of our strongest feelings. It is an internal sense of satisfaction to which, once we have experienced it, we know we can aspire. For having experienced the fullness of this depth of feeling and recognizing its power, in honor and self-respect we can require no less of ourselves" (Lorde 1981, 340). *Eaten by the Heart* is a container for participants to toe the line between discovering and asserting a sense of self, and the chaos of grief, heartbreak, and desire. By participating in the project, participants are given the opportunity to experience this internal sense of satisfaction that becomes a feeling that they can aspire to.

The people Saro-Wiwa chooses to interview have a range of skin tones, hairstyles, accents, and attire, and very rarely do they identify where in Africa they are from and whether they are "locals" or "diasporans." Tcheuyap examines how nation-building has become a less prominent motivation in African cinema, arguing that the early postcolonial goal to "write back" to colonial forces has given way to an interest in depicting what has historically been considered "non-representable" subject matter (Tcheuyap 2011, 33). Although Saro-Wiwa is Nigerian, her project is primarily a diasporic one, concerned with shared experiences and understandings of intimacy among African subjects. In this sense, "African" as an identity is a unifying principle for everyone who has chosen to participate, and yet it does not erase their differences. Because the project is by Africans for Africans, it goes without saying that Africa is a diverse and multifaceted continent.

How Do Africans Kiss? is not only about kissing. The film also actively disrupts the veil of secrecy around touch and intimacy, secrecy that Saro-Wiwa works both with and against, not only by asking individuals to speak frankly about love and intimacy but also by allowing viewers to see it in real time. The video ends with the man who shared about learning how to kiss in the United States:

> Everything is love in Africa starting from birth . . . even when you pass away . . . it's love. If I [think like of Ghana] I can take an example about funeral [sic]. It's amazing how many days it takes to get the body ready. That person is gone but you see the love and the connection there and all of the colors and seeing that body going underground 6 feet under and it's so much love so much passion and the elders are never forgotten they're there, they're part of the young generations life, they are everything and it's love.

The power in this video is its raw unfiltered vulnerability. *How Do Africans Kiss?* is permission to be a deeply emotional, feeling human African subject, and a reminder that the violence of colonialism does not strip the ability to love, to feel, to be soft.

Eaten by the Heart: The Installation (2012)

In 2012 Saro-Wiwa premiered a sixty-two-minute video installation of African and African diasporic couples and strangers making out at the Menil Collection (Saro-Wiwa 2012). The video opens with a rust-orange screen, indistinguishable sounds of people speaking , the heavy bass of afrobeat music playing in the distance, and cars honking. At the nine-second mark, a couple suddenly appears in the middle of the screen. The black static between their bodies and along the edges of their foreheads captures the mediated quality of the scene—it appears they are in front of a green screen. Both of their eyes are closed, and they kiss using ample tongue, as if unaware that they are in front of a camera. After four minutes, they pull away from one another and stare into each other's eyes before disappearing from the screen as quickly as they appeared. Saro-Wiwa writes of the performance, "So many of us cite with confidence that Love Is Universal. But the performance of love is, it seems, cultural. I wonder how the way we choreograph and culturally organize the performance of love impacts what we feel inside and who we become" (Saro-Wiwa 2012).

The video features a diverse group of kissing couples ranging in nationality, age, and sexual orientation. We recognize many of them from *How Do Africans Kiss?* Each couple was asked to stand in front of a green screen, which varied in color. In the third video, a man and a woman stand against a blue background with the sounds of birds chirping. They are both wearing pink, and the man digs his hands into the woman's afro as they kiss. There is a push and pull between the two of them, both of them expressing an equal amount of physical craving. When they are finished, they stare at each other, and then at the camera, implicating the viewer. What is most captivating about the piece to me is all of the ways we see African diasporic women exert sexual agency. They pull hair, they bite lips—they appear to be genuinely enjoying themselves. There are a couple of moments in the film where at the end of the kiss, the men appear slightly embarrassed or ashamed, whereas the women always seem self-assured. The piece ends with two women.

When the show premiered, museumgoers watched the film in an intimate dark room attached to the larger exhibit where the kissing pairs were projected larger than life. I on the other hand first watched the film on my laptop at a coffee shop. In an article by the *Houston Press*, Meredith Deliso writes, "It's a sweet concept, but I don't think most people can stand to watch an hour of other people making out. By the third couple, I had had enough" (Deliso 2013). Deliso's review exemplifies how the all-consuming nature of video installation forces viewers to encounter their own visceral responses. Isolde Brielmaier breaks down this relationship between the video installation and the visitor's body writing:

> The visitor's body is essential to the structure of video installation and the articulation of ideas. Within the context of the installation space, the visitor negotiates the specific site of the artwork as a way of experiencing and, in turn, creating meaning from the art. He or she quite literally and figuratively, takes a position vis-a-vis the work. The very quality of video installation makes the visitor intensely aware of his or her body, and all of its sensory functions form a complex entity that is intertwined, engaged, and capable of perceiving. (Brielmair 2008, 57)

The performance video is intense and uncomfortable. It feels almost intrusive. As a first-generation Nigerian American, at the point that I encounter this video, it is also the most I have ever seen Africans kiss in my entire life. The kissing is long and passionate. At times it includes lots of tongue. The couples vary in age, some appearing to be in their twenties and others seeming much older. Two of the couples appear to be same-sex pairings. In my view, the performance's objective is simple. While there is so much writing that claims to be about African sexuality and intimacy only to pathologize it, Saro-Wiwa's performance video throws us directly into the midst of hot, passionate, sometimes sloppy making out. It presents African intimacy and love with no pretense. It does not allow us to overly intellectualize it. Instead, the colors and sounds consume and transform us. Perhaps this is the reason Deliso could only stand to watch three of the couples. Tcheuyap writes in his chapter on how postcolonial African films have addressed sex that "neither open intimacy or sentimental confession is popular in African cinema." He argues that in African films, the body and sexual organs in particular "seem to avoid and be avoided by the camera" (Tcheuyap 2011, 194). *Eaten by the Heart: The Installation* plays with this trope by taking an act as "PG" as kissing, and allowing the viewer to experience it visually, emotionally, and intellectually. Saro-Wiwa pushes the act of kissing as far as possible and in doing so, reveals a great amount about sensuality, intimacy, and agency without the use of nudity. On the theme of "sentimental confessions," the style and content of *Eaten by the Heart* is exceptionally confessional in nature. Confessional art has been defined as "a form of contemporary art that focuses on an intentional revelation of the private self. Confessional art encourages an intimate analysis of the artist, artist's subjects' or spectator's confidential, and often controversial, experiences and emotions" (Jackson and Hogg 2010). While Irene Gammel argues that calling this type of art "confessional" is inherently problematic as it brings to mind the patriarchal history of the confessional and the priest, I argue that understanding *Eaten by the Heart* as a collective confessional speaks to the power of the piece, as well as the cathartic nature of the act of confessing (Gammel 1999, 3). In *Eaten by the Heart* the subjects do not confess sins in a dark room to a hidden man but are given an opportunity to release a range of often repressed thoughts and feelings they have been conditioned to carry as shame, publicly and in community, and have them shared as part of a project dedicated to creating a safe space to practice vulnerability. Saro-Wiwa's work illustrates Stuart Hall's assertion that representational art serves not as simply a mirror but presents new possibilities that constitute new kinds of subjects. In his words, "I have been trying to speak of identity as constituted, not outside but within representation; hence of cinema, not as a second-order mirror held up to reflect what already exists, but as that form of representation which is able to constitute us as new kinds of subjects, and thereby enable us to discover who we are" (Hall 1989, 80).

Eaten by the Heart is a space of radical intimacy and vulnerability, and Saro-Wiwa's disregard for the ways shame and tradition become obstacles and barriers, is precisely what allows her to approach people with the mission of filming them at their most vulnerable. Saro-Wiwa's films also create new worlds and ephemeral communities where Africans across the diaspora can discuss sex and intimacy openly, and connect across ethnicity, gender, sexuality, and age. In one interview, Saro-Wiwa asserts:

> The documentation also enacts something too and I think that's interesting to me. I mean after decades of watching certain types of Caucasian people kissing all of the time and being very used to that kind of intimacy in the world, I always wonder, well how does that effect who you become? You know that kind of exposure and that kind of performance, who do you become after that. It's not just oh you ingest it, but also you metabolize it. And it turns you into someone, it turns you into someone who has expectations, it turns you into someone that recognizes love in a format or a different format. (Saro-Wiwa 2020)

Here Saro-Wiwa describes the impact watching white people kiss and perform acts of intimacy has had on her own expectations when it comes to intimacy. Pulling on this experience, she uses *Eaten by the Heart* to create a new type of record that can shape the archive of what has been understood as acceptable African behavior. Saro-Wiwa does this by not merely tiptoeing around taboo or attempting to gently lure people into sharing, but by shattering the veil of secrecy, which allows for a brave and explicit naming of vulnerable emotions. Moreover, she creates an affective community within *Eaten by the Heart*, as we see the same individuals appear in all three parts of the series. They look like African aunties, mothers, uncles, and cousins but in a way that they are so rarely seen. Instead, Saro-Wiwa films them in such a way that gives room to move beyond our biases, habits, and "home training" to see African people differently than we've been told to see ourselves. To imagine a different way of existing.

By centering the erotic in her work, Saro-Wiwa demonstrates what careful attention to affect, vulnerability, and intimacy can reveal about the types of negotiations African diasporic individuals, particularly women, have to make, what parts of themselves they reveal and to whom, and how obligated they are to the needs and expectations of their families and communities. Saro-Wiwa visually maps these connections, as we are given the opportunity to see African diasporic people existing, feeling, and loving in ways that are both emotional and fully embodied.

Bimbola Akinbola is an assistant professor in the Department of Performance Studies at Northwestern University. Working at the intersection of performance and visual culture, her scholarly and creative work is concerned with conceptions of belonging and queer worldmaking in African diasporic cultural production. She can be reached at bimbola.akinbola@northwestern.edu.

Notes

1. Because the individuals featured in *Eaten by the Heart* are not named, all identity-based descriptions are a reflection of my own interpretation.

Works Cited

Ahmed, Sara. 2015. *The Cultural Politics of Emotion*. New York: Routledge.

Armitstead, Claire. 2018. "Interview: Zina Saro-Wiwa: 'For 10 Years I Didn't Cry About My Father.'" *The Guardian*, September 18, 2018. https://www.theguardian.com/artanddesign/2018/sep/18/zina-saro-wiwa-artist-for-ten-years-i-didnt-cry-about-my-father.

Berlant, Lauren. 2012. *Desire/Love*. Brooklyn, NY: Punctum Books.

Brielmaier, Isolde. 2008. "Transformers: Video Installation, Space, and the Art of Immersion." In *Cinema Remixed and Reloaded: Black Women Artists and The Moving Image Since 1970*, edited by Andrea Barnwell Brownlee and Valerie Cassel Oliver, 55–61. Atlanta, GA: Spelman College Museum of Fine Art/ Contemporary Arts Museum of Houston.

Cripps, Charlotte. 2014. "Zina Saro-Wiwa: Exploring My Father's Legacy." *Independent*, July 8, 2014. https://www.independent.co.uk/arts-entertainment/art/features/zina-saro-wiwa-exploring-my-father-s-legacy-9590268.html.

Deliso, Meredith. 2013. "The Menil Hosts a Big Show on Love." *Houston Press*, January 16, 2013. http://www.houstonpress.com/content/printView/6365778.

Diabate, Naminata. 2011. *Genital Power: Female Sexuality in West African Literature and Film*, PhD diss. University of Texas at Austin.

———. 2020. "Nudity and Pleasure." *Nka* 1, no. 46: 152–66.

Diawara, Manthia. 1992. *African Cinema: Politics and Culture*. Bloomington: Indiana University Press.

Epprecht. Marc. 2010. "The Making of African Sexuality: Early Sources, Current Debates." *History Compass* 8, no. 8: 768–79.

Esekheigbe, Itohan. 2021. "6 Nigerian Women Talk About Overcoming Purity Culture." *Zikoko*, May 6, 2021. https://www.zikoko.com/her/6-nigerian-women-talk-about-overcoming-purity-culture/.

Gammel, Irene. 1999. *Confessional Politics: Women's Sexual Self-Representations in Life Writing and Popular Media*. Carbondale: Southern Illinois Press, 1999.

Hall, Stuart.1989. "Cultural Identity and Cinematic Representation." *Framework: The Journal of Cinema and Media* no. 36: 68–81.

Jackson II, Ronald L., and Michael A. Hogg. 2010. "Confessional Art." In *Encyclopedia of Identity*. California: SAGE Publications.

Kenyatta, Jomo. 1961. *Facing Mount Kenya: The Tribal Life of the Gikuyu*. London: Mercury Books.

Lorde, Audre. 1981. "Uses of the Erotic: The Erotic as Power." In *Sister Outsider: Essays and Speeches*, 53–59. Berkeley, CA: Crossing Press.

Nalley, Yima. 2014. "Public Display of Affection? Not in Africa." *Waza Online*, May 20, 2014. https://wazaonline.com/en/speak-up/public-display-of-affection-not-in-nigeria.

Ngai, Sianne. 2009. *Ugly Feelings*. Cambridge: Harvard Press.

Saro-Wiwa, Zina. 2008. "This Is My Africa." ZSW Studios. 47:00.

———. 2009a. *Phyllis*. ZSW Studios. 15:38.

———. 2009b. *The Deliverance of Comfort*. ZSW Studios. 00:07:00.

————. 2011. *Sarogua Mourning.* ZSW Studios. 00:11:37.

————. 2012. *Eaten by the Heart: The Installation,* directed by Zina Saro-Wiwa. Houston: ZSW Studios, 62:00.

————. 2012/2013. *Eaten by the Heart: How Do Africans Kiss?,* directed by Zina Saro-Wiwa. Houston: ZSW Studios, 11:00. http://www.zinasarowiwa.com/video/eaten-by-the-heart/.

————. 2015. *Did You Know We Taught Them How to Dance?* ZSW Studios. http://www.zinasarowiwa.com/video/did-you-know-we-taught-them-how-to-dance/.

————. 2020. "The Archive on African Time: A Conversation About 'African Time' as a Nuanced Temporality That Not Only Creates But Demands New Ways of Negotiating with Archives," conversation between Zina Saro-Wiwa and Maryam Kazeem. *CalArts,* August 5, 2020. Video, 1:05:14. https://vimeo.com/444808692.

Tcheuyap, Alexie. 2011. *Postnationalist African Cinemas.* Manchester and New York: Manchester University Press.

University of Wisconsin–Madison, African Studies Program. 2012. "Eaten by the Heart: An Exploration of Love, Intimacy and Heartbreak in Africa and the African Diaspora." https://africa.wisc.edu/events-intro/events-special-events/eaten-by-the-heart/.

Van Dyke, Kristina, and Bisi Silva. 2012. *The Progress of Love.* Houston, TX: The Menil Foundation.

Going with the Gut: Fatness and Erotic Knowledge in Black Feminist Theories of the Body

Ana Quiring

Abstract: I argue that several Black feminists theorize fatness as a marginalized form of embodiment that should be reclaimed as a source of pleasure and abundance. Tracing the history of anti-fat bias back to its roots as a vehicle of racialized bodily control, we learn that the fat Black body has always served as a threat to white colonial power. Turning to Black feminist texts, from the writing of Audre Lorde and bell hooks to Zadie Smith's 2005 novel *On Beauty*, offers alternatives to this account of fatness, finding instead beauty, self-love, and political solidarity in fat Black women's bodies. **Keywords:** Black feminism; fatness; embodiment; racism; Zadie Smith; Sarah Baartman; *On Beauty*

In her essay "The Uses of the Erotic," Audre Lorde reflects on the erotic through a memory involving an elaborate play with margarine. She writes,

> During World War II, we bought sealed plastic packets of white, uncolored margarine, with a tiny, intense pellet of yellow coloring perched like a topaz just inside the clear skin of the bag. We would leave the margarine out for a while to soften, and then we would pinch the little pellet to break it inside the bag, releasing the rich yellowness into the soft pale mass of margarine. Then taking it carefully between our fingers, we would knead it gently back and forth, over and over, until the color had spread throughout the whole pound bag of margarine, thoroughly coloring it. I find the erotic such a kernel within myself. (1984, 45)

Lorde identifies a ration butter replacement, margarine, as the ideal metaphor for the transmission of erotic knowledge. The parcel of margarine takes on the language of a body—a body comprised of fat. Lorde kneads color

WSQ: Women's Studies Quarterly 50:1 & 2 (Spring/Summer 2022)

gently into the "soft pale mass" of the margarine. Her language derives its power from the intimacy it evokes, leaving no corner of the margarine uncolored or untouched. Lorde writes elsewhere that "growing up Fat Black Female and almost blind in america requires so much surviving that you have to learn from it or die" (1980, 32). Lorde collects fatness, Blackness, gender, and disability as categories of difference that induce a kind of desperate education. This account of her adolescence casts a different light on the margarine metaphor, evoking the material conditions of many Black women's formation: the intertwining of fat, color, and intimacy. Lorde and other Black feminists' theories of embodiment and erotic knowledge offer a route to the potentials afforded by fatness. A thin-obsessed white majority culture characterizes fatness as the vice of the uncontrolled and dissipated, a sign of a failing will. In contrast, Black feminist texts like Lorde's works and Zadie Smith's novel *On Beauty* (2005) offer us a method by which to view the heavy body as an accumulation of wisdom and intimacy—often gained over slices of pie. To take Lorde's metaphor both literally and figuratively is to imagine the erotic and political potential of touching the color of fatness: to claim for Black fat women a unique source of embodied knowledge and self-love.

In this essay, I analyze fatness as a specific form of erotic knowledge. Lorde describes the erotic not as specifically sexual but rather a variety of sensations and intuitions that come from the body, often signaled with the phrase "it feels right to me." Other Black feminists have also emphasized the linkage between knowledge and the body. bell hooks, for instance, writes that "there is a particular knowledge that comes from suffering. It is a way of knowing that is often expressed through the body, what it knows, what has been deeply inscribed on it through experience" (1995, 91). hooks describes the body as an archive of its experiences; the body carries with it a record of pain that can recognize familiar circumstances. A culture that associates fat with overindulgence would agree that the body is an archive of suffering, and that association has permeated some academic communities. Cultural theorist Lauren Berlant perceives indulgent eating as a soothing response to trauma; fat thus represents "the congealed form of history that hurts" (2011, 142). While Berlant writes to critique the income inequality that has increased "obesity" rates in poor Black communities, they risk reading fat Black bodies as histories of indignity, pain, and self-sabotage. Berlant's concern for fatness and (sometimes) affiliated health problems in poor Black neighborhoods is demonstrably genuine, but their argument suggests an overdetermined linkage between fatness and pain. Lucas Crawford echoes hooks when he writes back to Berlant, "When all bodies are archives that do not just remember their pasts but are built of these pasts, why are fat bodies given nearly mythical powers to signify traumatic experience?" (2017, 454). If all bodies carry memories of suffering, fat bodies can also carry other memories. The rhetorical choices used to describe fat in these disparate accounts also tells diverging stories; Berlant's fat "congeals," soggy and tepid. By contrast, Lorde describes margarine, ostensibly a synthetic, inferior war-era ingredient, as the vehicle for vibrant color, plied by gentle hands.

An interdisciplinary approach to the intersections of race, gender, and fatness can explicate the contrast between these two representations. Crawford's question, ostensibly rhetorical, has an answer that the young Audre Lorde, who wrote being "Fat Black Female and almost blind in america," would understand. Fatphobic rhetoric in popular, medical, and academic culture all evince anxiety over the excessive body. Moreover, excess in the form of thick thighs and heavy breasts always recalls other forms of excess— namely of femininity and racial otherness.[1] Indeed, fatness has long served as a metric for eugenicist categories in American culture. Kathleen LeBesco notes that fatness has often limited Americans' access to whiteness, and thus to citizenship (2004, 59). This inadequacy has had implications for Latino and poor white communities but has concentrated with greatest intensity on Black Americans. Anna Mollow traces the eugenicist imbrication of fat shame and racism, writing, "The behaviors to which fatness is commonly attributed replicate stereotypes of Black people as undisciplined and unable to control their appetites (2017, 106). The behavior most associated with fatness, of course, is what I call "exuberant eating," an umbrella for meals (and snacks) that prioritize pleasure, fullness, satisfaction, convenience, and community, over the strictest definitions of healthful fuel. Exuberance refers not only to enthusiasm but also to abundance and proliferation—in this case, to excess. Kyla Wazana Tompkins has argued that Black communities and subjects have often used the trope of excess to resist white oppression; this excess often comes in the forms of literal and metaphorical eating. "The Black mouth is a site of political intensity itself," she writes (2012, 9). Since the nineteenth century, diet proponents have associated "healthful" eating with other morality campaigns ordained by Christian and white supremacist standards, methods by which to suppress the pleasure and autonomy of the body (Strings 2019, 13). Exuberant eating refuses these standards, whether by gleeful choice or necessity. This kind of eating is not always joyful; sometimes it requires scarfing down a chocolate bar on a break during a long shift or eating at McDonald's in a food desert neighborhood.[2] However, exuberant eating of all forms narrates food and its impacts on the Black body in broader terms than nutritional value. Most pertinently, these terms involve the particular kinds of knowledge, care, and affection that fat, exuberant eaters can practice.

My answer to the question, "What can the fat body know?" comes through an omnivorous archive. In conjunction with histories of fatness and dieting and Black feminist scholarship, I read Black British author Zadie Smith's *On Beauty* as a source of theorizing in narrative form. Through her protagonist, Kiki Simmonds, Smith articulates an experience of fat Black womanhood that receives cruel dismissal from the white academic culture the novel frames, while serving as its own source of sustaining wisdom and love. As she navigates infidelity in her marriage and dismissals of her authority by her largely white community, Kiki learns to center embodied knowledge, a Black feminist commitment to "going with the gut." Sara Ahmed writes in her theory of coming to feminist consciousness, "A gut has its own intelligence. A feminist gut might sense something is amiss" (2017, 27). Smith builds on this claim; in her literary instantiation of the phrase, it is the gut as protruding stomach, hanging over a too-tight waistband, that provides the "gut instinct" of embodied knowledge. Smith writes, "[Kiki's] gut had its own way of going about things, and she was used to its executive decisions" (2005, 90). In this description, the fat body, especially the stomach, serves as a conduit to experience, evaluation, and community. Ultimately, Smith's intricate rendering of gut epistemology makes it a unique resource. In narrativizing gut knowledge, taking it from theory, statistic, metaphor, or anecdote to the novel form, Smith observes fat Black womanhood in both structural and intimate dimensions. Kiki's experience of her body reflects the long historical arcs of race science and misogyny; it also survives the embedding of those arcs in her most personal relationships. If we read Kiki as both protagonist and theorist, we can trace the imbrication of fatphobia and fat knowledge in institutions as vast as the American academy and as claustrophobic as a failing marriage. In her maneuvers through these institutions, Smith's Kiki joins Lorde and hooks in theorizing the political power of loving and knowing the Black body.

Historicizing the Threat of the Fat Black Body

Historian Hillel Schwartz's book *Never Satisfied: A Cultural History of Diets, Fantasies, and Fat* poses a foundational question: "How do Americans become convinced that weight reveals something desperately true about the person beneath the pounds?" (1986, 5). Schwartz inaugurates the field of fat studies by articulating an American preoccupation, and by echoing the racist history of physiognomy; fatness has the power to reveal inner character.[3] American culture reads fat as a physical manifestation of a moral failing. It thus frames fatness as an imagined biological and moral category that magnifies existing prejudices, especially those prized by American white supremacist culture: purity, the will, and individualism.[4] Tracing a history of this imagined category reveals its imbrication with race science and misogynoir.[5]

However, the fat body was not always treated as a threat to moralizing social orders. During the nineteenth century, the U.S. and Britain venerated buxom and full-figured women for their associations with abundant child-bearing and wealth. Accumulated fat served as a symbol of elevated status during an era of limited resources. As industrialization and global trade fueled by colonization began to bring a greater access to varied food, the reputation of fat changed. The implications for this change, at the start of the twentieth century, included more stringent definitions of femininity and whiteness. Laura Fraser writes that "well-to-do Americans of northern European extraction wanted to be able to distinguish themselves, physically and racially, from stockier immigrants" (2009, 12). Sabrina Strings argues that at the turn of the twentieth century, fatness recalled the vices of "primitive Africans" (2019, 4). A thin body, reinforced by constant dieting, became a way for white women to make themselves Western and modern.

Histories of the fat Black woman as archetype often begin with the image of the Venus Hottentot, a moniker applied to the South African woman Saarjtie "Sara" Baartman in the eighteenth century. White colonists brought Baartman to Europe to display her before huge crowds in London and Paris, drawn by tales of her primitive, voluptuous physique, especially the shape and size of her posterior. "She was," writes Samantha Pinto, "perhaps the most globally overexposed figuration of Black women's sexuality—and sexual subjection" (2020, 98). In addition to spurring the development of race science, Baartman embodied the simultaneous revulsion and sexual thrill so often projected onto Black women, especially those with bodies perceived as excessive or uncontrolled. The precedent set by Baartman's treatment would continue long past the eighteenth century, as fatness remained linked to primitivism, exaggerated sexuality, and Blackness in the Western imagination.

Over time, the race science that pathologized Black fat femininity joined forces with the medical panic over fat more generally. Historically, the increased medicalization of fatness over the twentieth century scarcely seemed to include Black women, who, according to Strings, "were rarely seen to matter at all" (2019, 195). Not until the later decades of the century did fat Black womanhood become both a cultural entity and a medical threat. The development of the Body Mass Index (BMI) by nutritionist Ancel Keys in 1972 spurred a new era of medical fat panic. The metric, long proved to be medically unsound, also tended to classify Black people with higher BMIs than whites. Nevertheless, String writes, the medical establishment alighted upon the higher BMIs of Black women as "evidence of disease," evidence that aligned with a long history of pathologizing their bodies (2019, 202–3). This development dovetailed with increased moralizing about the welfare state in the 1970s, which focused with disapproval on the figure of the freeloading Black mother, growing fat on the ill-gotten gains of state benefits.[6]

In the popular sphere, some highly visible Black women performed respectability by making weight loss and bodily control their platforms. Shirley Anne Tate notes a particularly American source of Black fat visibility, one Black British women could not quite share: the rise of talk show host and media juggernaut Oprah Winfrey, whose very public struggle with fat helped to cement the diet industry for American women of many backgrounds (2015, 68). On her talk show in 1988, Winfrey rolled out a wagon containing sixty-seven pounds of fat to demonstrate how much weight she had lost (Jefferson 2012). In 2015, she purchased a 10 percent stake in dieting company Weight Watchers, having served as a spokeswoman for years. Winfrey has personally profited from her own investment in the dieting industry as a compulsory aspect of modern femininity. Another exemplar of African American femininity, First Lady Michelle Obama, took her trademarks from health discourses of bodily restraint: her "Let's Move" anti-obesity campaign for children and her famously toned arms. For Black women, publicly aspiring to thinness becomes a powerful rhetoric of respectability.

Some responses to "obesity" rates in Black communities have pointed out the correlation between fatness and poverty. This reformulation makes fat people victims of income inequality rather than individual failures of self-control. Berlant's writing on the topic highlights the inequal distribution of ill health; it is the bodies of poor people, they write, "that fray slowly from the pressure of obesity on their organs and skeletons" (2011, 106). Berlant also points to real higher rates of heart disease and diabetes in Black communities, suggesting that the lack of access to fresh food and leisure time to exercise have shortened fat Black people's lives. It is, of course, relevant to consider the ways that late capitalism and environmental racism have made poor communities of color unhealthy places to live. And while fatness is affiliated with a number of health problems, especially heart disease and diabetes, many studies have shown that "obesity" itself is not a reliable indicator of health. Studies from *Obesity Review* have shown that somewhere between one-third and three-quarters of "obese" people are metabolically healthy (2014, 782). It is possible to critique the violence that poverty and racism wage on the body without reducing that violence to fatness or reducing fatness to violence. Berlant imagines "obesity" to "fray" the skeleton and organs, making fat not only a heavy weight but also an insidious solvent, dissolving the structure of the body. Scientific research cannot strictly reinforce this image, but its cultural implications are even more troublesome. Even in a sympathetic, antiracist frame of mind, Berlant risks conceiving fat people as victims, worthy of pity as their spines split hairs. Black feminists, taking stock of how the tropes of excess, savagery, and indulgence have dogged the steps of Black women for centuries, illustrate alternative images of the fat Black body that emphasize self-knowledge and community care.

Eros, Embodied Knowledge, and Gut Epistemology

Second wave feminism, in both mainstream and Black feminist iterations, saw the proliferation of theories of "the body." Feminists who endeavor to emphasize the authority of experience, Elizabeth Grosz argues, can claim that "the body provides a point of mediation between what is perceived as purely internal and accessible only to the subject and what is external and publicly observable" (1994, 20). Grosz acknowledges the devaluation of these epistemologies in the long history of philosophical body-mind dualism. However, feminists have insisted upon its value. Tompkins has argued that we should think of this mediation between the internal and external as permeable by "reading *orifically*," or focusing on the mouth and the process of eating. Critical eating studies, she writes, "theorizes a flexible and circular relation between the self and the social world" (2012, 3). Tompkins frames the mouth as the mechanism by which our inner selves meet the outside.

This juncture functions as a site of domination or subversive pleasure, or some mixture of the two. Tompkins follows a Black feminist tradition in narrating the white destruction of Black bodies through this metaphor; bell hooks foundationally called it "eating the other" (1992, 21). A central component of hooks's and Tompkins's arguments is reassigning, with an eye to the long-standing power of white supremacy, the characteristic of voracious (and savage) consumption from Black people to white ones, who "eat the other," making racial difference "seasoning that can liven up the dull dish that is mainstream white culture" (1992, 14). According to hooks and Tompkins, it is white mouths that consume and destroy with uncontrolled appetites. To attend to Black eating instead of white is to consider a subversive alternative to this violent consumption. Tompkins describes the Black mouth as a node of "political intensity"; fat studies would follow her path through the body to consider the consequences of that eating, to the stomach. By considering the work of Black feminists like Tompkins and Lorde, feminist science studies, and antidiet philosophies, we can consider the powers and attunements of the Black stomach—or rather the gut.

Lorde's theory of the erotic implicitly links sensual desire to other forms of craving. In so doing, she presages a fat-positive Black feminist politics.[7] Lorde writes,

> We have been raised to fear the *yes* within ourselves, our deepest cravings. But, once recognized, those which do not enhance our future lose their power and can be altered. The fear of our desires keeps them suspect and indiscriminately powerful, for to suppress any truth is to give it strength beyond endurance. (1984, 46)

Lorde describes erotic desire as a craving, a need for sustenance and satisfaction. Her theory evokes the resonance between representations of Black women's rapacious sexual and alimentary desires. To deny these desires, Lorde argues, is to renew their strength as forbidden and "indiscriminately powerful." This description recalls the anti-diet technique of intuitive eating. This philosophy implicitly follows Lorde's mandate by honoring the intelligence and sensations of the body, rather than the moralizing and strict confines of a weight loss diet. Those who practice intuitive eating listen to their bodies, eat when they are hungry, satisfy their cravings, eat foods that make them feel good, and do not follow rigid rules. This system is designed in part to prevent indulgent foods from developing the allure of the forbidden. *The Intuitive Eating Workbook* warns, "The psychological effects of deprivation—which uncannily fuels obsessive thinking about food, ultimately lead[s] to overeating and disconnection from your body" (2017, 61). While intuitive eating has recently emerged as a health practice, was popularized in the last five years, and has in no way permeated the fatphobic medical establishment, it has clear resonance with Lorde's philosophy. Denying one's cravings, whether erotic or carbohydrate-based, only alienates us from our bodies and gives those cravings unacknowledged power. Lorde's axiom "It feels right to me" has clear implications for an antidiet politics.

Both Lorde and proponents of intuitive eating attribute the body with the instincts to make evaluations on what "feels right," a faith in the intelligence of going with the gut. Feminist discourses on the body have historically rendered that body in conceptual, abstracted terms, but more recently theorists have sought to expand definitions of the body through scientific discourses. In *Gut Feminism*, Elizabeth Wilson encourages feminists to engage with biology more substantively, and invokes the multiplying instantiations of the word *gut*. For feminist theory, the gut is an instinct, a fat belly, the viscera of human embodiment (as in "blood and guts") and an incredibly intricate biological system. In emphasizing the role of biology in feminism, Wilson focuses her attention not on the neurological authority of the brain, but on the less obviously cognitive parts of the nervous system, and thus the body. "My argument is not that the gut contributes to minded states," she writes, "but that the gut is an organ of mind: it ruminates, deliberates, comprehends" (2015, 5). Wilson does not engage with Black feminist thought in detail, but the shared resonance across fields and disciplinary commitments can help us consider the gut as a vehicle for theorizing Black feminist thought.

While intuitive eating would emphasize the work of "making peace" with the body, and feminist biology of taxonomizing it, for Lorde, embracing embodied knowledge is always a route to love—personal, romantic, and communal. She chooses the term "erotic" for its etymological root in eros, deriving "the personification of love in all its aspects" (1984, 43). Thus, to trust the authority of the body is to identify the political power channeled through love for the self and, implicitly, for other Black women. As

Smith articulates in *On Beauty*, it is most often in community between Black women that the love and wisdom of the fat body emerges.

Fat Ladies Need Love Too

In *On Beauty*, Smith explores the experience of fat Black womanhood in middle age and the middle class. The novel tells the story of a liberal, interracial family, the Belseys, living in a university town analogous to Cambridge, Massachusetts. Conflict enters the Belsey marriage when Howard, a white art history professor, has an affair with a colleague. He justifies the affair in part because Kiki has gained weight. The novel follows Howard, Kiki, and their three children in and out of the university environment, satirizing contemporary academic culture and testing Kiki's patience with her unfaithful and superficial husband. The core tension of the novel exists between Kiki's personal experience of her middle-aged body and that of those who read and judge her. She experiences her bulk as a by-product of a full and complicated life, in which she feels at home, and which guides her to a variety of embodied insights. However, she is interpellated by a vast and often paradoxical set of racializing tropes, which are predicated upon and exaggerated by the American obsession with Black fatness. It is Kiki's refusal of these tropes, and her insistence upon embracing her body, that provide the novel's insight into Black self-love.

In one early scene, Kiki acknowledges the extent to which viewers project upon her body, a dynamic in which fatness and Blackness magnify each other. She attends a street fair with her son and barters with a man selling jewelry. As the conversation continues, Kiki identifies the role her body plays in the negotiation:

> Kiki suspected already that this would be one of those familiar exchanges in which her enormous spellbinding bosom would play a subtle (or not so subtle, depending on the person) silent third role in the conversation . . . The size was sexual and at the same time more than sexual: sex was only one small element of its symbolic range. If she were white, maybe it would refer only to sex, but she was not. And so her chest gave off a mass of signals beyond her direct control: sassy, sisterly, predatory, motherly, threatening, comforting—it was a mirror-world she had stepped into in her mid forties, a strange fabulation of the person she believed she was. (2005, 47)

This passage emphasizes the powerful and paradoxical implications that

Kiki's body, especially her "bosom," conveys. The size of her chest both amplifies and dissipates its sexual power. It is her race, Smith argues, that makes sexuality one among a contradictory "mass of signals." The list of adjectives that Kiki's bosom "g[ives] off" runs the gamut of racializing language applied to Black women over several generations. This is to say, Kiki knows that she carries, involuntarily, a form of somatic history with her bulk. In its associations with the "sassy," "predatory," and "threatening," her bosom references the Jezebel figure, a racist type associated with hyper-sexuality and seduction, so often blamed for the sexual transgressions of white men. In the alternating adjectives, "sisterly, motherly, comforting," it recalls the figure of the mammy,[8] a desexualized domestic laborer whose "body is grotesquely marked by excess," writes Kimberly Wallace-Sanders, and thus casts dainty white womanhood and childhood in relief (2011, 6). These two tropes, used as tools of cultural violence since the nineteenth century, purport to describe opposing forms of Black womanhood, although both are demeaning flat types. The conflations of these types arrive in the intersections of the Jezebel and mammy figures. As a result, Kiki, through the device of a large chest, must respond to both tropes. Fatness provokes paradoxical associations in its witnesses; Kiki's chest makes her desexual-ized and hypersexualized at the same time.

In this scene, Smith demonstrates how mainstream culture projects a narrative onto fat Black female bodies. Kiki perceives that this perception bypasses her own personhood and agency, knowing that her chest "[gives] off a mass of signals beyond her direct control" (2005, 47). Because Kiki understands these signals so fluently, she can separate them from her inner self, viewing them as "a strange fabulation of the person she believed she was." Kiki understands that her body bears a set of historical and semiotic signals outside her particular personhood. While acknowledging this phenomenon, the frustration of racialization, Kiki uses reactions to these signals as helpful diagnostics. Her body serves as a gauge, eliciting reactions from viewers that give her information about how to respond to them.

Smith's novel makes it clear that fatness can function as a channel to Black community and admiration in a way that white viewers would resist. Constructing a fat protagonist allows Smith to elucidate non-Eurocentric beauty standards. Black viewers, representing several different eras of enslavement and migration, often regard Kiki's body with enthusiasm, reflecting the value and admiration many Afrocentric cultures express for fat bodies. Smith's own background as a child of the Caribbean diaspora informs her transnational view of Black fatness. Andrea Elizabeth Shaw writes that in many West African communities, girls are prepared for adulthood and marriage by visiting fatting houses, where they receive social training as well as a rich diet to fill out their figures. Shaw argues that for these communities, the acquisition of maturity and education coincides with bodily expansion. She writes, "The physical fat that they take away with them on their bodies is a symbol of the cultural immersion that fatting houses represent and locate the girls in a specific aesthetic realm with Afrocentric roots" (2006, 7). A large or voluptuous figure, then, signals maturity, education, sexuality, and inclusion in the dominant culture.

In the novel, Kiki's Black interlocutors bear out this Afrocentric value system by reading her body as sexually compelling, insightful, and worthy of love. Kiki's unlikely friend Carlene Kipps, a conservative woman from the Caribbean, compliments Kiki on her body, saying, "It looks very well on you. You carry it well" (2005, 91). When Kiki's own daughter decries her mother's lapsed beauty, the rapper-poet Carl reproaches her, saying, "'Fat ladies need love too'" (2005, 139). Most directly, Kiki herself understands how different communities will read (or rather impose) different associations on her body.

> But then, thought Kiki, they were brought up that way, these white American boys: I'm the Aunt Jemima on the cookie boxes of their childhood, the pair of thick ankles Tom and Jerry played around. Of course they find me funny. And yet I could cross the river to Boston and barely be left alone for five minutes at a time. Only last week a young brother half her age had trailed Kiki up and down Newbury for an hour. (2005, 51)

Here Kiki demonstrates her awareness of the mammy type and how thoroughly white Americans have been taught to recognize it. The truncated images of Aunt Jemima and the Tom and Jerry maid crop parts of the Black woman's body as iconography for domestic labor. The thickness of the disembodied ankles only emphasizes the dehumanized caricatures. The whole body—especially the sensual curves of the torso—are eliminated. But young Black men who have received a more Afrocentric education can ogle the aspects of her body that are invisible or undesirable to white men, rendering her a locus of desire. However, they may then objectify and harass Kiki for the same traits that made her nonsexual to others.

While some may hypersexualize her body, other Black characters provide Kiki with the opportunity to exercise and trust her gut instincts. She most often has the chance to demonstrate this intelligence in conversation with another Black woman, her friend Carlene Kipps. In one scene, Kiki brings a pie to Carlene's house to apologize after a misunderstanding. Carlene, who is in ill health, doesn't touch the pie, but at the end of the conversation, Kiki "discover[s]" that she has eaten three pieces. Exuberant eating has served as a facilitator to the reconciliation between them. In another conversation, Carlene asks her politely, "You are not a little woman, are you?" (2005, 91). Kiki reflects that her unbothered response to the question comes from her expansive body itself: "Her gut had its own way of going about things, and she was used to its executive decisions; the feeling of immediate safety some people gave her, and, conversely, the nausea others induced" (2005, 91). Here, a discussion of Kiki's literal bulk also illuminates the figurative powers of the gut. Kiki's stomach has the authority to make its own "executive decisions," a phrase that professionalizes the more colloquial "going with the gut." In this scene, Kiki's gut is a sensing organ, which gives her signals about the trustworthiness of people she meets. Simultaneously, the gut is a vehicle for reaction; she can gauge others' character by the censure or affirmation with which they react to the fat body.

Over the course of the novel, Kiki's friendship with Carlene and fraught relationship with her husband lead her to a greater experience of self-acceptance and love for her fat body. She identifies weight gain as a component of a wider experience of evolution, aging, and growth that has led her to middle age. During a painful marital argument, she pleads, "I don't want someone to have contempt for who I've become. I've watched you become too. And I feel like I've done my best to honor the past, and what you were and what you are now—but you want something more than that, something new. I can't be new" (2005, 398). In rejecting "contempt" for her expanding body, she denounces newness as a misogynistic desire for sexual novelty and viability in male fantasies of slim, compliant women. In this instance, embodied knowledge teaches her that her husband prizes sexual gratification and feminine deference over their marriage bond. In a bit of cruel irony, fatness serves as a diagnostic tool; Howard's refusal to cherish her voluptuous body gives Kiki painful insight into the viability of their partnership at middle age. At the same time, Kiki refuses to bow to this insight. She tells him, "I'm not going to be getting any thinner or any younger, my ass is gonna hit the ground, if it hasn't already—and I want to be with somebody who can still see me in here" (2005, 398). Kiki's declaration is profoundly antidiet; it is not necessarily true that Kiki "can't be new"; rather, she refuses to try. Despite how her body has changed, she perceives it to be a hospitable home for herself, as she is still "in here." Her friendship with Carlene, and the confidence she has built in middle age, give her the authority to say with authority what "feels right" to her, and to reject her husband's fatphobia. She declares her right to a partner who affirms her ongoing identity and beauty in a fat body.

Conclusion

In Lorde's description of the erotic, she chooses margarine as the ideal metaphor for the diffusion of erotic knowledge. The margarine, in its synthetic paleness, absorbs and conveys the brilliant color of the yellow dye, the "kernel" of the erotic. For Lorde, massaging dye into margarine exemplifies what Anh Hua calls an "embodied erotic memory," one that calls to mind the sensation of soft fat in plastic and its historical context, the rationing of butter during World War II (2015, 113). Most presciently, however, Lorde alights upon margarine as an exemplary *medium* for color; a vehicle through which she can watch the "rich yellowness" of the dye infuse. The image of infusion exemplifies Lorde's theory of the "kernel of the erotic" within herself, which, when acknowledged and cultivated, can color and infuse her entire life. Lorde thus views fat, however synthetic, as the pliable, touchable substance that can transmit eroticism and self-knowledge. She conveys a similar elevated status to fatness with regard to her own body in *Zami*, where she writes, "There was Muriel. . . . And I was beside her, full of myself, knowing I was fat and Black and very fine. We were without peer or category" (1982, 223). Accessing—kneading and massaging—the erotic within oneself leads to self-love for the Black body as well as to a potential for lesbian eroticism and community.

Smith's framing of the character of Kiki Simmonds, in a different historical moment and class position, would certainly eat real butter rather than margarine. However, she, too, conceives fatness through exuberant eating with a diffusive, expansive quality. In one scene, at Howard and Kiki's anniversary party, full of white academics Kiki does not know well, she serves entirely soul food. The narrator opines, "Soul food has a scent that fills you up even before your mouth gets near any of it. The sweet dough of the pastries, the alcoholic waft of a rum punch" (2005, 84). Kiki uses fattening food, aerosolized deliciously through the air, to anchor her Blackness at a daunting party. Since her future is uncertain, the food that pads and cushions the body becomes comfort and community. Through their images of diffusion through fat, Lorde and Smith center the fat Black body as a conduit to community and love that extends beyond the boundary of the body itself. These images far exceed a simple narrative of "self-acceptance" or fat representation. Instead, Black fatness necessarily involves relationality—through touch, caress, feeding, and remembering. Through these actions, the kernel of the erotic expands, grows rich and broad in its ability to share embodied love.

Ana Quiring is a PhD candidate in English literature at Washington University in St. Louis. She is working on a dissertation on feminist modernisms. Her public-facing writing has appeared in the *Los Angeles Review of Books*, *Avidly*, and *Full Stop*. She can be reached at quiring@wustl.edu.

Notes

1. Health warnings about so-called ethnic foods often reflect racist divides; consider, for instance, the overstated concern about MSG in Asian American cuisine. Claire Jean Kim (2015) has written on the racist condemnation of Asian live animal markets in United States Chinatowns.

2. The term *food desert* denotes a neighborhood without easy walkable access to fresh foods.

3. For more on the origins of racist pseudoscience in physiognomy, see Lucy Hartley, *Physiognomy and the Meaning of Expression in Nineteenth-Century Culture* (2001).

4. Sabrina Strings argues that the rise of fatphobia in the United States derives from two interlocking historical events: the transatlantic slave trade and the rise of Protestantism. According to Strings, Protestantism's investment in work ethic and self-control, as well as its affiliations with white supremacy, had concrete impacts on the status of fatness as moral and racial failing.

5. *Misogynoir*, a portmanteau coined by Moya Bailey and popularized online, specifies the particular oppressions that Black women face. See *Misogynoir Transformed* (2021).

6. The "welfare queen" has become a stock type in Black feminist and queer theory, including significant roles in Cathy J. Cohen's "Punks, Bulldaggers, and Welfare Queens" (1997), Ange-Marie Hancock's *The Politics of Disgust: The Public Identity of the Welfare Queen* (2004), and mentions in Berlant's work on "obesity" in *Cruel Optimism* (2011).

7. Cherie Ann Turpin has written about Lorde's representations of the sensuality of food in *Zami*. See Turpin's *How Three Black Women Writers Combined Spiritual and Sensual Love: Rhetorically Transcending the Bounds of Language* (2010).

8. The fact that the mammy is a racist white fiction is perhaps emphasized by the consolidation of the trope over time; Wallace-Sanders writes that before the publication of *Uncle Tom's Cabin* in 1852, no mammy characters were described as fat (2011, 7). Afterward, this characteristic became a central component of the type.

Works Cited

Ahmed, Sara. 2017. *Living a Feminist Life.* Durham, NC: Duke University Press.

Bailey, Moya. 2011. *Misogynoir Transformed: Black Women's Digital Resistance.* New York: New York University Press.

Berlant, Lauren. 2011. *Cruel Optimism.* Durham, NC: Duke University Press.

Cohen, Cathy J. 1997. "Punks, Bulldaggers, and Welfare Queens: The Radical Potential of Queer Politics?" *GLQ* 3: 437–65.

Crawford, Lucas. 2017. "Slender Trouble: From Berlant's Cruel Figuring of Figure to Sedgwick's Fat Presence." *GLQ: A Journal of Lesbian and Gay Studies* 23, no. 4: 447–72.

Fraser, Laura. 2009. "The Inner Corset: A Brief History of Fat in the United States." In *The Fat Studies Reader*, edited by Sondra Solovay and Esther Rothblum, 11–14. New York: New York University Press.

Grosz, Elizabeth. 1994. *Volatile Bodies.* Bloomington: Indiana University Press.

Hancock, Ange-Marie. 2004. *The Politics of Disgust: The Public Identity of the Welfare Queen.* New York: New York University Press.

Hartley, Lucy. 2005. *Physiognomy and the Meaning of Expression in Nineteenth-Century Culture.* New York: Cambridge University Press.

hooks, bell. 1992. *Black Looks: Race and Representation.* Boston: South End Press.

———. 1995. *Teaching to Transgress: Education as the Practice of Freedom.* New York: Routledge.

Hua, Anh. 2015. "Audre Lorde's *Zami*, Erotic Embodied Memory, and the Affirmation of Difference." *Frontiers: A Journal of Women Studies* 36, no. 1: 113–35.

Jefferson, Whitney. 2012. "Oprah Winfrey Rolls Out a Wagon of Fat." Buzzfeed, September 18, 2012.

Kim, Claire Jean. 2015. *Dangerous Crossings: Race, Species, and Nature in a Multicultural Age.* New York: Cambridge University Press.

LeBesco, Kathleen. 2004. *Revolting Bodies? The Struggle to Redefine Fat Identity.* Amherst: University of Massachusetts Press.

Lorde, Audre. 1980. *The Cancer Journals.* San Francisco, CA: Aunt Lute Books.

———. 1982. *Zami: A New Spelling of My Name.* Berkeley, CA: Crossing Press.

———. 1984. *Sister Outsider: Speeches and Essays.* Berkeley, CA: Ten Speed Press.

Mollow, Anna. 2017. "Unvictimizable: Toward a Fat Black Disability Studies." *African American Review* 50, no. 2: 105–21.

Pinto, Samantha. 2020. *Infamous Bodies: Early Black Women's Celebrity and the Afterlives of Rights.* Durham, NC: Duke University Press.

Rey-López J.P., LF de Rezende, M. Pastor-Valero, and B.H. Tess. 2014. "The Prevalence of Metabolically Healthy Obesity: A Systematic Review and Critical Evaluation of the Definitions Used." *Obesity Review* 15, no. 10: 781–90.

Schwartz, Hillel. 1986. *Never Satisfied: A Cultural History of Diets, Fantasies, and Fat.* New York: The Free Press.

Shaw, Andrea Elizabeth. 2006. *The Embodiment of Disobedience: Fat Black Women's Unruly Political Bodies.* Lanham, MD: Lexington Books.

Smith, Zadie. 2005. *On Beauty.* New York: Penguin.

Strings, Sabrina. 2019. *Fearing the Black Body: The Racial Origins of Fat Phobia.* New York: New York University Press.

Tate, Shirley Anne. 2015. *Black Women's Bodies and the Nation: Race, Gender, and Culture.* New York: Palgrave Macmillan.

Tompkins, Kyla Wazana. 2012. *Racial Indigestion: Eating Bodies in the Nineteenth Century.* New York: New York University Press.

Tribole, Evelyn, and Elyse Resch. 2017. *The Intuitive Eating Workbook.* Oakland, CA: New Harbinger Publications.

Turpin, Cherie Ann. 2010. *How Three Black Women Writers Combined Spiritual and Sensual Love: Rhetorically Transcending the Boundaries of Language (Audre Lorde, Toni Morrison, and Dionne Brand).* Lewiston: Edwin Mellen Press.

Wallace-Sanders, Kimberly. 2011. *Mammy: A Century of Race, Gender, and Southern Memory.* Ann Arbor: University of Michigan Press.

Wilson, Elizabeth. 2015. *Gut Feminism.* Durham, NC: Duke University Press.

PART II. **BLACK POWER LOVE**

Dear Angela, *a/k/a Mrs. George Gilbert*: Coco Fusco's Love Letter to an Icon

Kimberly Lamm

Abstract: This article examines Coco Fusco's 2004 experimental video essay *a/k/a Mrs. George Gilbert* and its Black feminist return to the events that made Angela Davis an icon of Black struggle and liberation at the onset of the 1970s. Tracing Fusco's "epistolary aesthetic," I argue that *a/k/a Mrs. George Gilbert* can be read as a love letter to Davis that evokes the subjective singularity that often disappears behind her iconicity. **Keywords:** icons; Black feminism; video essay; idealization; epistolary aesthetic; interiority

I. Introducing *a/k/a Mrs. George Gilbert*

In her 2004 experimental video essay *a/k/a Mrs. George Gilbert*, Coco Fusco stages a Black feminist return to the events that made Angela Davis a global icon of Black struggle and liberation. She does so by composing a moving archive of the texts and images that emerged out of the pursuit, capture, and acquittal of Davis that began on August 7, 1970. On that day, seventeen-year-old Jonathan Jackson entered a San Rafael courtroom to free James McClain, and four people (including Jackson and judge Harold Haley) were killed. Davis met Jonathan while working for the release of his older brother George from the Soledad State Prison. He became one of the bodyguards who protected her against the death threats Davis received after she declared, while working as a philosophy professor at the University of California, Los Angeles (UCLA), that she was indeed a member of the Communist Party. The guns Jackson brought to the San Rafael courtroom were registered to Davis, which gave law enforcement justification to issue a warrant for her arrest, and she went underground.

While *a/k/a Mrs. George Gilbert* narrates the events that, in Fusco's

WSQ: Women's Studies Quarterly 50: 1 & 2 (Spring/Summer 2022) © 2022 by Kimberly Lamm. All rights reserved.

words, "catapulted Davis into a media circus," it does not document the ordeal Davis experienced as a fugitive of the U.S. nation state. This lyrical video essay collages together archival footage, interior monologues, simulated surveillance shots, and fictional dialogues to explore the desires that made Davis into an icon. *a/k/a Mrs. George Gilbert* is a love letter to Davis that addresses what often disappears behind her iconicity: her singularity.

As the exhibition *Angela Davis—Seize the Time* (2020) shows, artwork that expresses love for Davis is almost its own genre. Pieces such as Faith Ringgold's lithograph *Women Free Angela* (1971) or Elizabeth Catlett's screen print *Angela Libre* (1972) not only demonstrate their solidarity with Davis in visual form but also replicate the style—the striking designs, bright colors, and bold patterns—of the many posters, banners, signs, T-shirts, broadsides, and buttons that circulated through global visual culture to shape public opinion into a vision of justice for Davis. These artworks capture the love people from all over the world poured into their demands for her freedom. Fusco's video is unique because it reveals the image of Davis to be a site for confirming the expectation that Black women create collective feelings of political belonging. Tracking the fears and fantasies expressed through visual depictions of Davis, *a/k/a Mrs. George Gilbert* exemplifies the video essay's work "mak[ing] the very process of perception visible" and suggests that voyeurism and aggression are not exclusive to those who sought to demonize her (Biemann 2003, 10). Fusco certainly makes the case that many of the representations of Davis in dominant U.S. media were created to transform the accusation of guilt into an irrefutable fact. In her voice-over, Fusco argues that images of Davis crystallize American culture's inability to comprehend the reality of a young Black woman of extraordinary intellectual stature. My interest here is Fusco's slightly more subtle and counterintuitive point: whether produced to make her an identifiable target, or to express loving support for her struggle against the white carceral state, icons of Davis betray the assumption that images of Black women can be easily incorporated as the psychic glue of collective political life. Exploring the places where surveillance, research, and love overlap, the video writes a love letter to Davis that foregrounds her subjective singularity, her interiority, her unknowability, and her resistance to the imperative that she serve as an image that can be made to serve other people's needs.

a/k/a Mrs. George Gilbert is a meditation on surveillance and the kinds of seeing it produces. It begins with a grainy, shaky black-and-white image of a window pane and a keyboard score that creates an eerie, enigmatic

Fig. 1. Woman at window. Still from Coco Fusco's *a/k/a Mrs. George Gilbert*, 2004, video. Image courtesy of the artist.

atmosphere. From a sidelong angle situated below the window, viewers see the window's white wooden frames, the reflections of trees on the glass, and a Black woman who resembles Davis wearing a white nightgown. Her nervous pacing projects shadows on the glass. These images call attention to the layers of mediation at work in the perception of Davis, but they also allude to the many Black women who were scrutinized, arrested, and imprisoned in the effort to capture her, a historical event that represents the surveillance that is a daily experience for Black women in the United States. Warily, the woman approaches the side of the window and looks out of it, perhaps seeking to confirm that someone is watching her (fig. 1). This shadowy image of a window and a Black woman pacing behind it is the video's visual refrain. It announces its optics of fear and suspicion as well as its attention to the instability of vision and the shadowy undercurrents of historical memory.

In the voice-over accompanying these images, Fusco states, "I could say that our encounter happened by chance, but people who look for similar things often find each other along the way." As this provocative sentence about parallel looks concludes, the image of the woman behind the window

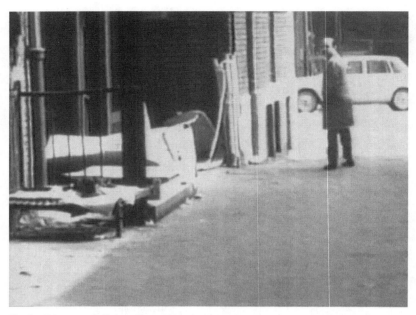

Fig. 2. FBI agent. Still from Coco Fusco's a/k/a *Mrs. George Gilbert*, 2004, video. Image courtesy of the artist.

fades to black. What follows is a depiction of a middle-aged white man in an alley wearing a trench coat and holding a pipe in his mouth. Placed in the upper far-right corner of the frame, he looks at the camera and then walks hurriedly away. He turns around to look again, as if worried he is being followed (fig. 2). This sequence, a parodic citation of film noir paranoia, implies that it was this man's gaze that Fusco replicates at the video's opening. He is the one watching the Black woman at her window.

In *a/k/a Mrs. George Gilbert,* Fusco plays a woman investigating Davis and her history. Fictionalizing the research process that animates her work, Fusco enacts the self-differentiation that her video argues for and makes the artist's desires a part of its material. In the process of her research, she begins a conversation with a former FBI agent. "I was following her shadow when he found me," Fusco explains. To the sound of an electronic type-writer and the image of letters typed on a piece of paper, Fusco remarks that "his note interrupted her private investigation." This note is one of many images of writing that appear in *a/k/a Mrs. George Gilbert,* and it provokes anxiety. How did he find out that she is researching Davis? With an image of a window pane in the background, viewers see the opening of a yellow mailing envelope. Inside it, the typed note appears, paper-clipped to the *Life* magazine from September 11, 1970, which features a shadowy photograph of Davis on the cover, an explicit symbol of the propaganda campaign intent on turning her into a dangerous criminal. The note reads: "I HAVE MORE MATERIAL RELATING / TO MISS DAVIS. IF YOU ARE / INTERESTED PLEASE CALL / 766-490-7639." Despite her fear, Fusco's character is curious about the material he holds. She dials the number on a white telephone receiver and the sounds of the pushed buttons correspond to flashes of black on the screen. The phone becomes part of the video's acoustic and visual texture and, like the image of typing, imprints the image with the desire to address others. In a series of conversations, the FBI agent explains his work for the "Bureau." He was assigned to monitor Davis after she was fired from UCLA in 1969. He confesses to the obsession he developed for his target, whom he calls "the philosophy professor," a formality that creates a cover for the agent's erotic attachment to his state-sanctioned invasion of her privacy.

a/k/a Mrs. George Gilbert is a video essay that exhibits the defining features of the genre. Instead of "documenting realities," it "organiz[es] complexities" (Biemann 2003, 10). While materializing the impulses that made Davis into a symbol, the video's supple visual aesthetic proposes an alternative vision. It therefore challenges expectations to see positive images of strong Black women, and foregrounds instead the "messiness of subjectivity," the unpredictable configurations of power and subordination that, as Jennifer C. Nash (2008, 4) argues, dominant definitions of intersectionality do not fully take into account. Recently bolstered by the discursive prominence of intersectionality, the necessity of creating and seeing positive images of Black women—unequivocally strong, assured, and shorn of victimization—is a Black feminist premise that has filtered into public consciousness, impacting it for good. Fusco does not reject the value of positive images, but explores how they might be animated by idealizations that indicate unconscious needs. The video suggests that the demand to see strong, positive images that counter systemic racism translates into forms of labor for Black women that are visual, symbolic, and affective.

Through its textual address, *a/k/a Mrs. George Gilbert* opens spaces where the singularity of Davis's subjectivity can be glimpsed. It refuses to let those openings be eclipsed by the project of making images of Davis into consumable symbols, however positive or productive. In other words, Fusco's video expresses its love not through idealization, but by reflecting upon the appetites and aggressions the love for an icon can express. In her more recent reflections on intersectionality, Nash expresses her wish for an iteration of Black feminist theory that "name[s] the tiredness, and even the violence that comes with always being made a symbol, even if that symbol is seemingly a productive one" (2019, 138). She also addresses the presumption that Black women will "save" women's studies as an academic discipline and mirror back an image of its "virtue" (2019, 138). In turn, Fusco reflects on the visual dimensions of the demand to serve as an icon of political virtue and explores what that iconicity excludes from the historical picture.

II. The Loving Vision of the Letter

Fusco places a discomfiting parallel at the center of *a/k/a Mrs. George Gilbert*. She links the narrator's private research into Davis to the agent's obsessive pursuit of her. While reproductions of headlines, newspaper articles, telegrams, manifestos, and book covers appear in a jagged pattern across the screen as though they are moving through a microfiche reader, Fusco states: "At first I thought my search was different than his. I thought I was looking *for* someone and he was looking *at* someone, but I realized we were poring over things. Some things that had been hers. Some things that spoke of her." These pieces of ephemera offer perspectives on Davis, and though they are "pored over" by others, they cannot be mistaken for the archive of experiences she uniquely embodies. The connection Fusco draws between "looking for" and "looking at" destabilizes the presumption that the researcher's relationship to the object of her investigation is benign. There are obviously significant differences between them—FBI surveillance is often the prelude to an assassination—but Fusco reveals the voyeuristic impulse they share.

The textual objects that Fusco uses to compose *a/k/a Mrs. George Gilbert* interrupt the ease with which images of Black women are consumed and internalized. They are also the materials through which she crafts an epistolary aesthetic, an imaginative practice in which the address of letter writing, its call for correspondence and response, informs the artist's formal choices. The epistolary aesthetic can be found in mail art, a quirky subgenre of contemporary art in which artists send their work through the mail to circumvent the restricted channels of art institutions and address viewers directly. Making the artwork into a letter, mail art draws on the dialogic dimension of language, the fact that it is imprinted with the voices and histories of others. And while the letter exemplifies a primary insight from semiotics—that words have an arbitrary, even distant, relationship to the things they represent—it also materializes the desire for presence, proximity, and connection. Indeed, the words of a letter can reveal the desire to *touch* another across spatial and temporal separations. While *a/k/a Mrs. George Gilbert* shares mail art's attention to language, address, correspondence, intimacy, and reciprocity, it counterintuitively makes the distance of the letter an expression of love.

Fusco includes multiple letters in *a/k/a Mrs. George Gilbert*. The camera pauses on the haunting conclusion of "An Open Letter to My Sister, Miss Angela Davis," an epistolary essay in which James Baldwin stresses the ominous significance of her arrest: "For, if they take you in the morning, they will be coming for us that night" (1971). Fusco also cites and narrows in on a telegram sent to President Nixon that expresses shock about Davis's acquittal, posing the question: "Will we ever be able to stop the lawlessness in our nation?" Fusco's video is aligned with the love Baldwin's letter expresses, and is critical of the delusional association between "lawlessness" and Davis's acquittal, but it also asks viewers to think about the weight of symbolizing Black collectivities under threat.

Love letters played a significant role in Davis's story. When Fusco reflects on the "things" that "spoke" of Davis, the camera lingers over the corner of a magazine or newspaper article titled "The Prison Love Letters of Angela Davis to George Jackson." The correspondence between Davis and Jackson were illegally seized and cynically deployed by the prosecution in the trial against her. The state's attorneys transformed the private unfolding of love, vulnerability, and subjectivity in the letters into evidence of a criminal appetite that Davis would stop at nothing to satisfy. Needless to say, weaponizing the Davis/Jackson correspondence in this way was an intrusion, and demonstrates that from the perspective of the U.S. legal system, Black people are not presumed to have physical or psychic coherence, never mind privacy or interiority, a premise that has its roots in chattel slavery. *a/k/a Mrs. George Gilbert* draws attention to how widespread and unconscious this premise is.

Though they now stand for that violation, the love letters of Davis and Jackson also exemplify an epistolary Black love. Traces of a relationship that formed through Davis's work advocating for the Soledad brothers, they show that love is the affective ground and virtual glue of radical solidarity. Rich with feeling and sensuality, the letters write to a world beyond the systemic racism the prison materializes, and they draw on the history of Black people writing to each other to maintain loving bonds despite the deliberate destruction of families and kinship structures. They are evidence that for Davis and Jackson, the feeling of love and acts of imagining are inseparable in the project for imagining a more just world in which Black people can have private, interior lives and share them on their own terms. As Robin D. G. Kelley writes in his introduction to *Freedom Dreams: The Black Radical Imagination* (2002, 4), "There are few contemporary political spaces where the energies of love and the imagination are understood and respected as powerful social forces." The correspondence between Jackson and Davis is one of those rare political spaces where the feelings of love and acts of imagination are not only respected but inseparable.

The letters Jackson wrote to Davis testify to his emerging voice as a writer, activist, and intellectual. Exemplifying the intimate connection between prison and epistolary expression (Maybrin 2000, 151–77), they substantiate the claim that when prisoners have little or no contact with the outside world, their written letters become their voice. Jackson had been imprisoned since he was eighteen and the letters to Davis express his desire to have love, not prison, define him. Near the conclusion of a letter with only the year 1970 as the date, he writes with humility and charm as he claims the love slavery denied: "In the event that you missed it (my writing is terrible, I know), I think a great deal of you. This is one slave who knows how to love" (Jackson 1994, 285–86). At the beginning of the next letter, he stresses how much he thinks about Davis and how deeply happy that imaginative act makes him: "I think about *you all of the time.* I like thinking about you, it gives me occasion for some of the first few really deeply felt ear-to-ear grins" (Jackson 1994, 286). Jackson composes an image of his loving feelings from the inside out.

Scholars who study the epistolary practices of the imprisoned comment on their visual and tactile qualities, as they often become containers of experience that prison nullifies (Wilson 2000, 179–98). Jackson's letters illustrate this aspect of prison correspondence. He expresses a strong desire to not just see Davis but be in her presence. In the letter from May 29, 1970, Jackson begins by stating, "I'm thinking about you. I've done nothing else all day. This photograph that I have of you is not adequate" (Jackson 1994, 300). Similar to Fusco's attention to the limitations of visual depictions, Jackson desires a presence that a photograph cannot capture. The desire for intimacy and touch shapes how he presents himself, and when he describes the surveillance of his correspondence, he places himself in the here and now of writing. After describing how his mail is interfered with and delayed, Jackson writes, "I'm going to write on both sides of this paper, and when I make a mistake I'll just scratch over it and continue on" (Jackson 1994, 280). Explaining how he will write on the recto and verso of a sheet of paper and identifying the marks he will inscribe over his errors, Jackson makes the letter into a material, textual, and visual object that holds both the traces of his presence and his imaginative act of thinking about Davis.

Jackson's desire to see Davis opens onto imaginative play with doubles that connects to Fusco's riffs on her aliases, both actual and presumed, and the dispersal of Davis's name and image through their hypercirculation. In the final paragraph in the letter from 1970, Jackson writes to Davis about "Yvonne," which is her middle name: "Should you run into Yvonne tell her that I love her also and equally. Tell her that I want to see her, up close" (1994, 286). This play with the idea of Davis's double registers the imaginative capacities they were cultivating in their letters. In the context of the prison-industrial complex and its dehumanizing violence, playing with the double has a political significance. For what one sees in Jackson's letters to Davis is the heartfelt wish that she can keep an image of him as a tender and kind human being. This wish seems to be part of Jackson's struggle to resist the inhumanity forced upon him, and the possibility that Davis can imaginatively hold on to that difference is crucial. While this desire aligns with the expectations that Black women will nourish and cohere communities, it emerges from reciprocal expressions of love. Near the conclusion of the 1970 letter, after declaring "[t]his is one slave that knows how to love," Jackson states, "It comes natural and runs deep. Accepting it will never hurt you. Free, open, honest love, that's me" (1994, 286). Jackson enacts in writing the "open, honest love" through which he defines himself. The "me" at the end of that sentence asks Davis to recognize and receive his love and shows that the letter is an imaginary space in which they can see themselves mirrored and held in their own words.

Davis's side of the correspondence complicates the familiar icons that depict her as a figure of Black militancy and reveals her becoming other to herself. At the closing of the letter addressed to Jackson on June 10, 1970, she writes about her defenses, and how their love had begun to erode them: "For the moment I'll unleash my thoughts and allow them to go in their instinctive direction toward wild wanderings, fantasies. . . . Something in you has managed to smash through the fortress I long ago erected in my soul" (cited in Apetheker 1997, 214). These expressions of sexual passion—"wild wanderings" and "fantasies"—suggests that the erotic has become, in Audre Lorde's words, a "resource" of deep knowledge that allows her vulnerability to emerge, freeing her from the expectation to embody strength (1984, 53).

As allegories of freedom, the love letters between Davis and Jackson connect to Black people's collective desire for transformation. In *Blues Legacies and Black Feminism* (1998b), Davis argues that after emancipation, despite its unfulfilled promises, sexuality was a vital expression of freedom. As she explains:

> For the first time in the history of the African presence in North America, masses of Black women and men were in a position to make autonomous decisions regarding the sexual partnerships into which they entered. Sexuality thus was one of the most tangible domains in which emancipation was acted upon and through which its meanings were expressed. Sovereignty in sexual matters marked an important divide between life during slavery and life after emancipation. (1998b, 4)

The Davis/Jackson correspondence tapped into this historical transformation, which made sexuality a practice of political articulation and a claim to agency.

Sexual, historical, and political, the Davis/Jackson correspondence was also an intellectual exchange. The letters build on the theoretical insights of Herbert Marcuse, with whom Davis worked as an undergraduate and PhD student, and put them to work for imagining a free Black world. In *An Essay on Liberation* (1969), Marcuse argued that the sensuous affects unleashed by the counterculture movement in the 1960s realized new political sensibilities that were capable of transforming the deadening distortions of late capitalism. Building on Sigmund Freud's theory of the drives and how the repressive force of civilization shapes them, Marcuse argued that the "individual reproduces on the deepest level, in his instinctual structure, the values and behavior patterns that serve to maintain domination" (2007, 162). For Marcuse, the aesthetic is a realm where the drives and needs of individuals can become unhinged from patterns of aggression and domination. He sees in art a commitment to love and Eros, a "deep affirmation of the Life Instincts in their fight against instinctual and social oppression" (1978, 11). As Marcuse asserts, "Art cannot change the world, but it can contribute to changing the consciousness and drives of the men and women who would change the world" (1978, 32–33). This is the transformation Fusco's video seeks as it models reflecting on the aggression brought to icons like Davis.

Davis and Jackson began the process of transforming the world by working through the pernicious idea that Black women were impediments to revolutionary change, except as subordinates, an idea Jackson rehearses. In a letter from June 1970, he writes about Black mothers holding their boys back, disclosing the punitive restraints the mythical Black matriarch is imagined to wield in order to sustain her emasculating power (Jackson 1994, 4). Davis crafts a passionate refutation and makes the claim that unless the Black male "purges himself of the myth that his mother, his woman, must be subdued before he can wage war on the enemy" the racist structure of society will not be overturned (cited in Apetheker 1997, 211). The letters enact the possibility of this purging, and Davis asserts the centrality of women to revolutionary struggle: "Only when our lives, our total lives, become inseparable from the struggle can we, Black women, do what we have to do for our sons and daughters. . . . We cannot be dismissed as counterrevolutionaries" (cited Apetheker 1997, 209). This exchange is a sketch of the arguments that would become central to "Reflections on the Black Woman's Role in the Community of Slaves" (Davis 1998c). Composed in jail and dedicated to Jackson, "Reflections" announces Davis's commitment to undoing "reified images" of Black women based on "grossly distorted categories" (1998c, 111). Fusco pursues Davis's scrutiny of "reified images" and the distortions upon which they were founded.

The Davis/Jackson correspondence aligns with bell hooks's arguments about love as a neglected but necessary element in political transformation. For hooks, love is a way to see and understand another's perspective and create a dialogic space in which hardened instincts and cemented viewpoints can soften. As she writes, "When women and men understand that working to eradicate patriarchal domination is a struggle rooted in the longing to make a world where everyone can live fully and freely, then we know our work to be a gesture of love" (1989, 27). *a/k/a Mrs. George Gilbert* contributes to the love of Davis's work by examining the idealization that love can often carry and translates into symbolic burdens for Black women. In the section that follows, I analyze how the video rewrites the aggressive desire for icons, an instinctual demand inscribed into sight that shapes how Black women are perceived. Drawing on Davis's own written meditations on the appropriation of her image in spectacle culture, Fusco opens places for seeing Black women's subjectivities, not as ready-made icons, but as texts that are dense with singularity and complication.

III. Seeing Singularity

a/k/a Mrs. George Gilbert builds on multiple aspects of Fusco's oeuvre: her engagement with the history of racist imagery, the militarized police state, and the imbrication of display and containment in the long durée of primitivism. The video also highlights the central role writing plays in her artistic practice. Fusco is first and foremost a visual artist, but she works out of a tradition that foregrounds the artist as a researcher, scholar, and intellectual. Fusco's writings are an extension of her creative work and serve as a paratextual reflection on its contexts and receptions.

Fusco's *Young British and Black: The Work of Sankofa and Black Audio Film Collective* (1988) exemplifies the generative roles writing and research play in her artwork and demonstrates how insightful she is about the work of her peers and predecessors. Reading the precision with which she describes the films of Sankofa and Black Audio Film Collective and the political contexts they emerged out of, one can see remarkable correspondences to *a/k/a Mrs. George Gilbert*. Delineating the various traditions these collectives interrupted and challenged, which includes institutions of "liberal enlightenment" and "mainstream images of Black identity," Fusco writes:

> Sankofa's reflections on the psychosexual dynamics and differences within Black British communities, and Black Audio's deconstruction of British colonial and postcolonial historiographies are groundbreaking attempts to render racial identities as effects of social and political formations and processes, to represent Black identities as products of diasporic histories. (1988, 8–9)

This emphasis on revealing racial identities to be effects of historical processes not only de-essentializes race but challenges the assumption that artists of color are, as Fusco writes, "unimaginative reporters of abject social realities" (2001, 129). Under the insidious guise of idealization, this conflation of artists of color with oppression blocks out their singular and subjective relationship to racial injustice.

a/k/a Mrs. George Gilbert traces the histories of racial injustice that made Davis into a global icon and follows them into the present tense of the video's construction. This shifts the focus from Davis to the U.S. police state and the mechanisms of surveillance that continue to wield enormous power. Near the opening of the video, Fusco suggests that the image-repertoire developing to justify the global war on terror recalls the images of an earlier

Fig. 3. Woman at subway stop. Still from Coco Fusco's *a/k/a Mrs. George Gilbert*, 2004, video. Image courtesy of the artist.

period. Without naming the pursuit of Osama Bin Laden, the attack on the World Trade Center, or the expansion of state powers through the Patriot Act, Fusco implies that the present is an echo of previous hunts; these reappearances are all the more ghostly and ungraspable since the visible articulations of resistance have been erased. Lingering images attest as much to what the narrator knows as what she has forgotten, but she states that the image of Davis is the exception to this more general rule of historical amnesia. In tandem with blurry images produced by an unsteady camera that attempts to come into focus at a subway platform in Brooklyn (the Central Ave. stop), Fusco states: "Though I could no longer match every face from that time with a name . . . I still recognized hers . . . Like most of those who had seen her, I hardly knew who she was. What I did know was that her image cast a long shadow." In tracing this historical shadow, Fusco creates parallels between the surveillance of those designated terrorists in the 1970s—as Davis was—and women of color living in the first decade of the twenty-first century. Indeed, across the subway platform, Fusco's camera spots a young Black woman, visibly anxious, who wears sunglasses and a wig (fig. 3).

Fig. 4. Portrait of Angela Davis. Still from Coco Fusco's *a/k/a Mrs. George Gilbert*, 2004, video. Image courtesy of the artist.

These parallels between the early 1970s and the first years of the twenty-first century reveal the historical tenacity of American fears and fantasies that reframe resistance to anti-Black racism as terrorism and force women of color to go on the run. They also highlight the need to revisit and reanimate the vital historical archive of revolutionary thought the icon of Davis encapsulates but also covers over.

When Fusco states, "I still recognized hers," the video shifts to a piece of black-and-white footage that creates a close-up of Davis (fig. 4). The camera watches Davis quietly looking and observing—viewers can see the movement of her eyes—without turning to what she sees. This cinematic portrait pays loving attention to Davis's beauty, but the focus on her active looking portrays a quality that is more elusive—a serene psychic composure, a capacity to hold on to her own perspective and self-image. This footage illustrates the "unrelenting scrutiny that magnified every detail of her being," as Fusco puts it, but it is also the first indication that *a/k/a Mrs. George Gilbert* will be devoted to creating images that suggest what is unknowable about her. The video indirectly renders the places where the acquisitive and aggressive dimensions of vision cannot go.

Focusing on Davis's perspective, but letting it remain inaccessible, this footage deflects the impulse to transform her into an icon. Highly recognizable and affectively charged images dense with symbolic meanings, icons function like cultural mirrors; they reflect the values and ideals through which collectivities see themselves. Icons most often do not portray the nuanced particularities of subjectivity. They are symbols that reflect the needs of the public who consumes them. Nicole Fleetwood identifies the significant role icons have played in Black cultural life. "[I]n light of historical and ongoing forms of racism," she writes, icons are a "plea for recognition and justice" (2015, 3), a description that clearly applies to those of Davis. And yet, as Fleetwood explains, with this plea and its "attempt to transform the despised into the idolized," Black icons "carry a sort of public burden" (2015, 4).

Overlaid with Fusco's reflection that she "hardly knew who [Davis] was," the footage of Davis that focuses on her looking connects to what scholars in Black studies identify as the Black interior. For poet Elizabeth Alexander, the Black interior is a psychic space that is not reducible to either the limited images of Blackness that serve the white imagination or the public images of Black resistance. The Black interior is a concept that recognizes the fact that while the white racist gaze is normalized in the field of vision, Black people live psychic lives that are not wholly determined by its violent intrusions. Building on Alexander's concepts, Kevin Quashie makes the Black interior a counterpoint to the "equivalence between resistance and blackness" (2012, 3). This equivalence is so pervasive, it is "practically unconscious," and, as Quashie explains, blocks out "vulnerability and interiority" (2012, 3). To attend to the Black interior, and the room it makes for experiences of subjectivity that are as singular and unpredictable as individuals, Quashie argues that it "requires a shift in how we read, what we look for, and what we expect, and even what we remain open to. It requires paying attention in a different way" (2012, 6). *a/k/a Mrs. George Gilbert* offers one iteration of the aesthetic for which Quashie calls.

Fusco's voice is central to the video's commitment to creating new ways of reading and seeing. She lends the texture of her slightly raspy voice to the script she cowrote with novelist Rick Moody, which gives the video an intimacy that underscores its emphasis on aspects of subjectivity that cannot be fully predicted or comprehended. With its dynamic array of pitches and cadences, Fusco's voice is distinct from that of the FBI agent. He habitually clears his throat, which suggests a process of consumption that has been blocked, but he also uses his voice as a tool to establish and reestablish—often with angry defensiveness—his knowledge of Davis, which his obsessions undermine.

The agent's obsessions reveal that Davis's defiance of available categories provoked the desire to capture her, which extended far beyond her trial. It seems the agent contacts Fusco to absolve himself of guilt. Clinging to his authority, he confesses to the crime of participating in her surveillance and criminalization, but also the guilt of becoming attracted to a woman who was an enemy of the state. As he took photographs of her with this Minox Spy Camera and listened to her phone conversations and speeches, he found her to be "well, you know, beautiful." Viewers can hear his grudging incredulity and the guilt that accompanied his attraction. He talks about her "incredible" hair and the beauty of her smile. The agent's attraction extends into expressions of paternalistic protection—he imagines he could have helped her at the Marin County shoot-out on August 7, 1970, though she was not there—as well as a deeply sadistic desire to witness her submission. He declares that "someone had to wipe the smile off her face" because it was "dangerous" and could convince anyone to do anything. The agent assumes that her smile would become less powerful if it was subordinated. Just after this confession, Fusco plays footage of Davis speaking to a crowd outside the courtroom after her acquittal (fig. 5). Speaking through her wide, irrepressible, "ear-to-ear" smile that echoes Jackson's (1994, 2086), Davis stresses that her release is not only the "happiest day of [her] life," but foresees "the victories that are to come" for all the people who "struggled so hard for [her] freedom." So broad, genuine, and deeply felt, Davis's smile expresses love for a just future.

As awful as the agent's confession is, Fusco does not completely separate her narrator from it. She listens to him talk about collecting articles about Davis from the Black press and describe what he likes about the photographs. With magazine covers and articles moving across the screen, he states his preference for the photographs of Davis that "looked like she wouldn't back down," but he also likes those that feature her "downcast eyes" and suggest sadness. Upturning the expectation that she will reject this white man's obsessive gaze, the narrator instead expresses her affinity with his fascination. "I was thinking about those pictures you mentioned. I agree. They are really extraordinary." By making the fascination for images of Davis into a space that the researcher and the FBI agent share, Fusco reflects on the multiple desires projected onto her image from across the political spectrum.

Fig. 5. Angela Davis smiling after her acquittal. Still from Coco Fusco's *a/k/a Mrs. George Gilbert*, 2004, video. Image courtesy of the artist.

For this reflection, Fusco engages with Davis's "Afro Images: Politics, Fashion, and Nostalgia," a short essay composed in 1994 that reflects on how her image was incorporated into the national imaginary and drained of its political context. In "Afro Images," Davis outlines the ways in which her image became so commodified that the historical context from which it emerged had been rendered practically invisible. After relaying an anecdote in which a person recalled who "Angela Davis" was through the afro, Davis writes about being reduced to a "hairdo" wrenched away from her ordeal as well as the communities of women with whom she shared histories of oppression. Discussing her appearance in the *New York Times Magazine* as one of the most influential "fashion trendsetters" of the last century, Davis writes: "I continue to find it ironic that the popularity of 'afro' is attributed to me, when, in actuality, I was emulating a whole host of women, both public women and women I encountered in my daily life, when I began to wear my natural in the late sixties" (1998a, 273).

"Afro Images" expresses Davis's disappointment with the ways specta-cle culture has diluted her image. For her, this dilution is a theft that continues a history in which Black women's capacities to claim ownership of their bodies has been systematically denied. And yet, at the core of "Afro

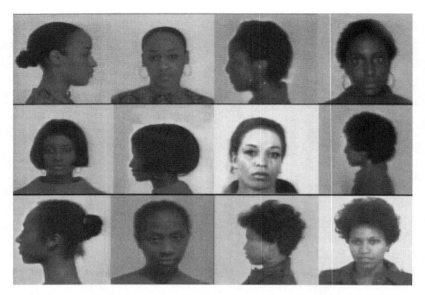

Fig. 6. Grid of mug shots and wanted photographs. Still from Coco Fusco's *a/k/a Mrs. George Gilbert*, 2004, video. Image courtesy of the artist.

Politics" is a dialectical tension about the reproduced image in the age of spectacle culture: both its nullification of history and its capacity to contribute to the emergence of unforeseen ideas and practices. While many images of Davis were taken and reproduced to create a culture of fear among Black women, these images also allowed a visual culture of resistance to emerge. As Davis explains, "The circulation of various photographic images of me—taken by journalists, undercover policemen, and movement activists—played a major role in the campaign that was ultimately responsible for my acquittal" (1998a, 274). At the end of her essay, Davis suggests the possibility of "actively seeking to transform [the] interpretive contexts" of photographic images (1998a, 278).

a/k/a Mrs. George Gilbert materializes the argument Davis makes in "Afro Images." The video replicates the gaze of surveillance and mimes how it collapsed other Black women into the image of Davis. Attesting to the power of video to put still images in motion, Fusco creates a grid composed of small square images—mug shots and wanted photographs—of Davis and women who look like her (fig. 6).

The images quickly appear, disappear, and reappear to enact the deep-seated assumption of Black women's sameness at the foundation of racist

Fig. 7. Women walking in the park. Still from Coco Fusco's *a/k/a Mrs. George Gilbert*, 2004, video. Image courtesy of the artist.

and sexist surveillance. After this grid of moving images, Fusco presents the target shape that brought them into this pattern of capture, containment, and substitution, which exhibits the Black women's collective vulnerability to the white male gaze. And yet, the connections premised on assumptions of their sameness were also re-created by Black women to align their own images with that of Davis and her defiance. Making her engagement with "Afro Images" explicit, Fusco explains, "Years after the war she averred that it was humiliating to be remembered as a hairstyle whose meaning fades out of collective memory with every revival." Near the end of the sequence, Fusco stresses the unknowability at the heart of Davis's hypervisibility when she states plaintively: "The agents had her pictures, her diaries, her doodles, and her letters, but they couldn't see her."

Fusco takes this hypervisibility, and its connection to the blindness of racism and sexism, and transforms them into a subtle vision that challenges the presumption of Black women's transparency. In the scene that concludes *a/k/a Mrs. George Gilbert*, Fusco depicts four young Black women in a park wearing afros and dashikis and going about the business of their everyday lives (fig. 7).

Portraying anonymous Black women and their decidedly undramatic dailiness, Fusco foregrounds the ungraspable mysteries and resistances singular individuals can evoke simply by living. Set to somber violin music, the shaky camera Fusco uses to shoot this scene might suggest the continuation of the agent's peeping-tom surveillance, but there is also an evocation of a Black feminist interior that is kept inaccessible. Perhaps in part, this group portrait reveals the "long shadow" cast by the image of Davis. The conclusion is not a depiction of an isolated icon produced by the process of forcing an individual to live as a target of a nation's fears, anxieties, and hopes, nor is it an explicit depiction of a political collectivity. An image of a few Black women walking and conversing suggests that reflecting upon the history that made Davis into a consumable image can open spaces in cultural vision in which the singularities of Black women's subjectivities can come into view without being exposed. That is, Fusco's evocation of Davis's love for the future of Black freedom allows these women to exist in spaces where they are not serving as symbols for others. A love letter to Davis that takes a step back from icons and the burdens they condense and cover over, *a/k/a Mrs. George Gilbert* creates the conditions for seeing Davis's radical gestures of love written into the present.

Kimberly Lamm is associate professor of gender, sexuality, and feminist studies at Duke University. She is the author of *Addressing the Other Woman: Textual Correspondences in Feminist Art and Writing* and is currently working on a new book devoted to Black women writers' representation of clothing and fashion. She can be reached at kkl9@duke.edu.

Works Cited

Alexander, Elizabeth. 2004. *The Black Interior: Essays by Elizabeth Alexander.* St. Paul, MN: Graywolf Press.

Apetheker, Bettina. (1975) 1999. *The Morning Breaks: The Trial of Angela Davis.* Reprint, Ithaca, NY: Cornell University Press.

Baldwin, James. 1971. "An Open Letter to My Sister, Miss Angela Davis." *The New York Review of Books.* https://www.nybooks.com/issues/1971/01/07/.

Beegan, Gerry, and Donna Gustafson, eds. 2020. *Angela Davis—Seize the Time.* New Brunswick, NJ: Zimmerli Art Museum, Rutgers, the State University of New Jersey.

Biemann, Ursula. 2003. "The Video Essay in a Digital Age." In *Stuff It: The Video Essay in the Digital Age*, edited by Ursula Biemann, 8–23. Zurich: Edition Voldemeer; New York: Springer Wien.

Davis, Angela Y. (1994) 1998a. "Afro Images: Politics, Fashion, Nostalgia." *The Angela Y. Davis Reader*, edited by Joy James, 273–87. Reprint, Malden, MA: Blackwell.

———. 1998b. *Blues Legacies and Black Feminism: Gertrude 'Ma' Rainey, Bessie Smith, and Billie Holiday*. New York: Random House.

———. (1971) 1998c. "Reflections on the Black Woman's Role in the Community of Slaves." In *The Angela Y. Davis Reader*, edited by Joy James, 111–28. Reprint, Malden, MA: Blackwell.

Fleetwood, Nicole R. 2015. *On Racial Icons: Blackness and the Public Imagination*. New Brunswick, NJ: Rutgers University Press.

Fusco, Coco. 1988. *Young British and Black: The Work of Sanofka and Black Audio Film Collective*. Buffalo, New York: Hallwalls, Contemporary Arts Center.

———. 2001. *The Bodies That Were Not Ours: And Other Writings*. London: Routledge.

———. 2004. *a/k/a Mrs. George Gilbert*. Written by Fusco and Rick Moody. Chicago, Illinois: Video Data Bank.

hooks, bell. 1989. *Talking Back: Thinking Feminist, Thinking Black*. Boston: South End Press.

Jackson, George. (1970) 1994. *Soledad Brother: The Prison Letters of George Jackson*. Reprint, Chicago: Lawrence Hill Books.

Kelley, Robin D. G. 2002. *Freedom Dreams: The Black Radical Imagination*. Boston: Beacon Press.

Lorde, Audre. 1984. "Uses of the Erotic: The Erotic as Power." In *Sister Outsider: Essays and Speeches*, 53–59. Berkeley: Crossing Press.

Marcuse, Herbert. 1978. *The Aesthetic Dimension: Toward a Critique of Marxist Aesthetics*. Boston: Beacon Press.

———. 1969. *An Essay on Liberation*. Boston: Beacon Press.

———. (1956) 2007. "Freedom and Freud's Theory of the Instincts." In *The Essential Marcuse: Selected Writings of Philosopher and Social Critic Herbert Marcuse*, edited by Andrew Feenberg and William Leiss, 159–66. Reprint, Boston: Beacon Press.

Maybrin, Janet. 2000. "Death Row Penfriends: Some Effects of Letter Writing on Identity and Relationships." In *Letter Writing as a Social Practice*, edited by David Barton and Nigel Hall, 151–77. Philadelphia: John Benjamin's Publishing Company.

Nash, Jennifer C. 2019. *Black Feminism Reimagined: After Intersectionality*. Durham, NC: Duke University Press.

————. 2008. "Re-thinking Intersectionality." *Feminist Review* 89: 1–15.

Quashie, Kevin. 2012. *The Sovereignty of Quiet: Beyond Resistance in Black Culture.* New Brunswick, NJ: Rutgers University Press.

Wilson, Anita. 2000. "'Absolutely Truly Brill to See From You': Visuality and Prisoner's Letters." In *Letter Writing as a Social Practice,* edited by David Barton and Nigel Hall, 179–98. Philadelphia: John Benjamin's Publishing Company.

Black Love Convergence: Reclaiming the Power of Black Love

Emanuel H. Brown and Michelle Phillips

Black Love Convergence is a multiday gathering hosted by Acorn Center for Restoration and Freedom, embodying bell hooks's call to "love Blackness as an act of political resistance." Participants come from across the U.S., Canada, and the Caribbean to "reclaim Black life" (hooks 1992), heal internalized oppression, and live into freedom. The collective weaves together movements, generations, and genders to experience Blackness as power, healing, and nourishment. Initially a reaction to the Trump administration, the work of Black Love Convergence has become a chamber resonating and affirming the wisdom of the Black diaspora. From the creator and a participant's perspectives, this piece explores the emotional-spiritual impact of this gathering on our narratives of Blackness, collective healing, and relationships.

The Conjurer

It began with needing to survive, and it became freedom.

Remember November 8, 2016. You are at a loss for words as you see your worst fears unfold. You watch a tyrant ascend to the highest office of a republic built on the idea of freedom. Your mourning is uncontrollable as you oscillate from rage to grief. You feel your heroes turning over in their graves; is this what they gave their lives for? Maybe your vote would have made a difference, but you are surrounded by Black people thick in their legacy in Kingston. You have been here for a little less than a month, running from everything you have lost. Yet tonight, as the results flow in, the absurdity of running is palatable. You are reminded, this is America. This betrayal and the inability to talk about it as backlash is America. This willingness to

WSQ: Women's Studies Quarterly 50: 1& 2 (Spring/Summer 2022) © 2022 by Emanuel H. Brown and Michelle Phillips. All rights reserved.

sacrifice Black bodies is America. You inhale this truth beside the others hiding in your cells, and it is like you can breathe for the first time in weeks.

Your exhale is staccato and labored and the first indication of what is to come. While you don't imagine white supremacists will march in the streets, gun down Black churches, or storm the Capitol, they will. Your breath is the harbinger for another summer of uprisings after a Black man, woman, trans woman, and trans man are all sacrificed for America. You don't know the details; you just know the apocalypse is coming. You get quiet. For a long time, you are eerily quiet. You find fear, doubt, confusion, and grief in your silence. You are barely managing the waves of rage. You wail in the sea, loud enough to wake your ancestors who never made it to America's shores. You will never know their names. Your voices commingle to unlock your courage. You know you must return to the world of the unknown and begin plotting for your emancipation.

Despite your resistance, you go back to the place conspiring for your death. A daily practice emerges of waking up and asking yourself, "What do you need to be free today?" You have been independent for less than a year, with no nonprofit job to hold you steady, as you try to shape your life around freedom. You start asking the question to as many Black people as you can find—your activist friends, spiritualists, healers, artists, children, and elders. You strike up conversations in airports, Lyft rides, and anywhere your curiosity leads you. The question consumes your dreams and pulls you into new places within your body. Soon you realize this was preparing you to make the leap beyond survival. You begin to believe what you heard about gathering, grieving, pleasure, creativity, curiosity, and remembering your practices. You have never tried to save your people before, so you are scared. You are intimately aware of the fragility of the promise of freedom, and you don't want to break them. You are not sure you know how to be the conductor. Your ancestors, the elements, and the moon become your secret keepers. You pull wisdom from bell, Audre, Harriet, Nanny, Octavia, and James. You get brave and name it: Black Love Convergence.

Your idea is simple: gather the most diverse group of Black folks you can, share practice, build connections, and get free. You want every element of it bathed in Black love; you root it in the South and invite those with power to co-hold the space. Just the sound of it—Black Love

Convergence—convinces you to keep going. You arrive at the land early to listen and consecrate yourself. You wonder if your Black transness is enough to hold the expectations of mothers, grievers, and the exhausted. You are easily convinced that people will decide your vision is not enough within minutes. You open your pores to drink in a full dose of what this moment is and summon your courage as you see the first car pull in.

You converge drums,[1] sound,[2] and Radical Self-Love,[3] creativity, pleasure, and shame. You do the traditional Black things: food, fire, singing, and remembering our sacrum is a holy pendulum. Mornings feel like family reunions filled with the familiar hum of dishes clamoring, setting the table, decoding your dreams, and demands for Black elixirs. Afternoons are spacious to allow for being together. You are elated when small groups are spotted frolicking with trees, praying in cotton fields, and laughing deep and whole. Stories of Caribbean, African, Southern, Midwestern, West, and East Coast Blackness weave together to remind us how we survived before. Evenings bring you deeper into your bodies, help you unlock pleasure in spirits, and bring peace. You find a rhythm that opens your imagination to dream beyond survival for two days. On the last day, you pack your bags with the sound of laughter, gyrating hips, a piece of cotton, new friends and lovers, a prayer from Oshun, and a blessing from a high priestess. You are bathed in sage, music, and words; these are your armor, sword, and shield for all that is to come. You weep knowing it is 2018, and the worst is yet to come. Your lamentations are alchemized into a joy only Blackness knows. The final offering seals in the medicine and makes you kin.

The leaving comes as waves of gratitude, lingering embraces, and promises to keep connected. You cement the agreements to conjure freedom with ashé, small pebbles in your pocket, and declaring, "I believe we are winning." Altars are broken down, and offerings to the land are given. You soften to knowing this is the beginning of something. Your vision of freedom is embodied here. You notice yourself be vulnerable, sink into bliss, and be excited about the limitless possibilities. The ease of your inhale and exhale becomes your new normal. As you drive away from this reclaimed space, tears roll down your face. Memories of all you have lost for this abundance to be possible. You whisper a silent prayer to your ascended ancestors for the strength to help us find our back to freedom.

Now, when you are asked how you know when you are free, your answer is simply, "Black Love Convergence."

The Participant

It was growing in mineral-laden soil, robust and earthy, retaining nutrients. By this time, you worshiped any element that brought life to Blackness— sun, water, wind, land as god. Lungs, trees, carbon, freedom.

You were always going to Black Love Convergence. You had been looking for this place your entire life—ancestral narrations alluded to a place where love and Blackness met inside of you. Love, if you thought hard, you could remember it light like trying to catch cottonwood fluff drifting from trees in spring. Blackness always had to be hard, immutable, masculine.

Remember? You were getting off the phone with Emanuel, where he described Black love in real time. Black Love Convergence, he called it. He said it was a practice space for all Black people to really be with one another. Wait. If we could practice being Black together, you didn't have to get it right.

You were twelve years into a marriage with a white woman. You knew she couldn't understand why Blackness, why love, and why they should converge. Later, you realized her question was really why not her because she would always put herself in any space between you two.

Exorcising your own anti-Blackness, you tearfully packed your suitcase for the weekend with equal parts expectation, trepidation, and exhaustion. Afflicted with the wounding of invisibility after long years of lying with whiteness, you knew there was no coming back from this place.

The West Coast would not save you even after twenty years. You imagined aeration better than humidity for your young lungs yearning to breathe free. Northwest in direction, you chased another wrong one away from home. Going back to the South felt like a retrospective on now incomprehensible drawls, collective phobias, and -isms. And still, it was only you that was afraid.

Having survived your first seventeen years of life in the South, you managed never to step foot on a plantation. You avoided them like graveyards as active as street corners. Your family, adept at avoiding grief like bad manners, asked you why you wanted to go there? Why host a celebration of love and Blackness on a plantation of all places?

In April 2018, outside of Raleigh, North Carolina, you were standing at the gates of the reclaimed Franklinton Center at Bricks[4] for the first annual Black Love Convergence. You can't even recount how you prepared for the space in which you were born arriving.

Freedom hit you altogether amid beautiful and Black relations, djembe drumming, walking through ghosts in cotton fields, and at the base of the enormous magnolia tree that memorialized the whipping post. You were free and didn't know it. The majestic magnolia you saw every day outside your bedroom window as a child felt different now. The one-hundred-million-year-old, leathery-leaved ancestor, the magnolia, is so old it is pollinated by sap-feeding beetles from the time before bees came to be. Only a tree so primordial, so sweet, was worthy of bearing the agony of our enslaved forepeople.

Every moment felt full of intention and, yes, love. There was a surprisingly easeful way you could exist outside colonial time. You were healing, feeling Black people up so close. You were taking your time as though it were finally your own. Weaving singing, humming, drumming, altars, and ritual throughout the weekend, you wondered if this love grew on trees. So free, you almost forgot yourself. Remember? Surrounded by other healing and loving Black people made the diaspora's illusion of distance, separation, and isolation feel smaller and smaller and smaller, yet again.

The Lesson

The last day you asked how I was getting to the airport. I told you I had to figure out where to stay the night because my flight left in the morning. You were full and bubbling over with the joy that only the circumstance of being fully seen and felt could bring. Your eyes were eyeing mine more than a few times over the weekend. I felt a distinct pleasure being the object of your gaze. I felt the palpable quickening in places that had not known love. I explored these places lavishly through the singing resonance of my voice at the firepit and in my bed, spent from dancing just before closing my eyes at night.

It made sense that you were engaging me and offering to stay the night with you; I had summoned you in a way. Your bluff and directness betrayed your empire's state of mind and island ilk. Still, this truth in volition could only follow the Convergence. Having never spoken to you, I agreed, somehow our shared attendance built credibility instantly.

The night went as we never imagined. Or maybe you did. Was the Convergence opening me to a way of holding Blackness, soft, deliberate, and trusting so soon? Was this the test? You told me you had never done this before. Something in your lilt had me ask, "This, a one-night stand, or this, this?" You replied, "This, this." Flashing back to moments we had workshopped on consent, touch, and relationship, you wondered aloud about my pleasure and ideation. We drew our bodies in shapes of desire breathing only at the tops of our lungs. I caught the innocence as it spilled from you, mouthing my deep and holy appreciation.

On the way to the airport the next morning, nor since have I ever wondered if I would see you again. Whether in New York, a hotel room, or plantation, it has never mattered. I had been to the consummate place where my free Black love was born, arriving on the leaves of sweet magnolia trees.

Emanuel H. Brown, MSW, is the founder of Black Love Convergence and the Steward of Acorn Center for Restoration and Freedom. He curates experiences that foster engagement and awakening by weaving together, storytelling, poetry, ritual, and music. As a Black Trans* leader in healing/arts/spiritual (HEARTS) Justice, he holds a unique point of view on the praxis of bringing our whole selves on the journey toward freedom. In 2021, BEAM and Lipton presented Emanuel with a Southern Healing Star Award and he has held fellowships with Pop Culture Collaborative, Resonance Network, and Praxis Project. You can find him on IG at @emanulhbrown and emanuelhbrown.com.

Michelle Phillips, LMHC-A, is the founder of Liberation Strategies and a Black Love Convergence participant. Michelle lives in Seattle, WA, and works as a therapist, healer, and facilitator specializing in grief, ancestral healing, and liberation. They are a 2020 National Board of Certified Counselors Minority Fellow for Clinical Mental Health Counseling and can be reached at info@liberationstrategies.com.

Notes

1. Held by Afia Walking Tree and Spirit Drumz.
2. Held by medicine woman Gina Breedlove and Vibration of Grace™.
3. Held by Sonya Renee Taylor, author of *The Body Is Not an Apology: The Power of Radical Self-Love*.
4. Franklinton Center at Bricks provides a nurturing home to local, national, and global programs and organizations seeking liberation on a reclaimed plantation, a first school to educate former slaves in the area.

Works Cited

hooks, bell. 1992. *Black Looks: Race and Representation*. Boston, MA: South End Press.

Loving with Their Consciousness: Black Women in Trinidad and Tobago Black Power

Keisha V. Thompson

Abstract: The exclusion of Black women's contributions to social movements has left a gap in the narrative of Black love as revolutionary action. This article addresses the historical narrative by centering Black women and their participation in the 1970 Black Power movement in Trinidad and Tobago as Black love. **Keywords:** Trinidad and Tobago; Black power revolution; postcolonial Caribbean; Caribbean women; Afro-Caribbean; Caribbean Black power

All the great movements for social justice in our society have strongly emphasized a love ethic.
                                                                    —*bell hooks*

A deep, abiding and unconditional love for Black people lay at the heart of the organizations and movements of the 20th century.
                                                                    —*Alicia Garza*

When one encounters the term "Black love," thoughts predominantly turn to romantic love. In a heteronormative society, images, literature, and research will take us into the discussions of gender dynamics and roles (Wanzo 2011; Randolph 2018). The archetypes present in society will point us toward both fictional and iconic Black couples (Charleston 2014). Beyond the romantic, we see, read, and hear about Black womanhood and sisterhood, and Black manhood and brotherhood, both in fictional accounts and scholarly inquiries. Occasionally we will see and read about family dynamics, intergenerational relationships and the impact on the individual in today's society (Nash 2013). Yet with all of these demonstrations and discussions, love remains difficult to define (Utley 2010). The concept of

WSQ: Women's Studies Quarterly **50**: 1 & 2 (Spring/Summer 2022) © 2022 by Keisha V. Thompson. All rights reserved.

133

political love—love that is present in public spaces and engenders activism and advocacy—is often eclipsed by heteronormative or sororal definitions. Yet understandings of Black love as essentially political are not absent.

While Nash (2013) describes a love politic based on feeling and affect, hooks (2018) offers that "to begin by always thinking of love as an action rather than a feeling is one way in which anyone using the word in this manner automatically assumes accountability and responsibility." Engaging in collective acts of resistance and revolution is more in line with hooks's definition, and thus will be the one used for this article. While most instances and expressions of Black love focus on the individual, this article focuses on the collective love rooted and centered in the resistance of the Trinidad and Tobago Black Power movement (Moore 2018).

Love in the context of Black resistance, revolutionary action, and activism goes beyond the individual. Revolutionary action in this movement means putting one's body, relationships, and resources on the line for the good of others, and for a cause that went beyond one's self (Chabot 2008). The Black Power movement in Trinidad and Tobago demanded racial equity and launched a grassroots campaign where they were raising the consciousness of the disenfranchised members of the population. This was a necessity in Trinbagonian society, creating awareness about inequities "demands that we always attempt to resolve contradictions" (Cudjoe 1984). The contradictions in the society to be resolved were the presence of racism and economic exploitation[1] in an independent nation with Black leadership (Barclay and Ralph 2011). By producing printed materials, holding teach-ins in neighborhoods, and large rallies throughout the country, the movement raised the consciousness of the masses. The individuals doing the consciousness raising were mainly from the educated middle class. They exemplified revolutionary love by reaching out to those on the margins of society. In breaking down the components of revolutionary love, Chabot (2008) offers that by enriching others without an expectation of reciprocity, we expand freedom while decreasing oppression and alienation. The ideals and actions of the participants in this movement embody revolutionary love. This article will explore this particular notion of Black love in terms of the participation of women in the Trinidad and Tobago Black Power movement.

Although having been active and significant participants, women have been largely ignored by scholars and observers in the history of Black nationalism and Pan-Africanism (Davies 2014; Reddock 2014; Pasley 2001). The leadership structure and existing narratives highlighted Black men as the leaders and the innovators (Reddock 2014). This paper aims to disrupt those narratives by highlighting the presence and contributions of women involved in the 1970 Black Power Revolution in Trinidad and Tobago. These women, like Amy Jacques Garvey[2] before them, were major contributors in a movement that reinforced patriarchy while also moving women's rights forward (Pasley 2001). Though this piece focuses on women, it is not to say that the men of the movement do not exhibit Black love. The movement as a whole depicted and was based on a love for a people, a nation, and for the poor and disenfranchised at that particular point in Trinbagonian[3] history. This movement ultimately shaped the concepts and appreciation of Blackness in the twin island republic. It also shaped hiring policies in the public sector and was arguably responsible for the changes in foreign interest in the nation's economy in the years immediately following the revolution (Barclay and Ralph 2011; Samaroo 2014). The existing narrative records show the contributions and leadership of the men of the movement, the military, the trade unionists, and many others (Samaroo 2014; Teelucksingh 2014). However, in conducting field research on the revolution, this author was able to gain rare firsthand accounts from both men and women on the pivotal role women played in the revolution.[4] Utilizing the aforementioned definitions of love and resistance, and firsthand accounts, this article will situate the women as not only being active participants but also being largely responsible for the existence of the movement beyond a governmental state of emergency and its lasting impact on Trinbagonian society (Cudjoe 1984).

Historical Context of Trinidad and Tobago

No one, it seems to me, likes to work hard for an employer and sing about how every creed and race can find an equal place in this country, when they all know instinctly that capitalism has gone steeringly and crazily mad in this isle of la Trinity.
                                                                  —*Selwyn Cudjoe*

Here every creed and race find an equal place.
And may God bless our nation.
    —*National Anthem of Trinidad and Tobago*

Trinidad and Tobago, the twin island republic situated at the southernmost tip of the Caribbean, is known as the land of the hummingbird, the land of calypso and steelpan (the only major musical instrument to be invented in the twentieth century). What is lesser known is the history of struggle by some of the population for equity and how it resonates throughout the society to this day. The issue is complex at various levels, as it includes the intersection of race and class in a postcolonial society (Blair 2013). Trinidad and Tobago, like much of the Caribbean, is made up of descendants of white European immigrants, formerly enslaved Africans, formerly indentured servants of East Indian and Chinese descent, descendants of the Native peoples, and various biracial individuals (Hine-St. Hilaire 2006). Those of African and East Indian descent make up the majority of the population in fairly equal proportions yet are often the ones battling for equality and equity (Teelucksingh 2014, 172). However, there are other layers of the population that wield economic power, traditionally those of white European descent and more recently Middle Eastern (Barclay and Ralph 2011, 178). Despite having gained independence from Great Britain in 1962, the vestiges of colonialism in the twin island were glaringly obvious to some concerned constituents, less than ten years postindependence (Samaroo 2014). Trinidad and Tobago in the late 1960s was wrought with discontent. The labor unions were unhappy, as evidenced by various strikes and demonstrations (Oxaal 1971). The unemployment rate among youth, particularly those of African descent, was high, and the newly independent government appeared to be lacking (Barclay and Ralph 2011).

Dr. Eric Williams, the first prime minister of the former British colony, rose to prominence in the mid-1950s as the political party the People's National Movement was formed. With a seemingly pro-Black rhetoric, Williams delivered several public lectures at Woodford Square, a location that ironically would be the rallying point for the Black Power movement of the 1970s. His most famous speech, titled "Massa Day Done," pointed out the racial inequalities that remained in the society as a result of colonialism (Cudjoe 1997). Despite his initial professed ideology, those of African and Indian descent felt as though his government was not looking out for the interests of the Black nationals. Under his administration, industry was run largely by foreign interests, and those of African and Indian descent[5] were often denied employment and education opportunities. Cudjoe posits that at some point during his rise to power and postindependence, Williams lost touch with the people and while appropriating their sentiments, stopped listening to their requests. Simultaneously, the civil rights movement taking place in the United States and then ultimately Canada trickled down to the small twin island nation. The constituents were ready to explode. And as we are about to see, the global nature of Black love as resistance and revolution informed, if not inspired, this movement.

The civil rights movement in the United States had such a global impact and spawned many leaders. One such leader was a son of Trinidad and Tobago, Stokely Carmichael, later known as Kwame Ture. Carmichael migrated to the U.S. at a young age and later became involved with the efforts of the Student Nonviolent Coordinating Committee (SNCC) while he was a student at Howard University (Joseph 2014). His call for "Black Power" during a speech in Mississippi in June 1966, quickly took root, not just in protest but in the very culture that remains today in the US, Trinidad, and all around the world. As the momentum of the movement built, Carmichael was banned from entering the country by prime minister Williams. There have been several accounts as to the concerns the government held about allowing Carmichael into the country, ranging from stirring up further dissention to a rumor that he would replace the prime minister if the government was overthrown. Dr. Williams certainly expressed concern about how the events in the United States were impacting those in Trinidad and Tobago. In an address to the nation on May 3, 1970, he stated:

> For some years now we have been aware of dissident elements in the society, especially among a minority of trade unions, seeking to displace the government. At first, they tried to do so by the electoral process, no one can have any quarrel with that. When that failed, however, they turned increasingly to unconstitutional means and armed revolution. This embraced certain sections of the Black Power movement copied from the United States of America.

The prime minister was correct, in that the involvement of the men and women in the 1970 revolution was largely due to a global chain reaction (Austin 2007). The profoundness of this political moment is captured in Dr. Williams's words, and there certainly is much to unpack from this statement and the political climate of that time. However, the significance of it for this paper, not in order of importance, points first to the global nature of the events of 1970, and second to the role of women during this particular place and time.

A Global Chain Reaction

Whites will not see that I, for example, as a person oppressed because of my blackness, have common cause with other blacks who are oppressed because of blackness.
                                        —*Stokely Carmichael*

Many students in the United States staged sit-ins and took over spaces on their college campuses throughout the civil rights era in protest against injustice (Schmidt 2015). In February of 1969, similar events were taking place in neighboring Montreal, Canada. A number of Caribbean students were involved in what is now termed the "Sir George University affair." Both Black and white students at the university were protesting the unfair and racist grading practices of a biology instructor and the inadequate response of the administration. For several days, students occupied the computer center (Austin 2007). The protest ended with the computer center in flames and students trying to escape the burning building. Fifty years later, *USA Today* would describe those events as Canada's civil rights reckoning (Friedman 2019). Of the students arrested, several were from various Caribbean countries, including Trinidad and Tobago (Greenidge and Levi 2019).

One year later, as they stood trial, a day of international solidarity was called by student activists at the University of the West Indies (UWI) based in Trinidad. The student activists and others took to the street to make their displeasure known (Greenidge and Levi 2019; Samaroo 2014). They marched across the nation's capital to several Canadian institutions and gave speeches in the same square where Dr. Williams rose to prominence. That day was the dawn of the movement in Trinidad and Tobago. The next day, nine of the leaders were arrested, and this set off many days of protests, meetings, marches, and a deliberate attempt to disrupt the status quo (Samaroo 2014). The governing body of the movement, the National Joint Action Committee (NJAC), was formed, comprised of students, university lecturers, trade union leaders, and other activists.[6]

For weeks, there were multiple marches across the nation. There was an attempt to have "Indians and Africans Unite," to fight against the power held by the traditional white elite and the government. This was evidenced by the historic march to Caroni on March 12, 1970, where an estimated ten thousand individuals joined in walking the miles from the nation's capital Port of Spain to the sugarcane fields in Caroni. The now famously dubbed

"University of Woodford Square," the place where prime minister Eric Williams rose to popularity and power, became the site of many lectures and galvanizing speeches on Black Power and the failure of Williams and his government (Greenidge and Levi 2019). It was also the site of the fatal shooting of Basil Davis, a young participant by a police officer during a rally (Samaroo 2014). An estimated thirty thousand mourners showed up to join the funeral procession through the streets on April 9, 1970. Tensions were high, and by several written and verbal accounts, Prime Minister Williams anticipated that there would be an attempt to topple the government (Wilson 2012). On April 21, 1970, the revolution reached its climax when Prime Minister Williams declared a state of emergency, and a mutiny was staged in the Trinidad and Tobago Regiment. The soldiers were being called upon by the government to march into the nation's capital to help keep or restore order. The mutiny was largely based on the soldiers' refusal to "turn on" their Black brothers and sisters at the request of the government. The police took over at the soldiers' refusal. All of the leaders of the movement were rounded up by the police and detained on an island off the coast of Trinidad called Nelson Island. After engaging in a fire fight with the Coast Guard, the soldiers who staged the mutiny were tricked into a negotiation that ended in them being detained at the Royal Gaol prison in Port of Spain (Oxaal 1971).

It was while interviewing one of the male leaders on his detention, that this author heard a statement that departed from the existing narrative of the Revolution and the movement: "The women saved us." This was the first time in weeks, after sitting with multiple interviewees and reading multiple written accounts, that the women were explicitly mentioned. When asked to elaborate, he fondly recalled learning of his mother being responsible for organizing food for the long marches. He explained how messages would be passed to the women secretly while visiting the detained men on Nelson Island. Years later at his home, he would share how both his first and second wives were persecuted by the authorities. He recalls with painful clarity the death threats that he still has that were written to his first wife. When these men and women decided to take a stance in 1970, the ramifications followed them and their loved ones for many years to come. Their revolutionary action went beyond themselves as individuals. He went on to detail how, because the male leadership was detained, the women continued the work of the movement under the organization NJAC. NJAC and the movement were one and the same at this point. With the leadership

Fig. 1. The author at an exhibition on Nelson Island commemorating the 1970 Black Power revolution in January 2016.

detained, and the state of emergency lasting seven months, that could have been the end of the movement. What is remarkable about their involvement at the point of the state of emergency is that their work had to occur covertly as they had to avoid the surveillance of the government. Many of the male leaders of the movement credit them with ensuring the continuity of NJAC. But as one pointed out, when the detainment ended, the male leaders returned to their positions of power within the organization.

Prior to this, the narrative of the events of 1970 and beyond had been decidedly male. There is some conjecture that this was because the media reporting everything from the Sir George Williams affair to the present moment was and is male. Most accounts cited thus far in this article come from male scholars and reporters, Pasley, Reddock, and Boyce-Davies being the exceptions. Pasley particularly centers the Caribbean women's movement in the events of 1970 and beyond. She points out that although the events of the movement have been described elsewhere with minimum exception of such names as Beverly Jones and Josanne Leonard, the active role that women played in the demonstrations and the guerilla struggle of the National Union of Freedom Fighters (NUFF) has been neglected. With such a declaration and this point of view, this author set out to tell the stories of the women whose actions resulted in the movement existing beyond April 21, 1970. Most of the information presented from this point forward primarily comes from the interviews compiled by the author for a documentary entitled *There All Along: The Women of Trinidad & Tobago Black Power* (Thompson 2020).[7] The title is based on the premise that the women didn't simply step up and acquire the skills and knowledge to run the organization and movement, but that they in fact, were there all along.

In Plain Sight: Firsthand Accounts

We must search history for a new element, something
that in a way is less familiar to us- ourselves.
                    —*Paula Giddings*

How could a young Black woman raised during the 1950s
find someplace to take collective action against the repressive
social conditions she faced, and bring about revolutionary change?
                    —*Kathleen Neal Cleaver*

Footage and photos of the events in 1968 into 1970 show the presence of
the women. They can be seen at the marches, listening intently to male
speakers, holding children in their arms. But what are their names? How
and why did they become involved? How were they able to maintain an
organization while the leadership was detained and they themselves were
under surveillance by the authorities? It is this author's contention that their
leadership abilities and knowledge did not emerge overnight, but that their
accounts and experiences have not been recorded and presented as a part
of the overall narrative up until this point. While Pasley (2001) situates
their participation as a precursor and instigator of a feminist consciousness
in the Caribbean, and presents a gender analysis of the Black Power movement ideology, most women who were active in the movement remain
anonymous in its recorded history, and the extent of their sacrifices are
unknown outside of NJAC. When asked, the men and women of the move-
ment/organization talk about women being present from the very beginning.
Aiyegoro Ome, a founding member of NJAC and former leader shares that
the women were present from the very beginning. Here are the origin stories
of the three women highlighted in the documentary film *There All Along*:

> We had women in the forefront of what we were doing because following
> the very first demonstration. And what we observed very prominently in
> all of the demonstrations, we didn't plan it that way, is that women tended
> to carry the flags. The people who carried flags, which would be at the head
> of the demonstrations were women. And then on the platform speaking,
> there were quite a number of women. I am proud to state that among those
> female speakers, in the early days was Liseli Daaga. (Ome 2018)

In 1970, Liseli Daaga was nineteen years old. She was raised in a middle-
class family and afforded a certain level of privilege due to her father's
position in the ruling political party of Trinidad and Tobago. She gave up

all of that privilege to join the Black Power revolution, which later on evolved into a movement. Liseli would eventually fall in love with the leader of the movement, Makandal Daaga, dedicate her life to the cause, and to this day, over fifty years later, continues to contribute to the organization that her late husband led. Hers is certainly a love story, but that is not the one to be told in this paper. Her elder brother Apoesho Mutope, the official photographer of the movement, is unwavering in his perspective to not view the women as separate entities within the revolution and the movement. He recalls working side by side with them in every aspect, and insists that they at times made sacrifices that "big hard back men" could not make. As pointed out earlier, revolutionary love is about what one can do for another. Liseli recalls that at this age in 1970, she had recently resigned from a committee at her church because she did not believe that enough was being done for "our people." She participated in a march to Shanty Town. Shanty Town, or Beetham Gardens as it is presently called, is an informal settlement that houses some of the poorest and most disenfranchised of Trinidad and Tobago (Forde 2018). During that first march to Shanty Town, she saw the manifestation of racial and economic inequity and heard who would later become her husband speak. It was during his speech that she recalls thinking, "Oh, this is what I want to do with my life" (Daaga 2018). When mention is made of her husband in the literature, the fact that she was a speaker at rallies is not mentioned. The fact that while working as a teacher she continued the work of going into communities and dropping off food and literature is not recorded elsewhere. Her presence as the wife of Makandal Daaga is known in the greater society, but, beyond her peers, her impact during 1970 and beyond is not.

Olabisi Koboni, born Joy Alfred[8] in the sister island of Tobago, was a recent college graduate when she became involved with NJAC. She credits her time at the Jamaica campus of UWI as being an impetus for her joining the movement upon her return to Trinidad. It was in Jamaica that she was exposed to the teaching of Walter Rodney,[9] and began having questions about the reality of postcolonialism. For Olabisi and the many students at UWI, he created a buzz. He engaged them in conversations and lectures about Black Power. He made them question whether or not independence truly happened in countries like Jamaica, Barbados, and Trinidad and Tobago. The economies of these countries, according to Rodney, still benefited the colonizers, and the experiences of Black people in this context were still largely marked by slavery. Olabisi believes that based on this

experience, her awareness of politics and economics increased. Her awareness of her Blackness increased; she recounts how at this point she started
wearing her hair in its natural state instead of straightening it. Upon her
return to Trinidad in 1969, she seamlessly fell into the recently formed
National Joint Action Committee.

> I was involved in a lot of the meetings there in Belmont. And so the state
> of emergency came and those of us, I think my involvement got deeper in
> that post-state of emergency, you know, period. When all the leaders were
> detained, some in the jail on Frederick Street, others on Nelson Island and
> so on. It involved . . . I never went on Nelson Island at the time, but making
> trips when they had their visits to see them, the people who were detained
> at the Frederick Street jail. And basically at that time it was more a ques-
> tion of holding together, holding the organization together. It was very
> trying for some people who had members of families who were outside still
> who had relatives inside the jail so it was more looking out for people and
> there was a lot of that, meeting people, looking out for people, seeing that
> everybody's life was in order and so on. And there was a certain amount of
> meetings and so on at the time but it was basically holding things together
> whether in terms of holding the organization together or in terms of look-
> ing out for people's families, you know because uhm, and holding ourselves
> together that was basically what. And so I think my involvement was deep-
> ened more during that period when the . . . during the period of the
> emergency when people were detained. (Kuboni 2018)

The compassion exhibited by Olabisi is demonstrative of the love that comes
with Black resistance. She became involved in a cause that would benefit
others more than herself. She speaks with great conviction about what the
families of those detained were experiencing at that time. It is as though she
not only took on some of the tasks required to keep NJAC going, but she
felt a responsibility to also take care of the families on the outside. As a
daughter returning to Trinidad with her bachelor's degree in French and
Spanish, she was not expected to join a revolutionary movement. On the
contrary, she was expected to take a position at a prestigious all-girls school
to make her family proud. She did both and believes that for this reason,
her family was in fact not proud but disappointed in her actions. She thus
sacrificed her familial status for the love of revolutionary principles.

Eintou Pearl Springer returned to Trinidad from England where she was
involved with the Black Panthers and immediately became involved. She
was friends with Althea Jones-LeCointe.[10] She recalls participating in many

marches in London before returning to Trinidad in November of 1969. Upon her return she became involved through her friendships with others in the movement. She worked full-time as a librarian, which she describes as being a class-ridden field. And she participated in the many marches and protests. She was involved with the publication of literature for NJAC, such as their liberation newspaper, walking through the more disenfranchised neighborhoods to recruit individuals to the movement and also educate them and increase their consciousness as Black people in Trinbagonian society. She recalls being trained by the leader, Makandal Daaga, in the art of public speaking, and being critically involved in the cultural arm of NJAC later on in the '70s.[11] Eintou would go on to become a poet laureate of Trinidad and Tobago, but not before she sacrificed some of her familial relationships, professional opportunities, and ultimately her own safety and well-being. As she says:

> I remember during the state of emergency being in a particular place, in an apartment on Duke Street and the police come in for us, come in with the ambulance. So intent were they on shooting and killing. (Springer 2018)

This quote from Eintou illustrates the nature of true love described by Moore (2018) as rebuking and binding structural impediments through which some Black people live and die. Her life was in danger, not only on this night, but on many others. She was surveilled for a significant portion of her life. And yet, she still showed up to keep the organization going, and gave her time, her body, and her talents to ensure that Black Trinbagonians had someone speaking up on their behalf, challenging the oppressive structures such as the private sector, the continued foreign interest in the economy, racism, and classism that kept them unemployed, underemployed, and disenfranchised.

A significant component of the women's involvement was educating those on the "blocks." They shared their education and skills with populations of disenfranchised individuals. Olabisi, Eintou, and Liseli recall going into Morvant, Laventille, Belmont, and various parts of the country:

> So I would be at the road side in the middle of the night in a meeting with people not acknowledged as big of my social strata. Right. Um, and so we had those discussions, those rap sessions, you know, to, to understand the society, uh, and so on and, and, um, and, and so that I think was successful, right. In terms of building awareness of the society. (Kuboni 2018)

The purpose of these sessions was to raise the consciousness of those living in marginalized parts of the country. To educate them about what was taking place in society, how it impacted them and encourage them to demand change. Eintou also has memories of spending many nights beside Olabisi hanging fliers "all over the place." Liseli recalls even during the state of emergency, leaving work and arranging to have cars and publications waiting for her and others to go door to door in the countryside "and continue our education." What is remarkable about their involvement at the point of the state of emergency is that their work had to occur covertly, as they had to avoid the surveillance of the government. Many of the male leaders of the movement credit them with ensuring the continuity of NJAC. But as one pointed out, when the detainment ended, the male leaders returned to their positions of power within the organization.

The Nature of Black Love

Revolutionary love requires consistent effort by everyone involved,
and it does not become meaningful until we leave our comfort zone
and exert ourselves for other people.

—Sean Chabot

Liseli, Olabisi, Eintou, and many other women exhibited and continue to exhibit the dimensions of love offered by hooks (2018), "a combination of care, commitment, trust, knowledge, responsibility, and respect." They left their comfortable homes, occupations, and used their privilege and knowledge to stand up for and against things that did not directly impact them. They were afforded the education that many of their counterparts were not, and although they held positions in society because of that education, they still felt a call to put down their titles and fight for those in the society who were without privilege and titles. They literally chose to put their bodies in harm's way through the demonstrations and by going into neighborhoods that were unfamiliar to them to educate others and to take care of the loved ones of those who were detained. They not only sacrificed their bodies but also their relationships with family members. Again, they did this not for themselves, but for their fellow citizens, and for the greater good of their country.

Olabisi is keenly aware of the impact her involvement had on her familial relationships. She was the first in her family to go on to secondary school, which at the time had recently been made possible by Prime Mminister Williams, and then on to college.

> And so we lived in tension. So one had to find a way of managing relationships, living literally in the same house with people who did not share the fact, who felt that you were letting down the family, um, who felt that this was an era of social mobility. And so I was the first to get a degree. As I said, my sister came soon after me. I was the first to get a degree. It meant something to my father and I was not living up to his expectations of the quality of life that I should have brought to the family. Having gained this degree and coming back into the family, I was not meeting the expectations of my family. (Kuboni, 2018)

In a class-based society like Trinidad and Tobago, individuals are able to elevate themselves and their families by gaining higher education. Being able to attend secondary school, and then university as a Black person were opportunities offered to a select few. Her choice to turn her back on the very government that made this possible and spend her time with members of the lower class was not understood or easily accepted. The expectations placed on Olabisi were further amplified by the fact her mother was deceased. She describes interactions where family members expressed that her mother would have been disappointed in her choices. Eintou also recalls that most of her family members were against her involvement in the movement. With the exception of a paternal uncle, they all felt as though she was "squandering the opportunities of the education she was given." Her mother in fact suffered greatly because of her involvement, as the police and other authorities would often visit the family's home with threats and intimidation.

> I have had my share of arrests and short-term detention. It did not get worse for me, because my first cousin, Theodore Roosevelt Guerra, who was a powerful criminal lawyer, would say, send the li'l girl home. I have had special branch and CIA surveillance. All of this led to my mother having nervous breakdowns, since the police promised her they had a bullet put aside for me. (Springer, pers. comm., 2018)

Constantly getting phone calls and visits by the authorities in connection with Eintou's involvement invoked fear and anxiety in her mother that ultimately would lead to her being institutionalized. However, Eintou and her counterparts did not retreat in the face of such threats. But they continued to selflessly put their bodies on the line for others in their society. In some ways they set the standard for how Black women in the Caribbean would show up in the Grenadian Revolution, and feminist activism across the region. These dimensions of commitment and responsibility are largely acknowledged within activist and Caribbean feminist circles, although not necessarily written about sufficiently.

Mr. Ome recalls that his second wife who was also involved in the movement prior to their marriage was displaced from her family as a result of her uncle with whom she was living being continuously pressured and threatened. Liseli describes growing up very "comfortable," as her father had a high position in Dr. Williams's People's National Movement (PNM) political party. She also points out that her way of living changed drastically with her involvement in the movement, and with ultimately marrying Daaga. She recalls being surveilled on her outings with friends, being intimidated in her home with her children while her husband was out, the numerous arrests faced by her husband in the years subsequent to the revolution, and even she herself being prevented from entering other Caribbean nations. Her brother sheds some light on the family dynamics, as he was involved earlier than she was and was a part of NJAC's leadership: "All the families of people, particularly the front-line people would have been affected. Quite a number of them, you know, were not openly confrontational, but you, had cases and say where sons or daughters get put out" (Mutope, pers. comm., January 2018).

He goes on to share that it was perhaps best that his father passed away in 1972, as he would not have been happy with Liseli's subsequent marriage to Makandal Daaga. Many others, like Olabisi, Eintou, and Liseli, similarly sacrificed their privilege and their very bodies for the cause. Immediately following the events of early 1970, for example, a fifteen-year-old Josanne Leonard could be seen and heard leading the Young Power movement that emerged out of the Black Power movement. She called for justice on behalf of those detained leaders, and the soldiers who were subsequently placed on trial for the mutiny within the army. Countless other women who may never be named joined in the demonstrations leading up to and beyond the climax of the movement. While the focus of this piece is on the events of 1970, among those countless others, there is a name that echoes in the hearts and minds of many participants: Beverly Jones. Beverly Jones was mentioned in each interview as she clearly left a mark on her elders. Beverly was a part of NUFF, a collection of youth who became disenchanted with the greater movement and felt like the revolution had fallen short (Sama-roo 2014, 103). They engaged in guerilla-style interactions with the armed forces. Beverly and her older sister Jennifer left their home and joined NUFF in the hills of Trinidad. On September 13, 1973, they were involved in a violent confrontation with the police, and Beverly died. She was two weeks shy of her eighteenth birthday, and it has been reported that she was also with child. Jennifer survived, was jailed, and she remembers the determination and resilience of her younger sister until the bitter end. She recounts the conflict their involvement created in the home they shared with their maternal grandparents, as both of their parents lived abroad in the United States. She speaks with profound sadness about the fact her sister died believing that she, Jennifer, was dead, and the way the ordeal left her mother heartbroken. Yet she speaks with conviction about their involvement and the greater cause to which they made a contribution. With varying degrees of conflict, sacrifice, and loss, these women were commit-ted to caring for and raising the consciousness of others. In caring for the greater cause and others, they also engender self-love in resolving the contra-dictory nature of being a Black woman in a patriarchal organization and movement.

Loyalty and Intersectionality

> *In linking racism to an attack on their masculinity,*
> *Black Power advocates failed to see how the construct*
> *of power and masculinity in itself oppressed women.*
> —*Victoria Pasley*

> *How does one uphold racial solidarity and oppose*
> *intraracial sexism at the same time?*
> —*Karen S. Adler*

While intersectionality is not widely used in Caribbean feminist literature, the spirit of it is certainly invoked in the lived realities of women in the Trin-idad and Tobago Black Power movement. In encouraging the use of Black feminist theories, Barriteau (2009) asserts that Caribbean scholars can benefit from some of its conceptual tools. Her argument is that although there is a marked difference in histories, both societies have a shared parent-age of being former British colonies, and therefore have shared trappings of racism and sexism. In this vein, and borrowing from Patricia Hill Collins (1996), "one rule in African American communities is that 'Black women will support black men, no matter what, an unwritten family rule.'" This "rule" can be seen displayed across the diaspora in the patriarchal nature of Black nationalist organizations, such as NJAC. The language used in recruiting women into the movement exemplifies this. Several handwritten pamphlets exist in the archives of the University of the West Indies that depict the fervor at which women were pressed to join. The following is an excerpt from a pamphlet calling on women to address the gambling issue among "their" men:

> Sisters, you must take keener interest in destroying the vice [of gambling] among the Brothers, because some of these Brothers are going to be fathers of your children. If they cannot support themselves on the gambling scene now, and do not intend to get put off this circle and look for something more progressive, how will they maintain you and your children in the future? You must do your thing also.

The women are given the responsibility to address the gambling as it directly affects the men's ability to support the women and children. The NJAC founder and deceased leader Makandal Daaga is quoted in more archived literature[12] stating: "Never underestimate the power of a woman where a man is concerned." And so NJAC and its constituents seemingly continued in the Black nationalist tradition of subsuming the woman's identity and needs under those of the Black man. While Black love in this tradition is largely one of women for men, it is much more than that. It is in fact a love for a people, and a nation. And although self-sacrificing, the duality of these women's reality demanded that they also love themselves.

Although they were involved in every aspect of the movement, they were still faced with chauvinistic attitudes and actions. Eintou recalls being called before the governing board by someone she ended a romantic relationship with: "And I went to the meeting and I told them in Trumpian language that I was responsible for my own body and I gave no credence to this body to even question or sanction. So I had those wars" (Springer, pers. comm., January 2018).

During the interview, her entire body and energy shifted when she uttered these words. It was very clear that she used clear language along with some choice curses to illustrate her point in that moment. When there was pushback in her adorning herself with makeup, she says "makeup was discovered on the banks of the Nile, I am an African woman." She also recounts her love for cooking and serving others, and how some people did not appreciate that aspect of her personality. She found herself in the classic bind of having others try to dictate and judge her expressions of womanhood. But what place does that have in a movement that is centered on and concerned with racial equality? While being ridiculed, while placing their lives in danger, Eintou and the women who fought as they did were still confronted with contradicting expectations due to their intersecting identities. Barriteau (2009) points out the origin of this contradiction: "Black men who are minorities in racist societies often seek control and manifest their desire to be patriarchs in ways that are pathological." Even the male leaders acknowledge the struggle among the membership:

> It was a difficult period for us. It was a difficult period, particularly for, for the leadership in NJAC. Some of them were very chauvinistic all right. I mean, there's no way around that some of them were and it led to confrontations I remember in the leadership between some of them and some of us and yeah, you know, the question of, of what sisters were capable of handling. And some of them had had reached the level of awareness where they, they were very conscious of the fact that they could handle anything that the men could." (Mutope, pers. comm., January 22, 2018)

As the official photographer of NJAC, a member of the executive, and an elder in the organization, Apoesho was able to view the women through multiple lenses. Literally, his camera lens captured many moments. He also was a man, who may have held traditional views prior to the revolution. He sagely added that although as an organization/movement they considered themselves to be thought leaders, (1) the same conflicts that were taking place in the outer society in terms of gender dynamics and power, were taking place within their organization, and (2) it was unfair to expect that the women who were placed in harm's way and made sacrifices to then not be given the opportunity to lead and attend to the administration of the organization. Aiyegoro Ome speaks of having confrontations with his male counterparts over the beliefs they held concerning the ways in which they felt the women should participate. Overwhelmingly, they leaned toward wanting the women to engage in domestic tasks. Both men speak to the unfairness of this, particularly as they observed that, in some instances, the strength and sacrifices of the women outweighed that of men within the organization. Nevertheless, these women remained loyal to the organization and its cause throughout this time. As the purpose and the ideology of NJAC evolved post-1970, the women eventually held positions on the executive arm of the organization, with Olabisi being the first post-1970, and ultimately they formed the National Women's Action Committee (NWAC). Throughout the years, these women also maintained key educational and leadership positions in Trinbagonian society. They carry themselves with a certain level of grace and strength that only comes from a place of love. Olabisi and Liseli have educated countless children and adults at various levels of instruction. Eintou has used her gift in the Black tradition in arts to portray history and current events in the society and also to train young people and even advocate for them in their communities.

Most of this paper has focused on the outward expression of love from these women, but along with the implied ideals of Black feminist love comes the concept of self-love. The events of 1970 caused Black people to question the origins of their ideals of beauty. As Eintou shares, the first time she was called beautiful was in 1970. She continues on:

> The first time African people's clothes were not regarded as costumes and natural hair and skin had its own beauty. . . . Although it was part of my upbringing and so on. It was never a part of regarded as the thing to be or have. So all of that changed, all of that perception changed and we created a generation of strong people, strong leaders. (Springer, pers. comm., January 17, 2018)

There is a level of awareness that these women have about the impact they've had. When one encounters Trinidadian society with its varied hues and cultures, the African heritage is firmly in place. Emancipation Day is celebrated on August 1 every year. Gaining the Emancipation holiday is a direct result of the lobbying and activism of NJAC. The day is marked with citizens donning African garb. But it is not an uncommon occurrence to see individuals dressed in this manner on any other day of the year. Natural hair is worn by women of various ages, and the names of the subsequent generations departed from the traditional British names. As these women learned to love themselves and their Blackness, as they took their place in society, they taught Black Trinbagonians to love themselves.

The Lasting Impact of Black Love and Resistance

When we choose to love we choose to move against fear
against alienation and separation. The choice to love
is a choice to connect to find ourselves in the other.
                                                    —*bell hooks*

At the root of Black resistance—the collective struggle
through which we might imagine and build a world
more just, more free, more equitable, more magical—is love.
                                            —*Darnell L. Moore*

The question is often asked as to the lasting impact of social movements such as the one in Trinidad and Tobago. Most people can point to the changes made by the government post-1970 that are directly tied to the revolution. Samaroo (2014, 108) argues that although the prime minister condemned the actions of the revolution, he used it to implement reform and change that he may have been considering prior to the events. Logically, it would appear that the revolution led to diminishing some of the foreign interest in the country. Many point to the banking industry as the premier example of reform. Prior to 1970, outside of service and janitorial positions, Black people did not work in banks. Being able to identify discrimination in employment and compensation led to positive changes for Black people in the labor force. Wearing natural hair and African garb became more widely accepted in the greater society. Sociologist Rhoda Reddock talks about how the acceptance of food even changed:

> In terms of food there had been a lot of food discrimination. Local food, for example, ground provisions were looked down upon as a slave food. For example, breadfruit, I mean you had to hide right to eat bread fruit before 1970. So it was only after 1970 that a lot of the local foods, bake and shark, bake and salt fish, even doubles and bara and chana and even roti, they gained a new status after 1970. (Reddock 2018)

There was a departure from the notion that "white is right." In its place was the idea that the ways of being and living that are native to Black people should be embraced and celebrated. The cultural shift that took place in 1970 was not temporary. Dr. Reddock also shares that an analysis of the census before and after 1970 showed more people identifying as Black.

Some say that the revolution and ultimately the movement failed because the government was not overthrown. But many would agree with the words of Liseli Daaga:

> You don't stop a movement. What we did in 1970, we really raised the consciousness of people throughout and once people's consciousness is raised, there is no stopping. People started talking about one topic and that that or we would listen to this speech and then people raise yes and expand more upon the topic. For example, be a brother, be a sister. People do not understand how profound that is and how much that changed our society. (Daaga, pers. comm., February 2018)

Aiyegoro Ome, a former head of NJAC, articulates how much people look upon these women with wonder that they have been able to maintain themselves and their commitment to Black people, not just in Trinidad and Tobago but across the Caribbean. Both Olabisi and Liseli have been responsible for educating generations of children and adults, and Eintou continues to leave her mark in the Black traditions and arts space in Trinidad and Tobago. Their care, commitment, responsibility, and respect continue to directly impact Trinbagonian society and individuals. Terry Ince was a high school student during the events of 1970, and she talks about how the movement impacted her, particularly as a darker-skinned child and now woman:

> I became more vocal as a person. I was a very shy child, very shy teenager. And while I didn't become vocal right away, I became more thoughtful in the way I did things. And when. I vocalized through writing, I used to write a lot as a teenager and my writing changed, I, I saw that. But as I became a young woman and I entered womanhood and went into other aspects of my life, I rec, I see the thread, I have a strong affinity to my African roots. I'm very proud of who I am as a Black woman. (Ince 2018)

Terry watched the movement unfold as a child. She remembers participating in the funeral processional for Basil Davis. She remembers listening to the older activists who would be around her school talk about the importance of the movement. She also was growing up in a family and during a time where and when her darker skin was not initially celebrated. Without the presence and the impact of women in the Black Power Revolution, women like Terry and ultimately this author would be without positive, strong models of Black womanhood. More than the words spoken by the women, their counterparts, and the scholars, this author has witnessed and experienced Black love from these women. Olabisi and Eintou made time for the interviews in the midst of their ongoing projects. Eintou coordinates a yearly reenactment of the Canboolay Riots (a historic event surrounding Carnival). Post-retirement, Olabisi is involved with online learning. I met with Liseli at the Butler Institute of Learning, where she retired as the principal but continues to work as the administrator for the NJAC-run high school. They gave their time, they connected me to their counterparts, they offered me refreshment and advice. What isn't captured in any of my notes and recordings are the moments where I literally sat at their feet, and they engaged in the age-old tradition of African griots and passed down their wisdom and knowledge to a young Black scholar. In the words of Dr. Deborah McFee:

> They were teachers, they became international public servants. They became NGO coordinators, they became lecturers. And I find that intriguing about these woman. It's like they, they scattered and the number of ways in which they influence us from the way they dress, the way they wear their hair. Just the fact that these women are located in all these different spaces for me meant that 1970 was a productive time because clearly the consciousness produced these diverse, diverse products. But they're all over shaping our reality both nationally and internationally, which is, I don't think we recognize how many of them are just all over. I spoke, I met, I spoke with Olabisi and I didn't know she taught at Bishop's and I think okay that is interesting. Sometimes I wonder. Clearly, how, how much, she must have given so much of herself to her students and the significance of her struggle. That's what I mean they're everywhere. They kind of permeate the society. And so then, we're living with them. We're living with their consciousness. (McFee 2018)

These women and many others, in the face of ridicule, alienation, and being placed in harm's way chose to love their Black brothers and sisters over several generations. They challenged the government to do more and do better for "our people." They used their education and positions to lift others up to educate generations of people. They saved a movement at a critical point, and their presence and presents of love permeate throughout Trinbagonian society. They have loved and continue to love with their consciousness.

Keisha V. Thompson is an associate professor of psychology at Kingsborough Community College, City University of New York. Her most recent research agenda is focused on the impact of the Black Power movement on Trinidad and Tobago's society and culture. She can be reached at keisha.thompson@kbcc.cuny.edu.

Notes

1. Based on the following excerpt from a pamphlet titled "Talking About Black Power" from a bound collection within the Alma Jordan Library of the University of the West Indies, St. Augustine. "To fight economic exploitation without fighting racism means that we fight the effect and not the cause. To fight racism without fighting exploitation means that we create a system of Black Capitalism that is even more harmful than White Capitalism, because it destroys the basic unity of Black people, that historically is our way of life; it means that one brother does psychological violence against another." We have to combine the two enemies of the Black man in our struggle, for they are combined in denying us our freedom. We must understand how they are related and how they enslave us.

2. Jamaican-born journalist and second wife of Marcus Garvey. Oftentimes credited with being responsible for his writing and running the UNIA when her husband was convicted of mail fraud in 1922.

3. A term used to unify and describe the people of Trinidad and Tobago instead of being island specific.

4. I traveled to Trinidad and Tobago in 2016 and again in 2018 to conduct audio and video interviews of individuals who participated in the revolution, gather archival data, and interview scholars in the fields of sociology and gender. The quotes in this piece are from those interviews.

5. This was particularly true for those who were of darker complexions.

6. This wasn't the first time NJAC mobilized in response to the Sir George incident. In late 1969, they blocked the entrance of UWI and prevented the Canadian governor-general from entering the premises in protest of the treatment of their peers in Montreal.

7. The untold story of women who participated in the Trinidad and Tobago 1970 Black Power revolution. The presence, importance, and impact of female participation in the events of 1970 is presented through the first-person accounts of women revolutionaries, their male counterparts, and scholars in the fields of sociology and gender. The film premiered at the Trinidad and Tobago Film Festival in September 2020.

8. A number of activists from the 1970s and into the 1980s changed their "colonized" names to ones of African origins. NJAC was instrumental in creating rituals around this both for adults and newborn children called

Naming Ceremonies. The choice of names was based on rejecting the colonized culture and a return to African traditions.

9. Walter Rodney was a Guyanese-born writer and lecturer at the University of the West Indies Mona, Jamaica campus. He is most known for his book *The Groundings with My Brothers*, and for teaching the students about the reality for Black individuals postslavery and independence in the Caribbean. He was declared persona non grata by the Jamaican government in 1968, and was dismissed from his position at UWI. This resulted in what is called the Rodney Riots.

10. She was the eldest sister to Beverly and Jennifer (mentioned later in the text). Well-known for her participation in the British Black Panther movement.

11. NJAC's ideology and function has evolved over the years. Post-1970 and into the early 1980s the focus was on being a cultural organization which still espoused ideal of Black power along with African spirituality. Eventually, they entered into the politics as a political party for a brief period of time, and has since returned to its cultural roots.

12. The following is from NJAC-produced literature given to this author:

> The Principles of NJAC, An Appeal to the Nation
> 1. Honor the Old
> 2. Love the Children
> 3. Be a Brother, Be a Sister
> 4. Protect and Prepare the Youth
> 5. Elevate and Respect the Woman
> 6. Build the Family
> 7. Unite the Nation
> 8. Truth must be the cornerstone of the Political System
> 9. We want the whole bread not the crumbs
> 10. Educate, discuss and persuade, thereby encouraging motivation, consultation, and participation
> 11. Love must be the basis of all relationships and work must be a right, not a favor, as man cannot find spiritual development and fulfillment without it
> 12. Let the people Decide

Works Cited

Adler, Karen S. 1992. "'Always Leading Our Men in Service and Sacrifice': Amy Jacques Garvey, Feminist Black Nationalist." *Gender & Society*: 346–75.

Austin, David. 2007. "All Roads Led to Montreal: Black Power, the Caribbean, and the Black Radical Tradition in Canada." *The Journal of African American History* 92, no. 4: 516–39.

Barclay, Lou Anne, and Henry Ralph. 2011. "Black Power and Equitable Business Participation: Forty Years on in Trinidad and Tobago." *Social and Economic Studies* 60, no. 3/4: 151–82.

Barriteau, Violet Eudine. 2009. "The Relevance of Black Feminist Scholarship: A Caribbean Perspective." *Feminist Africa* 7, Diaspora Voices: 9–31.

Blair, Erik. 2013. "Higher Education Practice in Trinidad and Tobago and the Shadow of Colonialism." *Journal of Eastern Caribbean Studies* 38, no. 3: 85–92.

Carmichael, Stokely. 1966. "What We Want." *New York Review of Books*, September 22: 5–8.

Chabot, Sean. 2008. "Love and Revolution." *Critical Sociology* 34, no. 6: 803–28.

Charleston, Kayla. 2014. "Act Like a Lady, Think Like a Patriarch: Black Masculine Identity Formation Within the Context of Romantic Relationships." *Journal of Black Studies* 45, no. 7: 660–78.

Cudjoe, Selwyn R. 1997. "Eric Williams and the Politics of Language." *Callaloo*: 753–63.

———. 1984. *A Just and Moral Society*. Grenada: Calaloux Publications.

Daaga, Liseli. 2018. Interview by Keisha Thompson. *Women of Trinidad & Tobago Black Power* (February 2).

Davies, Carole Boyce. 2014. "Pan-Africanism, Transnational Black Feminism and the Limits of Culturalist Analyses." *Feminist Africa* 19: 78–93.

Forde, Maarit. 2018. "Fear, Segregation, and Civic Engagement in Urban Trinidad." *The Journal of Latin American and Caribbean Anthropology* 23, no. 3: 437–56.

Friedman, Jordan. 2019. "1969 Sir George Wiliams Protest Was Canada's Civil Rights Reckoning." *USA Today*, March 27, 2019.

Garza, Alicia. 2015. "Black Love—Resistance and Liberation." *Race, Poverty & the Environment* 20, no. 2: 21–5.

Giddings, Paula. 1984. *When and Where I Enter*. New York: Harper Collins.

Greenidge, Adaeze, and Gahman Levi. 2019. "Roots, Rhizomes and Resistance: Remembering the Sir George Williams Student Uprising." *Race & Class* 61, no. 2: 27–42.

Hill Collins, Patricia. 1996. "What's in a Name? Womanism, Black Feminism, and Beyond." *The Black Scholar* 26, no. 1: 9–17.

Hine-St. Hilaire, D. 2006. "Immigrant West Indian Families and Their Struggles with Racism in America." *Journal of Emotional Abuse* 6, no. 2–3: 47–60.

hooks, bell. 2018. *All About Love: New Visions*. New York: William Morrow.

Joseph, Peniel E. 2014. *Stokely: A Life*. New York: Civitas Books.

Moore, Darnell L. 2018. "Black Radical Love: A Practice." *Public Integrity* 20, no. 4: 325–28.

Nash, Jennifer. 2013. "Practicing Love: Black Feminism, Love-Politics, and Post-Intersectionality." *Meridians* 11, no. 2: 1–24.

Oxaal, Ivar. 1971. *Race and Revolutionary Consciousness: A Documentary Interpretation of the 1970 Black Power Revolt in Trinidad.* New Jersey: Transaction Publishers.

Pasley, Victoria. 2001. "The Black Power Movement in Trinidad: An Exploration of Gender and Cultural Changes and the Development of a Feminist Consciousness." *Journal of International Women's Studies* 3, no. 1: 24–40.

Randolph, Antonia. 2018. "When Men Give Birth to Intimacy: The Case of Jay-Z's '4: 44'." *Journal of African American Studies* 22, no. 4: 393–406.

Reddock, Rhoda. 2014. "The First Mrs. Garvey: Pan-Africanism and Feminism in the Early 20th Century British Colonial Caribbean." *Feminist Africa* 19: 58–77.

Samaroo, Brinsley. 2014. "The February Revolution (1970) as a Catalyst for Change in Trinidad and Tobago." In *Black Power in the Caribbean*, edited by Kate Quinn, 97–116. Gainesville: University Press of Florida.

Schmidt, Christopher W. 2015. "Divided by Law: The Sit-Ins and the Role of the Courts in the Civil Rights Movement." *Law and History Review* 22, no. 1: 93–149.

Teelucksingh, Jerome. 2014. "The Black Power Movement in Trinidad and Tobago." *Black Diaspora Review* 4, no. 1: 157–86.

Thompson, Keisha, dir. 2020. *There All Along: Women of Trinidad & Tobago Black Power.* Documentary Film.

Utley, Ebony A. 2010. "'I Used to Love Him': Exploring the Miseducation About Black Love and Sex." *Critical Studies in Media Communication* 27, no. 3: 291–308.

Wanzo, Rebecca. 2011. "Black Love Is Not a Fairytale." *Poroi* 7 no. 2: 1–18.

Williams, Eric. 1970. "Prime Minister's Broadcast May 3, 1970" (transcript). Patricia Raymond's Eric Williams Collection. The Alma Jordan Library of the University of the West Indies.

Wilson, S. 2012. *Politics of Identity in Small Plural Societies. Guyana, the Fiji Islands, and Trinidad and Tobago.* New York: Palgrave Macmillan.

revolutionary love

Liseli A. Fitzpatrick

you said love
is revolutionary
so you
captured my
heart in your
fist transported
me around the
moon released me
in open space and
said star,

love is emancipatory!

Liseli A. Fitzpatrick is a Trinidadian poet and professor of African cosmologies and sacred ontologies in the Africana studies department at Wellesley College. Her penchant for poetry is driven by her deep-rooted desire to effect emancipatory change in the cocreation of an equitable, just, and breathable world. Love, ancestral reverence, embodied wisdom, nature, and liberation are central themes in her work. She can be reached at lfitzpa3@wellesley.edu.

WSQ: Women's Studies Quarterly 50: 1 & 2 (Spring/Summer 2022) © 2022 by Liseli A. Fitzpatrick. All rights reserved.

PART III. **MOTHER LOVE**

Love in Till's Casket

Teigha Mae VanHester

i
lay bare a boy
tattered
defiled
blurred by violence
yet arrestingly
clear

i
anointed
appointed
she loved him
now sorrowful vision
demanding change

tilling fields
the movement
communities
cultivated
loving justice

not today

tears graze
my every line
for our loss
for her sacrifice

WSQ: Women's Studies Quarterly 50: 1 & 2 (Spring/Summer 2022) © 2022 by Teigha Mae VanHester.

exposed
irreparable

love is humiliating
under voyeur shadow
emerge
devotion sprung
forth the soil

souls of the earth
loving anguish

we soar

upon salted waves
of black tears

torturous soul
eternal season
steeped sanctity
fidelity knows
the steadfast

midnight lullaby.

Teigha Mae VanHester (she/her/they) is a PhD candidate at Illinois State University in English and women, gender, and sexuality studies. Teigha utilizes her embodied experiences and codemeshed identity to contribute to the Black Femme Epistemological Sovereignty and Resistance. As a QTBIPOC Creative, the vast majority of her work focuses on Rhetorical Co-optation, Unapologetic Blackness, Collective Trauma, and Lordean Healing. She cultivates an urban homestead brand, Defiant Kinfolk, in Peoria Heights, IL, with partner, Ray, and their fur babies. She can be reached at tmvan@ilstu.edu or Instagram @teighamae.

Black Women Watchers

Wendy M. Thompson

I remember the first time I went into labor. It was as though I was being forced to dance to a new choreography. The pain gripped and twisted the whole of my body, my lower back folding inward, my five-foot body contorting to music only I could hear, moving on a stage only I could access. Each sudden lightning strike of pain reminded me that in that moment, my body was not my own but was shared by the small thing—a girl, they told me, who might have a congenital anomaly, so we were on high alert—pushing inside. My mother, who had given birth multiple times without anesthesia, reminded me of her mother, who had also given birth multiple (nine) times without anesthesia in a foreign country, and told me I was not the first woman to go into labor. She said this to me while panicked and driving to a hospital in Fremont at night, where I had intentionally chosen a young Asian American female doctor and knew that there would be Black female medical staff present, among many other nurses of color who would at the very least, see me and attend to my body.

Unlike in the videos and manuals I was given by the birthing center, there was no defining marker between the beginning of real labor and the moment when pain arrived to fight me for my body. There was no breaking of water. There was no voice outside of me that gently guided me into the golden meadow of motherhood. Just sharp violent pains that, if I were to describe it to a counselor later, had no color, no smell, and weren't even five minutes apart.

I barely remember standing in front of two panicked male front desk staff with swollen legs and feet, wearing a loose-flowing housedress while I struggled to pull my driver's license out of my wallet. One of the staff

WSQ: Women's Studies Quarterly 50: 1 & 2 (Spring/Summer 2022) © 2022 by Wendy M. Thompson. All rights reserved.

members, a young Chinese man, ran—literally, ran!—to get me a wheel-chair and quickly wheeled me up to my room. Then someone helped me onto the bed before leaving me alone.

Everything that came after that, the breathing, the rotating nursing staff, the pushing, the family members who stopped by, the white female doctor who came in to get my signature in the event that I died during delivery, ran together like watching a movie in fast-forward. Everything except for the Black nurse who I never saw at first but who came to me after I let out what I can only now describe as a wild animal sound. Alone in a room on the labor and delivery floor in this hospital, a cry was heard through my open door by another Black woman, a nurse, who wasn't even assigned to me but was conveniently (or divinely) right outside my room and who I would never see again during the rest of my stay at the hospital. I will never forget how she came in, looked at me, and immediately said, "Don't worry, honey. I'm going to go call the anesthesiologist to come right now."

No need to explain on a scale of one to ten. No need to prove my pain according to a white man's threshold. Just a matter-of-fact acknowledgment that a baby was coming, her mama was in great pain, and there needed to be some immediate action taken. With a little sugar on top.

Honey.

I thought about this birthing experience and the traumatic one that would follow seven years later in Minnesota after reading a post made by writer Kiese Laymon on social media on January 4, 2021.

Kiese wrote:

My mother had major spine surgery. It was terrifying. She's still trying to recover. When she finally woke up, all she could talk about was this Haitian nurse who told her it would be okay because there would be a Black resident in the operation room watching. We talked more and she made it clear that even if she would have had a Black surgeon, she really wanted a Black watcher to make sure she wasn't being treated like a nigger. I want to write an essay about Black watchers but I have deadlines. Have any of y'all found peace in knowing there was a Black watcher when you've gotten a procedure? Is it limited to medical procedures? I'm asking because now that she said it, I can't stop thinking about the peace that Black watcher brought my mama before and after surgery. And I'm thankful she had insurance, and you know she got that shit at the end of the year because of them damn deductibles.[1]

Reading Kiese's words, I felt them deep in my bones. In the parts of me that will never heal following the C-section that pulled out my first baby who got caught in my birth canal on her way into the world and the vaginal delivery of my son, legs splayed open, in a room full of white medical staff who were the antithesis of the Black watcher. Those nurses who threatened to withhold the epidural unless I disciplined my body to their convenience and the anesthesiologist who responded to my labor pains with anger, aggravation, and disgust were like every other white person who lives and operates in the hostile everywhere of Black haunting, who treads heavily and messily on Black vulnerability, who turns away and goes mute or demands the sheet be thrown prematurely over Black suffering and Black victims.

You're in a room, on a street, in an airport, at a gas station, at the liquor store, and the store clerk just called the police. Who do you want to be there to make sure you're good? Who do you want to be there when it becomes evident that you are going to die?

Thinking a bit more deeply about what Kiese describes as Black watchers, I immediately turn to Black women, and ways they engage in the constant labor of watching and witnessing. Arising from the kinship practices and childcare arrangements fostered during enslavement, Black women have long been a part of a Black family unit that extends "into the community" and connects through "a series of women-centered networks, including grandmothers, siblings, other relatives, neighbors, and even strangers, all of whom became . . . 'othermothers.'"[2] It is important to note that Black maternal care was "not limited to women" as young Black people were watched by "[g]randparents, aunts and uncles, and neighbors [who] were members" of these networks.[3] But due to the gendered nature of care, the majority of women were tasked with watching, and most of the watchers in Black communities continue to be Black women.

In the South, where my father's people are from, there was always a multitude of folks who gathered, especially around young people. Among them were Black women who watched them, "who nurtured them, who taught them life lessons, [and] who taught them how to act in Jim Crow society."[4] These women were an integral part of Black community life: feeding and watching other people's kids, guiding young adults, deescalating marital tensions, advocating for the good of the community, holding white people accountable, and preserving collective memory.

When they left the South and migrated to new cities and new norths, they brought these networks of care with them and continued their watch work, looking out especially for young people, even as they themselves battled redlining and overcrowding, job discrimination, unemployment, and police violence in the city. They would lean on each other, sharing the weight of personal, familial, and collective responsibilities, which "strengthened community bonds . . . [and] laid a foundation for activism."[5]

So many times, they would feel the web begin to fray under the weight of urban containment and renewal, deindustrialization, displacement, the time of crack, and gentrification, but, still, it never broke.

And Black women, in new souths, would remain constant in their watching.

Counting backward, I can recall specific incidents when Black women watched over and watched out for me when I thought I was already grown. Like the time I followed a man to Nashville to see if he could love me. He couldn't. And after an argument I found myself wandering the streets at night. It was and wasn't my first time in the South. I didn't know anyone else living there except him and his family. It must have been the summer. It must have been balmy. There must have been land and trees and crickets everywhere. Standing heart heavy on a street corner, I will never forget the car with two older Black women inside that turned slowly in my direction. I couldn't see—didn't want to see—their faces, but I heard the concern in their voices, inquiring from the passenger side window: *Are you okay?*

Black women have always wanted to know, wanted to make sure I was okay. Even when they couldn't and didn't ask me. The width of their gestures, the intent with which they watched, listened, and acknowledged me in passing, told me that they saw.

Throughout girlhood and into my reckless twenties, Black women defended and praised me as I grew awkwardly into my body and sexuality. They made sure I had enough change to ride public transportation and felt safe around older men. They told me that my shame was never mine. My favorite aunt Lisa told me this. And then took the time—years—to show me how to let it go and replace it with careful and gracious love.

I see you, babygirl.

To be a watcher is to stand at attention, to remain on guard, to be awake (woke), to take account in order to hold others accountable, to reserve oneself for the love labor of protecting others—a gun in one hand, the other parting the curtain ever so slightly. To force oneself to look even when the body wants to look away. To see what they did to Mamie's son. Sybrina's son. Lezley's son. Geneva's daughter. Valerie's son. Tamika's daughter. Larcenia's son. Watchers bear witness, remain willing to intervene, are eager to guard or block and guide and correct. Watchers stand by, prepared to console and to deliver the deepest and most urgent care even in the most brief and fleeting moments.

In some definitions, a watcher is a person who specifically attends to a sick or dying person at night. This latter definition seems to answer Christina Sharpe's question:

> In the midst of so much death and the fact of Black life as proximate to death, how do we attend to physical, social, and figurative death and also to the largeness that is Black life, Black life insisted from death?[6]

To this degree, Black women's watch work shares threads with Sharpe's interpretation and interrogation of wake work. Both are modes of/for "inhabiting *and* rupturing . . . with our known lived and un/imaginable lives."[7] To inhabit the corners of the public persona and to catch glimpses of the private interior as if background characters in a movie about every other Black person who doesn't realize they are being watched. And to step in and interrupt, rupture, and attempt to break violence, cycles, neglect, hesitation when absolutely needed, thus playing however small a part in another Black person's life story.

I feel beneath it all, is a cosmic desire to want to see oneself, the whole and all of us, moving forward, migrating to better norths, other Souths, finding the love and freedom we desire, or at least, to see the whole and all of us not have to suffer.

Anymore.

Rooted in the love and care for the collective *we*, the watch work of Black women becomes much more pronounced when forced to operate against state actors and in the context of state-sanctioned white supremacist violence. Usually already preoccupied with commuting, shopping, watching their own kids, or another mundane activity, Black women's awareness is first heightened in the presence of security or law enforcement agents. It is when those agents are activated against other Black people that Black women are required to be doubly present, their awareness piqued, as they find themselves being indirectly or directly called into an even more vigilant and sometimes confrontational form of watch work.

This is where Black women's watch work and attempts to rescue another Black person being pulled between fugitive resistance and prone submission can turn Black women into dangerous coconspirators. It is also where everyday Black women going about their business can find themselves thrust into triage and the treating of trauma or, in those circumstances that we can never be prepared for, providing comfort while holding the head and hands of a dying stranger made kin.

Watch work is at once so terribly loving—Black women choosing to move through the world with such abundance and care, extending their protective capacity to mother, to witness, to watch—and so terrible in that many Black women watchers remain overextended in the high demand that exists for their vigilance and care, forced to carry trauma in instances when they must watch what comes after the gun and before the white sheet.

There is ever a proximity between watch work and grief work.

As I've entered middle age, I have chosen to step into the role of watcher, a role that so many other Black women, othermothers, and ancestors freely took on before me; an intentional looking out for Black children, an affirming of Black young adults, an advocacy for the safety and basic human decency of my Black peers, and the greeting of and listening to our elders who have passed on the charge to us to faithfully keep watch. This means pausing one's work at any moment, allowing the course of one's day to be altered, sometimes drastically, and dropping one's immediate tasks to turn and watch in case one is needed to step in or do more.

But who watches and cares for the watchers?

During the pandemic, on a day that stretched from the one before it into the next, I was in my garden, digging out grass, pulling weeds, planting a mix of succulents, salvia, and other drought-tolerant perennials in the dirt, when I heard shouting coming from the BART platform that overlooks my yard. I glanced up and began to watch as a young Black woman physically held a southbound BART train by blocking one of the automated doors with her body, preventing it from departing from the Bay Fair Station. Her attention was directed at another young Black person who police officers were wrestling to the ground. She continued to berate the cops, forcing the train's passengers to also become watchers, although in a different capacity.

In this moment, I called out my children—the older one glad to be summoned away from the online learning screen—and told them that we were going to stand and watch, to make sure we could accurately report if anything happened to the young woman who was told to exit the train or face arrest. We watched her do so while continuing to record the officers with her phone and curse at them. We watched from below because I wanted my children to know the range and consequence and risk and urgency of watch work. We were watching because this is what you do for other Black people, especially when they are alone, without their people, our people, surrounding them, whether captured by the state, cornered in a courtroom, or left wide open on a hospital bed. You stand together. You make sure they know we are here with them. That they won't be taken or killed, alone and surrounded by our killers.

I want my children to know that this particular, specific, voluntary, (mostly) unrecognized, and uncompensated work of watching—over other Black people, communities, and movements—is the love language of Black women who have sustained us for generations. And for Black women who have assumed this role, who practice this skill of knowing when and where to be watching, which is unattainable through institutional training, to know that we see and appreciate you, and aim to model and reciprocate the love that you show us through your own watch work and care for other Black people who you encounter every day.

I want my children to know that to love one's people is to share in the labor of care. To always stay woke.

Stay watching.

In moments when white people stare or do nothing or look away from or refuse to notice Black crisis, Black suffering, Black hesitation, or Black potential, Black women start in, taking an inventory, an account, an assessment before taking action.

It is always a calculated risk.

But in the deft way that we as Black women hold our killers and other harmful, negligent characters accountable, in the multitude of ways we model collective agency and love, becoming a body of love, our watch is perhaps the best watch to be under when one is in danger, when one is about to lose their life.

Wendy M. Thompson is an assistant professor of African American studies at San José State University. She is the coeditor of *Sparked: George Floyd, Racism, and the Progressive Illusion.* Her creative work has most recently appeared in *Sheepshead Review, Funicular Magazine, Palaver, Gulf Stream Lit,* and a number of other publications. She can be reached at wttaiwo@gmail.com.

Notes

1. Kiese Laymon, Facebook, January 4, 2021, https://www.facebook.com/kiese.laymon
2. Stephen Berrey, "Resistance Begins at Home: The Black Family and Lessons in Survival and Subversion in Jim Crow Mississippi," in *Black Women, Gender & Families* 3: 67.
3. Berrey, "Resistance Begins at Home," 67.
4. Berrey, "Resistance Begins at Home," 67.
5. Berrey, "Resistance Begins at Home," 67.
6. Christina Sharpe, *In the Wake: On Blackness and Being* (Durham, NC: Duke University Press, 2016): 17.
7. Sharpe, *In the Wake,* 18.

deep sea diving

Ashia Ajani

imagine, beyond the crest of some sailboat sunken to depth
                            fishkin of godless proportions
gloat gleeful praise of ships saddled to sand.
yes, godless, rolling in the prestige of comfort
and the sheen of soulful medicine glistens in fins
too dark in depth to hold any light body.
my mother talks to fish;
she sings to them, open mouthed and gully lipped
observes their slender, enciphered movements
dares to make fantasy about their splendid magic.
she is no stranger to making stealth, survival.
this bitter marronage,
burdened bliss of exile—the ocean floor remembers
every bone and tooth that pried freedom from a busted
floorboard
monsters made sacred live,
                    down
                        here.
and in satisfaction, it's magnificent depths unearthed,
unwatered in bejeweled splendor, recall the eulogized
pleas for deliverance back eastward, these new bodies
make room for a rebirthed migration built of desire, not demand
these spirits flitter between planes of scale and skin
souls tethered in a shared sense of melanin
                        at last, become immovable.

WSQ: Women's Studies Quarterly 50: 1 & 2 (Spring/Summer 2022) © 2022 by Ashia Ajani. All rights reserved.

Ashia Ajani (they/she) is a Black storyteller hailing from Denver, CO, Queen City of the Plains, and the unceded territory of the Arapahoe, Cheyenne, Ute, and Comanche peoples. They are a UO doctoral student in environmental studies and an events coordinator for Mycelium Youth Network. Her words have been featured in *Frontier Poetry*, *Sierra Magazine*, and *Southern Humanities Review*, among others. Follow their work @ashiainbloom on socials and on their website ashiaajani.com. They can be reached at ashiaajani22@gmail.com.

PART IV. COMMUNAL LOVE

Cultivating Habits of Assembly: Black Womxn's Communal Writing as a Gathering Practice and a Love Letter to InForUS

Desireé R. Melonas

Abstract: This work is a reflection on the value of Black womxn participating in rich and vibrant writing communities among one another, not only for the purpose of producing work but also for the possibility of healing and joy such gatherings may yield. **Keywords:** Radical care; Black feminist praxis; liberatory praxis; afro-centric communities

I was not meant to be alone and without you who understand.
                                                                   —Audre Lorde

She is a friend of my mind. She gather me, man. The pieces I am, she gather them and give them back to me in all the right order. It's good, you know, when you got a woman who is a friend of your mind.
                                                                   —Toni Morrison

This piece is written in dedication to a writing group of which I am a part, and help(ed) cocreate. Together, we have given it the name InForUS. To my InForUS group members and coconspirators, Onyekachi, Tara, Tiffany C., and Tiffany Jean: thank you for gift of showing me exactly how beautiful, joyful, and abundant writing and creating can feel when done alongside and with friends.

The Invitation

In early spring 2020, right after having asked her to serve as my mentor during my 2020–2021 Woodrow Wilson fellowship year, political scientist Tiffany Willoughby-Herard asked what is perhaps one of the most important questions that had been posed to me by a colleague and friend up to that moment. After spending time together outlining my goals for the year

WSQ: Women's Studies Quarterly 50: 1 & 2 (Spring/Summer 2022) © 2022 by Desireé R. Melonas. All rights reserved.

and arriving at a shared agreement on time and other commitments, she pivoted and gently prodded: "What kind of networks do you have in place?"

Looking back, I realize that the question did not immediately compute. It just hung there for a time. This was evident in my noticeably long pause in the ensuing moments, as well as in my initial clumsy efforts at attempting an answer. I was gripping at words for a response I just did not have but wished I did. I then stopped and asked for clarification as to what she was aiming to know.

She said something along these lines: "Networks. Who do you have around you to hold you accountable? Who are those people for you?"

Networks. Networks?

A longer, more vexed pause

I rested with her question for a moment, and then rooted around for an answer that I thought might satisfy her and somehow leave me feeling both undisturbed and justified. I wanted my answer to convey a sense of my having deep roots in other people, and them in me. I suppose I wanted to appear properly and thoroughly professionalized, that I had done an adept job at working the conference circuits and marketing myself to others.

I went on: "Well, there is . . ." "Oh! And, I know [X], who I talk to from time to time." "I almost forgot about [X]." After engaging in some mental and rhetorical gymnastics to conjure the appearance of a robust network that really just did not exist for me, I openly confessed that I did not actually possess a strong web of people to help support my scholarly pursuits in a sustained way. I had in my professional circle folks who I could rely on to look at drafts of my work here and there, sure, or those who would without hesitation write strong letters of reference on my behalf. But these points of contact were disparate and sometimes felt transactional.

I do not think Tiffany knew/knows this, but I was embarrassed by that admission. I thought perhaps that her knowing that would stir regret over her decision to work with and mentor me. I suppose that I considered my having thin networks of association in the academic context as evidence of an individual failing at some level. I now realize that this is a reality for many scholars of color. Not only are many of us socialized (perhaps disciplined is the more appropriate word) into conceding the value of engaging in academic labor according to a dominant standard organized around principles of individualism, competition, and martyrdom, but many of us arrive into graduate programs that are not properly fitted for our arrival. That is, it is often the case that not much thought and care is given over to cultivating a graduate experience that takes seriously the fact that students of color enter into spaces that were not designed to inhabit us. The outcome of this is that many of us leave feeling alienated and unmoored from meaningful academic relationships that might contribute to the development of us as scholars and to our overall well-being. Worst yet, some of us walk away from these experiences believing that this is simply just the way of things. We then sometimes participate in recreating these very same problematic conditions, dragging on a very dangerous cycle.

Even though I expected to somehow be shamed for my not having knit together a tight sphere of support (to be absolutely clear: I had no evidence at all indicating that this might have been the case), Tiffany responded without judgment. It was as though she had simply logged information that she would later put to use.

And, she did.

After that conversation, I received a phone call from her asking my thoughts about convening a writing group along with her and a couple of other Black scholars who are at different career stages, individuals who she thought could also benefit from having this level of support, accountability, and community. I was not at all opposed to the idea, but I had wrestled with envisioning how this would work during the COVID-19 pandemic, at a time when so much of our lives have come to be mediated through virtual platforms, by viewing one another's worlds through the outlines of those now-oh-so-familiar Zoom, FaceTime, and Google chat squares. I thought it might be a challenge to cultivate intimacy, trust, connection, and community with folks whom I had not met in person and when done through a rather impersonal medium.

Still, I agreed. I thought that perhaps having the group as a regular touchstone could help provide structure and lend to productivity during the fellowship period. This group, to my surprise and joy, has transcended those aspirations. It has transformed into a site of sacred friendship, inspiration, care, radical dreaming, creativity, support, and, importantly, love.

It is clear to me now that Tiffany's nudging, "What kind of networks do you have in place?," was not simply a question, but an invitation. It was an invitation to participate in and set a robust standard for an ethics of care around how we—Black womxn—engage each other and one another's work in an academic context in a way that is both rigorous and compassionate. It was an invitation to reflect on the vital need for others in this work we do—that is, to consider accompaniment as a necessary condition to birthing our ideas. It was an invitation to reject the belief that "real" scholars labor in solitude.

And so, this invitation constituted part of the beginning of a writing group that we would later name InForUs, a place of respite, collaboration, generativity, community, and love. In what follows, I will telescope some of what our journey has looked like.

The Gathering: The Formation of InForUS

And we must constantly encourage ourselves and
each other to attempt the heretical actions that our
dreams imply and so many of our old ideas disparage.
    —Audre Lorde, "Poetry Is Not a Luxury"

Our first meeting was sometime in April 2020.

On that inaugural day, four of us gathered together over Zoom. Our shared connection was through Tiffany, so for me and the two other group members, that session constituted our first time meeting each other. Present at that meeting were my now friend-colleagues: Tiffany Caesar, Onyekachi Ekeogu, and Tiffany Willoughby-Herard. A few months into our journey, we graciously welcomed another scholar to join us; her name is Tara Jones.

The details of that first meeting are a bit hazy, but what I do vividly remember is the intense formality that characterized these initial interactions. We referred to each other by our titles—you know, Dr. So-and-So and the like—and seemed to enter into conversations with much circumspection. Or, at least that is how I experienced it. It felt tight, like we had put on a pair of pants that did not yet fit. Oh, it makes me chuckle a bit to recall this, especially because of how our interactions between one another are now carried out with such sweet ease. It was clear to me, even then, that we had entered into something that would take work, sculpting, and care.

One of the first things we tabled was the project of establishing a name for our group. We took a couple initial passes at assigning the group a name; I think the first one we gave ourselves was "The Quarantine Group" or something approximating that. That felt more like a placeholder than an actual title we claimed. We then seemed to have implicitly decided that it would not be right to settle into a name until we had shared adequate time with one another and gathered a sense of what sort of collective we aimed to become. In this way (and without necessarily foregrounding it as such) we committed ourselves to participating in an Afrocentric-inspired naming ritual, where the idea of naming something or someone is not simply about attaching to a person or a thing a title for the sake of distinguishing this thing from that, or this person from another. But we recognize that a name can also be, at the same time, an annunciation or mode of address (a declaration of who this thing or that person has shown themselves to be), an expression of intention (what one aims to become), as well as a site of return (the place to which one retreats when having lost one's way by some means).

I cannot locate the precise moment when we established ourselves as InForUS, but I know that we wanted the name to reflect both who we are and who we sought to continuously become as a group. The name is, in other words, both descriptive and aspirational in quality. In that sense, I suppose that we chose InForUS to announce that we *had* cultivated a practice of generously and thoughtfully holding space for one another, for creating room enough for each other's scholarship and ideas to be lovingly and intentionally held and impressed upon. The aspirational quality contained in the name, then, expresses a desire to continuously set the conditions for us to recreate that type of space as we evolve, one in which we are all enabled to both fit and thrive (Lorde 1988). The name announces, as hooks writes in *Sisters of the Yam* (2015), that we are focused on "building community [that] necessarily challenges a culture of domination that privileges individual well-being over collective effort" (117). "InForUs," as a claim of intent, therefore presses us to assume a practice of constantly reconciling our actions to our aims, where we repeatedly ask ourselves: What does it look like to invest into this co-writing community in a manner that reflects a responsibility to the well-being, success, peace, and happiness of the whole?

In practice, this has looked like taking care in reading each other's scholarship, and delivering feedback in a way that centers on uplift rather than on tearing down. Each one of us has witnessed how, in the academy, demoralization and abuse sometimes gets explained away as motivation, tough love, and thinning the herd behavior. We also know that these tactics are often targeted and are tacit and express attempts aimed at silencing, and running/wearing out those among us who are recognized as not belonging. Our group is in full agreement that we will leave no room or quarter for this kind of behavior to breathe. We have chosen instead to celebrate each other as writers, for sharing our ideas with the world, and mustering enough strength to put words to a page, especially during a time when one could easily and justifiably be immobilized by the sadness and despair from witnessing and experiencing the devastation exacted by the multiple pandemics of, among others: COVID-19, police violence, climate change, and environmental injustice.

It is therefore common for us to tell each other that our work is beautiful, or to lift up how brave one is for writing what it is they have. It is customary for us to speak to the range of feelings that one of our works might have powerfully elicited, or how it may have provoked a set of visceral responses. It is a part of our normal parlance to indicate how the ideas one has conveyed contain the potential to shape the future in ways that have liberatory implications. We are not just being polite; we mean what we say. It is in that sense that our practice of taking care necessarily involves making known that one's ideas matter, that we each have something to say that is worth being heard. This is important, because we know that this message is one that is not consistently delivered to Black womxn academics. Sometimes, what we are told, in a manifold of ways, is quite the opposite. Black womxn speaking love and affirmation into each other is thus a crowding out mechanism; it is labor necessary to divest of any meaning the lies we have been told are true about ourselves. I do not need to inventory them because many of us know what such lies remain in circulation. bell hooks, in fact, remarks on the importance of forging such a way of being among one another when she writes that it is "important for Black women to practice speaking in a loving and caring manner about what we appreciate about one another. For such an action makes it evident to all observers of our social reality that Black women deserve care, respect, and ongoing affirmation" (hooks 2015, 28).

We also recognize that writing is a practice that benefits from a certain level of homeostasis of the body, mind, and spirit. Try as we might, when we write, we cannot totally cloister off or disassociate parts of ourselves so that our writerly personas may come through. The way we minister to our physical bodies, for instance, has deep implications for our capacity to sustainably exercise our creativity and produce scholarship. We need sleep, good gut and heart health, and dental hygiene (have you ever tried to write while having a toothache?!) to help stay engaged in this work we do. This wisdom is particularly salient for Black womxn, individuals whose bodies often bear deep and cutting traces of racism and sexism's thoroughgoing effects. It is in that sense that when my group members and I make space at the beginning of each gathering to share openly about the various goings-on of our lives, and encourage one another in our diverse health journeys—*before* we get to writing or workshopping papers—we are quite literally doing work to help enable one another's survival. To that point, I'm reminded of a profound insight shared by one Woodrow Wilson faculty mentor when facilitating a summer 2020 self-care professional development workshop for the fellows. He implored: "We cannot write from broken vessels." Mmm, yes. Our collective writing practice of care is vessel work.

Taking care of one's vessel not only signifies attending to one's physical body in healthy ways; that is important, of course. But it also involves doing those activities and establishing and nurturing relationships that contribute to one's overall well-being, allowing one to enter back into one's work and into the various communities of which one is a part with their full(er) selves. In that way, our group takes seriously the idea that the ability to express ourselves through academic prose is perhaps strengthened by engaging in other forms of creative expressions—that is, when we permit ourselves the space to be playful and in discovery around developing new ways of translating our ideas. We usually reserve ten to fifteen minutes during each writing session for engaging in some form of creative writing or in some other activity that taps our creative nerve. This practice is rooted in the belief that writing is an activity that sometimes takes work to enter into. Sometimes we just need to muse, wander, saunter, and work things out a little before beginning the task of writing. Moreover, we appreciate that creative expressions like writing poetry, dancing, drawing, painting, singing, or listening to some music may, in fact, allow us to gain access to an array of feelings and perspectives that are otherwise difficult to grip at and articulate. These creative expressions may offer a portal to extricate those ideas, dreams, and visions we pressed down because we were told the world lacks room for them (Lorde 2007).

What has come out of this commitment is the creation of a collective poem we entitled "May Our Presence Be a Balm." This poem is laced with visions for how we want to inhabit the world and our work, and makes known the values that keep us each in motion or, in some instances, those that keep us steady. It opens with a biographical sketch of our writers collective, wherein we claim a multiplicity of intersecting identities that encompass and exceed our identity as "scholar." It then moves through a series of segments that, while different, all lift up the idea that we are multifaceted people whose work and scholarship reflect that. Our poem announces, as my InForUs sister Tiffany Caesar proclaimed in one stanza, that we are each "a whole scholar."

We delivered this piece together at a spoken word event held during a virtual national academic conference. Goodness. Let me tell you about that night: it was electric. It felt as though we had, through raising up our voices together to give collective utterance to our visions and proclamations, engaged in an act of consecration. We created the space for us all to share and manifest how we desire to show up in the world, for our work, and for others, and, man, did it feel good. Together, we made room enough to accommodate all of the various aspects that constitute who we are; all of those pieces that, gathered together, bring a uniqueness to our work; all the pieces we need, but that we are sometimes told do not fit. That night—and during our regular weekly meetings—we facilitated a much-needed moment to gather ourselves, something of critical importance for Black womxn because of how we often find ourselves having to negotiate spaces that are designed to alienate and fracture us. That being said, I am grateful to be able to say of my friends, as Toni Morrison reflected in *Beloved*—writing in the voice of the character Sixo—that they "gather me, man" (2004, 321). We are gathered through our gathering.

Thank goodness for that.

This is a very small snapshot of all that our coming-together has involved. There is much, much more I could and wish to say, but hopefully this window into our world will tempt others—other Black womxn—into summoning similar gatherings of their own.

That is the hope.

The Invocation

We have to renew our habits of assembly. We have to really practice getting together in that double sense of the word "practice"—you know, it's a praxis, it's a thing that we engage in constantly. But we also have to keep trying to get better at it. We have to renew it; we have to regenerate it.
—Fred Moten

It is difficult to capture in words how profoundly this group has touched me and what we mean to one another. To say that we are just a writing group would be misleading. What we have become transcends that.

We've given each other companionship and created beloved

community during a time when so many of us across the globe are experiencing intense isolation, alienation, and longing for connection.

We've grieved together the loss of relationships, dashed opportunities, loved ones, and particular visions for how some of us thought our lives might take shape.

We've celebrated monumental professional successes, birthdays, health breakthroughs, and even a virtual wedding!

We've held space for each other's pains as well as each other's joys.

We've learned much from one another; our writing bears traces of those impressions.

We've shared survival tactics and resources of a varied sort, embodying the words Audre Lorde penned in a letter to her dear friend Pat Parker: "Whatever I have/know that is useful to you is yours" (2018, 88).

We've embraced the idea that writing can be joyful, abundant, and, as bell hooks reminds us, a practice that heals (1989, 9).

Together, we claim, over and over, that we are writers, and empower each other to imbibe the mantra: "I've got something to say!"

We have cultivated an environment that is so immensely loving, compassionate, and rigorous that I have not the faintest desire to journey alone. To this point, I can recall a short exchange I had with political theorist Jasmine Syedullah during a panel at the 2018 Western Political Science Association annual meeting. During the discussion segment of the panel, after Jasmine had presented on the prophetic undertones inherent in Assata Shakur's work, I asked a question as a follow-up to something she said during her talk. Jasmine accentuated how Shakur's approach to liberation was not to locate or portend to a discrete end point, but her politics centered on setting the conditions that would enable oppressed folks to stay in the struggle, to continue on in what Jasmine called "journeying through the wilderness." From a place of earnestness and exhaustion, I asked: "How does one find the fortitude to keep journeying, and not tire out?" She responded with such gentle ease and assuredness, saying something along these lines: "Oh, she never insinuated that one must journey alone. We journey alongside people." Ah, yes. That is it. We do *not* have to journey alone. That wisdom has stayed with me.

This insight rests at the center of all that we do as a group. Not only do we accept that we do not *have* to journey alone, we simply do not wish to. We have found that there is much joy, healing, generativity, and life in (compassionate) accompaniment.

Now, if Tiffany were to ask me again, "What networks do you have?" I would lift up InForUS. This is my support, my space of accountability, reprieve, and sisterhood. Importantly, this gathering has impressed upon me the necessity of cultivating habits of vibrant and loving assembly. My supplication is now: *May I always have friends and sisters with whom to journey, so that I may never again be alone. May I continue to encourage others to find rest and joy in accompaniment.*

Asé.

Desireé R. Melonas is an assistant professor of political theory and coordinator for the Distinction in Black Studies program at Birmingham-Southern College in Birmingham, Alabama. She researches and teaches at the intersections of contemporary political theory, Black political thought, human geography, and Black feminist thought. She is also a 2020–2021 Woodrow Wilson Career Enhancement Fellow. She can be reached at drmelona@bsc.edu.

Works Cited

hooks, bell. 1989. *Talking Back: Thinking Feminist, Thinking Black*. Boston: South End Press.

———. 2015. *Sisters of the Yam: Black Woman and Self-Recovery*. New York: Routledge.

Lorde, Audre. 1988. *A Burst of Light and Other Essays*. New York: Ixia Press.

———. 2007. *Sister Outsider: Essays and Speeches by Audre Lorde*. Berkeley: Crossing Press.

Lorde, Audre, and Pat Parker. 1989. "Sister Love: The Letters of Audre Lorde and Pat Parker 1974–1989." In ed. Julie R. Enszer. New York and Dover: A Midsummer Night's Press and Sinister Wisdom.

Morrison, Toni. 2004. *Beloved*. New York: Vintage Books.

Moten, Fred. 2015. "Interview with Fred Moten." Interview by *South Journal*. Accessed April 2, 2021. https://southjournal.org/fred-moten/.

BIPOC Solidarities, Decolonization, and Otherwise Kinship through Black Feminist Love

Sewsen Igbu, Shanna Peltier, Ashley Caranto Morford, and Kaitlin Rizarri

Abstract: Black, Indigenous, and People of Color (BIPOC) solidarities in colonially called North America are frequently theorized within the ongoing histories of white heteropatriarchal supremacy and colonial ideologies and structures. Within these discourses, whiteness continues to be centered while the voices, theorizations, lived experiences, and contributions of Black peoples are overlooked, a perpetuation of the anti-Blackness embedded within colonization. The centering of whiteness also subsumes differences across BIPOC communities and frames kinship relations as emerging solely from the shared goal of dismantling systemic violences experienced across BIPOC communities. But, Black feminist theorizations of love recognize that differences and incommensurabilities are integral to positive and meaningful BIPOC solidarities. Thus, decolonization and BIPOC solidarities must center Black feminist theorizations of love as integral to building decolonial otherwises of freedom. **Keywords:** BIPOC solidarities; Black feminism; Black love; decolonization; colonialism

Introduction

The university can be an utterly hostile, disheartening, and energy-depleting space for Black, Indigenous, and People of Color (BIPOC) students, faculty, and staff. Embedded in the very walls of the university are the violent ideologies of colonialism, white supremacy, and racism. The authors of this piece—Sewsen Igbu, a diasporic Eritrean settler; Shanna Peltier, an Anishinaabe kwe; Ashley Caranto Morford, a diasporic Filipina-British settler; and Kaitlin Rizarri, a Filipina settler with Mi'kmaw and mixed European ancestry—have experienced this pain and oppression firsthand. And yet,

WSQ: Women's Studies Quarterly 50: 1 & 2 (Spring/Summer 2022) © 2022 by Sewsen Igbu, Shanna Peltier, Ashley Caranto Morford, and Kaitlin Rizarri. All rights reserved.

inside the walls of an institution that was never built nor intended for us, and that never sought for us to survive let alone to thrive, we found each other. Together, we formed a community of care that would fill the grooves and crevices of the university with a radical, revolutionary, transformative, and decolonial love—a love committed to building a thriving and joyful future for the beauty that is BIPOC communities and lives.

In 2020, the four of us created and cofacilitated an online reading, writing, and dreaming group on BIPOC solidarities, which was hosted at our university but open to scholars, organizers, community members, and nontraditional academics throughout Turtle Island.[1] In this collective, we reflected on, contended with, and discussed what it means to build sustainable, long-lasting, respectful, and ethical solidarity across BIPOC communities. We explored what principles should guide this work, what is currently nourishing BIPOC solidarities, and what is currently limiting or preventing meaningful BIPOC solidarities. We continue to dream, dialogue, be dedicated to, and live this work into being. We seek for our commitment to include and extend beyond academic scholarship and theorizing into everyday life, community organizing, and day-to-day concrete practice. Furthermore, we come to this paper with the deep understanding that Black feminist love is absolutely integral to building better presents and futures.

We seek to challenge the common framing that BIPOC relationships and their communities' livability are contingent on, defined by, and must be framed within/through the ongoing histories and violences of white supremacy, colonial ideologies, and institutions. Too often, when BIPOC solidarities are discussed, it is through the centering of whiteness and white experiences, as if our kinship and collaboration can only, and do only, occur because of the violence of white supremacist structures and systems. As the BIPOC Project articulates, too often solidarity and kinship-fostering efforts across systematically oppressed communities "still focus only on combating white supremacy" ("About Us," par. 3). When our coming together is tied to whiteness, our relationality is tied to violence, destruction, and oppression. Certainly, the pain in our communities can bring us together in collective pursuits of justice. However, our kinship connections and desires to be in community are not—and should not be—inextricably bound to whiteness and violence. Our relations as BIPOC communities have existed, do exist, and will—and must—exist beyond whiteness, colonialism, and patriarchy in all its forms. Our aspirations for love and community must not be bound to survivalist narratives. They must not be defined by whiteness and colonial oppression. Our dreaming must not be bound to a colonial context. We create communities with one another because we want to be in these relationships forever—in the here and now, and in the future elsewhere beyond whiteness. Black feminism and Black feminist love envision worlds that are not binaries bound to being in opposition to white colonial patriarchal supremacist ideologies.

At the same time, we recognize that, far too often, People of Color and Indigenous communities have absorbed and accepted narratives of anti-Blackness, heteropatriarchy, ableism, and settler colonial violences. As a result, non-Black Indigenous and People of Color often enact, condone, participate in, and perpetuate violences against Black communities. Black feminism is critical to the rejection of these legacies. Black feminist love and Black feminist thought challenge us to recognize the intersectionality (Crenshaw 1989) of anti-Black racism and the ways anti-Blackness is intimately connected to white colonial states and other forms of white supremacy that harm other systematically oppressed communities. Black feminist theory emerges from the on-the-ground lived experiences of Black women. Black women have powerfully articulated their lived experiences through Black feminism; Black feminism developed to speak to the daily realities of living as a Black woman in a settler colonial state, under the ongoing violences of white supremacy, heteropatriarchy, and misogynoir (Bailey 2010). Black feminist theory is a powerful and active good medicine in the face of settler colonial structures; it offers both thought and action. As bell hooks writes, "I came to theory because I was hurting—the pain within me was so intense that I could not go on living. I came to theory desperate, wanting to comprehend—to grasp what was happening around and within me. Most importantly, I wanted to make the hurt go away. I saw in theory then a location for healing" (1991, 1). Any challenge to settler colonialism, any move to decolonization, and any act of future world-building must center Black feminist voices and theorizations.

We recognize there are existing tensions within attempts to establish BIPOC solidarities in pursuit of justice or world-making within and across our communities. There is often a move among organizers to build relationships based on commonalities—common experiences under (settler) colonialism. Audre Lorde has said, "As women, we have been taught either to ignore our differences, or to view them as causes for separation and suspicion rather than as forces for change [. . .] But community must not mean a shedding of our differences, nor the pathetic pretense that these differences do not exist" (2007, 112). This move to commonality yet again frames relationships as contingent on and centralizing whiteness. Further, this move to focus on sameness risks decentering Black communities, when any movement for liberation, justice, and futurity must center and be guided by Black feminism, Black voices, and Black experiences.

BIPOC Incommensurability

Speaking to the ways in which incommensurability across BIPOC communities can enact harm, Lethabo King (2019) recognizes "the agonizing texture and horrific choices that often had to be (and have to be) made [by colonially oppressed communities] to survive under relations of conquest" (xi), resulting in our enacting violence against one another. Too often, the mechanism solidifying incommensurability between Black, Indigenous, and People of Color communities is the settler colonial state and the various nuanced but interlaced ways in which colonialism is enacted against our communities. Furthermore, Lethabo King (2019) writes about the various iterations of colonialism as having "edges, yet each is distinct. Each form of violence has its own way of contaminating, haunting, touching, caressing, and whispering to the other. Their force is particular yet like liquid, as they can spill and seep into the spaces that we carve out as bound off and untouched by the other" (x). To offer a specific example of incommensurability across BIPOC communities, we might consider how the shadows of colonialism and empire push many Black and People of Color communities from their homelands and into the Indigenous lands colonially called Canada.[2] North American enterprise and imperial endeavors overseas destroy Black and People of Color homelands, which results in Black people and People of Color emigrating to colonially called North America (Mutamba 2014, 2; Morford 2021, 4; Walia 2013). The colonial system that drives Black people and People of Color from their homelands then enwraps racialized immigrants in the tensions existing between Indigenous sovereignty and state manipulations of immigration, citizenship, and desirability. Caranto Morford writes that, frequently, racialized immigrants

> arrive in [colonially called] Canada without truly comprehending that [they] are arriving on stolen Indigenous territories, without understanding the ongoing colonization and dispossession occurring within these

lands, and without recognizing [their] positioning as settlers and treaty people in these territories. This lack of realization is deeply embedded in the colonialism of Canadian immigration policies and processes. Entrance into [colonially called] Canada requires that one be well-versed in the mainstream Canadian system and narrative, and that one can demonstrate their ability to be indoctrinated into the status quo. (2021, 5)

Here the colonial system seeks to legitimize its right within Indigenous lands by absorbing racialized immigrants and their descendants into the settler colonial status quo imposed within the Indigenous lands it occupies. This incommensurability becomes further visible in the tensions between immigration, state threats of deportation, and resultant immigrant desires for citizenship from the settler state. Such desires for citizenship stem from the desire to survive and live in safety, but further perpetuate settler colonial processes because they legitimize and empower a settler state that continues to infringe upon Indigenous sovereignty.

At the same time, we believe relationality and being in good and responsible kinship with one another should honor and, indeed, can be empowered by and across our collective differences and incommensurability. We believe the language and honoring of incommensurability and "stuckness" can assist us in moving away from settler colonial, survivalist relationalities—that is, the commonality of white supremacist oppression and resistance to this violence—as solely tying together BIPOC solidarities (although this resistance may be part of the overarching vision and dreams for thriving Black, Indigenous, and People of Color communities). Exploring BIPOC relationalities through an honoring, a holding of truth for, and an organizing with accountability to incommensurability presents the possibility of an otherwise world, or otherwise spaces, that embrace the nonfixed and not easily knowable nature of complex relations, for instance, between Indigenous genocide, anti-Blackness (Lethabo King, Navarro, and Smith 2020, 2), and border imperialism (Walia 2013). Non-Black Indigenous and People of Color need to witness and sit in the tensions and discomforts of how they/we participate in actions that enact harm against Black communities—actions that run in opposition to the healing and kinship-making power of Black love.

Indeed, Black feminist thinkers recognize the importance of kinship making through differences. Speaking specifically to Black and Indigenous solidarities, Lethabo King, Navarro, and Smith state:

> Incommensurability [. . .] asserts a lack of commonality/relationality
> between Black and Native folks. This project emerges from us thinking that
> all of these modes are insufficient. While certainly solidarity, antagonism,
> and incommensurability are distinct and no one mode of relationality can
> be presumed, at the same time, it is illogical to presume we can talk about
> any mode without doing it in relationship with one another. If we submit
> momentarily to the popular position that Black and Native peoples, and by
> extension, Black and Native politics are at an impasse represented by their
> incommensurability, then the flip side of being stuck together—or this
> stuckness—is already a form of relationality. (Lethabo King et al. 2020, 1)

Scholars of color have extended this discussion of incommensurability and
kinship solidarity to encompass Black, Indigenous, and People of Color
relationalities and solidarity work, more broadly, engaging with Black feminist studies and Crenshaw's concept of intersectionality to argue:

> intersectionality mean[s] challenging the ideas that communities are
> brought together by commonality and that identification is the only or
> even the primary basis for collectivity [... Black, Indigenous, and] Women
> of Color activists, writers, and artists have developed an analytic of differ-
> ence that became the foundation for their relationships within movements.
> They have addressed the ways languages of struggle did not, and still do
> not, translate across geographical contexts and historical trajectories, but
> asserted that solidarity and coalition could still be based on, rather than
> built in spite of, these incommensurabilities. (Hong 2018, 28)

Black feminism unpacks how anti-Blackness is not just singularly anti-Blackness but is interconnected with every facet of the state's oppression of
systematically oppressed peoples and its perpetuation of colonial-capitalist
endeavors. Anti-Blackness, ableism, heteropatriarchy, capitalism, colonialism—each of these oppressive systems (and others) works together
in conjunction, and as Black feminism helps us to understand, we cannot
unpack these other systems without refusing and dismantling anti-Blackness.

Black love recognizes, honors, and is accountable to the differences
and incommensurability—and, indeed, understands the sheer transformative power and radical, revolutionary love—that can be held and enacted
through and across differences. Black love is a call-to-action to non-Black
Indigenous and People of Color to do better and to be better kin to Black
communities. Black love is a necessary pathway to decolonial futures.

The Politics and Ethics of Black Love

Black feminist theorizations of love are political and revolutionary, radically outside of the domain of neoliberal discourses of love. Neoliberal systems, institutions, and bodies all too often wield and weaponize the word and language of love as individual, as apolitical, as an eraser and dismisser of difference, and as a unifying balm that excuses rather than works through, holds accountability toward, and dismantles systemic violences. In short, the language of love under neoliberal systems becomes a tool to (re)produce violent colonial systems of inequality and oppression. Counter to this conceptualization of love, Black feminist theorizations are ethical and collective theories of justice and transformation (Nash 2013). As emphasized by Patricia Hill Collins, Black love is especially significant and transformative given the current conventional social context that "is so dependent on hating Blackness" (2004, 250). Furthermore, with regard to the process of dismantling these violent social contexts, we see Black feminist theories of Black love as a path toward an "Otherwise World" (Lethabo King et al. 2020, 5). We argue this pathway is created through the embracement of the Black love currently in practice and in aspiration of future making, with hopes to "model practices of reading and listening that create new possibilities for thinking of, caring for, and talking to one another" (Lethabo King et al. 2020, 5). Thus, Black love is necessary in pursuits of justice and toward collective, long-lasting, and revolutionary healing.

Non-Black Indigenous and People of Color have much to learn from Black feminist wisdom and truth around Black love. Indeed, non-Black Indigenous and People of Color have the responsibility to not only witness but also to breathe in and embody Black love with every breath they/we take and in everything they/we do, in an ongoing way. Black love is a political action that is simultaneously about reconditioning and transcending self. Black love is about the collective, the community, the making of a better world emerging from, grounded within, and centering the beautiful wisdoms and truths of Black feminisms. Specifically, we suggest to work from a place of Black love is to embrace a politics that names and dismantles non-Black Indigenous and People of Color's internal fears of difference—and, more particularly, how these fears of difference stem from a fear to confront and overcome one's own complicities in anti-Blackness and colonialism, thus, as a fear to work on and ultimately move beyond the self.

An ethics of Black love recognizes, names, honors, and appreciates differences across BIPOC communities by actively laboring to dismantle internal fears of colonial complicity often held by non-Black Indigenous and People of Color. We would like to bring forth frameworks of Black love theorized by Black feminists as a way to sit with incommensurability (or modes of "stuckness" in BIPOC relations)—to not be fearful of the incommensurable, to not be approval-hungry or reconciliation-hungry for smoothing tensions in BIPOC relations, and to do better and be better relations to Black communities. Furthermore, we are critical of the propensity for BIPOC organizing and solidarity to occur only in contexts that resist violence. We see Black politics and Black ethics of love as revolutionary and transformative possibilities for theorizing meaningful, long-standing, and decolonial solidarities across BIPOC communities—solidarities not tied to whiteness, that move beyond simply surviving the colonial state, and stretch into eternal futures where whiteness and colonialism no longer exist. We take inspiration from June Jordan's work on potentialities of love that are life supporting and actionable—for it is "always the love [. . .] that will carry action into positive new places" (Jordan 2009, 269).

In our view, "Where is the love?" is a question that applies to the "horrific choices" (Lethabo King 2020, xi) made within BIPOC contexts. These choices made among BIPOC communities, against one another, are rooted in settler relations of conquest. These "horrific" choices ultimately reinforce colonial hierarchical systems that socialize BIPOC peoples and communities to enact violence within and across their communities to survive violent (un)livable existences. These choices denote the "absence of love" theorized by bell hooks (2014), who states that we are taught to survive unrelenting conditions of state violence, but through this survival, we as BIPOC communities (and in hook's theorizing, specifically referencing Black women) (re)produce a denial of love. hooks (2014) describes a mode of living not full because societal and structural anti-Blackness, and the internalization of this anti-Blackness, denies that Black women should be and need to be loved. In hooks's perspective, embracing and reciprocating love is necessary for transformation and for thriving beyond survival as Black women—and, in the context of our work, for solidarities across and within BIPOC communities. Furthermore, hooks (2014) forewarns the instability of political endeavors and radical aspirations that proceed without an ethic of love. When love is invisible or noncentered, political projects risk becoming "seduced, in one way or the other, into continued allegiance to systems of domination—imperialism, sexism, racism, classism" (hooks 2014, 1).

We extend this work to encapsulate BIPOC communities, and the solidarity and cross-collective political organizing we aim to envision, as needing transformative modes of love that move our relations beyond existing only in contexts of survival—for hooks (2014) warns when we focus only on what we "feel is hurting us," we move farther away from the collective transformations of society. There are a few ways in which we understand "us" in this context: the "us" can be the BIPOC community as a whole, wherein BIPOC organizers focus so centrally on something that hurts *all of us*, we risk subsuming, erasing, ignoring, or dismissing our differences and the power dynamics that come into play with these differences. We witness this shortcoming through organizing tactics like strategic essentialism (Spivak 1990; Spivak in Chakraborty 2010), which creates a pressure toward sameness. Strategic essentialism is a political organizing method that essentializes our specific unique positionings and identities for the purpose of fighting toward a shared specific goal. Or, the "us" can refer to specific groups within the BIPOC umbrella, wherein certain peoples under this umbrella only focus on what particularly hurts *them*, and, in so doing, potentially harm other communities within the BIPOC umbrella. An example of this is when immigrants focus on gaining citizenship protection without considering whose land they are on and how citizenship legitimizes the settler state. Another example is when Indigenous nations argue settlers can go back to their homelands without consideration of how refugee settlers may have fled death in their homelands. By ameliorating what hurts "us," collective organizing risks being transformed into a mode of self-reparation that perpetuates harm. These particular forms of individually oriented pursuits of "justice" and "reform" do more to align with the existing structures of domination than to dismantle them. The ways we end up realigning ourselves with these structures enable the ideologies, practices, and violences of these structures being reproduced within our communities, families, and collective attempts at organizing.

According to Nash, "The labor of crafting a collectivity constructed around difference requires a 'serious . . . undertaking'" (2013, 11; Lorde 2007; Jordan 2009). For non-Black Indigenous and People of Color, the task of working on the self means perhaps even working against the self by recognizing and naming one's privileges through colonial proximities to whiteness and then naming and refusing one's complicity in—even one's acceptance and validation of—colonial processes that hinder and work against Black love. By working against the self and toward Black love in this way, the self transforms and embraces the "possibility of a politics organized not around the elisions (and illusions) of sameness, but around the vibrancy [. . .] complexity," and necessity of naming, accepting, and holding one's differences as a means of acting accountably, responsibly, and through a politics of Black love (Nash 2013, 11).

Black love, particularly Lorde's (2007) work on differences and "recognizing the vibrancy and complexity of differences" (Nash 2013, 11), acknowledges that reconciling differences risks enacting another form of violence for BIPOC solidarity. The relationality from the stuckness (Lethabo King et al. 2020), in concert with Lorde's conceptualization and embrace of difference, challenges the desire for reconciling or erasing differences in hopes of developing common ground for a collective pursuit of justice. But this hyperfocus on sameness ultimately maintains the status quo by ignoring how certain communities benefit from privileges and participate in systemic complicities that harm others.

Rather, the relationality from the stuckness and the embracing of differences enables us to nourish across our communities by honoring an ethics of Black love—one that encompasses and transcends self to redress the materiality and political systems necessitating "horrific choices" (Lethabo King 2020, xi) and sameness. Moreover, we endeavor in our work and through this writing to ask: What are the new choices that can be made when Black feminist theorizations of love are taken seriously in BIPOC communities, to imagine an otherwise world and be in relation? We recognize the violences occurring across our communities, and the "horrific choices" being made on all BIPOC sides, that are grounded in the limitations (and "unlivability") placed upon colonially oppressed communities. In our view, horrific choices and survivalist organizing (although perhaps necessary at times) negate love and the possibility of joy that could arise when BIPOC solidarities practice love intentionally and purposefully.

Complicating Settler Futurity, Decolonization, and BIPOC Solidarity through Black Feminist Love

Colonization in so-called Canada is a process not only built through the genocide and dispossession of Indigenous peoples from their lands; it is *also* built on and fuels itself through anti-Blackness. Thus, Black love is critical to decolonization, and Black love has been bringing decolonized futures into being every single day. Yet, conversations about processes of decolonization in the context of so-called Canada often neglect to recognize and center Black experiences and voices, even as anti-Blackness ignites colonization. In our experience, academic circles, Indigenous community organizing, and decolonizing discourses all too often leave out Black voices in conversations on decolonization. Or Black communities—and legacies of slavery—are misrepresented in decolonization discourse (Garba and Sorentino 2020). These invisibilities and missteps play a role in maintaining anti-Black racism.

Jaye Simpson (Two-Spirit, Oji-Cree) writes that "Indigenous people were killed for the land, but it was so often enslaved Black people who built the cities we now call home" (2020, par. 11). Shanese Steele (2020), an Anishinaabe-Métis-Trinidadian organizer, has also emphasized processes of land back in Canada must include Black, Afro-Indigenous, and Indigenous peoples. Simpson agrees with this assertion, stating, "To fail to include our Black peers in our Land Back movement speaks to our legacy of anti-Blackness" (2020, par. 11). In response, and as a critical step in the direction of an Otherwise World (Lethabo King et al. 2020), we must cease eliminating Black voices and communities from pursuits of, and collective dialogues and planning's toward, decolonization. We assert that the exclusion of Black histories, peoples, communities, and theorizations from these lands and from decolonization processes in these lands sustains systemic colonial anti-Blackness. Furthermore, if decolonization processes do not include the dismantling of anti-Blackness and the recognition that Black peoples are "colonized and displaced Indigenous people" (Ziyad 2017, par. 7), then they are not truly decolonizing. We ask in this work and explore below what it means to enact decolonization in a way that centers theories and practices of Black love. Furthermore, we reflect on how theories and practices of Black love dismantle anti-Blackness in processes of decolonization.

If we embrace Wolfe's (1999) reading of colonization as an ongoing structure, we need to recognize that this structure encompasses enslavement, anti-Blackness, the prison industrial complex, the child welfare system (of which many Black families have experienced violence from), migrant (including Black migrant) labor under oppressive conditions, and exclusionary (racist, anti-Black) immigration practices. This conceptualization goes beyond colonization as an event that occurred temporally upon the first European settler landing on these Indigenous shores (which denotes a reductive interpretation of colonization as implicating an Indigenous/White Settler oppositional binary). Furthermore, the common focus of decolonization in North America as solely the repatriation of Indigenous lands and life (Tuck and Yang 2012) overlooks the reality of Black place and relationality with/in these lands. Garba and Sorentino (2020) note, "Slavery cannot be added as an afterthought without diminishing the historical-geographical scope of modernity and leaving the constitution of the material and symbolic conditions of conquest unthought" (775). While Garba and Sorentino importantly discuss how slavery is a violent metaphor with real-world impacts, and resist being sidelined to an afterthought in theories of decolonization, enslavement must also be understood as an ongoing and lived reality experienced in concrete ways in the current day. These real-world impacts are part of the colonial Canadian settler future-making project. Oftentimes, discussions of settler future-making are limited to an Indigenous/white binary (Lethabo King 2019, xv). And, indeed, settler power and settler futurities in Indigenous lands are built and fueled by "white human self-actualization," which is contingent on the project of maintaining and extending the genocide and dispossession of Indigenous peoples on their lands (Lethabo King 2019, xv). But, as Lethabo King emphasizes, settler power and futurities also include the anti-Black violences impacting Black peoples and communities within and through the colonially established Canadian nation-state.

The legacies of slavery continuing on through contemporary anti-Black colonial systems are the consequence of "the afterlife of slavery" as "Black lives are still imperiled and devalued by a racial calculus and a political arithmetic that were entrenched centuries ago" (Hartman 2007, 6). Within this afterlife, Black lives are fungible, in which "the person underneath is imprisonable, punishable and murderable" (Maynard 2017, 13). The "racial calculus" (Hartman 2007, 6) (re)produces conditions intimately intertwined with the conquest of Black people, which encompasses both metaphor and materiality in colonial and decolonization processes. Thus, a decolonial project on these lands must be one that intentionally pulls and removes anti-Blackness from the fabric of society. Pursuits of decolonization must be purposeful in threading something new, imagined, and rooted. More specifically, decolonizing pursuits must resist and refuse the continuous absenting of Black people in colonially called Canada. This marked absence often occurs through a conceptualization of Blackness as "unrooted," an act that erases meaningful Black connections to place, geography, history, spaces, and time (McKittrick 2006). We argue that, alongside Indigenous voices and scholarship, decolonization in colonially called Canada and

North America needs to center Black, including Afro-Indigenous, voices and scholarship, and particularly the writings and work of Black and Afro-Indigenous feminists and their theorizations of Black love.

There is a long and ongoing history of decolonial Black joy in the face of and despite colonization, and this joy has deep and ever-growing roots in these lands. These roots are exemplified in the central ways in which Black women in colonially called North America have helped to develop political thought that envisions livability beyond the nation-state, embraced and centered relations of collectivity and revolutionary love, developed intimate relationships with these lands, and created rich Afro-Indigenous presences within Indigenous communities (Taylor 2020; betts et. al 2020; hooks 1991; hooks 2014; Lethabo King 2019; Nash 2013). The centrality of Black women in envisioning nourishing pasts, presents, and futures in these lands means Afro-Indigenous and Black feminisms are absolutely critical to refusing and moving beyond colonization. Indeed, we can never truly dismantle colonization and will only serve to renact its erasure of Black peoples in these lands if we do not center and amplify Black feminisms in our kinship and futurity building against colonization. As the Combahee River Collective recognizes, "Until Black women are free, none of us will be free" (Taylor 2020).

Conclusion

Black love is central to decolonizing, not because love is only about the self but because it is transcendent. Black love generates a "politics of love" that is generous (Nash 2013, 3) and implicates "both people we know and strangers" (hooks 2014, 109). As such, Black love always necessitates the collective in a way that is political and not tied to maintaining (colonial) structures and power. Black love theorizes ways of living, and living well, that surpass current societal organizing and processes of oppression, marginalization, and violence. Black love as theorized by Black feminists is, at its core, about feeling and experiencing freedom. It is a radically different way of living, in which different ways of being can come together.

We hope the preceding critique—the care-filled unpacking of the limitations of dominant discourses of decolonization—is a feature of love at work. The processes of thinking through these issues, and writing this work, were practices of love that centered "acknowledging the truth of our reality, both individual and collective, [as] a necessary stage for personal and political growth" (hooks 1994, 295). Bringing to the forefront the missteps and "horrific choices" made within the contexts of the various BIPOC communities we are part of—and, in this case, interrogating theories of decolonization—involved an intentional and "care-ful" trekking through "the most painful stage in the process of learning to love—the one many of us seek to avoid" (hooks 1994, 295). In this work, we refused and resisted the allure of avoidance that comes with unpacking the messiness of BIPOC relations. We will only sustain systems that perpetuate division and violence, and further enact harm against each other, if we continue to practice avoidance or depend on solidarities built on the idea of sameness. By actively seeking and laboring to love, we create relations that may be messy and perhaps incommensurable—but it is through such processes that we may one day find ourselves in an otherwise relation (or world). This otherwise world we wish to live in requires confrontation and moving beyond pain and complicity, so we can embody an ethics of love that envisions ours and others' freedom, livability, and joy-filled futurities: "Moving through the pain to the other side we find the joy, the freedom of spirit that a love ethic brings" (hooks 1994, 295–6).

This pursuit of moving through and beyond the pain will be messy and difficult. Anything worth doing is messy because relationships, learning, and love-building—these living and ongoing gifts—are messy. That is why they are so difficult, so worthwhile, and so beautiful. That is why they are and must be ongoing commitments. By moving through this messiness with Black love always at the center and the forefront, we are offered pathways to embodied and transformative BIPOC solidarity-making (Cendana 2020; DRUM 2020). We are offered solidarity-making that seeks to breathe in, act from, move with, spread, and sustain—in eternal ways—the virtues and values of the communities we love and wish to be in solidarity with. We are gifted a type of solidarity-making wherein we embrace and are guided by the messiness as a way for us to be accountable to, and to ultimately refuse, our complicities in colonial and systemic harms. By sitting with and nourishing incommensurable realities, we can move beyond these systems and transform our worlds into a decolonial otherwise. BIPOC solidarities must emerge from, center, and be rooted in Black love and Black feminist thought, alongside Indigenous—including Afro-Indigenous—thought, or else the solidarity work will fall short, not be done ethically, and will not bring into being a better future and decolonial otherwise.

It is our view that meaningful, respectful BIPOC solidarities can exist when we center love. June Jordan's question, "Where is the love?" which emphasizes the revolutionary community-building potentials and politics of Black love, must underpin theories and processes of decolonization, future-making, and BIPOC kinships and relationalities. It was in the writing of these words that we wanted to convey to each other (as an Anishnaabe kwe, diasporic Eritrean settler, diasporic Filipina-British settler, and mixed Filipina settler) where the love is amid the messiness of our BIPOC solidarities work. This writing is a small step toward otherwise relations—a demonstration of a commitment to love "myself well enough to love you (whoever you are), well enough so that you will love me well enough so that we will know exactly where is the love" (Jordan 2009, 4).

Sewsen Igbu (she/her) is an Eritrean diasporic settler living in Tkaronto/Toronto. Her scholarly work is situated on Black family studies, specifically on East African Canadian families navigating the child welfare system. She is a PhD student in adult education and community development at the Ontario Institute for Studies in Education, University of Toronto. She can be reached at sewsen.igbu@mail.utoronto.ca.

Shanna Peltier (she/her) is an Anishinaabe kwe from Wiikwemkoong Unceded Territory located on Mnidoo Mnis (Manitoulin Island), Ontario. Shanna is a PhD student in school and clinical child psychology at the Ontario Institute for Studies in Education, University of Toronto. She can be reached at shanna.peltier@mail.utoronto.ca.

Ashley Caranto Morford (she/her) is a diasporic Filipina-British settler. Her scholarly and organizing work asks how Filipinx/a/o settlers in Turtle Island can be better relations to Black and Indigenous communities in Turtle Island and in the Philippines. She can be reached at amorford@pobox.pafa.edu.

Kaitlin Rizarri (she/her) is a mixed Filipina settler living in Tkaronto/Toronto. Kaitlin is a MA student in adult education and community development at the University of Toronto. She is coming to reclaim her Mi'kmaw (from Ktaqmuk) roots and sees this as a responsibility she is still learning to enact in good ways. She can be reached at kaitlin.rizarri@mail.utoronto.ca.

Notes

1. This group was part of the Jackman Humanities Institute working group program at the University of Toronto.
2. We were inspired to use the term "colonially called" because of the work of Mitcholos Touchie (Nuu-chah-nulth), which highlights how important it is to destabilize and challenge colonial place naming as part of a tactic of honoring and remembering that all of so-called North America is Indigenous land.

Works Cited

Bailey, Moya. 2010. "They Aren't Talking about Me . . ." *The Crunk Feminist Collective* (blog). Accessed April 30, 2021. http://www.crunkfeministcollective.com/2010/03/14/they-arent-talking-about-me/.

betts, edxi, Mahlikah Awe:ri, Shanese Steele, and Bonn, host. 2020. "Stolen Kinship: Confronting Anti-Blackness in Indigenous Communities." *Indigenous Action.* Podcast audio. November 20, 2020. https://www.indigenousaction.org/podcast/ep-5-stolen-kinship-confronting-anti-blackness-in-indigenous-communities/.

Cendana, Greg. 2020. "Delawang Bagsak: How Can Filipinas/xes/os Be in Solidarity for Black Lives?" Zoom panel.

Chakraborty, Mridula Nath. 2010. "Everybody's Afraid of Gayatri Chakravorty Spivak: Reading Interviews with the Public Intellectual and Postcolonial Critic." *Signs: Journal of Women in Culture and Society* 35, no. 3: 621–45.

Crenshaw, Kimberlé. 1989. "Demarginalizing the Intersection of Race and Sex: A Black Feminist Critique of Antidiscrimination Doctrine, Feminist Theory and Antiracist Politics." *University of Chicago Legal Forum* 1, no. 8: 139–67.

Collins, Patricia Hill. 2004. *Black Sexual Politics: African American, Gender, and the New Racism.* New York: Routledge.

DRUM—Desis Rising Up and Moving. 2020. "Four Levels of Solidarity." Movement Hub. Accessed December 20, 2020. www.movementhub.org/resource/four-levels-of-solidarity/.

Garba, Tapji, and Sara-Maria Sorentino. 2020. "Slavery Is a Metaphor: A Critical Commentary on Eve Tuck and K. Wayne Yang's 'Decolonization Is Not a Metaphor.'" *Antipode* 52, no. 3: 764–82.

Hartman, Saidiya. 2007. *Lose Your Mother: A Journey Along the Atlantic Slave Route.* New York: Farrar, Straus and Giroux.

hooks, bell. 1991. "Theory as Liberatory Practice." *Yale Journal of Law and Feminism* 4, no. 1: 1–12.

———. 1994. *Outlaw Culture: Resisting Representations.* London: Routledge.

———. 2014. *Sisters of the Yam: Black Women and Self-Recovery.* New York: Taylor & Francis Group.

Hong, Grace Kyungwon. 2018. "Intersectionality and Incommensurability: Third World Feminism and Asian Decolonization." In *Asian American Feminisms and Women of Color Politics,* edited by Lynn Fujiwara and Shireen Roshanravan, 27–42. Seattle: University of Washington Press.

Jordan, June. 2009. *Some of Us Did Not Die: New and Selected Essays of June Jordan.* New York: Basic Civitas Books.

Lethabo King, Tiffany, Jenell Navarro, and Andrea Smith. 2020. "Beyond Incommensurability: Toward an Otherwise Stance on Black and

Indigenous Relationality." In *Otherwise Worlds: Against Settler Colonialism and Anti-Blackness*, edited by Tiffany Lethabo King, Jenell Navarro, and Andrea Smith, 1–23. Durham, NC: Duke University Press.

Lethabo King, Tiffany. 2019. *The Black Shoals: Offshore Formations of Black and Native Studies*. Durham, NC: Duke University Press.

Lorde, Audre. 2007. *Sister Outsider: Essays and Speeches by Audre Lorde*. Berkeley: Crossing Press.

Maynard, Robyn. 2017. *Policing Black Lives: State Violence in Canada from Slavery to the Present*. Nova Scotia: Fernwood Publishing.

McKittrick, Katherine. 2006. *Demonic Grounds Black Women and the Cartographies of Struggle*. Minneapolis: University of Minnesota Press.

———. 2017. "2017 Feminist Theory Workshop—Katherine McKittrick (Keynote & Seminar Leader)." Duke GSF. YouTube Video, 51:12. May 8. https://www.youtube.com/watch?v=ggB3ynMjB34

Morford, Ashley Caranto. 2021. "Settler Filipino Kinship Work: Being Better Relations within Turtle Island." PhD diss., University of Toronto.

Mutamba, Moyo Rainos. 2014. "Resisting Inclusion: Decolonial Relations Between Peoples of Afrikan Descent and Original Peoples." *Decolonization: Indigeneity, Education & Society*: 1–5.

Nash, Jennifer C. 2013. "Practicing Love: Black Feminism, Love-Politics, and Post-Intersectionality." *Meridians: Feminism, Race, Transnationalism* 11, no. 2: 1–24.

Simpson, Jaye. 2020. "Land Back Means Protecting Black and Indigenous Trans Women." *Briarpatch Magazine*, September 10, 2020. https:// briarpatchmagazine.com/articles/view/land-back-means-protecting-black-and-indigenous-trans-women.

Simpson, Leanne. 2014. "An Indigenous View on #BlackLivesMatter." *Yes! Solutions Journalism*, December 6, 2014. https://www.yesmagazine.org/social-justice/2014/12/06/indigenous-view-black-lives-matter-leanne-simpson.

Spivak, Gayatri Chakravorty. 1990. "Criticism, Feminism, and the Institution: An Interview with Elizabeth Grosz." In *The Post-Colonial Critic: Interviews, Strategies, Dialogues*, edited by Sarah Harasym, 1–16. New York: Routledge.

Steele, Shanese. 2020. "August 24, 2020 Meeting." Black Literature Reading Group. Zoom meeting.

Taylor, Keeanga-Yamahtta. 2020. "Until Black Women Are Free, None of Us Will Be Free." *The New Yorker*, July 2020. https://www.newyorker.com/news/our-columnists/until-black-women-are-free-none-of-us-will-be-free.

The BIPOC Project. "About Us." https://www.thebipocproject.org/about-us.

Tuck, Eve, and K. Wayne Yang. 2012. "Decolonization Is Not a Metaphor."
    Decolonization: Indigeneity, Education & Society 1, no. 1: 1–40.
Walia, Harsha. 2013. *Undoing Border Imperialism.* California: AK Press.
Wolfe, Patrick. 1991. *Settler Colonialism and the Transformation of Anthropology:
    The Politics and Poetics of an Ethnographic Event.* London: Cassell.
Ziyad, Hari. 2017. "Why We Need to Stop Excluding Black Populations
    from Ideas of Who Is 'Indigenous.'" *Black Youth Project: BYP.* http://
    blackyouthproject.com/need-stop-excluding-black-populations-ideas-
    indigenous/.

no

monét cooper

sounds a lot like know
which can look like now
I announce what I will not
do on the anniversary of Freddy Gray's death
when was the moment his captors looked
in horror at his body
to exclaim no
spine is more twisted than the fossil
of this city
how do they know
of prehistoric pain
moving from womb to corner
street to block
the length of his back buckled
as news turned off
just after his mother wails no
over her boy discovered
strewn between law and vernacular
we mow like lawn
marking their property lines
what wreckage do I
lick from the day's
obituaries
in my feed
familiar crows
mark ears
wails follow me
to work where I coax
sensations of my severed
sound underneath smile
and simile attempt to twist

WSQ: Women's Studies Quarterly 50: 1 & 2 (Spring/Summer 2022)

my mouth's vertebrae
into what does not shake
when I open it to eat
or speak or announce I am fine
just fine or ask how do
I keep making babies
with these death notes
clenching our air
I issue exquisite refusals
from this mortal skin
my eyes look at us
alive and crumbling
see how my baby
prepares to be divined
alive mouth unmasked
without bit or reins
pulling life into itself
adjusting my mouth
into a thousand celebrations
we are alive and moving
crumbling as every living
thing must do
falling together
we suckle life's death
that recalcitrant blossom

monét cooper is a doctoral student, poet, and educator in the joint program in English and Education at the University of Michigan. She is the 2021 Hurston-Wright Foundation College Poetry Award winner and has work forthcoming in *This House Will Not Dismantle Itself: Critical Futures in Education*. She can be reached at monetc@umich. edu.

Blk Anger

Roya Marsh

It is the night after the election and I don't smile.
I lie
awake. Wondering what kind of ancestor I will be.

I, the child of a hard father that only wanted soft daughters,
learned to make a perfect fist on my own. Learned to swing by watching,
    by feeling.
I bark, like the dogs do, loud and in the face of danger.
Gnash my teeth & secure all things vital.
I learned to fight before I learned to speak.
My hands grew into grenades.
I learned I hold the pin,
tight.
Learned, To explode only when necessary.
Learned, 'tho I'm always at war not every room is a battlefield.

I shout: *Black Joy* across the world and folks with smiles the smell of
    green bean casserole praise me for not being
"angry."

The definition of angry: having a strong feeling of or showing
annoyance, displeasure, or hostility.

I been angry.
My fists paint holes into walls.
I was 14 the first time I stomped a man's face into mashed potatoes.
I used to pray
to a god who would not come home.
A Black butch with a slick tongue
and a hunger for freedom
I'm the kind of sorry no one teaches us to forgive.

WSQ: *Women's Studies Quarterly* 50: 1 & 2 (Spring/Summer 2022) © 2022 by Roya Marsh. All rights reserved.

I Say: Blk Joy
They Hear: shuck & jive
Think me palatable (good black).

Nah, This ain't what enlightenment looks like. I got a backpack full of
    screw ups and screw yous.

There came a point where tears were no longer able to cleanse.
There are still days I want out, but I'm no better if I only save myself. And
    right now, There are people lining the floors of arenas to hear me tell
    them
losing is at capacity.
Guess we going
to win.

Someone gave me a pen
I wrote a spine into a sack of skin.
Imagine me not angry
explaining to white folks anti-racist work ain't hashtagging or posting a
    black box not fit to hold my last breath.
Or raising me up by your white guilt straps.
Antiracism means you're willing to die for my kind of Black.
That built the country, you wrote me out of.

What good is writing poems to my unborn when I got nieces and nephews?

They shutting down 1 prison to build four and got a bunk with our last
    name on it.
They waiting for us to forget we were chosen
While I'm god's daughter
my godson's father is locked in a cage.

I don't write metaphors about caskets and burials.
Just another way for the world to hold us hostage.

Tell the dead I am still here
Tell the here I am still fighting
I live and learned to walk on the seas beneath and between us.

The ship is sinking, but I'm teaching us to swim.
To wade in the warzone.

Where our joy endangers us.
Buying groceries.
Playing video games.
Enjoying ice cream.
In bed.
In a backyard.
In a parking lot.
On a wine train.

The men in my family are still breathing and that is not a crime.
The women in my family are reproducing and that is not a crime.

I say: *We gon' make it*
Someday we'll all be free
Be real Black for me
Alright
& I'm talking to god
on repeat

I was born Black, woman & American
Bitterness beckons, inspired by my mere existence
Born waiting for *the land of the free* to bust a capitalist in my head.

You think me being angry is the problem?

I Say: *Black Joy*
And I mean, I forgive my father.
I mean, F the police.
I mean, dismantle white supremacy.
I mean I was zip tied one night,
Kettled on the manhattan bridge the next,
and lived to teach your kids in the morning.

I am everything
america threatens

to break
and the threat
and the break
and america itself.

What I'm saying is,
Nah, I'm not angry.
I'm coming.

I say: Black Joy and I mean,
who are you
when I start taking
what I am owed?

Bronx, New York, native **Roya Marsh** is a nationally recognized poet, performer, educator, and activist. She is the author of *dayliGht* (MCDxFSG, 2020), a finalist for the Lambda Literary Award in Lesbian Poetry, and works feverishly toward LGBTQIA justice and dismantling white supremacy. She is the cofounder of the Bronx Poet Laureate initiative, a PEN America Emerging Voices Mentor, and the awardee of the 2021 Lotus Foundation Prize for poetry. She can be reached at bookroyathepoet@gmail.com.

The Years They've Taken: Systemic Oppression, Black Bodies, and the Materiality of Grief

M. Carmen Lane and Sondra Perry,
with introduction by Kendra Sullivan

On October 1, 2020, artist, writer, facilitator, birth and end of life doula, M. Carmen Lane and artist Sondra Perry convened with a live, virtual audience to carry a private conversation into public realms. Intimacy and friendship accelerate intellectual and spiritual bravery as the artists weave and dart through a conversation that spans death and interruption, the work of the artist and the work of the arts institution, being human and thingly being, and how "what is" also contains "what is possible." An extension of their friendship forged when the artists met during Perry's installation of "A Terrible Thing" at the Museum of Contemporary Art Cleveland and shortly after the death of Lane's grandmother, this discussion deepens their inquiries into Blackness, grief, mourning, vengeance, humor, and the physicality of survival. Taking place seven months into COVID times, the artists talk about how to create meaning out of the uprising for racial justice while managing their own grief as it both contracts and expands during a protracted, global pandemic whose end feels like a receding horizon.

The Years They've Taken: Systemic Oppression, Black Bodies, and the Materiality of Grief was presented virtually with ATNSC: Center for Healing & Creative Leadership in Cleveland, Ohio, and EFA Project Space, New York. The conversation was moderated by Arthur Russell of ATNSC and is represented in *Black Love, Women's Studies Quarterly*, with footnotes and edits for readability by Kendra Sullivan of the Center for the Humanities at the CUNY Graduate Center, with the guidance Dr. Rashida Harrison of the *Black Love* editorial team and Michigan State University. Readers are privileged to enter the conversation in medias res. It began long before the "here and now" of the talk, and is no doubt evolving in the long, "right here, right

WSQ: Women's Studies Quarterly 50: 1 & 2 (Spring/Summer 2022) © 2022 by M. Carmen Lane, Sondra Perry, and Kendra Sullivan. All rights reserved.

now" of the present tense as it unfolds in and through Lane and Perry's transformative art practices.

M. Carmen Lane: This conversation is an invitation to be who we are in our practice and in our friendship right here, right now. Our humor, our joy, our creative imagination, our Blackness, our queerness, our living-alone-ness is all material. The conversation builds on our friendship, but also a media image, a still shot from John Lewis's body being taken over the bridge where he was beaten one last time.[1] As if through this ritual, a Black body might escape being beaten on the bridge, beaten by the system. It was indulgent. It enraged me. Instead of wrestling with his life and work, I was left reacting to how we handled his body.

Our art practices share a material and physical attention to the labor required to understand what it means to live in a Black body in this environment, in this experiment, we call America. There is a distinction between *death* for people of African descent in the Americas, and *interruption* by this white supremacist system. Its cultural attitudes, behaviors, beliefs, practices, rituals, and ideologies interrupt our lives and leave no space for grieving. The next step is always symbolic and in service of white culture. We're asked to perform care and aliveness even in our death for this system. In private, we talk about the difference between death and being interrupted. This is a conversation that you and I have had "out there," and that I'm bringing "in here." We talk about it to support each other, to be friends, and to care for ourselves. How and why do we stay alive in a historical moment where people who live in bodies like ours are dying at a higher rate than others? How and why do we do the thing that we need to do, which is make art?

Sondra Perry: I want to touch on what we talk about "out there." One thing that [*laughter*] Carmen and I do is get together on the weekends and have fellowship over the phone or via Zoom with a little bit of coffee. To start out the week, I like a Sunday coffee with Carmen. It was one of those Sunday mornings that you brought up the idea of the interruption, and it completely shifted how I thought about this past six months and the ways that I was formulating my work around efficiency and productivity. The idea of the interruption has permeated my thinking about what my body is doing in the world and what is happening to my body in the world.

You were there for me when my grandfather passed away from COVID in April 2020 as I kept trying to make sense of what happened to him. The way that I made sense of it was, "oh, well, he was older." He was eighty-six. I kept saying that to my mom and to my aunts when we were talking about his passing and what to do, whether to go to the hospital, or to the funeral, or to watch it on Zoom. Some of those decisions were made for us, meaning that we couldn't engage in—my family couldn't engage in the ways that they wanted to—but I kept trying to make sense of his death and I kept thinking of his age. As soon as you said the word "interruption," I thought, "Wow, isn't that interesting," I tried to wish away (the violence of) his death because of his age. Would I have done that if I was another race? Would I have done that if I was white or if he was a white man? Or would I have had more anger? His life was taken away. I think that I internalized this interruption in his life as something natural. And I'm really concerned about that, about naturalizing Black murder. When our bodies are interrupted, what happens to us afterwards? What happens to our legacies? What happens to the images of people who are interrupted? This is something that we both work through in our artistic practice. And as people who are living, how are we able to see when our lives get interrupted? Each time you get pulled over by the cops. Each time you're getting a passive aggressive email from a curator because they are racist. Each time you have to pay more out of pocket for your health care. Each time. How are we able to acknowledge those interruptions?

CL: For me, the answer is art. It's what we make. It's what we talk about. It's how we use ourselves in our practice. Not to explain. But to show . . .

It was an honor and a privilege to be present for you after the death and the interruption of your grandfather's life. I hear you saying that his age didn't matter—his death was an interruption. The choice to close ourselves out of the experience of living in our bodies is something that gets taken away from us in this system. The cumulative impact of continual interruptions also contributes to the diseases that develop in our bodies, which then impact our ability to make work. I think about Camille Billops having Alzheimer's. I think about my own grandmother, who died just before we met. Her closing out opened up this potentiality for me to meet you. I would not have an art practice without grief, without mourning as a material to catalyze my practice.

When my great-grandmother died, I was sixteen years old. This is my first understanding of what it meant to lose a relative, somebody who had cared for me. At her funeral, a woman named Jesse Reader was the choir director of the church handling her service. I only met Jesse this year. I didn't know that Jesse was the choir director, but I experienced Jesse's intervention in that role. When we went to the cemetery to put my great-grandmother's body into the ground, we were all surrounded by a large group spread across the cemetery. When her body was lowered into the ground, the choir started to sing. I don't know what the song was. I just remember the vibration, the shift in atmosphere, and the sound of these voices covering the group of people who were mourning my great-grandmother. That catalyzed my first questions around death. That continues to catalyze this practice right here and right now.

My grandmother is from Lorain, Ohio. She graduated from Lorain High School before Toni Morrison. She was the first Black student to be in the National Honor Society at Lorain High and the first Black student to be allowed in extracurricular activities at Lorain High School. So, her experience cracked open the potentiality for what Toni's experience was in that space. If you meet Black people from Lorain, particularly elders, they might have passed through that opening too. There is something geophysical about how Blackness and meaning-making are expressed from that landscape.

When my grandmother died, I had the ability to be present with her, to hold her hand until her pulse was absent. She stopped breathing before her heart stopped beating. What does it mean for a Black body in this system to stop breathing first? The white nurses came in, and for thirty minutes, they tried to clock her end-of-life time and couldn't do it because her heart was still beating. That was a form of communication to her loved ones. And I had the ability to receive it. So what is the communication that your grandfather is having with you? Given your practice, given the materiality of your practice, what does it mean for you to witness his ritual of end through Zoom? How is that feeding your work? How is that a gift to you? It does not erase the interruption.

SP: In my practice, I work a lot with my family. After he passed, I watched a video where he was on the porch and I wanted him to stand behind my aunt. So I'm asking him in the video to stand behind my aunt, and he's just not listening. I'm asking him over and over again, "Grandpa, please stand behind us." The last time I saw him was on the same computer that I was watching that video on.

Did I tell you about the night before he passed? I felt that there was someone in my apartment. I don't have a giant apartment, so I opened every door that I could. I just knew that there was someone in there. There was no one. The next morning, I got the news that he was gone. I know that was a gift, that was something that he left.

I want to talk about your doula-ing. Carmen is a doula. Carmen is an end-of-life doula and a birth Doula. I am so curious to hear you talk about your doula-ing in relation to your art practice. What does it mean to usher a life into the world, usher one out of it. I'm thinking about the altar work that you make, the interstitial space of the in and out, the in between, ushering between life and the great beyond, and making space there.

CL: It's all birth, Sondra. What comes up for me is being a two-spirit person. One teaching regarding two-spirit people is that we are both male and female. But more significantly the teachings tell us that two-spirit people are stewards of the edge. Birth, death, naming, healing, making of art, these are some of the gifts of being a two-spirit person. I look to make contact with you at the edge of meaning, at the edge of possibility, at the edge of transformation. And paradoxically, in order to birth anything, you have to be deeply present in the here and now. In the deepest and clearest ways. Because if we cannot be right here, right now, there can be no transformation. There can be no change.

That is what enrages me about oppression. It is a distraction and it interrupts your ability to be in the here and now, the fullness of your power and the fullness of your potentiating energies as a maker, a doer, an artist, a human being. All the distraction and the busywork keeps me out of the here and now. Clean this, fix this, explain this, who are you? Looking at communications with curators and museums and galleries, the work of calling an institution a white institution is distracting me from making work. It is not my job as an artist to fix, heal, or even condemn an institution that we, in this ecosystem, have imbued and reified with whiteness. I am an artist. You are an artist. Either they steward our work or they get out of the way. But it is not my work to fix these institutions, because that takes years off of my life. It is an interruption.

SP: It takes years off your life. I think about that all of the time now. About the years that are gone. The years of making, the years of love, the years that were taken.

CL: Even before we were born, Sondra.

SP: Mhmm.

CL: I had dry skin when I was born. How is someone living in a water environment born with dry skin? If that isn't systemic oppression . . .

SP: It permeates everything. Including the embryonic sac.

CL: When you said "embryonic sac," I saw an image of your work. In your video installations, it feels like the stuff of creation bubbling up. It's primordial.

SP: It's in-between space where there is immense possibility. A lot can bubble from that spring. And I want to be cautious of what I conjure. *Flesh Wall* has been coming back into the work and back into my studio recently. It won't go away because it's my body. But it's my body in a way that I haven't been able to see myself, it's an unruly being; *The Flesh Wall* is an unruly being and I think I want to be an unruly being.

CL: It also makes me think about the Candomblé orixa Omolu, who is an orixa of plagues and on the body. You and your practice are moving through and getting to the other side of this experience. You called your work flesh.

SP: I feel like I'm like a cog in a machine that the work is using to show up in the world. But the system can make that world feel very small. Flattening it. Condensing it. Taking away from it. Carmen, in your work, how do you deal with the interruption and this taking away?

CL: One of the things I've been thinking about is vengeance as a material. I'm claiming vengeance as a form of grieving. Catharsis is required. One of the things the system is asking me to do is reconcile and heal and repair without this other ritual. The physicality of the altar work reclaims vengeance, because I'm giving space to what's been taken from those who have come before me. The altar installations are doorways between the seen and the unseen. I feel like there's a certain level of creativity that's required in vengeance. Have you ever seen *The Wife, the Thief, the Cook, and Her Lover*?

SP: It's on the list.

CL: In the film, Helen Mirren's love is murdered, and she cooks him and serves the body of her lover to the folks who caused the violence. It's very beautiful, visually. What is the ritual required to get us to a place where we then can integrate the learning and move towards reconciliation? And who needs to witness the ritual? In the video, *Some Notes on Racism*,[3] I ask how art can be a material for vengeance, to get it all out of the body. To give it back. There is a force larger than the forces of the oppressor that art can access. Art can do that. Our practice can do that, individually and collectively. I collaborate with my ancestors. They're with me right now, in this conversation with you. I'm sitting in my grandmother's chair.

SP: Mhmm.

CL: I've been thinking of that in relation to my sound work. What is the sound of vengeance, the vibratory quality of it? There's an anger that I carry that doesn't belong to me. It needs to be attended to. There is grief, there is sadness that does not belong to me; it's been passed on. The circle has not been completed because of ongoing interruptions.

SP: They don't need an exorcism. It's something else that they need.

CL: They need to be seen.

SP: They need to be seen. They need to be in a body of their own.

CL: I'm thinking of your work with exercise equipment.[4]

SP: The machines are just trying to live their lives. They're trying to prolong their lives. They know that they are made to be used, and they say, "Hey, hold up, hold up." I know what this means. You're here to use me. That means that at one point, I will get used up. I am trying to make sure that I live a long, prosperous life. So that means when you use me, I'm going to make it difficult for you. I'm going to make it really difficult for you to try to use me in the ways that you want to. That's why the pedals are on backwards. That's why there's hair gel in the rowing machine.

CL: You make me think about the differentiation between my human experience and being a Black body in this system. They will take me in as an object but not as a human being. Breonna's body was murdered, and then in her death, she became an icon. In this system, her body and her image are objects. When does she get to be a human being? And what does it mean for us as Black artists? To be asked to collude in that level of objectification? We're neither kings and queens or enslaved people. We get to have the multiplicity and variance of all of creation. My practice cannot reify what this art world is, what this system is, what this microcosm wants us to be. My practice has to be "here and now" potentiality, not a reflection of what someone wants to buy.

The flesh in your work grows; it's alive. When I think about bodies and being Black bodies in this system, I think about structural location, not embodiment, not my embodied experience as a human being. Have you ever seen the film *The Dark Crystal,* Sondra?

SP: Oh, yeah.

CL: Blackness in this culture is the equivalent to the Indigenous (pod) people in the film. The Skeksis stuck them in chairs and sucked out their life force. That is how racism works and Black bodies are used in this culture. Blackness is the elixir of life in this experiment we call America. That's my experience, Sondra. And although it seems ugly, it resonates for me. There's a theory in Gestalt therapy that Arnold Beisser coined, "that change occurs when one becomes what he is, not when he tries to become what he is not."[5] And for me, that's the function of art: to embody what is, to wrestle with it, for the potentiality to do something different.

In the Q&A, someone asks, "I wonder what an end-of-life processional might have looked like with vengeance in mind?" What we are left with in America is John Lewis's traumatized body doing work for the system that killed him. Expressions of grief are not just kindly.

SP: Mhmm.

CL: You're saying a lot of *mhmms.* What's going on? I feel like something just bubbled up for you, even if it's raggedy in scope and it's not fully formed, I'm still curious.

SP: Might be raggedy, but I'm thinking about all the work that the dead are asked to do. It just made me sad, that's all; it just made me a little bit sad.

CL: Mhmm. Yes.

SP: You convinced me to get this book about the meaning of different afflictions in the body.[6]

CL: It's a book of patterns. The patterns can be applied at the systems level, the group level, or the individual level. Why do people of color have certain illnesses like high blood pressure, diabetes, and prostate cancer? When you ask me to keep my rage and my grief and my sadness inside of me, and take away opportunities to express myself, I might develop high blood pressure. If the longings of my heart are never attended to . . .

SP: There's nowhere for it to go, so it causes harm in the body. I feel that we aren't thinking about the psychic component of physical illness. One of the ways to get this stuff out of the body is through the making of art.

CL: I'm thinking of the value of friendship for artists of color. One of the reasons that I'm enjoying this conversation with you right now is that I really don't want another Black cis-het male to explain art and race and our community without understanding that it's a gendered experience that they are having about our people, of our community, of their practice. It is not my experience. Institutions want to do the antiracist work quickly. But none of it tracks back to anyone's practice. Their work shouldn't be to disrupt or interrupt or take away from our practice. The work of the institution is to create space for people and for art to interact. That's it. But that's not a sexy enough job title, Sondra.

SP: Institutions are supposed to leave space for artists to make work.

CL: I think their goal is power. In proximity to certain places, spaces, and institutions, I lose my teeth, so to speak. What do I have left?

SP: Everything's happening so fast. Yes, Black Lives Matter, but do it quickly. Yes, do it without investigating how your institutions function in the first place, without asking how they harm Black people in the first place, without asking how many Black people are coming in through your doors? What kind of outreach are you doing? How many Black people work there, outside of your education department?

CL: In our city, instead of talking about Black bodies, they talk about zip codes. When we talk about infant mortality in our city, we talk about zip codes. When we talk about access to the Internet, we talk about zip codes. We don't talk about the systemic intervention of denying access based on what kind of body you were born into.

Think about the quote, unquote controversy of the Philip Guston exhibit, not being installed in a couple of museums. The system wants to show work by Black people talking about Black lives. They don't want work critiquing whiteness or white supremacy. That's not the conversation they're interested in. So, of course, it's going to be shuttered. The potentiality to make new and more profound meaning in his work lives right here, right now. This is the time to give people like you and I opportunities, to show our work, to have solo shows, and to be in conversation with each other.

SP: Let's open to Q&A.

Arthur Russell: On behalf of everyone at ATNSC[7] and EFA Project Space,[8] thank you for having that conversation with us and calling us in to listen.

Dylan Gauthier: Sondra, you had work in *Sick Time, Sleepy Time, Crip Time: Against Capitalism's Temporal Bullying* curated by Taraneh Fazeli. Carmen, I got to know you and your work through Jillian Steinhauer's exhibition *In the Presence of Absence*. Both exhibitions at EFA Project Space extended conversations that I really appreciated around care. Carmen, can you speak a little about the Center for Healing & Creative Leadership?

CL: Healing often hurts more than the wound. A particular kind of space needs to be created to support what it means to heal. I want to shift the question over to Arthur Russell and Imani Badillo so they can talk about ATNSC, a predominantly African American urban retreat and residency space in an historically Hungarian neighborhood in Cleveland, Ohio. I founded the project in a residential space for artists and creatives and change catalysts. It's a space that nobody wanted, and now, it's something again. Imani is our inaugural intern, so I'm excited that they are with us.

Imani Badillo: I'm struck by the liveliness and the momentum of ATNSC. Spending time at ATNSC is also knowing you and spending time with you and your knowledge, Carmen.

AR: There is something about creating space and platforms to propel the longings of the heart, to give voice to those longings, and to give material resources to those longings. I'm grateful for ATNSC and I'm happy to be a part of the many projects that we have going on there. Here's another question from the Q&A: If art cannot (should not) explain oppression, what are the alternatives?

CL: What do you think, Sondra?

SP: One alternative is protest and other forms of activism that aren't embedded within museum culture but within civic life. Engaging in art, or making art that isn't about explaining, requires a lot of institutional back and forth. Pushing institutions to think about Black artists requires an immense amount of administrative function and curatorial imagination. The pushing and pulling of that takes just as much work as the art does. I've learned that from Carmen and all of the things that they've had to go through to make work. It requires an immense amount of administrative engagement, but what you're gaining is a form of expression that can, that can utilize, the things that are trapped in your body, in a way that other things can't, other types of engagement can't, does that make sense? I hope that makes sense.

CL: I think white people need to make art about being white people in order to disentangle or disembowel themselves from white culture and a white worldview. That's not my work, and it's not your work, but I'm curious to see what that work would look like.

SP: Matthew Barney makes work about whiteness all of the time. No one ever talks about it in that way, ever.

CL: One of the most interesting pop culture films I've seen about whiteness was *Terminator Genesis*. It's amazing! Got to watch. I mean Linda Hamilton. They are beating down on those white machines you know, just tearing constructs up. And of course, Arnold Schwarzenegger has to sacrifice his white body.

SP: Wow, wow.

AR: Sondra, one of the themes you touched on in your last response was the way things trapped in the body find their way out. Could you talk more about maybe an art practice of excavation?

SP: The title of my exhibition came partially from *A Terrible Thing Happened*, a picture book about trauma for children. I adopted "A Terrible Thing" as the title because of the history of MOCA Cleveland.[9] When Carmen and I first started talking on a regular basis, it was about our bodies and how it felt to be in our bodies while trauma was building up in dangerous ways, and we were trying to figure out how to get rid of it. I've been thinking about death a lot. I've been thinking about interruption a lot. I got sick in March, and I'm pretty sure it was coronavirus because I had all the symptoms, but then the antibody test came out negative. I have a preexisting condition of being a fat person, a fat Black woman. I could die. Is this a good death? I don't think so. And I was afraid. I was very afraid of dying, and then my grandpa passed away. I'm thirty-three years old, and he's the first person in my family to pass away and to be interrupted. Now I'm thinking about the objects that I make, these machines, these creatures that permeate the worlds of my installations, and I'm trying to understand them as beings that can be prolonged inside of the care of an institution, an installation space, or a studio. I'm thinking about the lives of the artwork. In dealing with my own mortality, prolonging the lives of the artworks feels more urgent than it ever has before.

CL: What you're sharing and the intensity with which you're sharing it resonates with me because I almost died in January of this year. That's as close to the edge as I can get, and it catalyzed an urgency in the making. I sometimes wonder how I'm able to wake up and function. The reason that I have the capacity to speak plainly about the conditions of our lives here and now is because I'm aware of what is possible for this world. I know what is possible, and nothing this system does to cause anger, pain, rage, and grief, takes away from that knowing. It all is happening simultaneously. But unless you give yourself the gift of the experience of what is possible and allow yourself to take it in, then you will succumb to the powers of empire, imperialism, and capitalism. That's what the work is. That's what art is.

SP: It's knowing what possibility is.

CL: And showing people what is possible, letting them embody it and investigate it in themselves, if they choose to.

Audience Member: The crossroads is the intersection of what is and what is possible. Can you speak about liminality and the crossroads as a functional space or force of potential within your practices and lives?

SP: For me, the crossroads exist in the thingly being, the ability to morph and transmute. I think about the flesh again. I think about all the possibilities of the flesh.

CL: It also makes me think about temporality and the notion of space-time. Assuming experience is a straight line versus an accumulative mound is a limiting belief.

Audience Member: Sondra, can you speak about the idea of the possible in relation to the recurring motif of the chroma key in your work?

SP: The chroma key is the space of postproduction where everyone gathers to create a new world. It's a space that needs direction. It's a space that needs ushers. It's a space of possibility, but you gotta watch it a little bit. You gotta watch it because it's the possibility of anything.

CL: To me, that's the edge of the woods. Conceptually, my practice cannot be at the center. Even the construct of inclusion is at my cost at my peril.

SP: Yes.

CL: I don't want to be included. The moment I move to that comfortable place, my power is gone. I refuse. I think the chroma key is also a space of refusal, which is why I do not have a gender pronoun. I am Carmen.

SP: Hmm.

CL: Did you watch *Lovecraft Country* the other day?

SP: I am in two episodes. I am two episodes behind.

CL: The point of it is, what's the medium for experimentation? And do we as Black people get to experiment and do weird, you know? So this is actually how Sondra and I talk for real.

SP: There are some silences. There's some mmms and ahhs and all that. But that's truly how it goes down.

CL: Pretty soon we're going to start talking about hair.

SP: Yeah, I redid it.

CL: One thing we are showing but not talking about in this conversation is the function of humor in a creative practice and in friendship as a pathway to our sense of freedom in our body. In my work, I want more humor the more difficult the subject matter. Would you say your work was funny?

SP: I would definitely say that my work is funny. But I don't know what other people consider funny.

CL: No one would say it was funny.

SP: I think I'm hilarious. Humor is really needed in these spaces of difficulty. It's about multiplicity of being. It's about being able to hold many things in your body at the same time, which is what we have to do.

CL: Well, we can close ourselves out, Sondra. It's always a pleasure to talk with you and to be inspired by you.

SP: Carmen, you're the best. I always love speaking with you and always leave with so much to resonate with. I appreciate your friendship.

M. Carmen Lane, MSOD, is a two-spirit African-American and Haudenosaunee (Mohawk/ Tuscarora) artist, writer, and facilitator living in Cleveland, Ohio. Lane is founder and director of ATNSC: Center for Healing & Creative Leadership, an artist led, socially engaged urban retreat, residency, research, and exhibition space located in the historic Buckeye-Shaker neighborhood. Lane can be reached at mcarmenlane@gmail.com.

Sondra Perry was born in Perth Amboy, New Jersey, in 1986. Perry holds an MFA from Columbia University and a BFA from Alfred University. Perry has participated in residencies at the Skowhegan School of Painting and Sculpture, Vermont Studio

Center, Ox-bow, and the Experimental Television Center. Perry can be reached at
sondra.r.perry@gmail.com.

Notes

1. Accompanied by a military honor guard, the body of representative John
Lewis was carried over the Edmund Pettus Bridge in Selma as part of a
state-orchestrated processional marking his death on July 26, 2020. More
than half a century prior, the congressman was among the civil rights
movement demonstrators attacked by police while attempting to march
across the bridge toward Montgomery on "Bloody Sunday," March 7, 1965.
2. Sondra Perry's *Flesh Wall* (2016–2020) was a temporary, monumental
installation of digital displays on 70 billboards across Times Square, New
York City, that lit up every midnight in February, 2021. The work used
video, animation, magnification, and highly processed, digital manipulations of images of the artist's skin to explore notions of individual and
historical Blackness, being, and identity at scale.
3. M. Carmen Lane's *Some Notes on Racism during a Global Pandemic, for
Daniel (2020)* is a sound piece with original composition, "Center the
Medicine," by Jennifer Elizabeth Kreisberg (Tuscarora) and illustration and
animation by Katherine Freer. The video poem explores the intersection of
race, police violence, whiteness, and the complex histories that contribute
to systemic violence—created in response to the murder of George Floyd.
4. Sondra Perry included nonfunctional exercise equipment in recent video
installations, offering viewers an embodied experience of the ways in which
intentional, counterinstitutional design might disrupt the flow of productivity, conformity, and labor within racist regimes. The machines were
included in *Graft and Ash for a Three-Monitor Workstation* (2016) and *Wet
and Wavy—Typhoon coming on for a Three-Monitor Workstation* (2016).
5. Bessier, A. 1970. "The Paradoxical Theory of Change." In *Gestalt Therapy
Now*, edited by J. Fagan and I. L. Shepherd, 77–80. New York: Harper &
Row.
6. The book is *You Can Heal Your Body* by Louise Hay.
7. ATNSC (pronounced *ata-en-sic*) is an artist-run urban gathering space that
facilitates healing and creative leadership. Located in the historic Buckeye-Shaker neighborhood of Cleveland, ATNSC seeks to reclaim this place
for people to heal, create, read, collaborate and forge relationships. For more
information: https://www.atnsc.org/.
8. EFA Project Space is a program of the Elizabeth Foundation for the Arts.
Conceived as a collaborative, cross-disciplinary arts venue founded on the

belief that art is directly connected to the individuals who produce it, the communities that arise because of it, and to everyday life; and that by providing an arena for exploring these connections, we empower artists to forge new partnerships and encourage the expansion of ideas. For more information: https://www.projectspace-efanyc.org/.

9. Sondra Perry presented *A Terrible Thing* (2019), a video and installation-based work about the submerged architecture, labor, and infrastructure of exhibitions, institutions, and urban development projects in and around MOCA Cleveland.

PART V. **RECOLLECTING LOVE**

Memoirs of the Colored Girls Museum: For Blackgirls Everywhere to Remember That Our Love Is Enuf

Loren S. Cahill

Abstract: This article is a nonconventional archival repository for the Colored Girls Museum in Germantown, Philadelphia, wherein I posit that the museum space is a radical love site through its curation of social relationships, spatial capacities, and navigation of time. Through the transformation of oral history with the museum's founder, Vashti DuBois, I fashioned an avant-garde memoir about how DuBois's own life story is a curation toward radical love that is held by a space. Specifically, I argue that radical love cultivated through the museum space provides a nexus for affective potential, interaction, and interdependence. The creative methodological approach has allowed me to provide a mirror, dynamic archive, and letter for Blackgirls to bear witness to themselves being centered and loved through narrative. **Keywords:** radical love; Blackgirls; memoir; Philadelphia; spiritual; spatial; community archive

I understand the ways in which my girlhood was interrupted and messed over and, [long pause] and hard. And, I now have this opportunity to care for that girl . . . Because girlhood is always with us. I'm hoping, in presenting the Colored Girls Museum, to others, particularly others, like my Colored Girl self that I offer as a reminder that girlhood is a sacred space. And it deserves protection, praise and grace. And we can give it.

—Vashti DuBois[1]

Radical love as practiced by Blackgirls is ritualized work that allows us to (re)member our past and (re)imagine our future (Cahill 2021). As Vashti DuBois, founder of the Colored Girls Museum (TCGM) explains in the epigraph above, girlhood is always with us, and intentional loving spaces can remind us of this sacred embodiment. Jacqui Alexander implores us to

WSQ: Women's Studies Quarterly 50: 1 & 2 (Spring/Summer 2022)

engage in "crafting interstitial spaces beyond the hegemonic where feminism and popular mobilization can reside" (Alexander 2005). To do this, she wrote, "would mean building . . . a meeting place where our deepest yearnings for different kinds of freedoms can take shape and find rest" (Alexander 2005). TCGM is one such space that honors the creative potential of Blackgirlhood (Brown 2009; Wright 2016; Butler 2018; Cox 2015).

This article is a nonconventional archival repository for the Colored Girls Museum in Germantown, Philadelphia, wherein I posit that the museum space is a radical love site through its curation of spirituality, spatial capacities, and navigation of time. Through the transformation of an oral history with the museum's founder, Vashti Dubois, I fashioned an avant-garde memoir about how DuBois's own life story curates radical love to be held in space. I will first explain why I choose memoir as my methodology. I will then detail a spiritual-spatial memoir that centers DuBois's lived experience while simultaneously tracing the cultivation and curation of the museum. The creative method has allowed me to not only document a story of how love is made manifest in a particular space but also gives me room to craft a love letter to Blackgirls reading this article to see themselves reflected and connected to people and place.

Blackgirl—One Word, No Space

I deliberately write Blackgirl as one word. This choice rejects compartmentalization of Blackgirls' lives, stories, and bodies and serves as a symbolic transgression to see them/us as complex and whole. Robin Boylorn (2016), the creator of this term, articulates:

> It speaks to the twoness and oneness of my raced and gendered identity. I am never only Black or only girl/woman, but always both/and at the same time . . . I merge the words to make them touch on paper the way they touch in my everyday existence.

Boylorn (2016) further describes the intentionality and multidimensional use of Blackgirl. She writes:

> *Blackgirl.*
> *So that the words look the way they sound on my tongue.*
> *Blackgirl,*
> *not*
> *Black*

(then)
girl.
There is no pause in my identity.
Blackgirl,
not
Black
(space)
girl.
There is no space left in me.
Blackgirl
(no space).
because there is no protection between my race and sex.
Because I am never seen or experienced as Black by itself or a girl without race.

Boylorn's epistemological premise of Blackgirlhood gathers intersectional, indivisible, and intergenerational expertise that can be gleaned from our unique positionality. Blackgirls of all ages routinely learn that "no matter how good we are from the beginning that . . . femaleness in patriarchal culture marks us unworthy of love" (hooks 2002). Blackgirls during every phase of their lives are unlearning this universally practiced falsehood. It is for that reason that this article continues like the scholarship of Boylorn and hooks by my earnest attempt to collapse temporal distinctions between Blackgirls/women to capture our fullest embodiment and the breadth of our identity, our capacity to love, and create space for ourselves.

Memoir as Method

I root my methodological choice in the theoretical premise of Vashti DuBois, the founder of the Colored Girls Museum, which is that museums can and should be understood as memoirs. It is rooted in the belief that those with situated knowledge and a radical standpoint have the most to offer toward composing an authentic memoir and rendering. Memoirs historically and contemporarily are a medium that Blackgirls have used to author counternarratives but also curate archives of the fullness of our lived experience (Ward 2013; Brown 1994; Lorde 2011; Shakur 2020; Davis 2019; Broom 2019; Cullors 2018). Blackgirl memoir when viewed as methodology is "an ontoepistemological data tool to analyze our cultural and spiritual way of being, doing and performing" (Evans-Winters 2019). This article stands alongside the other critical scholars, artists, and activists who seek to honor and acknowledge the full humanity, complexities, and nuances of Blackgirls (hooks 1996; Ford 2021; Davis 1974; Lane 2020). As Collins (2000) suggests, "analyzing and creating imaginative responses to injustice" is at the heart of Black feminism. In this memoir, I aim to remedy the dearth of literature that holds both the survivance, birthed out of institutional harms and personal betrayals, alongside the indefatigability of one Blackgirl who chose to love and models through her spirit and space how other Blackgirls can follow suit.

I chose memoir for my method because it allows for a unique opportunity to accessibly describe a Blackgirl's life but also challenges Blackgirl readers on how we might see her through analysis of social structures, spaces, and systems of power relationships. In the following sections, I compose a memoir largely weaved together from the transcripts of my oral history with the museum's founder, Vashti DuBois. It traces spiritual dimensions of love by analyzing (re)memory, ritual, and (re)imagination. It concludes by cartographing spatial love by mapping the dimensions of physical, virtual, and love space. In the spiritual section, I pull apart my radical love definition into (re)memory, ritual, and (re)imagination, then examine whether these processes are employed. Whereas in the spatial section, I survey if physical, virtual, and love space is curated at TCGM. In the table below, I describe my working definitions of the memoir's themes. Each of these listed definitions helped to frame spiritual processes and spatial dimensions I used to compose the memoir. By letting method be a mirror to the

SPIRITUAL	SPATIAL
(Re)memory: A process of complex reflection to memories in ways that affect the experience of the present.	*Virtual:* Online platforms where digital communities can be fostered that allow for connections, camaraderie, and care.
Physical: In-person, three-dimensional spaces, where folks can gather to meet and learn together inter/(intra)generationally.	*(Re)imagination:* Daring creative visioning and subsequent praxis of healing, sacredness, and freedom in the past, present, and future.
Ritual: A way for creating and expressing meaning tied to legacies of the past to be carried into the future.	*Love:* A physical or virtual plot that allows Blackgirls to a mother, daughter, and sister that is filled with opportunities for (re)memory, ritual, and (re)imagination.

Colored Girls Musuem's actual praxis, we get closer to actualizing and fully understanding what the love project and freedom dream truly entail. Radical love is also how we dream and imagine beyond our present to create spaces, relationships, and ideology that affirms and honors us.

The Colored Girls Museum

The Colored Girls Museum, located in the historically Black neighborhood of Germantown, Philadelphia, beautifully embodies Collins's *Black Feminist Thought*. Closely related to intersectionality (Crenshaw 1989), Patricia Hill Collins (2002) conceptually developed and wrote extensively about the theory and praxis of Black feminist thought. She cites that Blackgirls participate in multiple oppositional knowledge projects situated within intersecting power relations of race, gender, class, sexuality, age, ability, ethnicity, religion, and nationality. The Colored Girls Museum centers healing in its sanctuary space, which is open on Sundays, inside the home of its founder and executive director, Vashti DuBois (she/her). DuBois personally worked with local Philadelphian curators and Blackgirl artists across the nation to populate each room of her home with multidimensional "artyfacts" (DuBois 2019), objects, and information about Blackgirlhood. DuBois's home functionally operates as a memoir museum that honors the stories of celebration, experiences of violence, and herstory of ordinary Blackgirls (DuBois 2019). She invites guests to investigate local histories and identities, as well as how they can bring them into their lives through their words, bodies, and art. By exploring the spiritual-spatial praxis, I use the memoir below to empirically document the cultivation and curation of radical love at the Colored Girls Museum and simultaneously write to Blackgirl readers who see themselves situated in this narrative as well.[2]

Spiritual

Blackgirls have a legacy of using any and all resources available to them to obtain freedom. Their radical loving practices have included (re)membering their past (Morrison 1987), performing rituals to transform their realities (Teish 1985), and (re)imagining our future (Lillvis 2017). This section weaves together analyzed oral responses of the Colored Girls Museum's founder, Vashti DuBois. Specifically, this section navigates the praxis of the three major elements of my radical love definition: (re)memory, ritual, and (re)imagination as modeled by the Colored Girls Museum. It traces the life story of Vashti Dubois and into the story of the museum with selected quotations for Blackgirl readers to digest for their own love pursuit. It explores the museum's unique choreography of ritual for her protection, praise, and grace. It lastly complicates the definition of (re)imagination to offer that listening back and looking forward is a process of Blackgirl space reclamation. In order to properly orient ourselves to the Colored Girls Museum, we must first begin with the story of how the founder found love and shared it with others.

(Re)memory

Every Blackgirl is a walking, talking museum.
                                        —*DuBois*

(Re)membering, in the Morrisonian (Morrison 1987) sense of the word, is the process of complex reflection on the past in ways that affect the experience of the present. This memoir stands in this legacy by seeking to ask what the collective memory of Blackgirlhood is and how our existence and resistance furthers our freedom. Black feminist knowledge via productions and artifacts that push for consideration of deliberately silenced, marginalized, or hidden voices are necessary for transformational visions of the future (Troutman and Johnson 2018). Such works potentially can take artwork cultivated from our lived experiences and use them to guide us on a journey of our collective memoir through the power of the visual, the historical, and the counternarrated. Vashti's story helps to unsettle and challenge colonial logic and politics of domination through discourses of accountability, pedagogies of rememory, and critical remaking.

Our movements, conversations, and bodies are repositories of our memories. They each hold the multifarious artifacts that we have used to create homes wherever we are. Society has forced us to become our own museum because refuge is often not found for us in other spaces in the world. In lieu of us not being represented in predominant archives, our embodied spirit intuitively serves as our (re)memory's record. If we were to follow the path of the spirit, one entry point for the Colored Girls Museum begins about sixty years ago in Brownsville, New York, when the mother of Vashti DuBois, then fourteen years old, put her out of her home.[3]

She was not pregnant. She was not running the streets. She was recently awarded full tuition to a Catholic school. She did not talk back or lie. She was a shy girl and a good student who truly only wanted to please her mother. Existing as a Blackgirl with four brothers and a complicated, nuanced mother[4] left Vashti to create her own version of Blackgirlhood that allowed her to survive. With a notebook in one hand to stand in for a jump rope, jacks, and books, she held the many parts of herself together. Her notebook portal, community, and rigorous education became her lifelines. Vashti was a chronic couch surfer who bounced around living with friends, teachers, and school administrators. Her nonbiological aunties counseled her while waiting at bus stops while she commuted across the city. Her cafeteria's lunch ladies coached her to keep her head held high. Jackie Lee, her only Blackgirl teacher, pushed her to learn to understand why she does not like something before she rejects it. These ordinary people held her humanity and saw her potential. Each person she came in contact with transfigured into mirrors, allowing her to visualize the volume of her own internal museum's curation and her future life's work.

This self-possessed visionary, Aquarius dreamer was clairvoyant enough to see beyond her physical circumstances and be admitted into the prestigious Wesleyan University in Connecticut. She was grateful that a full scholarship covered her classes and room and board because it resolved the unpredictability of her living situation. At Wesleyan, she also began to recognize that so many of her peers and comrades, while not pursuing it as their major, were truly gifted artists. She convened a monthly gathering called "Womyn's Work" that rotated through the special interest cultural houses for Black, Latinx, and Asian students. Every month, participants would cook, perform, and share their most beloved artifacts from home. Vashti did the best she could at Wesleyan, but by sophomore year she was on academic probation and was not allowed to return her junior year.

Vashti ultimately left Connecticut and sought reprieve to what felt familiar by returning to New York. There, she found work to support herself and found other ways to continue to make art and community. She lived in Brooklyn in a "funky brownstone on Hancock Street" (Dubois 2020). Again, she returned to her monthly practice of experiential art. Fashioned after A'Lelia Walker's Dark Tower during the Harlem Renaissance, she convinced all of her neighbors in her converted building to open their doors to others. Each floor became a different cultural exposition. Starting from the bottom floor where you can grab your home-cooked food, guests were able to climb each floor to listen to and dance to different forms of music. Each floor hosted a different genre: jazz, house, and opera. She invites others, wherever she has lived, to engage in this reflective practice of (re) memory of who they are, where they come from, and what they embody. The invitation also caused her to remember that she still desired to be a student. The physical embodiment of persistence, Vashti returned to Wesleyan exactly ten years after she first began and finished her bachelor's degree at the age of twenty-eight as a single mom to a newborn daughter. She made a promise to the universe that if she finished school, she would summon sanctuary for others most in need, transient extensions of her radically loving spirit. That promise turned into her personal mission.

After September 11, 2001, and having her homelife shaken, Vashti decided with her husband to relocate to Philadelphia. Vashti used her social work degree to lead the Congresos Girls Center, a space for adjudicated and delinquent girls between the ages of thirteen and seventeen. The Congresos Girls Center's girls led and asserted themselves in a particular way. No place felt sufficient to holistically recognize all the parts the girls possessed. She determined that their summer employment would be to transform the center into a space to reflect them and their humanity. Had Vashti not run into issues with the executive leadership of the Congresos Girls Center, it was her initial vision to turn the center into the Colored Girls Museum. Her dreams were momentarily deferred but far from over. Vashti harnessed the lessons from her life experiences to move past her fears of not having enough money and resources to just begin. Led by the call of her past, future ancestors, and her inner Blackgirl, Vashti launched the Colored Girls Museum in her Germantown home on Sunday, September 11, 2015.

Ritual

Whenever, wherever or however you engage with the Colored Girls Museum, you are being enrolled in a ritual for her protection, praise, and grace.

—*DuBois*

As people of the African Diaspora, many aspects of our culture, including language, song, traditions, and foods, have been systematically stripped from us. In an attempt to reclaim some of our cultural productions and connections, we offer rituals. Rituals can be understood as a basic way of creating and expressing meaning (Miller 2005). Stories and narratives of our individual and community experiences are expressed in ritual. Story-telling is a ritual practice—it is through story that lineage, survival skills, community, and religion are conveyed. This section describes how rituals at the Colored Girls Museum are constructed in ways that help us to analyze our identity, as well as heal and celebrate ourselves.

The Colored Girls Museum is an influential radical love site that is demanding that "Philadelphia meets its moral obligation" (DuBois 2020). The power of work lies in the choreography of her ritual of experiential storytelling of Blackgirlhood. The ritualistic hope is that "when you leave the dwelling or log off her social media, that intention is inscribed upon you" (DuBois 2020). The Colored Girls Museum, unlike other sterile muse-ums divorced from community, "opens a portal" (DuBois 2020) for Blackgirls to feel safe because the story is held in a home by curatorial griots—not wall captions. While viewing her curated physical or virtual rooms, Blackgirls are encouraged by curators to recognize our power, be present to our culture, and witness the totality of the record of our lived experiences. We also are reminded through both stories and artifacts that "the goal for our lives is to ensure that our powers are left intact, that seek-ing survival [alone] is of little use at this moment" (DuBois 2020). The alchemy of the Colored Girls Museum's ritualized work allows us to be inti-mately aware of the fact that a space exists for our protection, praise, and grace. The museum's existence licenses us to curate space and time into a sanctuary for ourselves as well.

(Re)imagination

Blackgirls do not use linear time.
—*DuBois*

Black lives have been policed by the white toxic imaginaries (Rankine 2014). Routinely, our future has been decided for us under the guise of systems of racialized terror, historical looting, disinvestment, and violent policy. The Black Radical Imagination(s) have attempted to ameliorate our social condi-tions by exploring healing, sacredness, and freedom. There is an underrecognized archive of Blackgirls who have asserted that we belong in all spaces and all times (Samatar 2017). This Afrofuturist claim interrogates both Afro-optimism and Afro-pessimism to assemble visions of collectiv-ity, freedom, and radical love across temporalities (Womack 2013). The

Colored Girls Museum also wrestles with this idea that the past and future are not cut off from the present—both dimensions influence the whole of our lives, who we are, and who we become at any particular point in space-time. The museum reminds us of our position from the present creates what that past and future look like and what it means at every moment.

What grounds the work of the Colored Girls Museum is that their work honors all that an empty space holds. When interlocutors of the museum do that well, they begin with an understanding "that even with nothing visibly there, a space still has a story" (DuBois 2020). There is an underlying imprint that wants to be known. Stories from the past, present, and future exist in empty or full rooms. So the museum's many circulating curators are required to begin with thoughtful listening and introspective reflection rather than rushing to put stuff up on the walls. The museum asks us to listen to what past ancestors and future ancestors want and honors the answers that we hear. This approach to (re)imagination bends dominant conceptions of spatio-temporalities to curate with and for the benefit of Blackgirls collectively. With this lens, she operates in drag, a public health engine disguised as a museum. She strategically does this to invite a wide range of Blackgirls to heal gloriously. She presents as a museum to be an unassuming learning site gifting restoration, often unconsciously needed by her guests. She also takes on the form of the museum because it is a force field that provides a certain kind of protection to her visitors. Vashti reminded me that, "once we have our home, we can start revolutions" (DuBois 2020). The Colored Girls Museum is a home to us all and provides a backdrop to anchor us in place long enough to imagine, build together, and to resist.

Spatial

As you have become acquainted with the Colored Girls Museum's praxis of radical love, you will now learn how she operates as a physical, virtual, and love space. Viewing space for Blackgirls through a lens of love brings about new ways of understanding and relating to our environment. Womanist geographies such as these illuminate the social, political, cultural, natural, and built environments placed around Blackgirls instead of looking at them only as isolated beings. Physical, virtual, and love spaces all remind us that Blackgirls are forever entangled and enmeshed with the space surrounding us. Our ability to experience freedom must not just contend with our psychological and social relations, but also create interstitial rooms for being, connection and recognition.

In this last and final section, I will detail the Colored Girls Museum's general physical trappings and decor. I will also explain how TCGM has moved virtually during the coronavirus pandemic. Lastly, I end this section with the connection between her affective curation of love space. TCGM is spatial execution of radical love and aims to be a resource to Blackgirls everywhere.

Physical Space

You know, we danced up in this piece. We hang stuff. We bond. We jump. We play. We eat. She's a house. And she never stops being a house. I think that's really important.

              —*DuBois*

Early innovators such as Patricia Hill Collins (2004) and bell hooks (1992) have mapped and theorized spaces that Blackgirls create, reconfigure, and maintain to contend with and subvert the simultaneous forms of racist/white supremacist and heteropatriarchal violence and oppression to which they are often subjected. For instance, in her essay, "Homeplace: A Site of Resistance," hooks (1992) argues that the homeplace is a space in which Blackgirls who are marginalized by larger society are free not to be the intruder, the interloper, or the Other (as they often are outside of it). Instead, in the homeplace, Blackgirls are the standard, the norm, and the model by which all other things are measured. Homeplace is a space that is continuously forming and where roles and identities are chosen rather than assigned, an active domain of resistance to racism/white supremacy.

The choice of the Colored Girls Museum to exist inside an homeplace was quite intentional. The Colored Girls Museum is a 130-year-old, red brick, blue-trimmed house in Germantown, Philadelphia, standing on a double lot. The first floor of this home is like a patchwork cloth stitched together by hung artwork from the floors to the ceilings. The bedrooms are decorated with collage artwork, African textiles, a wooden dresser, several mirrors, and a stunning fireplace. Each room makes you feel full, whole, complete, and seen. In between the middle of the two bedrooms, stands a small all-white parlor that is adorned with white clothing hanging from laundry lines and pins, pearls, gloves, washboards, and steel iron. These simple artifacts pay homage to Blackgirl domestic workers who cleaned for others for a living to ensure our survival today. There is also a small prayer closet that has a floor-to-ceiling mosaic inside. These two rooms are the only constant within the museum's ever-evolving backdrop. Each room holds our prayers for our inner Blackgirls and answers for our healing. The Colored Girls Museum holds our many past and future memories.

The house dresses herself up from head to toe in her Sunday best decor for the occasion, to be seen and bear witness to Blackgirls much like herself. She has comfy tufted chairs and beds in each room to remind us to rest. She has visually stunning pictures and sculptures of us to offer mirrors to our lived experience. She has dolls and action figures in each room to remind us of the joy that can be found in play. Healing herbs grow in her victory garden. The lamppost outside guides Blackgirls to their Philadelphia home. While her physical attributes often change and shift to honor different exhibits and themes, she always centers and invites Blackgirls to affirm their cosmological being.

Virtual Space

The Colored Girls Museum asked, "Where are our people?" And Vashti told her, "They are in someplace in this place called the internet."
                                                                        —*DuBois*

Virtual space has also become vital for gathering, ceremony, and healing, especially amid a global pandemic, for millennials in general, by and large. Over the past decade, virtual space for Blackgirls provides various platforms for counternarratives to alter the flawed dominant narrative that exalts white supremacy as definitive. For instance, the cultural, economic, political, and social presumptions of #Blackgirlsaremagic (Thompson 2013) inform other social media campaigns begun by Black queer femmes, such as #Blacklivesmatter (Garza 2020), #Sayhername (AAPF 2014), among others, and ring true to the necessity to project positive images of Blackgirls in a global society that would otherwise objectify, critique, and make invisible the Black female body, mind, and spirit. Similarly the Tiffany Lethabo King (2019) theorization in *The Black Shoals* outlines analogy to demonstrate how the digital world offers a liminal space for Blackgirls to gather, reassemble, and come together or apart.

When the pandemic first began, COVID-19 brought an abrupt halt to the exhibit's showings. After feeling very lonely in the middle of the coronavirus pandemic, the Colored Girls Museum asked, "Where are our people?" And Vashti told her, "They are in someplace in this place called the internet" (DuBois 2020). The Museum countered by saying, "Take me there. I want to be on Instagram Street." A physical exhibit first inspired by Toni Morrison's books shape-shifted to the virtual world by inviting "ordinary Blackgirl curators to invite six to fifteen of their ordinary friends to submit objects of significance to them for a time like this, that are teaching them how to survive, offering them joy, making them laugh, helping them get through, or just offers them the opportunity to simply name what is in their hands." *The Songs of Toni Morrison: Psalms for a Time Like This* virtual exhibit turned into a beautiful patchwork quilt, both comforting and providing survivance strategies for Blackgirls transnationally. While it is a new practice and one that felt at first unfamiliar and somewhat uncomfortable, the Colored Girls Museum moved from physical to virtual space and has opened yet another spatial pathway to lead us steadily closer to radical love.

In addition, in the summer of 2021, TCGM hosted a summer program entitled Galaxy Girls, another brainchild of Vashti. Youth participants met virtually on Zoom for almost the entirety of the program with the exception of a few socially distant hikes. Over Zoom, they were led through abolitionist curriculum on ecology, sculpture, and creative writing. Much of their summer work was radically assembled into a guerilla podcast and digital zine. All of the participants this summer were new and none of them have physically been inside TCGM. Virtual space (as a result of the pandemic) has complicated, challenged, and reaffirmed, Blackgirls' place(s) in the world.

Love Space

> *This house was like this is the longest I've lived anywhere and in truth this the only home I've ever had and I love it. And so I turned this love that I have to share with other ordinaries like myself.*
>
> —*DuBois*

In a love space, Blackgirls of all ages can be a mother, daughter, and sister. In a love space, collective, cultural, and creative memories are unleashed to connect us directly with our ancestors. The love space ritualizes work, play, and food. The love space allows our imaginations to be Black, radical, ratchet, and to live in the boundless territory of Afrofuturism. The love space is physical, virtual, and ethereal. To interface with the Colored Girls Museum in any spatial form is to be greeted by love. Vashti beautifully stated, "If you ever have the privilege of seeing her in person, you sense it immediately walking up the path." The museum tells Blackgirls as Harriet Tubman did before her death, "I go to prepare a place for you." In order to understand the impact of the museum, you have to recall for yourself what it feels like, "when a friend invites you over with full knowledge that you are having a particularly hard time and you arrive to find that they have done everything that they can think of to make sure that you feel at home. They go out of their way to make sure that you feel safe and cared for and seen." The Colored Girls Museum is embodied love in place.

Vibrating at the frequency of love, she chronicles and celebrates our centuries' long experience of joy and pain with her interior design, artifacts, and artwork. She, even with the boundaries enacted by COVID, time travels and shape-shifts to channel her mission through the internet to provide resources and relief on how to get over the obstacles in front of us. The Colored Girls Museum is spatially modeling how to return to our innate practice of loving ourselves: where we come from, what we have experienced, and where we are headed next. By offering a space for Blackgirls to unpack womanist spatial-temporalities, we are gifted with the opportunity to engage and recreate sanctuary in our homes, schools, organizations, and communities. The love space gives us the strength to transform whatever boundaries stand in the way of us having a place in the world. By her greeting us with love, we learn that love is what we deserve everywhere we go. She reminds Blackgirls daily that we "are our own best things" (Morrison 1987). Our brilliance, our magic, and even our undesirable parts have subaltern pathways that lead to great treasure if we dare to listen and remember. Upon visiting Blackgirls' physical or virtual spaces, you immediately get a sense of their spiritually driven mission. You are also able to readily understand their unique abolitionist curation, theory, and pedagogy embedded within their space. Those fortunate to speak with Vashti can feel love reverberate from her dreams of freedom (Kelley 2002) for Blackgirls everywhere. The Colored Girls Museum affirms that Blackgirls' temporality is boundless between the past, present, and future, existing in all places and all times. In that way, she, like Vashti herself, stands as our pillar, a choreography of care, our safe harbor and home.

Loren S. Cahill is an assistant professor at Smith College's School of Social Work. Her research interests attempt to achieve Blackgirls their radical love praxis as well as their navigation of their social, spatial, and temporal realities. She can be reached at lcahill@smith.edu.

Notes

1. All quotes from Vashti DuBois are derived from a personal Zoom correspondence with the author in 2020.
2. Watch an eleven-minute audio collage depicting Vashti's entire oral history at this YouTube link: https://www.youtube.com/watch?v=woxYGuZDt4M.
3. I wrestled about acknowledging Vashti's complicated relationship with her mother. She mentioned, "One of the most hurtful things was having people say to me what did you do? Why do we as Black folks who come from a history of rape and violation against Black girls still blame her? But to this day when I tell people my mom put me out when I was thirteen, they ask me what I did. I did nothing—but they are asking the wrong question every time." I chose to keep it because I believe that her lived experiences are a major driving force behind her work.
4. Vashti also mentioned to me: "My mother had a mental illness (I think), but I don't really know. Is there a *DSM-5* code that covers the stress and strain of being a Black, single mom trying to raise five children? Always working but always being the "working poor," the effects of diabetes, high blood pressure, racism, sexism, colorism, growing up in the South, having an abusive father and a mom who was physically ill—all things which contributed to how she saw me—raised me as her only girl." Undiagnosed mental health issues run rampant throughout the African American community for a plethora of reasons. Her mother is still human and to only view her as a villain is to underappreciate her situated knowledge.

Works Cited

African American Policy Forum. 2014. #SayHerName Campaign. Retrieved from https://aapf.org/sayhername.

Alexander, M. Jacqui. 2005. *Pedagogies of Crossing: Meditations on Feminism, Sexual Politics, Memory, and the Sacred.* Durham, NC: Duke University Press.

Broom, Sarah. 2019. *The Yellow House: A Memoir.* New York: Grove Press.

Brown, Elaine. 1994. *A Taste of Power: A Black Woman's Story.* New York: Anchor.

Brown, Ruth Nicole. 2009. *Black Girlhood Celebration: Toward a Hip-Hop Feminist Pedagogy*. New York: Peter Lang.

Boylorn, Robin M. 2016. "On Being at Home with Myself: Blackgirl Autoethnography as Research Praxis." *International Review of Qualitative Research* 9, no. 1: 44–58.

Butler, Tamara T. 2018. "Black Girl Cartography: Black Girlhood and Placemaking in Education Research." *Review of Research in Education* 42, no. 1: 28–45.

Cahill, Loren. 2021. "Radical Love Unlimited: A Biomythography." *Visual Arts Research* 47, no. 1: 89–100.

Collins, Patricia Hill. 2000. "Gender, Black Feminism, and Black Political Economy." *The Annals of the American Academy of Political and Social Science* 568, no. 1: 41–53.

———. 2002. *Black Feminist Thought: Knowledge, Consciousness, and the Politics of Empowerment*. New York: Routledge.

———. 2004. *Black Sexual Politics: African Americans, Gender, and the New Racism*. New York: Routledge.

Cox, Aimee Meredith. 2015. *Shapeshifters: Black Girls and the Choreography of Citizenship*. Durham: Duke University Press.

Crenshaw, Kimberlé. 1989. "Demarginalizing the Intersection of Race and Sex: A Black Feminist Critique of Antidiscrimination Doctrine, Feminist Theory and Antiracist Politics." *University of Chicago Legal Forum* 1: 139.

Cullors, Patrisse. 2018. *When They Call You a Terrorist: A Black Lives Matter Memoir*. New York: St. Martin's Press.

Davis, Angela. 1974. *Angela Davis: An Autobiography*. New York: International Publishers Co.

Davis, Bridgett. 2019. *The World According to Fannie Davis: My Mother's Life in the Detroit Numbers*. New York: Little, Brown.

DuBois, Vashti. 2019. *About Us*. https://www.thecoloredgirlsmuseum.com.

Evans-Winters, Venus E. 2019. *Black Feminism in Qualitative Inquiry: A Mosaic for Writing Our Daughter's Body*. New York: Routledge.

Ford, Ashley. 2021. *Somebody's Daughter: A Memoir*. New York: Macmillan Publishers.

Garza, Alicia, Opal Tometi, and Patrisse Cullors. 2014. "A Herstory of the #BlackLivesMatter Movement." In *Are All the Women Still White?: Rethinking Race, Expanding Feminisms*, edited by Janell Hobson, 23–28. Albany: SUNY Press.

hooks, bell. 1992. "Yearning: Race, Gender, and Cultural Politics." *Hypatia* 7, no. 2.

———. 1996. *Bone Black: Memories of Girlhood*. New York: Macmillan Publishers.

———. 2002. *Communion: The Female Search for Love*. New York: Harper Perennial.

Kelley, Robin D. G. 2002. *Freedom Dreams: The Black Radical Imagination*. Boston: Beacon Press.

King, Tiffany Lethabo. 2019. *The Black Shoals*. Durham, NC: Duke University Press.

Lane, Cassandra. 2021. *We Are Bridges*. New York: Feminist Press.

Lillvis, Kristen. 2017. *Posthuman Blackness and the Black Female Imagination*. Athens: University of Georgia Press.

Lorde, Audre. 2011. *Zami: A New Spelling of My Name: A Biomythography*. California: Crossing Press.

Miller, G. E. 2005. *Experience, Narrative, and Ritual in Black Women's Writing: A Womanist Perspective in Pastoral Care*. Available from ProQuest Dissertations & Theses Global.

Morrison, Toni. 1987. *Beloved*. New York: Plume.

Rankine, Claudia. 2014. *Citizen: An American Lyric*. Minneapolis: Graywolf Press.

Samatar, Sofia. 2017. "Toward a Planetary History of Afrofuturism." *Research in African Literatures,* 48, no. 4: 175–91.

Shakur, Assata. 2020. *Assata: An Autobiography*. Chicago: Chicago Review Press.

Teish, Luisah. 1985. *Jambalaya*. New York: HarperCollins.

Thompson, Cashawn. 2013. "Cashawn Thompson." http://cashawn.com/.

Troutman, Stephanie, and Brenna Johnson. 2018. "Dark Water: Rememory, Biopower, and Black Feminist Art." *Taboo: The Journal of Culture and Education* 17, no. 3: 8.

Ward, Jesmyn. 2013. *Men We Reaped: A Memoir*. New York: Bloomsbury.

Womack, Ytasha L. 2013. *Afrofuturism: The World of Black Sci-fi and Fantasy Culture*. Chicago: Chicago Review Press.

Wright, Nazera Sadiq. 2016. *Black Girlhood in the Nineteenth Century*. Chicago: University of Illinois Press.

"Everyone Has a Pic Like This in the Album!": Digital Diasporic Intimacy and the Instagram Archive

keisha bruce

Abstract: In this essay, I examine how the Black digital diaspora have found belonging online by imagining intimate kinships with one another. Building on my personal experiences of following and engaging with the popular Instagram archive, @BlackArchives.co, I offer the term *digital diasporic intimacy* to describe the ways that the Black diaspora have used social media to come together and creatively participate in the construction of online communities. **Keywords**: digital diaspora; social media; intimacy; kinship; archives; time; memory

On February 26, 2020, @BlackArchives.co, an Instagram account that documents Black experiences through archival images, uploaded a series of photographs taken by New Orleans street photographer Sthaddeus "Polo Silk" Terell. The ten-part series comprised of snapshots of the New Orleans community at his ephemeral street studios in the early 1990s. In the first image, a young woman stands in the center of the frame with her legs slightly parted and her left hand confidently hooked into her waistband. The other hand is placed on her thigh, fingers spread slightly to draw attention to her long, white, curved acrylic nails. She wears black leather trousers, a navy-blue button-up checked shirt, and an oversized leather-look chestnut bomber jacket with "POLO" written in large white letters down the visible sleeve. Her skin—a deep reddish brown, a shade darker than her jacket—shines against the hand-painted white material that frames the ephemeral street studio dedicated to Ralph Lauren Polo. As we look at this photograph, we look back on a particular moment of New Orleans' cultural history, and the woman's fashion transcends time and space to signal a Black diasporic, temporal style politic. While her glossy black hair styled into a

WSQ: Women's Studies Quarterly 50: 1 & 2 (Spring/Summer 2022) © 2022 by keisha bruce. All rights reserved.

Fig. 1. Sonia Fraser and Keisha Fraser, circa 1996/1997. Courtesy of Sonia Bruce.

curled half-updo signals the eighties, her clothing, which fuses together elements of streetwear, country, and punk, encompasses the innovative and blended style of the early nineties that we still recognize, reuse, and repurpose today. When I scrolled down my Instagram feed that morning, this post immediately caught my attention. There was something about this photograph and its visual vibrancy that instilled a feeling of warmth, familiarity, and closeness within me. But as a 1994 baby, born and living in Britain, I struggled to understand how that was possible. So, I wondered, what was it about this snapshot that commanded my attention and intimately pulled me to a space and a time where I could feel connected to the unnamed woman?

During the summer later that year, I had been searching through my mother's photo albums, and as we rummaged together through the boxes, we found an album that documented her time spent living in New York City in 1997. One photograph reminded me of the image of the unnamed woman I had seen on Instagram months before. In the photo, my mother poses with one hand on her waist as she leans against the doorframe inside of our Bronx apartment. At two years old, I stood beside her in a silver puffer jacket, leg bent in what appears to be an attempt to imitate her pose. Similar to the photograph of the unnamed woman, my mother couples her oversized sweatshirt with leather-look pants. While these photos were taken a mere few years apart, in different geographical spaces with different contextual histories, there is an energy that travels between the stillness of the snapshots, an intimate diasporic synergy that captures these women's ability to "empower [them]selves through representation" (hooks 1995, 60). Seeing this photograph allowed me to articulate what I had experienced months before when I scrolled down my Instagram feed: I had felt intimately connected to the photograph of the unnamed woman as I was reminded of my mother.

I was not the only Instagram user who imagined intimate kinships in response to the photo series. Black viewers used the Instagram comment section to discuss the ways that Silk's photographs felt familiar to them, and many yearned for that era even though they expressed that they had not been born at that time. Some viewers tagged friends and family members, writing that these images reminded them of one another. Some celebrated the Black aesthetics in the images. Some commented that they wished they were there in these photographs because it looked "lit af."[1] Collectively, these comments and my own experience reveal the ways that some viewers of @BlackArchives.co's posts have projected ourselves, our lives, family members, friends, and our contemporary realities onto the archival photographs and the stories that we perceive them to hold. In doing so, we had oriented our identities in ways that destabilize the binaries of past and present. In other words, within these moments, the past and present are joined in a delicate dance of diasporic worlding and self-imagining. It is within this disruption of linear notions of time, enacted through the viewers responses to the photographs, that I posit "digital diasporic intimacy" takes shape.

Concerned with the ways that love and diasporic kinship are practiced across the @BlackArchives.co account, I suggest that digital diasporic intimacy provides a lens for us to see the ways that Black online communities are rooted in experiences of encounter, the negotiation of difference, and celebration of Black life through time. In doing so, this essay asks: What is digital diasporic intimacy? How might digital diasporic intimacy be organized around visuality and diasporic temporalities? And finally, how might we understand digital diasporic intimacy as a loving practice for sustaining Black solidarity on the Internet?

I begin this essay by mapping out a genealogy that connects my conceptualization of digital diasporic intimacy to theories of the Black diaspora, digital communities, and global Black intimacies. I argue that the term offers a lens to better understand the diasporic connections that are fostered through online community building. From there, I demonstrate how digital diasporic intimacy is engaged across @BlackArchives.co, and I argue that it is experienced through temporality. This research stems from my autoethnographical project on Black women's digital visual cultures. Drawing on my own experience of engaging with the archive in my everyday life, I have selected photographs and comments that represent moments where familial kinship or concerns with time and intimate memories were expressed by Black viewers. Through an analysis of these, I suggest that across @BlackArchives.co, digital diasporic intimacy is achieved through a strategy of what I call "speculative remembering." Attentive to the ways that Black Instagrammers have used the archive to orient their identities in relation to one another, I use speculative remembering to highlight the ways that digital diasporic intimacy is created through acknowledgements of time, memory, and affect. I use the term "diasporic temporalities" to signal the ways that time is enmeshed in the creation of Black diasporic worlding. It suggests that Black diasporic identities can be articulated through an untethering of Western notions of time.[2] Instead, time is an orientation that can be wielded to create intimate kinships. Afterward, still drawing on this, but focused on how some viewers have used respectability politics to orient their memories and diasporic identities, I demonstrate that tension is fundamental to digital diasporic intimacy for the mediation of conflict. Finally, I conclude with a discussion of how digital diasporic intimacy sustains the formation of diasporic socialities necessary for understanding and responding to contemporary social realities.

Digital Diasporic Intimacy

I use digital diasporic intimacy to describe the effect of a range of Black diasporic encounters and practices on social media platforms that celebrate transnational community, center joy, and enact love through quotidian digital practices (bruce 2022). It builds upon Paul Gilroy's claim that "playful diasporic intimacy" is a "marked feature of transnational black Atlantic creativity" to explore how everyday digital play might forge diasporic kinships (1993, 16). While Gilroy looks to literature, music, and politics to explore a hybridized Black culture, my conceptualization focuses on digital technologies to explore how these creative kinship practices are mediated on social media.

Scholars in cultural studies, social studies, and anthropology have understood the creation of a diaspora as a result of geographical displacement, dispersal, and migration (Kalra, Kaur, and Hutnyk 2005). These theories commonly situate the formation of a diaspora in relation to an attachment to, or longing for, an original or imagined homeland (Basch, Schiller, and Blanc 1994). However, researchers of the Black diaspora recognize that the requirement of a geographical homeland does not apply as cohesively to the Black diaspora where forced migration and land dispossession shape spatial experiences, nor does this framework recognize the privileges and powers that some might have with access to that homeland (Campt 2002; Brown 1998). With a focus on the Black diaspora, Paul Gilroy and Stuart Hall have complicated dominant understandings of diasporas to account for the ways that they might instead be articulated through a shared set of political and material resources and practices (Gilroy 1992; Hall 1990). While some argue that the Black diaspora is created out of a shared oppression (Ellison 1972; Shelby 2002), it is this acknowledgement of a shared experience of anti-Black racism, but also shared cultural expressions and experiences such as art, fashion, language, and play that I argue fuels transnational socialities within digital diasporic intimacy. Thus, the diaspora in my conceptualization illustrates the ways that materials, ideas, experiences, and creativity travel across transnational borders. However, it also acknowledges the hypervisibility of Black American cultures and experiences within these digital diasporic worlds.

Social media has long offered a space for the geographically disparate Black diaspora to create belonging, organize politically, and negotiate our identities (Sobande 2020; Everett 2009). It also provides a space for the Black diaspora to create intimacy through everyday dialogue, expressions of joy, and digital play. Black digital media researchers have explored the ways that Black identity and community are mediated online through joy, humor, and expressive cultures (Brock 2020; Lu and Steele 2019; Sinanan 2017; Steele 2016). However, many of these studies prioritize Black American digital publics in their analysis. A diasporic framework to explore this can offer us an insight into how these practices might facilitate the construction of a Black digital diaspora, necessary for intimate community building. A digital diaspora describes a phenomenon whereby a diaspora of people uses the Internet as a means of building community, connecting to other members of the diaspora, and negotiating disparate identities (Brinkerhoff 2009; Leurs and Ponzanesi 2011). With a specific focus on the Black digital diaspora, Anna Everett argues that the Internet offers a space for the formation of a distinctive diasporic Black consciousness. She argues that on the Internet, national borders "are replaced by new kinship structures now predicated on the fluidity of cybernetic virtual communities and homelands" (2009, 33). In doing so, she situates a fluid diasporic connectivity at the crux of a digital Black identity. My understanding of the Black digital diaspora builds on Everett's argument to suggest that kinships are created through quotidian digital play and creativity.

Although I situate playfulness and enjoyment as central to digital diasporic intimacy, I do not wish to suggest that it only arises in these moments. Digital diasporic intimacy is also created through mundane conversation, sharing digital material, and even passive participation enacted through little direct engagement, such as reading comments or viewing the online material. It is found in the exchange of ideas, shared experiences, cultural meanings, and the desire for connectivity. Like Gilroy, researchers of the Black diaspora recognize the ways that diasporic identities and communities are intimately formed. While Bianca C. Williams (2018) uses "emotional transnationalism" to analyze the ways that Black women have created diasporic networks through practices of solidarity, reciprocity, happiness, and leisure, Keguro Macharia offers "frottage" to describe how the Black diaspora intimately imagine and create belonging together:

> Frottage tries to grasp the quotidian experiences of intraracial experience, the frictions and irritations and translations and mistranslations, the moments when blackness coalesces through pleasure and play and also by resistance to antiblackness. More than simply proximity, it is the active and dynamic ways blackness is produced and contested and celebrated and lamented as a shared object. It is bodies rubbing against and along bodies. Histories rubbing along and against histories. It is the shared moments of black joy and black mourning. (2019, 7)

Macharia's frottage highlights the ways that diasporic connectivity emerges from this interplay of joy and refusal, harmony and difference. Like frottage, digital diasporic intimacy recognizes that diasporic connectivity is not always harmonious, and this is especially prevalent on the Internet where differences are rapidly made visible.

In conversation with Gilroy, Everett, Macharia, and Williams, my conceptualization of digital diasporic intimacy asks how diasporic intimacies shape and are shaped by social media. It is concerned with the ways that digital kinships are imagined online, the ways that Black culture is celebrated transnationally, and how diasporic community can be created through not only shared experiences but also sites of difference.

Archives, Photographs, and @BlackArchives.co

Scholars have routinely noted that institutional archives are not neutral spaces and even within Black archival spaces, Black women are violently erased (Carter 2006; Hartman 2008; Olusoga 2016; Schwartz and Cook 2002). This concern about *who* and *what* becomes a part of the archive is a discussion that runs parallel to concerns about who the architects of these institutional archives are (Farmer 2018). In response to archival silences, lack of representation, and accessibility issues, those marginalized by institutional archives have turned to social media methods to curate archival spaces that disrupt the limitations of institutional archives.[3] Nehal El-Hadi refers to this as "radical curation," which she describes as an intervention on the limitations of institutional archives as it centers, validates, and celebrates marginalized groups (2015). Within these spaces of radical curation, intimacy is fostered, as people can come together to collaborate and create new worlds.

In 2015, researcher and curator Renata Cherlise founded the popular visual project and digital archive, Black Archives, previously known as Blvck Vrchives.[4] On the project website, the archive is referred to as a "gathering place for Black memory and imaginations" where visuality is used as a tool for, and a process of learning about and encountering diasporic Black histories (2021). In an earlier iteration of the website Cherlise states that the archive's purpose was to create a counternarrative to mainstream misconceptions of Black life. To do this, she intended to "replace [these misconceptions] with collective memories of everyday life shared through fictive kinships" (2020). In both iterations, the archive is positioned as a site to rearticulate memory to create intimacy. And so, within this space of the Instagram archive where the utilization of memory and imagination is encouraged, digital diasporic intimacy is engaged temporally to curate fictive kinships.

Shortly after the website was founded, Cherlise began an accompanying Instagram account, @BlackArchives.co, previously known as

@BlvckVrchives. The Instagram account broadened the reach of the archive and allowed members of the public to not only submit their own photographs to the page, but also engage with the archive through its social media functions. I argue that it is within this space of the digital archive where radical curation and social media tools makes diasporic intimacy available through processes of visuality. Black feminist scholars have illustrated the ways that visual media can be used as a tool for (re)imagination, to revise narrative scripts, respond to displacement and oppression, and claim a diasporic identity (Campt 2012; Raiford 2009; hooks 1995). I extend this to argue that Black folk have used the photographs posted to @BlackArchives.co as conduits, or "diasporic resources" (Brown 1998, 298), for intimacy, and I suggest that this is achieved through a process of speculative remembering.

Speculative Remembering and Digital Diasporic Intimacy

When I used Silk's photograph of the unnamed woman to call upon my mother, I participated in an intimate practice that would connect us all through what I understood to be a diasporic memory. To theorize this as a practice of digital diasporic intimacy, I propose that we use a term that encapsulates how viewers have used their own memories and knowledges—drawn simultaneously from their personal archives and @BlackArchives.co's posts—to imagine stories that root us within the visuality of the photographs, while simultaneously lifting what was captured into the present. Thus, speculative remembering describes the act of imagining what *might have been* in relation to *what has been* and *what is*, while drawing on digital "diasporic resources" to help us to access a shared memory (Brown 1998, 298). It fuses together the acts of speculation and memory, guessing and recalling, to create diasporic socialities that prioritize intimate kinships. I use speculative remembering to describe the act of looking at the present while looking at the past and then proceeding to imagine the relationship between the two. The term is in conversation with other Black memory and archival practices, including Saidiya Hartman's "critical fabulation" (2008, 11), where narrative fiction is used to fill the gaps caused by archival erasure, and Toni Morrison's "rememory" (2019, 324), which describes the act of recalling something previously forgotten and reassembling memory. While there is not one singular example of what constitutes speculative remembering, I argue that it is a strategy used to engage with material in a way that facilitates intimate diasporic community and identity building temporally. It is this engagement with time, memory, and the imagination that distinguishes speculative remembering from Hartman and Morrison's terms.

On the @BlackArchives.co account, the comment section underneath the posts are repeatedly used as a means for the viewers to locate themselves within an axis of space-time where they can imagine kinships with those featured in the photographs and with one another. As they respond to the photographs, they expose the limitations of fixed linear time as they speculate, remember, imagine, and create digital belonging together and with the people captured in the images. We witness this play out in the ways that viewers identify, negotiate, and wrestle with their identities together. The following few examples illustrate some of the ways that the viewers intimately engage with the digital community archive through speculative remembering in order to articulate their diasporic identities. Additionally, they illuminate how the fixity of time does not impede on the ability to develop and sustain digital diasporic intimacy.

A photograph published to @BlackArchives.co in November 2019 features a young man and woman seated in a home music studio in 1977 Midland, Texas. They both wear short afros and their cross-legged seated positions imitate one another. His arm is wrapped around her shoulder in a warm embrace, and they both bare teeth, smiling at the camera. The photograph was submitted to the archive by a member of the public who detailed that it captured her parents four years prior to her birth. Retold through @BlackArchives.co's caption, she shares that although her parents are no longer in a relationship, their love still lives on through her. Other followers write in the comment section that this image epitomizes Black love, using raised fist and black heart emojis to signal a diasporic solidarity expressed through love and intimacy. Thus, snapshots move and are moved by our engagements with them, physically and emotionally.

In response to this image, an unrelated follower writes, "omg everyone has a pic like this in the album [sparkling heart]."[5] This response, as well as my experience detailed at the opening of this essay, indicates that for some followers, @BlackArchives.co is navigated and approached with an experience of flicking through family photo albums. While the tactile materiality of photo albums is remediated through technologies and their affordances, a haptic resonance remains, and I suggest that this forms the basis of digital diasporic intimacy across @BlackArchives.co. Campt argues that photographs across the Black diaspora have "haptic registers," which are structured by a "tripartite sense of touch" that is indexical, physical, and affective (2012, 43). It is this tactility that sustains intimate acts of curation, engagement, and the transmission of Black family photos.

Within her comment, this follower refers to the genealogies of Black family photo albums as a singular entity: "the album." In doing so, she draws together geographically and culturally disparate Black families' photographic and archival practices to propose that they are collaborative, as though together we are quilting a collective diasporic memory through our photo albums. Suggesting that there are universal similarities between disparate Black family photo albums, this follower's comment implies that a diasporic kinship exists between Black families globally and that it can be traced through photography and memory. As one of Cherlise's original aims for @BlackArchives.co was to help curate "fictive kinships," this comment suggests that there is nothing fictive about it; it is a reality that can be seen and felt through our creation, curation, and engagement with photographs. Using the analogy of "the album," this follower orients herself in a way that positions her as part of a wider diasporic story and memory. She intimately connects herself to the couple featured in the snapshot as well as to "every-one" else. However, this use of "everyone" to address other Black folk may homogenize Black memory as it leaves little room for the stories, memories, and family dynamics that do not align with the narrative determined by the image. Instead, I propose that this follower refers to the *feeling* that the photographs captures and not its actual composition when she writes that "everyone has a pic like this." She recognises and draws upon the snap-shot's haptic resonance to speculate the ways that she might be oriented alongside other Black folk. Thus, the digitally mediated photograph becomes a resource to *feel* diasporic intimacy.

In another photograph, taken in the 1970s by African American photog-rapher Jimmie Mannas, two teenage boys are pictured in a New York City subway. In the black-and-white image, one boy who wears his afro picked stands over the other who is seated on a bench, and they both look intently into the camera lens. In response, one viewer writes: "I be feeling hella connected to all these photos."[6] Without providing any context to explain why, he uses this space to express his intimate feelings of familiarity with this photograph and others featured on @BlackArchives.co. His comment alludes to the way that the archive has been used to find diasporic belong-ing and create intimacy multidirectionally.

Another comment left on this photograph might offer an explanation of multidirectional belonging and intimacy. In the comment, a middle-aged viewer writes: "They could be your dad your uncles or any of my friends from the block those 70s [raising hands, raising hands]." Addressed to the readers of her comment, she iterates that these boys could either be her friends, or "your" elder family members. In doing so, she not only presumes @BlackArchives.co's audience to be Black, but also imagines a familial relationship between herself and other viewers. She enacts speculative remembering to imagine an intimate intergenerational diasporic kinship. While she locates the boys in the present-time as grown men, either as "your dad" or "your uncle," she simultaneously positions them in the 1970s as she reminisces about her own childhood and speculatively remembers them as her friends. For this viewer, these boys concurrently exist in the past and present, and are both young and old. This duality allows her to also exist in the past and present as she speculates on what could have happened during her youth and how these boys might be socially coded today. She melds together the interior time of the photograph with the exterior time of Instagram to imagine a space and time where the boys and herself become *we*. Furthermore, by referring to them as "your" dad or uncle, she separates herself from what she assumes to be the dominant generation of Instagram users. She scripts an intergenerational kinship in which she positions herself alongside authoritative family members, thus places herself in a position of intimacy and authority, as if she were a digital auntie.[7]

On some occasions, searching for family members does not solely rely on speculation and imagination. Instead, there are actual restorative possibilities for connection that are enabled by the archive. One viewer wrote to Cherlise via the comment section to announce her realization that one of the boys in this photograph is her father: "@blvckvrchives this is my dad (sitting down) and his friend. my mom just confirmed for me." There are multiple examples of Instagram users finding old photographs of family members, locating previously unknown family members, and tracing surnames in the comments of the digital archive. For some, Cherlise's archive is used as a network that allows for intimate connections to be discovered and celebrated. Within this curated archive, digital diasporic intimacy represents a possibility to unite families, real and fictive, who are separated by space and time.

A series of photographs taken by Susan Meiselas in 2004 capture Black life in a small town northwest of Lisbon, Portugal. These were posted onto @BlackArchives.co in July 2019, and many comments from Black

American viewers expressed their surprise that Portugal has long had a Black community. Despite this, viewers map similarities between their own lives and those photographed to cultivate diasporic intimacy. The first image in the series captures a young woman who is having her hair braided by two other women. As she holds the black and blonde braiding hair in either hand, one woman parts the back of her hair while the other finishes a braid. Drawing on similarities between Black communities separated by the Atlantic, followers of @BlackArchives.co used the comment section to articulate the ways that diasporic memory exists irrespective of geographical space. As one Black American follower writes: "Growing up around my mom, Gmom & aunts this was always seen in the kitchen! [Smiling face with heart eyes emoji; raising hands emoji, medium skin tone; raised fist emoji, medium skin tone]." He recognises the four Afro-Portuguese women in the photograph as his family members and is transported to his childhood family kitchen, interpreting the scene to represent an intimate Black diasporic social ritual. He moves between this act of viewing the scene depicted in the photograph and his memories of observing the scene in his childhood kitchen to identify a time and space where the two diasporic memories meld together. The combination of emojis emphasizes their familiarity with the scene and the use of the fist symbolizes Black solidarity, celebrating their similarities despite the geographical difference.

Although I have illustrated how digital diasporic intimacy is celebrated, not all interactions on @BlackArchives.co are harmonious. Macharia's frottage reminds us to be attentive to the ways that intimacy is created vis-à-vis friction. For instance, some viewers use the archival photographs to perpetuate narratives of the Black diaspora that are steeped within respectability politics, an aspirational practice that uses narratives of respectability to reject stereotypes for the purpose of enacting social change (Higginbotham 1993). Some viewers left comments on @BlackArchives.co posts that employed respectability politics as a way to distance themselves with what they perceived to be the damaging present and align themselves from a romanticized past. These viewers use speculative remembering to position their ideas of what it means to be Black and to police the ways that Black folk *should* act. The following comment was left on a post that captures children swimming in a river in Mali in the 1970s: "With all the rump shaking and black on black disrespect that is flooding this platform your page is my favourite and a breath of fresh air. Keep on elighing [sic], inspiring and reminding me of our people's greatness!"

While this viewer acknowledges tensions within Black digital communities, they create their own tension here by proposing that "rump shaking" and "black on black disrespect" is antithetical to Black "greatness." In doing so, they position the past, as perpetuated by @BlackArchives.co, as a romanticized reality that represents the best of the community. Similarly, the following comment left in response to a photograph of a college band in Atlanta, Georgia, in the 1980s echoes this sentiment, but blames the media for denigrating Black folk: "Not trying to be funny . . . but I didn't see not one breast hanging. no ass showing . . . the men were all polished. No pants hanging off the ass . . . wow what a difference 2 decades and others controlling our media makes." While this viewer rightly acknowledges the ways that dominant media perpetuates harmful images of Black folk, they employ respectability politics to undermine the agency of those Black folks as it relates to gender, sexuality, and class. According to this viewer, time evidences a linear narrative of declining respectability within the Black community. Their projections fetishize the past as an intimate reality and reject Black ratchetness in the present.[8] Thus, their relationship to digital diasporic intimacy is shaped by their own politics and the ways that they privilege linear progress narratives.

The presence of respectability politics across @BlackArchives.co is reflective of a wider culture of misogynoir that is expressed almost routinely on social media platforms. Moya Bailey coined the term to describe "the anti-Black racist misogyny that Black women experience particularly in U.S. visual and digital culture" (2021, 1). Misogynoir is perpetuated and circulated online via search engine results (Noble 2018), memes (Jackson 2014), and through conversation, and although it is damaging and denigrates, Black women respond to and confront its perpetuation through a variety of digital practices (Bailey 2021). For instance, those comments posted onto @BlackArchives.co did not go unchallenged. Black women had responded to them directly and recognized their roots in misogynoir and classism. This intracommunity tension evidences the frictions of intimacy and lack of harmony that reside within Black online spaces. In the two examples above, the commenters—who are cis men—project their ideologies onto the photographs in ways that help them to orient their identities in relation to diasporic temporalities; however, their views are contested. These interactions demonstrate how experiences of digital diasporic intimacy are entangled with the intersections of one's identity, including gender, class, sexuality, and citizenship. My conceptualization of digital diasporic intimacy does not negate the existence of harmful interactions, but it also does not deny the existence of joy and connection because of them. Instead, these conversations, where people are interrogated and held accountable for their harmful views, is an intimate part of creating and mediating diasporic communities through conflict.

Digital Diasporic Intimacy and Diasporic Solidarity

Throughout this essay, I have illustrated how speculative remembering is used to produce digital diasporic intimacy. Combining autoethnography with analysis of viewers' comments, I explored how diasporic memories and imagination might be shaped by the photographs and how they simultaneously shape meanings of the photographs as a process of diasporic worlding. I also recognized that the Black community is not homogenous and acknowledged how speculative remembering is utilized differently depending on the person, their memories, what they perceive from the photographs, and their understanding of time.

While I have been attentive to the ways that kinship and temporality are enmeshed in this curation of intimacy by way of the digital visual medium, my personal engagement with the material had an impact on the research direction. This research emerged as I sought to articulate phenomena that were occurring on social media when I attempted to find diasporic community. This means that my own social media behaviors impact the sites of focus and images I encountered and explored. However, I propose that this further demonstrates the diasporic capacity of digital intimacies in this context. Overall, this essay argues that digital diasporic intimacy is affected by and experienced through time. I argue that speculative remembering underpins this form of intimate world-making, which is untethered from the constraints of Western, linear time, as it has the capacity to bring us together to celebrate lineage, honor Blackness and community, and invite us to grapple with diasporic difference in generative ways.

The two weeks that bridge together May and June of 2020 were especially difficult times to navigate the Internet, and especially as a Black person.[9] Within this time, the world watched as George Floyd was killed by an officer from the Minneapolis police department and ensued Black Lives Matter protests and riots erupted across cities in the U.S. and around the globe. Social media sites were flooded with digital ephemera focused on the protests, anti-Black racism, and memeable activism. This was all in the midst of a global pandemic that forced the world to rely on the Internet for work and our social well-being, a pandemic that disproportionately took the lives of Black folk living across the globe. Amid these periods of Internet trauma, logging out of social networking sites entirely can be a strategy of self-preservation and self-care. During these times, the proliferation of traumatic images constitutes depression, anxiety, and feelings of helplessness (Torres 2016); however, some people have used visual mediums as a source of healing, and @BlackArchives.co offered such a space.

During this difficult time, @BlackArchives.co became a space for the Black diaspora to discuss the contemporary climate and come together in solidarity. During the protests, the page largely remained unchanged and continued to do the work of reminding us of our histories and connecting us to one another through time. Viewers expressed gratitude for Cherlise's curational account and recognized the way that it operated as a digital healing space: "Thank u for introducing us to our past and sending us into the future with power and strength of our ancestors. Makes shit feel less lonely and very possible. Thank u soo much." This comment demonstrates how the curation of digital diasporic intimacy via @BlackArchives.co creates space for Black solidarity necessary for surviving these times. Another viewer situates the fictive kinships enabled by the platform as central to her healing:

> The joy these pictures bring to me are indescribable . . . its like looking at pictures of your love ones who you've never met yet you cherish them and hold them dear to your heart. Though the individuals in the photos are strangers to me, the connection I feel to their beautiful faces has been so comforting during these times. Thank you! From a Black girl coping in these trying times [pleading Face].

These comments make apparent that the imagined bonds created through digital diasporic intimacy can be returned to in times of trauma and healing. These intimate connections are the foundation for diasporic solidarity and the bedrock for digital socialities. Being connected to one another through image, through time, and on the Internet, creates the terrain for digital diasporic intimacy to grow. Through this practice of care, kinship, and accountability, the Black diaspora can create digital belonging, together.

keisha bruce (they/she) is a PhD candidate in Black studies at the University of Nottingham. They research and write about the intersection between Blackness, technology, intimacy, and visual culture. Their research has been funded by a Midlands3Cities doctoral training partnership. They can be reached at keisha.bruce@nottingham.ac.uk.

Notes

1. In African American Vernacular English (AAVE), "lit" refers to something that is exciting and energizing. "AF" is an abbreviation for "as fuck."
2. This Western construction of time relies on the concept of linearity, so it often prioritizes a progression narrative to understand the Black diaspora. This is explored in Michelle M. Wright's *Physics of Blackness* (2015).
3. Other examples of Black women, queer and nonbinary folk doing this type of work include Cecile Brown's Facebook page "Our Jamaica," where she gathers stories of the Jamaican diaspora; Karis Beaumont's Instagram account @BumpkinFiles, which visually explores Black British history and culture beyond London; and Marc Thompson and Jason Okundaye's @BlackandGayBackInTheDay, a digital archive honoring Black queer life in Britain.
4. Some of the comments featured in this essay refer to @BlackArchives.co as @BlvckVrchives. For accuracy, I will refer to the archive in accordance with how it was referred to in the original comments.
5. Where emojis are used in the comments, I will insert them textually between brackets. The names of emojis are taken from emojipedia.org.
6. In AAVE, "hella" is a word used for emphasis. In this example, the viewer is expressing their deep connection with the archival photographs.
7. It is commonplace in Black diasporic digital networks for users to refer to unknown Black children online as their nieces, nephews, and cousins. I use "digital auntie" here to signal that practice of imagining diasporic kinship online. It also builds upon Black diasporic worlding where the auntie figure signals intergenerational knowledge-making.
8. Black ratchet is an antirespectability practice. It describes behaviors and cultural expressions that sit outside of middle-class, heteronormative codes of respectability.
9. I am in no way suggesting that navigating the Internet is easy for Black folk outside of these periods of heightened trauma. Safiya Noble (2018), and Ruha Benjamin (2019) demonstrate how anti-Black racism is digitally mediated through technology and on the Internet.

Works Cited

Bailey, Moya. 2021. *Misogynoir Transformed: Black Women's Digital Resistance*. New York: New York University Press.

Basch, Linda, Nina Glick Schiller, and Cristina Szanton Blanc. 1994. *Nations Unbound: Transnational Projects, Postcolonial Predicaments, and Deterritorialized Nation States*. Newark: Gordon and Breach Science Publishers.

Benjamin, Ruha. 2019. *Race After Technology: Abolitionist Tools for the New Jim Code*. Cambridge: Polity.

Black Archives. 2021. "Black Archives Is a Gathering Place for Black Memory and Imaginations." https://www.blackarchives.co/about.

Blvck Vrchives. 2020. "A Curated Visual Journey Through History." Accessed July 6. http://www.blvckvrchives.com/.

Brinkerhoff, Jennifer M. 2009. *Digital Diasporas: Identity and Transnational Engagement*. New York: Cambridge University Press.

Brock, André. 2020. *Distributed Blackness: African American Cybercultures*. New York: New York University Press.

Brown, Jacqueline Nassy. 1998. "Black Liverpool, Black America, and the Gendering of Diasporic Space." *Cultural Anthropology* 13: 291–325.

bruce, keisha. 2022. "Black Women and the Curation of Digital Diasporic Intimacy." PhD diss., University of Nottingham.

Campt, Tina. 2002. "The Crowded Space of Diaspora: Intercultural Address and the Tensions of Diasporic Relation." *Radical History Review* 83: 94–113.

———. 2012. *Image Matters: Archive, Photography, and the African Diaspora in Europe*. Durham, NC: Duke University Press.

Carter, Rodney G. S. 2006. "Of Things Said and Unsaid: Power, Archival Silences, and Power in Silence." *Archivaria* 61: 215–33.

Ellison, Ralph. 1972. *Shadow and Act*. New York: Vintage Books.

El-Hadi, Nehal. 2015. "Radical Curation: Taking Care of Black Women's Narratives." *Model View Culture*, no. 21. May 19, 2015. https://modelviewculture.com/pieces/radical-curation-taking-care-of-black-womens-narratives.

Everett, Anna. 2009. *Digital Diaspora: A Race for Cyberspace*. New York: SUNY Press.

Farmer, Ashley. 2018. "Archiving While Black." *Black Perspectives*. July 8, 2018. https://www.aaihs.org/archiving-while-black/.

Gilroy, Paul. 1992. *There Ain't No Black in the Union Jack*. London: Routledge.

———. 1993. *The Black Atlantic: Modernity and Double Consciousness*. London: Verso.

Hall, Stuart. 1990. *Cultural Identity and Diaspora*. In *Identity: Community, Culture, Difference*, edited by Jonathan Rutherford, 222–37. London: Lawrence and Wishart

Hartman, Saidiya. 2008. "Venus in Two Acts." *Small Axe*, no. 26: 1–14.

Higginbotham, Evelyn Brooks. 1993. *Righteous Discontent: The Women's Movement in the Black Baptist Church, 1880–1920*. Cambridge, MA: Harvard University Press.

hooks, bell. 1995. *Art on My Mind: Visual Politics*. New York: The New Press.

Jackson, Laur. 2014. "Memes and Misogynoir." *The Awl*. August 28, 2014. https://www.theawl.com/2014/08/memes-and-misogynoir/.

Kalra, Virinder S., Raminder Kaur, and John Hutnyk. 2005. *Diaspora and Hybridity*. London: SAGE Publications.

Leurs, Koen, and Sandra Ponzanesi. 2011. "Mediated Crossroads: Youthful Digital Diasporas." *M/C Journal* 14, no. 2. https://doi.org/10.5204/mcj.324.

Lu, Jessica H, and Catherine Knight Steele. 2019. "'Joy Is Resistance': Cross-Platform Resilience and (Re)Invention of Black Oral Culture Online." *Information, Communication & Society* 22, no. 6: 823–37.

Macharia, Keguro. 2019. *Frottage: Frictions of Intimacy Across the Black Diaspora*. New York: New York University Press.

Morrison, Toni. 2019. *Mouth Full of Blood: Essays, Speeches, Meditations*. London: Chatto & Windus.

Noble, Safiya. 2018. *Algorithms of Oppression: How Search Engines Reinforce Racism*. New York: New York University Press.

Raiford, Leigh. 2009. "Photography and the Practices of Critical Black Memory." *History and Theory* 48, no. 4: 112–19.

Schwartz, Joan M., and Terry Cook. 2002. "Archives, Records, and Power: The Making of Modern Memory." *Archival Science* 2: 1–19.

Shelby, Tommie. 2002. "Foundations of Black Solidarity: Collective Identity or Common Oppression?" *Ethics* 112, no. 2: 231–66.

Sinanan, Jolynna. 2017. *Social Media in Trinidad: Values and Visibility*. London: UCL Press.

Sobande, Francesca. 2020. *The Digital Lives of Black Women in Britain*. London: Palgrave Macmillan.

Steele, Catherine Knight. 2016. "The Digital Barbershop: Blogs and Online Oral Culture Within the African American Community." *Social Media + Society* 2, no. 4: 1–10.

Torres, Monica. 2016. "Instant Replay: The Most Powerful Gifs Are More Than the Sum of Their Repeated Parts." *Real Life*, November 22, 2016. https://reallifemag.com/instant-replay/

Williams, Bianca C. 2018. *The Pursuit of Happiness: Black Women, Diasporic Dreams, and the Politics of Emotional Transnationalism*. Durham, NC: Duke University Press.

Wright, Michelle M. 2015. *Physics of Blackness: Beyond the Middle Passage Epistemology*. Minneapolis: University of Minnesota Press.

May I?

Jameka Hartley

If you were a well, may I
dip into your waters and drink you

If you were a pipe, may I
put you to my mouth and smoke you

If you were a car, may I
climb behind your wheel and drive you

If you were soil, may I
dig my hands in and till you

If you were mine, may I?

Jameka Hartley is an interdisciplinary Black feminist poet and scholar. She is an assistant professor of history, philosophy, and social sciences, and currently holds a Schiller Family Assistant Professorship in race in art and design at the Rhode Island School of Design. Her work centers on issues of Black motherhood, popular cultural representations of Black women, child to adult outcomes, and stigma. She can be reached at jhartley@risd.edu.

WSQ: Women's Studies Quarterly 50: 1 & 2 (Spring/Summer 2022) © 2022 by Jameka Hartley. All rights reserved.

PART VI. **LOVE CULTURE**

Embracing a "Big, Black Ass" at a "Tiny, Tiny Ass Desk": Lizzo's Affective Performance of Choric Self-Love

Myles W. Mason

Abstract: This essay analyzes Lizzo's 2019 Tiny Desk Concert as an affective performance of call-and-response that provides insight into pleasurable transgressions of hegemonic boundaries to performatively spread love. Lizzo invites a transgression of these norms, eliciting a response from her physical and digital audiences to embrace the fat, Black, feminine abject as a means of self-love. Turning to the Black communicative technique of call-and-response, the essay illustrates the contours of the choric self-love Lizzo establishes with her audiences that transformatively reimagines a self-love that centers Black women's joy. **Keywords:** affect, Black rhetorics; call-and-response; choric communication; digital media

If you can love my big, Black ass at this tiny, tiny little desk,
you can love yourself. . . .
Can I get one more "Hallelujah!"?
[audience: Hallelujah!]
Can I get a "Ya-Ya-Yee"?
[Ya-Ya-Yee]
Can I get a (growling) "Ya-Ya-Yee-ee-ee"?
[Ya-Ya-Yeee]
Whoo! My name is Lizzo, thank you!
                                        —Lizzo, *Tiny Desk Concert*

On August 5, 2019, National Public Radio (NPR) Music published the newest episode of the Tiny Desk Concert series to their YouTube channel featuring hip hop artist Lizzo (NPR Music 2019). The performance lasts just under seventeen minutes (16:59) and features three songs from Lizzo's acclaimed 2019 *Cuz I Love You* album: the title track, "Truth Hurts," and "Juice." Unlike most of her shows, Lizzo performed with a backing band,

WSQ: Women's Studies Quarterly 50: 1 & 2 (Spring/Summer 2022) © 2022 by Myles W. Mason. All rights reserved.

comprised of Devin Johnson (keyboard), Dana Hawkins (drums), Vernon Prout (bass), and Walter Williams (guitar), all of whom present as Black men (Thompson 2019). In just over two years, the video garnered over eleven million views, making it one of the "most popular" Tiny Desk Concerts (Tiny Desk hereafter) on the NPR Music YouTube channel (NPR Music n.d.). The affectivity of Lizzo's performance, "all charm, vibrant, and gracious" (Thompson 2019), quickly generated discussion among digital audiences, in the over twelve thousand comments on and over 338,000 reactions to the YouTube video (NPR Music 2019). Much of the discourse surrounding Lizzo's performance focuses on the above call-and-response quote and its themes: self-love and embracing her self-testimony as a means of spreading self-love for all through identification with her transgressions and joy (NPR Music 2019).

Born Melissa Viviane Jefferson, Lizzo notes her persona cohered in 2015 with the release of the single "My Skin." The song celebrated a "big, Black girl . . . saying, 'I'm in love with myself!,'" which took audiences aback (Coscarelli 2019). Solidifying this, Lizzo's 2019 *Cuz I Love You* album has been heralded as a testimony of self-love and body positivity, complete with the artist posing nude for the album cover (Rose 2019; Irby 2019). Because Lizzo is a fat, Black, woman, her emphatic embrace of her body is a violation of the hegemonic discourses that seek to abject her body. Black women's bodies are regularly recoiled from as a means of (racist) self-preservation in both physical and digital spaces (Lorde 2007, 147; Ahmed 2013; Silva 2019; Towns 2016), constraining Black women into impossible, immobilized social locations (Crenshaw 1989; Hull, Bell-Scott, and Smith 1993; Hartman 1997; Collins 2004; Camp 2002). And yet, Lizzo's performance generates an atmosphere of embrace, desire, and love between herself and the Tiny Desk audiences.

Tiny Desk's multimodal nature offers an excellent avenue to appreciate the dynamics of self-love more fully as a transformational act in popular culture. Desires for intimacy with artists guided the start of Tiny Desk, which offered "unadulterated and raw" performances, that built previously unavailable affective connections (Crockett 2016). However, Tiny Desk tends to privilege building these connections with white artists—hosting twenty-eight concerts before the first Black male performer was featured (Raphael Saadiq), and nearly twice that before a Black female performer was featured (Omara Portuondo, who is Afro-Cubana) (Boilen 2009; Contreras 2010). Further, like Lizzo's being "alien" to everything around her (Thompson 2019), Black artists are regularly regarded as misfitting to the space of Tiny Desk in any number of ways (Boilen 2009, 2015; Thompson 2013; Contreras 2010). And yet, in the face of this perceived misfitting, the most popular and well-received Tiny Desk performances are from Black and other nonwhite artists (NPR Music n.d.). Tiny Desk and the popularity of performances by Black artists illustrates the affective potential in transgressing the hegemonic performances of abjection. In other words, Lizzo's permeation of the physical and digital NPR spaces resists the fat antagonism and misogynoir within scenarios of abjection. The Tiny Desk audiences' embrace of Lizzo illustrates the affective investments at play as audiences respond to Lizzo's call for self-love and the capacity of this collective affect to rupture oppressive norms.

This essay outlines the contours of a choric self-love, which rest upon *performances of embrace* that unseat the raced and gendered hierarchies of abjection. An embrace illustrates the pleasurable potential of transgressing hegemonic norms of embodiment and space. Thus, self-love, like abjection, is always already contextually dependent on the specific spaces in which bodies and objects are co-present with one another. The affective investments of protecting the self from the abject are troubled in the dynamics of choric self-love. Embracing the abject deploys a "powerful force that challenges and resists domination" and offers new possibilities for theorizations of self-love that centralize Black women (hooks 1989, 26; 2001; Collins 2004). Lizzo's embrace of her "big, Black ass" within the confines of the "tiny, tiny ass desk" operate as a call for the audience's response of mirroring this embrace from which they can love themselves.

A Tiny, Tiny Ass Desk: Bodies and Objects *in situ*
Within the spatial turn of women's and feminist studies, spaces can be thought of as constellations of relations between objects and bodies that actors orient themselves toward (Beebe, Davis, and Gleadle 2012; Ahmed 2006; Massey 2013). The copresence of various objects and bodies produces felt boundaries of self and Other (Ahmed 2006, 54; Kristeva 1982). The abject emerges from within the constitutive spaces between bodies and objects as they orient toward one another (Ahmed 2013; 2006). What is abject is not necessarily universal but contextually contingent upon the co-present bodies and objects. The felt entanglements of bodies and objects index "a multi-faceted negotiation of power" as certain bodies

find themselves misfitting to the spaces they inhabit (Pezzullo 2003, 349; Garland-Thomson 2011). Non-normative bodies, or those bodies that fail the norms of the given space, experience discrepancies in their capacity to act—the body and the objects it encounters are misfitting to one another (Garland-Thomson 2011). Thus, as Raka Shome argues, space is a technology of power that operates through "marking off space" as for certain bodies, objects also become a means of "containing bodies" by misaligning non-normative bodies (Shome 2003, 47; Ahmed 2006). In other words, our embodiment is sensed through the *in situ* relations of space.

The norms of space facilitate the extension of bodies that align within the instituted boundaries while presenting obstacles for marginalized actors. Linda McDowell and Joanne Sharp (1997) note scholarship has recognized the "more or less appropriate, more or less socially sanctioned in particular spaces and at different times" has nuanced the "complexity . . . of positionality and contextual nature" of embodiment (2). Further, as Kathryne Beebe, Angela Davis, and Kathryn Gleadle (2012) illustrate through their reading of Henri Lefebvre, the practice of space extends to the objects that become part and parcel to the lived experience of various social actors. The spatial dynamics of embodiment require attention to the co-present objects and bodies, which influence the experiences of space by constraining or extending bodies as they orient within contextual, contingent relations.

As *in situ* relations facilitate the actions of body, the boundary between the two begin to blur, only becoming noticeable again when one fails the other (Ahmed 2006, 47–49). The failure to extend through a space produces a felt border. The relationality of fat to nonfat, Black to non-Black, and woman to nonwoman constitutes borders between bodies of these categories, to abject the bodies that fail hegemonic norms (David and Cruz 2018; Schalk 2013; Hartman 1997). Samantha Dawn Schalk (2013) notes that Black and/or fat bodies are constituted "as nonnormative, sometimes excessively so," and it is this excess that marks them as disgusting or unbeautiful (David and Cruz 2018; Havlin and Báez 2018; Strings, 2015, 2020). The relationality of subjection animates constitutions of whiteness, which according to Saidiya Hartman (1997) only sustains itself through the abjection of Blackness and other colonized subjectivities. Armond Towns (2016) pointedly argues that contemporary white space is built upon the specific immobilization of Black women, which is evidenced by their treatment in shared digital and physical space. Black women's bodies, like Lizzo's, are not typically afforded the space to extend, being constantly placed in misfitting contexts that seek to render them abject.

As mentioned above, Lizzo performed with a backing band rather than her usual accompaniment by a DJ—typically her friend and oft-collaborator Sophia Eris, another Black woman hip hop artist. At the behest of producer Bob Boilen, four Black male-presenting artists were instead assembled within the space between the bookshelves and eponymous tiny desk, which is Boilen's (Thompson 2019). This immediately impressed upon the actions of two separate Black women, creating a boundary to the space for one (Eris) and constraining how another (Lizzo) was allowed to inhabit the space. The desires of white male actors and primarily white physical audiences for normative conceptions of a concert or music were placed before options to reorient the space to fit the Black woman's desires and standards. Lizzo's performance was still expert but was not how she would have typically staged her set, as she was forced to align within the desires of the space. The band only met Lizzo at sound check a couple hours before the Tiny Desk recording, and yet the group performed with a sense of community, with Lizzo calling out to multiple members of the band and them responding, or vice versa. Their co-present bodies facilitated the actions demanded of the performance in a space that had already created multiple borders against Lizzo's body.

The most referenced border throughout the performance is the Tiny Desk's abjection of Lizzo's body, physically preventing her from extending to fit with the desk. At least seven times throughout the performance, Lizzo references the *tinyness* of the desk (NPR Music 2019). A boundary is produced as Lizzo's body fails to align with a proximate object, the desk (Ahmed 2006). In the interlude before "Juice," which is heralded as her anthem of body positivity, Lizzo directly articulates her misfitting to the desk. She says:

> So here we are, I got the final song for yo' (beat) ass (beat) at this tiny, tiny little ass desk. [Audience whoops] This desk is so damn small (laughs) *my thigh barely fit underneath it* (laughs) but we're so happy to be here. (my emphasis, NPR Music 2019)

Lizzo's misalignment with the objects around her prevents her from using the desk as intended. The relationality of objects and Lizzo's body, as well as the band members' bodies, produce a boundary between her and the space, seeking to constrain her actions to hegemonic desires. However, Lizzo subverts the space into one of joyous embrace. Constituting this abjection as joyous presents the discursive space needed to resist hegemonic norms of space—the space needed to embrace the abject.

A Big, Black Ass: Embracing the Abject as Self-Love

Lizzo transgresses the hegemonic discourses and norms of space through joyous performances of embrace that unseat the raced and gendered politics of recoil and extension. Recoiling from bodies and/or otherwise rendering them abject works to "[re]produce the spatial and material terrain" of marginalization and facilitate the extension of normative bodies (Havlin and Báez 2018, 18; Ahmed 2006; 2013). Stephanie Camp's (2002) work argues bondspeople "slip[ping] 'way" from plantations to the "rival geographies" of outlaw parties as a means of "creat[ing] space and time to celebrate and enjoy their bodies as important personal and political entities" (572). Transgressing the boundaries and measures of containment to party, Camp (2002) illustrates tactical means of everyday resistance to the white male supremacist hierarchies of oppression. Lizzo mirrors these transgressions to "take pleasure in [her] own bod[y]" by embracing her "abject" qualities (Camp 2002, 534). Embracing necessitates an undoing of the surfaces abjection constitutes permeating the boundaries of self and abject. When bodies embrace, they become so "entwine[d], encircle[d], . . . enclose[d]," they are indistinguishable from one another (Oxford English Dictionary n.d.). When the abject body becomes the central embrace of self-love, actors resist the corrupt desires of self-preservation to blur the boundaries of self and Other. Within the spaces of this blurring, bodies are forced to become entwined with what is fundamental for renegotiations of love. Rather than being recoiled from, the fat, Black, feminine body becomes central to the embrace, permeating the boundaries of self and O/other.

The perceived unruliness of fat, Black, feminine bodies causes them to fail various societal norms and expectations of beauty and comportment, but this same unruliness also presents the potential for desire (David and Cruz 2018; Schalk 2013; hooks 2001; Collins 2004). Sabrina Strings (2015; 2020) argues that fat, Black feminine bodies have been constituted as "social dead weight" through medical discourses of sexual disease and obesity. These discourses claim fat, Black feminine bodies must be avoided to maintain the safety of those around them, as they threaten the sanctity of bodily hygiene and national purity (Strings 2015; 2020). Just as Saartjie

Baartman's exploitation as Venus Hottentot has been continually positioned within the liminal space of disgusting and desirous (Hobson 2018; Gentles-Peart 2018), Lizzo also troubles facile distinctions of abjection by positioning her "excessive body" as desirous.

Lizzo's "Juice" exemplifies a desirous yet abject body that loves itself. This self-love is shorthanded to "juice," which is "kinda freaky . . . spiritual and special. I think—um—I think it's Black pussy [laughs]," Lizzo says (Coscarelli 2019). Lizzo's laughing after linking juice to Black pussy illustrates a tactic of joyous self-love. In an episode of the *New York Times'* "Diary of a Song" YouTube series, Lizzo, along with the writer and the producer of the track, explain how the song was made and the background of the lyrics. Lizzo explains a line in the prechorus, "I was born like this, don't even gotta try," as meaning "I love me at—for me no matter what make up I have on, what weave I got on, whether I got my lash extensions on or not" (Coscarelli 2019). Here, self-love is positioned as outside the valuations of standard beauty practices and centers the first-person Black woman in its formulation (Phillips 2015; David and Cruz 2018). This self-love is directly centered on, per Lizzo, Black pussy, which has been the site of varied historic, white supremacist violence (Camp 2002). However, the *I* who loves their self is a resistive form of "personal agency" that speaks back to "historical silences and targeted violence" that have rendered Black women abject (Phillips 2015, 36; Strings 2020; Camp 2002).

Throughout the Tiny Desk performance, Lizzo physically embraces her fat, Black feminine body, illustrating the possibilities of pleasure if her audience mirrors her actions. Lizzo hugs her arms around her body and smiles as the audience cheers for a sustained ten seconds after "Truth Hurts" (NPR Music 2019). In this action, Lizzo is marking her abject body as desirous. The abject is never meant to be loved; indeed, we are taught to disdain the abject for our own sake. Centering Black women at the heart of self-love turns the "corrupt" distancing of the abject—I love myself because *I'm not them*—to an entangling "mixture of bodies" that needs the abject—I love myself because *I love them* (Pough 2016; Silva 2019; Deleuze 1978). Lizzo embodies the utmost abject within the space: sweating, fat, Black, hysterical. However, through rooting herself at the center of self-love through her juiciness and physical embrace, Lizzo constitutes abject self as the crux of self-love.

Negotiations of *in situ* bodies are integral to the scenarios of abjection and reimagining them. Camp's (2002) arguments center analyses of space, embodiment, and subjection to understand how Black actors can resist fore-gone conclusions of oppressive logics. Actors must adapt the structured plotlines of recoiling from the abject and constructing boundaries that thwart the extension of non-normative bodies to new ends of embracing the abject a pleasurable transgression (Taylor 2003; Ahmed 2006). The threat of the abject is its potential to leave its trace upon its abjectors (Kristeva 1982; Ahmed 2013); thus, to take seriously the possibilities of challenge, critique, and recreation of norms (hooks 1989; Pough 2016; Collins 2004), we must resist hegemonic urges to reject the abject. The affective investments needed for an embrace of the abject do not necessar-ily require a reconciliation of the disgusting; rather, we desire the abject's capacity to undo bodily boundaries because we want it to leave its trace (Ahmed 2013). Hegemonic scenarios of abjection would constitute Lizzo's "flashing flabby brown skin onstage" as repulsive, pushing her away from normative, desirous bodies (David and Cruz 2018, 30). However, the inven-tional space constituted through these structured plots create the possibilities of embracing Lizzo as a means of solidarity and rethinking self-love for all.

Lizzo's juicy theorizations of self-love center the abject, but they hold radical potential to challenge hegemonic recoils by *embracing* the abject and drawing upon an honored Black rhetorical tradition of call-and-response. Hegemonic scenarios of abjection would lead us to believe the audience would recoil from Lizzo, whether due to her Blackness, her fatness, or her excessive femininity, constituting her as disgusting; however, they embrace her. Lizzo's own self-love operates as a call the audience responds to.

Can I Get a Ya-Ya-Yee: Call-and-Response as Choric Self-Love

Twenty-six seconds into the Tiny Desk Concert recording, Lizzo solicits a response from the obliging audience by asking, "Can I get an 'Amen'?" (NPR Music, 2019). The rhetorical technique of call-and-response is rooted in the traditions of Black communication and African cosmology aimed at fostering a sense of collective identity (Daniel and Smitherman 1976; Alke-bulan 2014). Further, call-and-response operates as a conductor of affective attachments to mobilize participants to various ends (Alkebulan 2014; Rand 2014). Throughout her performance, Lizzo issues a total of twenty-eight calls for response, which facilitates building a sense of unity and harmony from which the audience can love themselves.

The traditions of call-and-response are derived from African traditions and proliferate diasporic Black cultures (Alkebulan 2014; Daniel and Smitherman 1976; Keegan 2009). Jack L. Daniel and Geneva Smitherman (1976) argue call-and-response constitutes "an interactive network" that requires the "active participation of all" to resist hierarchies of oppression (33). Adisa A. Alkebulan (2014) further underscores the concept of *nommo*, or performative life-force that seeks and constitutes spiritual harmony, within call-and-response to illustrate the affirming potential of collective affects. Call-and-response confirms co-presence with other bodies and emphasizes communality over individuality (Daniel and Smitherman 1976). Within the Black diaspora borne of the Atlantic Slave Trade, call-and-response was appropriated by white captors to ensure a "consistency to fieldwork" (Keegan 2009, 10). However, the roots of call-and-response built a strong(er) sense of community among enslaved Black folks, which resisted some of the alienation slavery insists upon (Daniel and Smitherman 1976; Keegan 2009; Hartman 1997; Camp 2002). The "embodi[ment of] communality" achieved through call-and-response allows for the constitution of collective affective attachments that transgress hegemonic hierarchies (Daniel and Smitherman 1976, 34; Camp 2002).

Love, as a concept, necessitates an intentional, joyous relationality between actors (hooks 2001; Utley 2010; Butler 2011). bell hooks notes that love is not just a connective relation but also a set of practices and affective attachments that can be life-affirming (2001, xvii, 4–5). However, the discourses of love often abject Black women's bodies and/or present "new forms of domination and forced submission as opposed to self-actualization," forestalling the transformative powers of love hooks (and others) outlines (Utley 2010, 292; hooks 2001).

As actors transgress the boundaries constructed around loving Black women, they reimagine love through the politics of embracing the abject and create more welcoming spaces for marginalized bodies (Hester and Squires 2018; Pough 2016; Camp 2002). Love that centers Black women is a "rebellious" affective force that forefronts a sense of communality that "enhances life's joy" (Utley 2010, 292; hooks 2001, 140; Collins 2004).

Call-and-response and the unity it enacts resists oppressive hierarchies to emphasize the common good, wherein what affects one person affects the entire community (Daniel and Smitherman 1976). Abjection operates as a hierarchy "with those on the bottom being disadvantaged by the full array of factors, up to the very top [to] . . . those who are not disadvantaged in any way" (Crenshaw 1989, 152). Bodies at the top of this hierarchy conform to what Audre Lorde outlines as the mythic norm—white, cisgender, heterosexual, able-bodied, neurotypical, wealthy, Christian man—and perform oppressive scenarios of recoil to preserve their selves from the abject (Lorde 2007, 115–16; Ahmed 2006; Silva 2019). However, call-and-response offers the discursive space wherein the "I" forms synergistic affective attachments with the "we" (Daniel and Smitherman 1976). These collective affects of harmony lend efficacy to the caller's message among the respondents (Alkebulan 2014). In other words, call-and-response rearticulates the oppressive impulses of abjection to blur boundaries of self and Other for the pleasurable transgression of hegemonic norms.

I argue Lizzo's use of call-and-response performs a choric self-love wherein self-love becomes a "collectivity [of] synchronized action, [that] does not assume similarity or uniformity of identity" (Rand 2014, 30). The heterogeneity of participants enhances the affective potential of the call-and-response, as community and solidarity are built across lines of difference (Rand 2014, 41). Within this collectivity, choric performance envelopes subject in a joyous affective state that drives the welfare of the communal whole (Alkebulan 2014; Nelson 2000; Daniel and Smitherman 1976; Rand 2014). Lizzo's performance builds the rapport of call-and-response throughout the performance, which facilitates the final call for the audience to love themselves because they already love her. The co-present physical audience readily accepts Lizzo's calls, as evidenced by this essay's epigraph and other quoted moments from the performance; but Tiny Desk performances present inroads to understanding the digital possibilities of call-and-response within choric self-love.

Both call-and-response and digital media hold the power to trouble distinctions of space and time (Daniel and Smitherman 1976; Rand 2014; Towns 2016; Pezzullo and de Onís 2017), meaning digital viewers of Lizzo's Tiny Desk performance can still feel as if they are co-present at the time of filming. Further, digital audiences can respond to Lizzo's calls just as her physically co-present audience did. To illustrate, I focus on the comments to the YouTube video of Lizzo's Tiny Desk performance. As mentioned above, there are over twelve thousand individual comments to this video, which are arranged to feature those with the most engagement via likes and replies. Digital actors answer Lizzo's explicit calls for "Hallelujah"s, "Amen"s, and even one response to "Ya-ya-[y]ee" (NPR Music 2019); however, they also respond to the implicit calls to embrace Lizzo's abject qualities.

Lizzo's presence is hard to miss, where it be due to her "gale force . . . voice" or being unnecessarily "dressed to the nines" in a "stunning . . . bright orange dress" with matching nails and earrings (Thompson 2019; NPR 2019). Camp (2002) notes that dressing in bright colors and matching accessories are important factors while embodying rival geographies of pleasure for Black women. However, the color orange often issues calls of emergency and caution, positioning Lizzo as a threatening or dangerous presence. Many commenters (such as Corderral Lewis, ThinWhiteAxe, and Candace S.) liked Lizzo's styling because it is a natural fit or complement to Lizzo's complexion, and Kailey Ryan even asserted, "Lizzo invented the color orange" (NPR Music 2019). The perceived naturalness of articulating Lizzo's fat, Black body to danger illustrates the ease with which hegemonic actors can perform routine scenarios of abjection (Strings 2015; 2020). Detracting, or "troll," comments (such as the ones by eatc12 and Phill Helbig) regularly compare Lizzo and her styling to the sun due to her size (NPR Music 2019); one commenter (Asron 12) cluing us in that "the joke is that she's very overweight" (NPR Music 2019). In rendering Lizzo abject due to her size, commenters like Asron 12 perform this scenario as expected by recoiling. Importantly, though, comments rendering Lizzo abject are mostly *in response to* positive comments. Put differently, comments that dissent from or do not complete the call-and-response of choric self-love are seeking to disrupt the collective embrace being performed.

This same strategy of disrupting the embrace of Lizzo also emerges in relation to her sweating during her performance of "Truth Hurts." White spaces often use the sensorial, such as fear or smell, to abject nonwhite bodies from shared space (Lorde 2007; Ahmed 2013; Strings 2015; 2020). Racialized and fattened tropes of smell are played into in a comment thread on the video. Commenter Starri'a embraces Lizzo because she "smells like shea butter and vanilla," garnering over 6,100 likes. However, a now deleted racist reply (summarized by Starri'a) contradicted this by insinuating "heavier set people . . . only smell like sweat," and a still-posted comment (Blue&Green) extends this by saying "smells like diabetes more like" (NPR Music 2019). In the face of an embrace of Lizzo's abject body, hegemonic actors attempt to reassert the recoil from her abject qualities of race and fatness (David and Cruz 2018; Gentles-Peart 2018; Schalk 2013). Ronald Coleman concisely asserts detractors "can't handle that much blackalicious black queen," gesturing to their inability to answer Lizzo's calls for embrace (NPR Music 2019).

Digital audiences complete the performance of call-and-response in their embrace of Lizzo, submitting to the collective joy and harmony of choric self-love. La Guardia Gross and Thera Webster commented that Lizzo's "energy, . . . passion, . . . [and] connection to the audience" serves as a "balm to all the sadness and negative messages out there" (NPR Music 2019). Much like a balm that seeps into the skin, blurring the boundaries of self and not-self, the performance "cures" the dis/eases of the digital audience (see comments by Katie Jus-Katie, Maddy Street, and Roxanne Water) (NPR Music 2019). In the collective affect built through call-and-response, digital audiences are incorporated into the harmonious community that resists hierarchies of abjection. This incorporation, in turn, constitutes inventive ways of feeling and understanding self-love that troubles the "stigmatiz[ation of] Black women as unworthy of love" (Collins 2004, 250). Rather, Black women become central to the constructions of love: and it is through loving *Lizzo* that audiences can love *themselves*. In responding to Lizzo's calls of "Can I get a ya-ya-yee?" the audience constitutes a choric collective of diverse bodies that are performing a unifying embrace.

Conclusion

Self-love is not naive; it cannot be. Whether corrupt—as in the case of the recoiling racist body—or transformational—the choric embrace of an audience—self-love is relational and deeply concerned with boundaries (Silva 2019; Lorde 2007; hooks 2001; Rand 2014). To be transformational or even healing (see Miller qtd. in Butler 2011), love must transgress hegemonic boundaries of oppression to offer abject subjects liberatory potential (Utley 2010, 304–5). The specific embrace of Black women offers a radical reimagining of self-love that resists the instantiated hierarchies of abjection to create a more harmonious world (Alkebulan 2014; hooks 2001; Hester and Squires 2018). This essay has analyzed Lizzo's Tiny Desk Concert performance to illustrate the possibilities of this embrace of the abject body to reimagine the norms of self-love.

In her reaction video to Lizzo's *Cuz I Love You* album, fat, Black woman YouTuber Maya Tomlin, known as KioshiWarrior, says, "This self-love stuff is so hard . . . [but] I'm finally ready to embrace *myself* and seeing [Lizzo] . . . love herself so outwardly and so proudly, is just—it's *healing*, bruh" (KioshiWarrior 2019). Lizzo's performances of self-love—just as the NPR's audience's choric love of Lizzo—theorizes a self-love that necessitates the embrace of Black women. Embracing the abject adapts contextual scenarios of abjection to new ends that seek the blurring of bodily boundaries between self and Other. Lizzo facilitates building this collective affect through the use of call-and-response, which incorporates speakers and audiences into a single, though heterogenous, whole (Daniel and Smitherman 1976; Rand 2014). The communal embrace desires the entanglement of self and abject because it ultimately leads to a love of the self. This self-love illustrates the pleasurable potentials of transgressing hegemonic spaces.

NPR's Tiny Desk series' impetus as a desire of physical intimacy between artists and NPR audiences and ancillary digital audiences offers an archive of the affective dynamics of physically and digitally co-present bodies that can respond to one another's calls. Through analyzing Lizzo's Tiny Desk Concert, I have traced how both digital and physical audiences' affective attachments to Lizzo have been because of her transgressions of hegemonic spaces. She is a fat, Black woman, crying out of love and sweating from a performance at a constraining desk, and yet she is embraced by audiences. What remains to be explored are the affective shifts of o/Other bodies—of Indigenous bodies, of queer/quare bodies, of dis/abled bodies, of migrant bodies—in the spaces of the NPR Tiny Desk. As hegemonic discourses seek to constrain non-normative bodies through various strategies, transgressions of these discourses, such as a playful call-and-response for self-love, become the affective grounds upon which community across intersectional identities of abjection may be reimagined.

Myles W. Mason is a postdoctoral fellow at the University of Colorado, Boulder, in the Department of Communication. They can be reached at myles.mason@colorado.edu.

Works Cited

Ahmed, Sara. 2006. *Queer Phenomenology: Orientations, Objects, Others*. Durham: Duke University Press.

———. 2013. *The Cultural Politics of Emotion*. New York: Routledge.

Alkebulan, Adisa A. 2014. "The Spiritual Essence of African American Rhetoric." In *Understanding African American Rhetoric: Classical Origins to Contemporary Innovations*, 23–40. New York: Routledge.

Beebe, Kathryne, Angela Davis, and Kathryn Gleadle. 2012. "Introduction: Space, Place and Gendered Identities: Feminist History and the Spatial Turn." *Women's History Review* 21, no. 4: 523–32.

Boilen, Bob. 2009. "Raphael Saadiq: Tiny Desk Concert." *NPR*, September 28,

2009. https://www.npr.org/2009/09/28/113214222/raphael-saadiq-tiny-desk-concert.

———. 2015. "Andra Day: Tiny Desk Concert." *NPR*, October 13, 2015. https://www.npr.org/2015/10/13/448289941/andra-day-tiny-desk-concert.

Butler, Judith. 2011. "Response: Performative Reflections on Love and Commitment." *Women's Studies Quarterly* 39, no. 1/2: 236–39.

Camp, Stephanie M. H. 2002. "The Pleasures of Resistance: Enslaved Women and Body Politics in the Plantation South, 1830–1861." *The Journal of Southern History* 68, no. 3: 533–72.

Collins, Patricia Hill. 2004. *Black Sexual Politics: African Americans, Gender, and the New Racism*. New York: Routledge.

Contreras, Felix. 2010. "Omara Portuondo: Tiny Desk Concert." *NPR*, March 8, 2010. https://www.npr.org/2010/03/08/124284177/omara-portuondo-tiny-desk-concert.

Coscarelli, Joe. 2019. "Watch Lizzo Make 'Juice,' a Pop Anthem as Irresistible as She Is." *New York Times*, April 23, 2019. https://www.nytimes.com/2019/04/23/arts/music/lizzo-juice.html.

Crenshaw, Kimberlé. 1989. "Demarginalizing the Intersection of Race and Sex: A Black Feminist Critique of Antidiscrimination Doctrine, Feminist Theory and Antiracist Politics." *University of Chicago Legal Forum* 1989: 139–68.

Crockett, Zachary. 2016. "Tiny Desk: How NPR's Intimate Concert Series Earned a Cult Following." *Vox*, November 21, 2016. https://www.vox.com/culture/2016/11/21/13550754/npr-tiny-desk-concert.

Daniel, Jack L., and Geneva Smitherman. 1976. "How I Got Over: Communication Dynamics in the Black Community." *Quarterly Journal of Speech* 62, no. 1: 26.

David, Emmanuel, and Christian Joy P. Cruz. 2018. "Big, Bakla, and Beautiful: Transformations on a Manila Pageant Stage." *WSQ: Women's Studies Quarterly* 46, no. 1: 29–45.

Deleuze, Gilles. 1978. "Cours Vincennes." Translated by Timothy S. Murphy. *WebDeleuze*. https://www.webdeleuze.com/textes/14.

Garland-Thomson, Rosemarie. 2011. "Misfits: A Feminist Materialist Disability Concept." *Hypatia* 26, no. 3: 591–609.

Gentles-Peart, Kamille. 2018. "Controlling Beauty Ideals: Caribbean Women, Thick Bodies, and White Supremacist Discourse." *WSQ: Women's Studies Quarterly* 46, no. 1: 199–214.

Hartman, Saidiya V. 1997. *Scenes of Subjection: Terror, Slavery, and Self-Making in Nineteenth-Century America*. New York: Oxford University Press.

Havlin, Natalie, and Jillian M. Báez. 2018. "Introduction: Revisiting Beauty." *WSQ: Women's Studies Quarterly* 46, no. 1–2: 13–24.

Hester, Scarlett L., and Catherine R. Squires. 2018. "Who Are We Working For? Recentering Black Feminism." *Communication and Critical/Cultural Studies* 15, no. 4: 343–8.

Hobson, Janell. 2018. "Remnants of Venus: Signifying Black Beauty and Sexuality." *WSQ: Women's Studies Quarterly* 46, no. 1–2: 105–20. https://doi.org/10.1353/wsq.2018.0015.

hooks, bell. 1989. *Talking Back: Thinking Feminist, Thinking Black.* Toronto: Between the Lines.

———. 2001. *All About Love: New Visions.* New York.

Hull, Akasha, Patricia Bell-Scott, and Barbara Smith, eds. 1993. *All the Women Are White, All the Blacks Are Men: But Some of Us Are Brave.* New York: The Feminist Press at CUNY.

Irby, Samantha. 2019. "Lizzo: *TIME*'s Entertainer of the Year 2019." *TIME*, December 2019. https://time.com/entertainer-of-the-year-2019-lizzo/.

Keegan, Nathan. 2009. "Call-and-Response: An Ancient Linguistic Device Surfaces in Usher's 'Love in This Club.'" *Elements* 5, no. 2.

KioshiWarrior. 2019. "LIZZO: CUZ I LOVE YOU (ALBUM REACTION)." YouTube. https://www.youtube.com/watch?v=ZFLDsqSk2Zc.

Kristeva, Julia. 1982. *Powers of Horror: An Essay on Abjection.* Translated by Leon Roudiez. Reprint, New York: Columbia University Press.

Lorde, Audre. 2007. *Sister Outsider: Essays and Speeches.* Berkeley: Crossing Press.

Massey, Doreen. 2013. *Space, Place and Gender.* John Wiley & Sons.

McDowell, Linda, and Joanne Sharp, eds. 1997. "Introduction." In *Space, Gender, Knowledge: Feminist Readings.* New York: Routledge.

Nelson, Stephanie. 2000. "Choric Communication: The Case of a Togolese Women's Musical Organization." *Text and Performance Quarterly* 20, no. 3: 268–89.

NPR Music. 2019. "Lizzo: NPR Music Tiny Desk Concert." YouTube. NPR Tiny Desk Concert. Washington, D.C. https://www.youtube.com/watch?v=DFiLdByWIDY.

"———." n.d. *YouTube.* Accessed December 11, 2019. https://www.youtube.com/channel/UC4eYXhJI4-7wSWc8UNRwD4A.

Oxford English Dictionary. Oxford University Press. Accessed December 31, 2020. http://www.oed.com/view/Entry/60979.

Pezzullo, Phaedra C. 2003. "Resisting 'National Breast Cancer Awareness Month': The Rhetoric of Counterpublics and Their Cultural Performances." *Quarterly Journal of Speech* 89, no. 4: 345–65.

Pezzullo, Phaedra C., and Catalina M. de Onís. 2017. "Rethinking Rhetorical Field Methods on a Precarious Planet." *Communication Monographs* 85, no. 1: 1–20.

Phillips, Mary. 2015. "The Power of the First-Person Narrative: Ericka Huggins and the Black Panther Party." *WSQ: Women's Studies Quarterly* 43, no. 3: 33–51.

Pough, Gwendolyn D. 2016. "Do the Ladies Run This . . . ? Some Thoughts on Hip-Hop Feminism." In *Catching a Wave: Reclaiming Feminism for the 21st Century*, edited by Rory Dicker and Alison Piepmeier. Boston: Northeastern University Press.

Rand, Erin J. 2014. "'What One Voice Can Do': Civic Pedagogy and Choric Collectivity at Camp Courage." *Text and Performance Quarterly* 34, no. 1: 28–51.

Rose, Francesca. 2019. "Review: A Lesson in Self-Love, by Lizzo's 'Cuz I Love You.'" *Atwood Magazine*, April 29, 2019. https://atwoodmagazine.com/lzly-lizzo-cuz-i-love-you-album-review/.

Schalk, Samantha Dawn. 2013. "Coming to Claim Crip: Disidentification with/in Disability Studies." *Disability Studies Quarterly* 33, no. 2.

Shome, Raka. 2003. "Space Matters: The Power and Practice of Space." *Communication Theory* 13, no. 1: 39–56.

Silva, Grant J. 2019. "Racism as Self-Love." *Radical Philosophy Review* 22, no. 1: 85–112.

Strings, Sabrina. 2015. "Obese Black Women as 'Social Dead Weight': Reinventing the 'Diseased Black Woman.'" *Signs* 41, no. 1: 107–30.

———. 2020. "Fat as a Floating Signifier: Race, Weight, and Femininity in the National Imaginary." In *The Oxford Handbook of the Sociology of Body and Embodiment*, edited by Natalie Boero and Katherine Mason, 143–63. New York: Oxford University Press.

Taylor, Diana. 2003. *The Archive and the Repertoire: Performing Cultural Memory in the Americas*. Durham, NC: Duke University Press.

Thompson, Stephen. 2013. "John Legend: Tiny Desk Concert." *NPR.Org*. November 16, 2013. https://www.npr.org/2013/11/16/245218626/john-legend-tiny-desk-concert.

———. 2019. "Lizzo: Tiny Desk Concert." *NPR*. July 29, 2019. https://www.npr.org/2019/07/29/732097345/lizzo-tiny-desk-concert.

Towns, Armond R. 2016. "Geographies of Pain: #SayHerName and the Fear of Black Women's Mobility." *Women's Studies in Communication* 39, no. 2: 122–26.

Utley, Ebony A. 2010. "'I Used to Love Him': Exploring the Miseducation About Black Love and Sex." *Critical Studies in Media Communication* 27, no. 3: 291–308.

"Black Love Is a Saving Grace": An Interview with the *Black Love* Cover Artist, Lennox Commissiong

Rashida L. Harrison and Lennox Commissiong

This *Women's Studies Quarterly* (*WSQ*) special issue on *Black Love* features a photo of the artwork entitled *Be Still My Heart*. This vibrant piece was created by artist Lennox Commissiong, who graciously allowed the editors to use it as a frame for the issue.[1] He is a self-taught artist, committed to translating elements of Black lives and experiences, creating pieces of influential people of African descent who refuse to bend to the demands of "societal power structures" (Commissiong 2018). Born in St. Vincent, Commissiong, who is local to New York City, moved to Brooklyn when he was fourteen. His early experiences included joining the military, which helped shape his view of the world. He would later graduate from Brooklyn College with a degree that led to a career in IT.[2] Commissiong, however, understood that he was an artist and was committed to enhancing his natural abilities as an adult. He shared that he did not take a linear route on his journey, having his first show opening in 2014. The passion and *love* for being a conduit, and the strife to be a great artist, is what drives Lennox Commissiong.

During our interview, I learned that Commissiong is motivated by a love for the creative process, is dedicated to his craft, and works daily. He has a distinct appreciation for color in his artwork, which he gained while perfecting a signature technique. Commissiong utilizes pointillism for the cover piece, *Be Still My Heart,* as well as the several pieces mentioned in the interview. Pointillism is considered a Neo-Impressionist technique that involves using tiny dots of pure or unmixed colors to craft images (Sothebys 2018).[3] Commissiong's approach to pointillism, one where he uses a knife to cut tiny pieces of Color-aid paper, also has a politic. He declares, "My homage in small dots of color represents the many lives they have touched across

WSQ: Women's Studies Quarterly 50: 1 & 2 (Spring/Summer 2022) © 2022 by Rashida L. Harrison and Lennox Commissiong. All rights reserved.

various races and cultures and their political legacies (2018).[4] In this quote, he refers to the portraits of figures like Bob Marley, Muhammad Ali, and Thelonious Monk. The Monk piece entitled *Evidence* was a proud creation that Commissiong was asked to contribute for the 2017 Centennial, created utilizing the technique. He's extrapolating important meaning in his method and creates art that he hopes allows "the viewer to experience the sensation of a visual treasure hunt."[5]

Ultimately, *Be Still My Heart* was created with Valentine's Day in mind, and when Commissiong was made aware of this special issue on Black love, it was one of two pieces he felt compelled to share. The other work of art was a joint portrait of Ozzie Davis and Ruby Dee entitled *Solemnity*. Although the coeditors were enlivened by, and grappled with both creations, we chose the abstract piece. *Be Still My Heart* in its original conception was meant to have a vertical cocooned heart. The colors, shades of pink and purple, illuminate Black love in a way that appears at odds with popular narratives of Black love as necessitating struggle and heaviness. Lennox notes that he wanted the colors to feel light because that "just feels like love." The feeling of love was one this author took away when first viewing the art piece. I was excited to sit and talk with the artist that saw Black love as a constant pulse that radiated light.

Rashida L. Harrison: Tell me a bit about your background and how it shaped you to become the artist you are today.

Lennox Commissiong: I was born on the island of Saint Vincent. It's been in the news lately because a volcano erupted. I migrated to the United States when I was fourteen. I always yearned to be an artist. To me, that was the highest purpose I could achieve in life other than being a good father. I always wanted that, but it took me a while to figure out that what they call natural talent is only the gateway. You must work every day if you want to achieve greatness. It took me a while to figure that out. I've been on the journey ever since.

After I graduated from high school, I went to college to become a commercial artist. But I wasn't disciplined enough to get through it. The knowledge I learned was the background to what I needed. But I was impetuous. I just wanted to draw and paint. So I dropped out, and I went to the Marine Corps. I spent four and a half years in the Marine Corps, mostly stationed in Hawaii; that allowed me to travel most of Asia, Africa, Australia.

When I returned to the U.S., I went back to school to pursue a degree in business management, finance, and computer technology. My day job is in information technology. When returned to pursuing my art, it was for me to learn on my own. So, through books and experimentation, I developed my style, I just kept working every day.

RLH: Thank you for sharing your journey. When looking at your work, I noticed that you have three sections [on your website]: reality, abstract, and pointillism. I understand that pointillism is a technique that uses tiny dots of color, in this case, colored paper to create a larger image with variations of color. You utilize pointillism to recreate images of prominent figures. Tell me a bit about why you chose those figures and technique?

LC: While I was in the Marine Corps, in Australia of all places, I picked up a couple of posters; one was Muhammad Ali, the other Bob Marley. I knew I wanted to create pieces based on those images at some point in my life, but I didn't possess the ability to do it then. Those iconic figures resonated with me because of my respect for their contribution to world humanity and African American culture. My first subject, Bob Marley, brought reggae music to the world at large; his lyrics were infused with political commentary and spoke to the plight of ordinary citizens of the world, who he urged them to unite. Muhammad Ali was a favorite of mine even when I resided in St. Vincent. I was introduced to him by my grandfather. We listened to his early fights on the radio together as we did not own a TV set.

My technique was born out of necessity. The prospect of introducing color to my work was intimidating. When I attended college, Color-aid paper was used in color theory classes to mimic the different colors on the color wheel. It's also museum-quality and colorfast, (doesn't fade over time). With it I learned to recognize, categorize, and mix hues, shades, and tints.

I was comfortable drawing in pencil at the time and feared working in color because I hadn't attempted to do so before. The idea came to mind to use Color-aid paper because all the colors were readily available. When you look at a poster, a color is rarely just a hue, there are nuances within each color, especially mixed ones. For example, green can range from blue to yellow and in between. Inadvertently, pointillism taught me how to mix colors. The knowledge gained from my experimenting was applied to my painting studies. Thus, I began painting in color.

RLH: How do you create "dots" using the pointillism technique?

LC: I cut paper up into small pieces . . . an eighth of an inch, in some cases, a quarter of an inch square, infrequently using larger pieces up to a half an inch square. Once, during one of my shows, one of my guests approached me saying, "Oh my God, they got holes in them, they got holes in them!" "Where?" I replied. I thought I missed a spot on my "canvas." He was referring to the holes in each "pixel" where I inserted the X-Acto knife to transfer it to the canvas. I always laugh about that because he was so observant and intense.

RLH: When you submitted work for our review, you gave us an option. Although we loved the Ozzie [Davis] and Ruby [Dee], we went with the abstract to have a broader view that signaled the complexities of Black love and all its interpretations . . . Can you tell me more about *Be Still My Heart*?

LC: I feel love is caring. Honesty. Peace. Black love is special because it's what has encapsulated us against all the ills and woes that have been transcended upon us. That's why there is a cocoon. If you begin from the standpoint of love, spread it outward, you could solve a trove of issues across race, cultures. My pallet for the project was chosen because I wanted it to be light. Those colors to me, just feel like love. As you can see, I'm wearing purple. That's my favorite color. I've been attracted to that family of colors, pink and purple, for a while now. It just works.

RLH: I appreciate your clarification, especially about the colors you chose.

LC: It's just energy. Good energy. It's like the molecules bouncing off each other in a good way. It lightens the Spirit.

RLH: There were several other pieces in your pointillism collection [on your website] that drew my eye, including *First Lady* and *One Love*. How long does it take to create such pieces?

LC: The Bob Marley piece, *One Love*, was the first one I created. After I began, I reached a point where I was stuck on technique because I wasn't good enough with color. I went out and purchased a book on color (*Color* by Betty Edwards). I then revisited the piece. It took years to complete because I was using that image to work on my technique. Next was Muhammad Ali, *The Greatest.*[6] And as I worked on it, my technique improved, including being more intricate.

This called for smaller "pixels," some just barely fitting on the tip of my X-Acto knife. When I was finally able to depict the beads of sweat rolling off his face, I felt a sense of accomplishment. Initially, I stuck to portraits. I began doing abstracts in 2020. I always had in mind melding the two genres (portraits and abstraction). The Monk piece, *Evidence*, was my first attempt at that.

I'm at a point now where I can just go crazy. It's a wonderful feeling to be able to replicate what I can see and be able to lay down whatever is in my head.

The Michelle [Obama] piece, *First Lady*, took a year; in the middle of the build, I was asked to do the piece for the Thelonious Monk Centennial.[7] I took a break from Michelle to complete *Evidence*. I had two months to complete a piece that would normally take three months pedal to the metal, every spare second, to complete. I took a vacation from my day job and got it done. I initially intended to do just a portrait but decided to expand my vision because I thought Monk, for all he contributed to jazz, deserved it. I added some information in the background, including the original sheet music from the tune the piece was named after as well as the date and place where he performed the piece first. His family was present at the celebration, people who played with him were there . . . Around forty artists from around the country as well as some from abroad were invited to participate. It was a wonderful experience. I finally resumed work on *First Lady*. In total it took a year to complete. My *One Man* show featuring that piece was well-received by the public. And yes, that was a good year.

RLH: You mentioned that, for you, being an artist and getting to be an artist was your highest achievement. Can you say more about what it means to you? Why was this your highest achievement?

LC: I'm by no means a Bible thumper, although growing up, my grandmother dragged me to church often enough to be; however, regarding creation . . . I do believe there's a power . . . Whatever makes the flowers grow when you plant the seed, whatever makes the sun come up every day, whatever makes the birds sing, seasons change, that's God.

I believe artists, especially—God bestowed onto us the power of creation. I don't feel artists should beat their chests and feel like they're "the source" because we are just conduits. We take information from this form in the universe and can translate it into something tangible that others can enjoy. Some do it in the form of pictures, music, written words. We're simply the conduit . . . I'm simply humbled that I was chosen to be one of those conduits. I feel, given that blessing, I should work as diligently as I can to use my gift, to make society a better place. With rare exceptions, I create every single day that God gives. Every time I approach my canvas, I'm thrilled beyond belief that I'm able to do what I do.

RLH: What kind of legacy are you are creating?

LC: I strive not to be good, not to be "very good"; I want to be remembered as an *exceptional creative*. No middle of the road. I would like to be recognized as being the original Color-aid pointillist.

When someone is walking past my work, I want to compel them to stop and look further, whether they love or hate it. Hopefully there's a vibe that makes them want to explore the canvas, whether it be due to composition, color, design.

This anecdote illustrates what drives me. I hadn't started painting in color when I was given a gift certificate to attend a beginner's painting class on Saturdays, at my local library. When I attended my first class, I was told by the instructor to bring in earlier work so she could assess my level. After she addressed the class, she pulled me to the side to go over my work. And as I showed a different piece of work, I began hearing low sighs [signaling awe]. I looked around to see members of the class behind us looking at my work and taking it in. I don't know if you can imagine the feeling of being able to move an audience that way. It's what I feel at every show I participate in. This reaction is what I try to replicate, I know it won't be to that degree every single time. I was at a show not too long ago where this woman came over and shared with me that the Monk piece made her cry. I thought, "Wow, that's a little extreme, but also pretty cool." Moments like that, just make me want to put out my absolute best each and every time.

RLH: Given the constraints of publishing, the front cover of this journal features your piece pictured horizontally, but you originally created it vertically. We appreciate your willingness to allow us to print it that way. Was that a hard decision? Are you often attached to your motivations and intent of your artwork? I'm thinking about the abstract pieces, given those often provoke a variety of meaning.[8]

LC: It wasn't a difficult decision at all. I didn't feel that the reformatting of the piece subtracted from what I was attempting to say, in any way. I'm quite attached to motivation/intention. I don't let a piece go public until I feel that I've made my statement. That means composition, color, elements must be tight and balanced.

I once began to explain to a patron what my thought process was in creating a particular piece. I began pointing out the images that were "embedded." The person looked at me as if I had thirteen heads. Now I leave interpretation up to the audience. I enjoy listening to what people's interpretations are and sometimes they point out elements that they see in a particular piece that I didn't intend; I can usually see their reasoning. I do build a certain way and there are many symbols and elements there that you won't see with a cursory look.

RLH: Yes, I did not realize the center of your piece was a cocoon! And now it is so obvious. We really appreciate the time you've taken, as well as sharing the explanation about *Be Still My Heart.*

LC: Black love is definitely a saving grace.

RLH: Thank you so much for taking the time to interview.

LC: My pleasure.

Commissiong offers just a glance into the critical moments that go into an artist's love of craft and community. The vibrancy of *Be Still My Heart* is reflective of his passion for light and positive energy. His artwork, with the specific technique, and use of color he provokes sentiments of complexity, and envelopment in lightness and love. When asked to publish his art, horizontally, rather than the vertical heart he intended, Commissiong barely paused before agreeing. It is because he is at peace with the meaning-making process of his audience. He wants to inspire, and realizes that inspiration is translated differently for people. Black love is provoked, inspired, and realized in complex ways; it grows and spreads. *Be Still My Heart* illustrates that Black love envelops friends into family, neighborhoods into communities; it can inspire and turn anger into action, and shift oppression to justice. Black love is a constant pulse, radiating.

Lennox Commissiong visited Robin Roberts on *Good Morning America* to deliver her birthday gift in November 2021, a portrait he created for her. To see this piece, and learn more about Lennox Commissiong's work, please visit http://wizardhandsart.com/ or https://www.instagram.com/wizardhandsart/.

Rashida L. Harrison is an assistant professor of social relations and policy at James Madison College at Michigan State University. She is also one of the coeditors for this current issue of *WSQ* on *Black Love* and can be reached at harri516@msu.edu.

Notes
1. I interviewed Lennox via Zoom on June 2, 2021.
2. Commissiong's life trajectory is documented in several of the articles listed in his website, which features his 2018 *Wizard Hands* art exhibition.
3. Commissiong defines his technique in the "Artist's Blog" section of his website and explains how it works in this interview.

4. From "About the Artist" page on wizardhandsart.com.
5. "About the Artist," wizardhandsart.com.
6. Both *One Love* and *The Greatest* were released in May 2014 as documented on wizardhandsart.com.
7. *First Lady* was released in January of 2017, which is the centennial year of Thelonious Monk's birth.
8. As this issue was closer to publication, the artwork *Be Still My Heart* was changed to be portrayed vertically on the front cover as its original intent. There are two images of the piece side by side.

Works Cited

Art Daily. 2018. "Dramatic Mosaic Portrait of Michelle Obama Is on View in Harlem." https://artdaily.cc/news/106857/Dramatic-mosaic-portrait-of-Michelle-Obama-is-on-view-in-Harlem#.YZK0Rb3MKAk.

Commissiong, Lennox. 2018. *Wizard Hands Art by Lennox Commissiong.* https://wizardhandsart.com/.

Repeating Islands. 2018. "Art Bureau Mosaic Portrait of Michelle Obama by Vincentian Artist Lennox Commissiong at Dwyer for Harlem Week." https://repeatingislands.com/2018/08/14/art-bureau-mosaic-portrait-of-michelle-obama-by-vincentian-artist-lennox-commissiong-at-dwyer-for-harlem-week/.

Sothebys. 2018. *Pointillism: 7 Things You Need to Know.* https://www.sothebys.com/en/articles/pointillism-7-things-you-need-to-know.

Contemporary Love Stories:
Love in the Trap, Hookup, and Consumer Culture

Taylor Leigh Tate

Abstract: In Lindsey Stewart's work on social goods "akin to freedom," she shows that contemporary traditions for Black freedom and love have the capacity to be both liberating and limiting. This essay draws on Lindsey Stewart's on social goods "akin to freedom" to argue that bell hooks and Cornel West have a too-narrow understanding of freedom and love, so they miss out on practices and spaces they consider too "commodified/materialistic." Through this analysis, a different story about Black people, salvation, and love is told, one that compels us to see a resurgence of spirit work, of ancestral healing practices, in the trap, hookup, and consumer culture. **Keywords:** Black love; freedom; commodification; nihilism; bell hooks; Cornel West; hip-hop

When Black philosophers like Cornel West and bell hooks identify contemporary traditions of Black love and freedom, they recognize the traditions as something inherited, fragments of the traditions they used to have, but as traditions that have been snuffed out, scarred, and almost ruined by capitalism, commodification, reification, and materialism (West 1993; hooks 2001). When they articulate their evolution, they do not leave much room to acknowledge ways in which changes in Black love and freedom traditions are generative. They, instead, argue that overall, changes in Black love and freedom traditions have been to the detriment of Black people. This is evident in Cornel West's and bell hooks's analysis of the role that emerging market cultures like trap culture, hookup, and consumer culture have had in Black love and freedom traditions. West and hooks argue that the market cultures have called people to "put everything and everyone up for sale" (West 1993, 17; hooks 2014). They demand that people sell, advertise, and promote themselves in a way that weakens nonmarket values like nurturing,

WSQ: Women's Studies Quarterly **50**: 1 & 2 (Spring/Summer 2022) © 2022 by Taylor Leigh Tate. All rights reserved.

sharing, caring, and connecting. In arguing this, they explain that emerging market cultures like trap culture, hookup culture, and consumer culture are symptomatic of a spiritual blackout—an undeniable collapse of hope, meaning, love, integrity, honesty, and decency.

In this essay, I explain that while the historical analysis that West and hooks put forth is needed to articulate the ways healthy Black love can manifest, their frameworks limit our capacity to see how contemporary traditions for Black love and freedom have the capacity to be spiritually empowering. Their framework limits our capacity to see contemporary traditions of Black freedom and love as sources of healing, redemption, and salvation. In arguing this point, I tell a different story about Black people, salvation, and love, one which compels us to see a resurgence of spirit work, of ancestral healing, and hexing practices in changing social mores, and one that acknowledges ways love grows in trap, hookup, and consumer culture.

To do this work, I first discuss West's and hooks's contribution to the literature on Black love, life, and freedom. From there, I consider alternative stories that may have been unthought of or ignored bacause of the determinations of the myths, narratives, and paradigms put forth by West and hooks. I then identify significant moments in which existential and spiritual transformations have taken place in trap, hookup, and consumer culture. After analyzing my findings, I conclude that remarkable expressions of love exist where West and hooks thought there were none. My findings also illustrate that West's and hooks's frameworks limit our capacity to see how people, particularly those who grew up in the hip-hop generation (those that came of age in the 1990s or early 2000s or decades that can be considered post-soul and post–civil rights) engage in emerging struggles, missions, and visions, not faulty approaches to transcendence. This reading characterizes movements within trap, consumer, and hookup culture as integral in one's development. It locates generative avenues in these spaces and locates them within the dialectical struggle toward love and freedom. Moreover, it demonstrates that changes in Black love and freedom traditions mark an important transgression people undergo as they pass through different forms and stages to reach a higher development.

Competing Narratives

Cornel West argues that the white colonizers and settlers that fled to the Americas during the Columbian exchange experienced social disorientation and lostness regarding their identity, but that they ultimately decided to soothe their anxieties with cultural myths (1993). They supposed that their European brethren, religious individuals who had once tried to persecute many of them for being "impure" or "bad," were evil and that they were good. They also worked to define individuals outside of their group (Indigenous, Black, Chinese, among others) as bad and characterized Black people as threatening creatures (West 1993, 83; hooks 2001, 98). In keeping up with this narrative, Black men were portrayed as predators of white women. Black men also were portrayed as super performers, and as spineless, sexless, and impotent individuals. Black women, in contrast, were characterized as "licentious, lustful, and untrustworthy betrayers" (hooks 2001).

Cornel West and bell hooks argue that the myths constructed by white settlers and colonizers became dominant in the cultural ethos at the expense of Black life—at the expense of dominating, raping, enslaving, plundering, torturing, and murdering millions of Black people—particularly Black women and queer people. When making this argument, both West and hooks explain that America's Black foremothers and fathers developed Black institutions that were able to "ward off contempt" and "forge a mighty struggle against the white supremacist bombardment of Black people" (West 1993, 15–17; hooks 2001). They stress that America's Black foremothers and forefathers created powerful buffers to ward off nihilism and to equip Black folk with cultural armor to beat back the demons of hopelessness, meaninglessness, and lovelessness. These buffers consisted of Black spiritual institutions and Black civic institutions that stressed the value of service, sacrifice, love, care, discipline, and excellence. These practices continued on, in the 1950s, '60s, and '70s when the Black power struggle, sexual liberation, and feminist movement put "emphasis on accepting and loving the body." The "ideas from these three movements helped release Black women and all women from the tyranny of patriarchal women-hating" (hooks 2001, 99).

Moreover, they argue that in recent decades, market-driven forces have shattered Black civil society—Black families, neighborhoods, schools, churches, mosques—and in doing so, unchained Black subjects from the sacred and divine (West 1993, 16; hooks 2001, 3–5). More and more Black people have bought into the ever-growing market culture that puts everything and everyone up for sale. Like many of their white counterparts, many Black people have developed a habit of seeking "random nows," of fortuitous and fleeting moments preoccupied with acquiring pleasure, property, and power "by any means necessary" (West 1993; hooks 2018). They prioritize private aims over public aspirations, as well as prioritized market values like individualism, selfishness, and indifference over nonmarket activities like caring, sharing, nurturing, and connecting. In other words, they prioritize the provision, expansion, and intensification of pleasure, comfort, and stimulation above all else, just as white people have done. This has made it difficult for Black traditions of love, surviving, and thriving to find footing and combat vast senses of social despair, alienation, and lostness.

West and hooks claim that the spiritual blackout is reflected in changing social mores. They claim the spiritual blackout is evident in Black communities that have gone from being "the most civilized and humane in America—highly nurturing, caring, loving, and self-respecting" to "rootless, dangling people with little link to the supportive networks—family, friends, school—that sustain some sense of purpose in life" (West 1993, 85). They also hold the spiritual blackout is evident in obsessions with pleasure, power, and property, which have infiltrated, permeated, and, in some ways, devastated freedom traditions (West 1993). Black schools no longer operate as one of the primary spaces used to teach Black people about self-love, self-respect, and justice. Since the so-called desegregation period, Black youth have been forced to assimilate into white schools led by white educators that lack respect for Black people, culture, and ways of life. Black religious institutions no longer share their commitment to fighting injustice, to fighting white supremacy (West 1993; hooks 2018). Black music no longer functions as an expression of cultural defiance against white supremacy or an expression of the soul. Hip-hop and trap music, a contemporary genre of music that many Black artists have had a hand in creating, does not prepare people to fight for justice as the blues did (West 1993; Boggs 2011; Cone 2011; hooks 2014). At the same time, Black love and Black sexuality have, more and more, become taboo, fetishized, mythologized, exploited, and imperialized, leaving psychic scars and personal wounds in its wake (West 1993, 81–93; hooks 2001, 93–113).

In making this argument, both hooks and West have shown that the barriers that Black people used to ward off nihilism no longer function as they should (West 1993; hooks 2001). They also make evident that a pervasive sense of nihilism has grown into a full-blown spiritual blackout, and that evidence of our collective spiritual crisis is reflected in "troubled Black females" who "try to find a place for themselves within the existing paradigms by internalizing self-hatred" in trap, hookup, and consumer cultures (West 1993; hooks 2001, 106). They assert that such women "feel that the only options they have are to claim the roles of bitch and ho" and that in "embracing these labels they can feel a false sense of agency" (hooks 2001, 106). Moreover, they liken these women to "their enslaved counterparts" who find strength "through processes of disconnection and dissociation."

West and hooks also illustrate that contemporary pleasures of joy, sex, and love are often predicated on myths about Black sexuality, and argue that, though sexual empowerment and Black sexuality have become more mainstream, we cannot say that the old myths about Black sexuality have died out. The same tropes reside in our consciousness, and they make it difficult to interpret ourselves in terms of some unmythical truth content. As West explains, "what we have is white access to Black bodies on an equal basis—but not yet the demythologizing of Black sexuality" (85). Further, they show that we must recognize that changes in social mores have made Black people vulnerable, with little sense of self and fragile existential moorings (West 1993; hooks 2018).

Her-Stories

Cornel West and bell hooks characterize contemporary subjects as spiritually impoverished, but when analyzed in a different light, they may be seen as individuals enriched by spiritual traditions unbeknownst to West and hooks. They may even be seen as individuals who borrow from ancestral healing, hexing, and love practices. To understand this framing, we must first understand who enslaved men and women crossed to the Americas in the transatlantic slave trade, they brought with them knowledge of African cosmology and spiritual practices, and they passed these things down to their descendants. As Angela Davis explains, those who drew on their ancestors' spiritual rituals often used the rituals as a mechanism by which they gained a critical consciousness of their oppression (Davis 2010, 50–52, 67; Stewart 2017). This, in turn, encouraged "freedom of action," and the "liberty to move, to act in a way one chooses" (Davis 2010, 48; Stewart 2017). The enslaved Black female, for example, asserted a limited independence from slavery's pain, as well as "agency in forging community, personality, and place" (Hazzard-Donald 2013, 48; Steward 2017, 105) through hoodoo love rituals, and other sexual love rituals, passed down to her. In the process of gaining sexual autonomy, the enslaved woman underwent an inward emancipation, and "bit by bit" she "claimed herself" (Morrison 1987, 124; Stewart 105). In doing so, she learned to conceive the body, not as a site of suffering, or as her master's property, but as a site of resistance and potentially, transcendence. In this way, gaining sexual autonomy helped her develop a sense of self-love, heal from trauma, and develop a critical consciousness (Davis 2010, 128–30, 135).

In drawing on Davis's work, for example, Lindsey Stewart argues that hoodoo love rituals helped render lovers completely under direction and control. In doing so, the hoodoo practitioners would move from a position of powerlessness to one of immense command. In the third volume of Harry Middleton Hyatt's *Hoodoo, Conjuration, Witchcraft, Rootwork*, practitioners report that, through spiritual rituals, a woman could put her lover "firmly under [her] jurisdiction" (Hyatt 1973, 2514). Their lover's "whole heart and mind" would "fall right into her. . . . There's nobody else and he ain't contented until he's right with her" (Hyatt 1973, 2532). This created "crossroads thinking" and demanded a psychic distance be maintained to develop a critical consciousness. Further, it called practitioners of spirit work to imbue material objects with alternate meanings, and through this process, facilitate the struggle for liberation.

After making her case about the emancipatory capacity of hoodoo rituals, Stewart turns to blues women and argues that "the blues borrows from spirit work practices" (104). Drawing on what Kameelah Martin calls the "symbiotic" relationship between spirit work and the blues (Martin 2013, 128), she discusses the role spirit work plays in endowing sexuality with power to heal, enrich, or empower (Stewart 2017). She argues that it was common for blues singers to identify the mojo with female sexuality, a powerful, valued "charm" that all women owned, and all men wanted" (Chireau 2003, 47). She further argues that the "mojo" referenced within the blues often functioned as a "remedy" for the blues: "Only through the work of some powerful mojo can the blues woman relieve herself" of present misery (Martin 2013, 135). Indeed, mojo is a hoodoo term derived from the West African (BaKongo) minkisi, which translates, roughly, into "medicine of the gods" (Leone and Fry 1999, 380–2).

Given Stewart's characterization of the blues women and spirit work, we might think that spirit work is evident in contemporary demands for the feminist goddess adored in media, particularly hip-hop, trap, hookup, ballroom, and consumer culture. These spaces encourage and reward its participants for using their powers to bewitch, entice, seduce, and mesmerize as the blues women did. The resurgence of spirit work may also be exemplified in practices like twerking and strutting, and in the rise of trap artists like Nicki Minaj, Cardi B, Megan Thee Stallion, City Girls, and so on. Like the blues women, the trap artists challenge and empower women to take ownership over their bodies, sexuality, and pleasure.

In doing so, the artists affirm their right to pleasure, model real, enthusiastic consent to sex, and provide alternatives to narratives that encourage people to labor through uncomfortable, sometimes painful, sexual encounters or lie about their sexual experiences to appease or placate their partner's egos (Febos 2021). Black trap artist Megan Thee Stallion is especially gifted at giving people a language to express consent and dissent, as well as tools to refine techniques for expressing their wants and desires. In "Girls from the Hood," for example, Megan Thee Stallion discusses her experiences with casual sex after dabbling in hookup culture, saying, "I ain't lying about my nut just to make niggas happy." This declaration exemplifies her commitment to affirm her right to pleasure and her right to relationships where she can honestly express her likes, dislikes, interests, and discomfort. But also, through her declaration, she makes it known that she will not consent to touch she does not want or minimize herself for others benefit. In vocalizing these things with confidence, she encourages others to do the same—to vocalize their needs, to express, enforce, and even reinforce them, if need be.

Similarly, in "Crybaby," she gifts us with an entertaining and informative sex story. The story begins with Thee Stallion showcasing that she has used her mojo to get a man's "whole heart and mind" to "fall right into her." Thee Stallion's man fiends for her. He anxiously waits on her to text him. Then, on her time and at her pace, she decides to respond and hook up with the guy. As she recounts their sexual encounter, she boasts he was "moaning like a bitch when he hit this pussy. Damn, he probably wanna wear my hoodie." Her pleasure is soon disrupted however, and she speaks up about it. "Don't fuck me like that! Fuck me like this," she says. In doing so, she creates space for them to work together to figure out how they can pleasure each other.

Through their music, trap artists like Thee Stallion define their bodies outside of inherited definitions and characterizations of it, and work to reclaim the body as a site of pleasure (as opposed to a mere object, property, or means to fulfill the capitalist agenda). Moreover, their music compels people to acknowledge the raunchy, sexy, spiritual, powerful, needy, enchanting parts of the human spirit, and recognize that those parts of ourselves are just as important as our political, familial, or career identities. Those aspects of the human spirit need not conflict with other social identifications or be compartmentalized, suppressed, or erased, like they were in previous generations where respectability was prioritized above the need for genuine desirability. On the contrary, contemporary trap and hip-hop artists teach us that the nature of our human condition demands that those parts of ourselves be explored, nurtured, and unified with the other parts of our soul.

This is no small feat. It takes a profound amount of self-worth to enforce one's boundaries in a society that pushes Black women to ignore their needs. It takes immense inner strength to engage in quests to fulfill one's existential needs (like the desire to be wanted, or the need to stand in one's truth). It takes tremendous effort and courage to do this in a society that injects fear and inferiority complexes into Black people. Moreover, it takes a tremendous amount of self-love to treat one's body as a site that can be reclaimed, animated, politicized, personalized, and enjoyed in a patriarchal white supremacist society that devalues, disrespects, and demonizes Black women's bodies. That Black artists like Megan Thee Stallion are doing this work gives reason for hope that people can triumph in the struggle for bodily autonomy, freedom of thought, and love, but also in the struggle against nihilism.

It must be noted that the mind-numbing, cathartic, and potent features of contemporary trap and hip-hop music are like medicine to the soul for those alienated and exploited in capitalist societies. The beats, rhythm, lyrics, and dance the music calls for function like a pain reliever in that they soothe tension and stress created by capitalist and colonial powers. As Big Freedia explains in "Explode," encountering the rhythm and beats trap artists produce in their music makes it possible to "release ya anger, release ya mind, release the time, release the stress, release ya love, forget the rest" (Big Freedia 2014) Similarly, Frantz Fanon explains that Black music evokes movements that enable people to purge themselves of stress. As he notes in *The Wretched of the Earth*, "shakes of the head, bending of the spinal column, throwing of the whole body backward, may be deciphered as in an open book the huge effort of a community to exorcise itself, to liberate itself, to explain itself" (1961, 57). In this way, the cathartic features of Black music and dance alleviate pain and suffering brought onto people by capitalist forces.

The artists also aid in people's healing through advocating for consumerism through their music, interviews, and social media posts. The stars explain it is important to "treat yo self" to a wardrobe that inspires confidence in oneself. They also demonstrate that treating oneself to coveted material possessions can be cathartic and enriching. This is especially the case for those exploited and degraded by capitalism. Such subjects are often coerced into providing mental and emotional labor for their bosses, customers, and dependents. They often find it difficult to center their emotional needs, their happiness, or care for themselves. Efforts to treat themselves to luxury goods gives them the energy to continue another day.

Through trap, hookup, and consumer cultures, the artists create canopies; they create spaces that have the capacity to shield people from systematic violence and abandonment because it allows people to experience themselves as delightful or divine. This, in turn, gives them a sense of emotional security and self-validation, which often allows the ego structure to withstand the shattering impact of that rejection that capitalism engenders. At the same time, because they have mind-numbing and cathartic features that enable people to let go and release toxic energy, attitudes, and commitments, they provide compensation for being forced to live behind walls. That is, the canopies they create disrupt and challenge dominant narratives about Black womanhood and sexuality, myths that render women passive, demure objects for men's pleasure. In doing so, they allow the female gaze to take central stage. As Megan Thee Stallion has explained, while many assume that she dresses and performs with the male gaze in mind, she "values compliments from women far more than from men" (Thee Stallion 2020). Similarly, films like *Twerk* center the female gaze. There are no men in the film (though many of the financiers of the film, the production team, and onlookers watching the film are men). The women simply twerk and dance with and for each other.

While the artists often engage in liberatory practices through their spirit work, their movement and imagination are often limited. This is evident when we look at the ways the trap stars commodify themselves and their art to gain access to sexual, financial, and spiritual power. On a business level, it behooves them to hypersexualize themselves, have clear skin, wear their makeup a certain way, dawn their wigs a certain way, transform their bodies with plastic surgery, and signal that they can afford name brands (Foster 2019; Jouelzy 2021). These efforts allow them to create and maintain a demand for the sexy siren and alluring nymph images they strive to embody and profit off. On a personal level, or more spiritual level, their personal and public identities, their feminine identities, personal sense of self-worth, as well as their identities as artists are tied to their capacity to get people to buy into the feminist adored images they want to sale. This is because successful performances often ensure rewards in the dating market, in record sales, and cash flow. Given all this, their desire and capacity to do spirit-work is dependent upon their ability to get people to buy into what they sell. It is dependent upon whether they can get people to believe them when they say, "He will buy me Gucci if I ask for it," or say, "I bet your little sister want to look like me. I bet your little brother want to fuck on me" (Miami 2018). Moreover, it is dependent upon their capacity to signal to others that they can perform better (that they are more beautiful, sexy, and thus, more valuable) or through showing that others are less than them. This "signaling" allows them to place themselves on a spectrum where they are defined as more valuable than other Black women (Foster 2021; Joulzey 2021). So, on one hand, we see that "those fears which rule our lives and form our silences begin to lose their control over us" when we engage in spirit work as they do. On the other hand, we see that the quality of light by which they scrutinize their lives, has direct bearings" on how they "pursue their magic" and "make it realized" (Lorde 1985).

Competing Narratives

Under Stewart's framework, we see that those transported to the Americas brought their cultural practices with them, passed them down to their descendants, and they passed them down to their descendants. Each generation altered the practices, made it their own, and used them to create little canopies, to create little pockets of paradise, for themselves. Enslaved women utilized hoodoo love rituals, mojos, and menstrual-blood rituals. Their descendants, the blues women, altered the rituals, and made them their own, while maintaining the basics. Contemporary subjects enervate the practices. Spirit work practiced in mainstream media forums hardly resembles the form it once took. There are differences, for example, between Cardi B's and Megan Thee Stallion's brand of sexual empowerment and the kind of sexual empowerment the blues women would adopt. They do not evoke or invite the same sort of spiritual experiences or spiritual insights as blues women like Gertrude "Ma" Rainey, Bessie Smith, and Billie Holiday. They seem to operate on a different level of power and dignity as their foremothers and forefathers did. At times, their capacity to manifest ecstatic sensations through their art seems shallow. It is as if some sense of vitality has been lost through their efforts to commodify themselves and sell their art, and because they fail to showcase joy, sweetness, and gentleness like the blues did. Still, the contemporary artists, much like their ancestors, have mastered the art of conjuring ecstatic states, cathartic states, and heady senses of desire through potent beats, melodic sound, captivating movement, form, and sexual lyrics.

In contrast, the narrative put forth by West and hooks portrays the trap stars as individuals who seem empowered but are spiritually impoverished. They argue that their capitalist mindsets limit what they think is possible; it limits what they find hope in and what they think love and freedom are. In arguing this, they explain that the spiritual malaise at hand cannot be cured, but it can be mitigated with *love*, which hooks defines as "the will to extend oneself for the purpose of nurturing one's own or another's spiritual growth" and explains that it involves "a combination of care, knowledge, responsibility, and commitment" (2001, 20). Similarly, West explains that nihilism "is tamed by love and care" and that "any disease of the soul must be conquered by a turning of one's soul. This turning is done through one's own affirmation of one's worth—an affirmation fueled by the concern of others" (2001, 19). In making this argument, he shows that nihilism must be responded to by attending to oneself and others in a way that fosters tenderness, sweetness, and deep paideia or education.

The kind of social transformation we need, West argues, is best represented by leaders like Ralph Nader, Al Sharpton, Marion Wright Edelman, and Delores Huerta, and entertainers like Richard Pryor and John Coltrane in multiracial alliances, in programs like the Black Radical Congress and NAACP's ACT-SO programs for young people, in the movement for Black lives, as well as the Moral Monday Movement and Poor People Campaign, in media and television campaigns like Democracy Now! that "bear serious witness to revolutionary politics today," as well as with individuals within academia who "prefer to be a hope rather than talk about hope" (West 2017). In the face of spiritual impoverishment, we can pull on these rich resources, as well as resources within the Black musical tradition, LGBTQ communities, the feminist movement, Indigenous people's struggles, the environmental justice and other abled communities and anti-imperialist organizations. These movements, West argues, are full of individuals who act as beacons of hope with prophetic visions and a commitment to link social issues to global movements.

Unlike the trap artists, these individuals and organizations embody love in the concrete—that is, they respond to terrorism with compassion and justice, demand that the suffering speak, and wish joy upon others. They represent a love of truth, of veritas, showing that "the condition of truth is to always allow suffering to speak" (West 2011). They also represent a love of beauty and freedom in the face of overwhelming evil, institutional, structural, personal evil. To love the way, they love is to be involved in what Simone Weil calls "the formation of attention" where individuals move from superficial truths to the substantial, to the frivolous to the serious, and wrestle with truth, and thus, justice, sadness, sorrow, and joy (West 2011). It calls for "the turning of the soul," the cultivation of a self that respects reality (2011).

They encourage loving reconstruction projects that reassemble our fragments, our cracked heirlooms, heal scars and wounds created by colonialism, and bring broken people back together much stronger than what they were before. In doing so, they illustrate the power of love. As Derek Walcott writes, "Break a vase and the love that reassembles the fragments is stronger than the love which took its symmetry for granted when it was whole" (Walcott 1993, 9). In recognizing ways in which contemporary spaces are "about love," West and hooks acknowledge ways in which the spaces draw on their ancestral traditions. They recognize ways in which contemporary subjects, like their ancestors, ask after one another, make sure folks have what they need, respect the power of vulnerability, hold each other in dignity, and cultivate joy (West 2017).

What's Love Got to Do with It?

While the narrative put forth by West and hooks is needed to articulate what love can look like, it obscures the actual process by which real human beings, confronted with real and seemingly intractable problems, make decisions, and exercise their capacities to create new ways of living. The process by which real human beings achieve freedom and love can be messy, nonlinear, and iterative. At times, efforts to redefine the body outside of inherited definitions and characterizations of it has involved objectifying the body, reifying it, turning it into a thing, but it turns the body into a thing that is empowered, that negates and resists white-minded notions of the self. At other times, it has involved nonlinear trajectories toward love of self and others. Instead of learning to love in a linear path, from God to family to friends to spouse to community, many people learn to love via voluntary practice. Love is exercised on oneself and others, sporadically, spontaneously, inconsistently, in all kinds of relationships, and in all sorts of places. It has been practiced in trap, consumer, and hookup culture, but also in political protests and in voter booths consistently and inconsistently, with breaks, and in rare moments of inspiration. Evidence of this showcases that liberatory practices can be exercised in political protests, but also in clothing stores, bedrooms, music, on dating sites, and sex-worker sites like OnlyFans.

Through this analysis, we see that changing social mores are moving in the direction of progress and freedom. Such efforts are often messy, misguided, self-interested, vain, or based in capitalist logic, but they stimulate and cultivate a desire to resist unfreedom. At the very least, the efforts act as an imperative part of the process; a vital stage in the development toward love. We also see that it is not necessarily the case that, compared to earlier epochs in terms of spiritual content, contemporary subjects have diminished spiritually. Certainly, there is a difference between being immersed in the potency of a protest and the potency of casual sex. There are enough similarities, however, to see contemporary efforts, however clumsy or commodified, as a part of efforts to engage in spirit-work, because in both situations, one can find salvation, redemption, and empowerment, and in doing so, reap some sort of spiritual experience or insight.

Conclusion

> *What did you do to make a mark on this world? What mountains did you climb? Which angels gave you their wings? Which skies have you flown? When you reach the heavens, who was there to catch when you fell? And did they tell you that you saved them too, like you saved me? That they are mending their wings and holding them up to the sun, just to step back and watch you fly. So, go head, Lei, FLY!*
>
> —*Leiomy Maldonado*

Stewart's account of spirit work, its role in history, in the emancipation of Black people, challenges and disrupts West's and hook's myths about Black America. The master narratives and controlling images that they draw on "erases and excises in ways that foreclose possibilities of pleasure for Black female subjectivities" (Morgan 2015). This has resulted in "a mulish inattentiveness to Black women's engagements with pleasure—the complex, messy, sticky, and even joyous negotiations of agency and desire that are irrevocably twinned with our pain" (Morgan 2015). Through reflecting on the oral narratives of African American women's music, which contains elements of African cultural heritage, history, and philosophy, we can claim different myths, different ways of chronicling our current lives, our origins, our cultures, our conditions, and our worlds (Carter 2015). The recovery of these myths provides the philosophical space to recognize ways in which sexual love, as conceived in the blues and trap music, can become a terrain upon which emancipated Black people work out what their freedom means. Regardless of if efforts to do so are messy, misguided, and founded in capitalist logic, it might behoove us to treat individuals embarking on such journeys as spiritual practitioners with knowledge to share. In doing so, we might find that some are in the process of creating new stories, stories that help us better understand Black love, sexuality, and pleasure in the concrete. Their praxis might not call them to demythologize myths about Black love, sexuality, and pleasure completely, but they create new stories that move us closer to understanding about Black life, resistance, and love.

Acknowledgments

Special thanks to Darian Spearman and steve núñez for making this work possible.

Taylor Leigh Tate is a Houston native committed to creating spaces of beauty, belonging, rest, and love for all people. She works at the intersection of philosophy of religion, social and political philosophy, specializing on the topics of nihilism, spiritual impoverishment, African American religious existentialism, and the politics of language. She can be reached at taylor.tate@uconn.edu.

Works Cited

Alexander, M. Jacqui. 2006. *Pedagogies of Crossing: Meditations on Feminism, Sexual Politics, Memory, and the Sacred.* Durham, NC: Duke University Press.

Big Freedia, vocalist. 2014. "Explode." Track 8 on Big Freedia, *Just Be Free*, Queen Diva Music.

Boggs, Grace Lee. 2012. *The Next American Revolution.* Berkeley: University of California Press.

Boggs, James, and Grace Lee Boggs. 1974. *Revolution and Evolution in the Twentieth Century.* Monthly Review Press Classics. New York: Monthly Review Press.

brown, adrienne m. 2019. *Pleasure Activism: The Politics of Feeling Good*. Chico, CA: AK Press.

Camp, Stephanie M. H. 2002. "The Pleasures of Resistance: Enslaved Women and Body Politics in the Plantation South, 1830–1861." *The Journal of Southern History* 68, no. 3: 533–72.

———. 2004. *Closer to Freedom: Enslaved Women and Everyday Resistance in the Plantation South*. Chapel Hill: University of North Carolina Press.

Carter, Issac Martel. 2015. "The Discourse of the Divine: Radical Traditions of Black Feminism, Musicking, and Myth within the Black Public Sphere." PhD diss. Florida Atlantic University.

Chireau, Yvonne. 2003. *Black Magic*. Berkeley: University of California Press.

City Girls, vocalists. "Twerk." Track 4 on City Girls, *Girl Code*. Quality Control Music.

Cone, James H. 1972. *The Spirituals and the Blues: An Interpretation*. New York: The Seabury Press.

———. 2011. *The Cross and the Lynching Tree*. Minneapolis: HighBridge

Cooper, Brittney C., Susanna M. Morris, and Robin M. Boylorn. 2017. *The Crunk Feminist Collection*. New York: Feminist Press.

Davis, Angela Y. 1981. *Women, Race, and Class*. New York: Random House.

———. 1998. *Blues Legacies and Black Feminism*. New York: Vintage.

———. 2010. "Lectures on Liberation." In *Narrative of the Life of Frederick Douglass, an American Slave, Written by Himself: A New Critical Edition by Angela Y. Davis*. San Francisco: Open Media Series.

Fanon, Frantz. 1963. *The Wretched of the Earth*. New York: Grove Press.

Foster, Kimberly. 2019. "Beauty Is a Bad Investment." YouTube. https://www.youtube.com/watch?v=kQYb2VRQHWQ&t=433s

Glymph, Thavolia. *Out of the House of Bondage: The Transformation of the Plantation Household*. Cambridge: Cambridge University Press, 2008.

hooks, bell, and Cornel West. 1991. *Breaking Bread: Insurgent Black Intellectual Life*. Boston: South End Press.

———. 2014. "A Public Dialogue Between bell hooks and Cornel West." Unpublished lecture.

hooks, bell. 2000. *All About Love: New Visions*. New York: William Morrow.

———. 2001. *Salvation: Black People and Love*. New York: William Morrow.

Hyatt, Harry Middleton. 1970. *Hoodoo, Conjuration, Witchcraft, Rootwork*. Cambridge: Western Publishing.

Jouelzy. 2021. "High Value Man/Woman Does Not Exist." YouTube. https://www.youtube.com/watch?v=3rsljjEinWs&t=773s

Lorde, Audre. 1984. *Sister Outsider: Essays and Speeches*. Berkeley: Crossing Press.

Marcuse, Herbert. 1966. *Eros and Civilization: A Philosophical Inquiry into Freud.* Boston: Beacon Press.

Martin, Kameelah. 2013. *Conjuring Moments in African American Literature.* New York: Palgrave Macmillan.

McWhorter, Ladelle. 2013. "Post-Liberation Feminism and Practices of Freedom." *Foucault Studies* 16: 54–73.

Miami, vocalist. 2018. "Act Up." Track 7 on *Girl Code*, Quality Control Music.

Morgan, Joan. 2015. "Why We Get Off: Moving Towards a Black Feminist Politics of Pleasure." *The Black Scholar* 45, no. 4: 36–46.

Morrison, Toni. 1987. *Beloved.* New York: Vintage International.

Stewart, Lindsey. 2017. "Work the Root: Black Feminism, Hoodoo Love Rituals, and Practices of Freedom." *Hypatia* 32, no. 1: 103–18. https://doi.org/10.1111/hypa.12309.

West, Cornel. 1993. *Race Matters.* New York: Vintage.

———. 2017a. "Race Matters in Twenty-First-Century America." In *Race Matters.* Boston: Beacon Press.

———. 2017b "Spiritual Blackout Imperial Meltdown, Prophetic Fightback." Unpublished lecture.

PART VII. **CLASSICS REVISITED**

Scratching the Surface: Some Notes on Barriers to Women and Loving (1978)

Audre Lorde

Racism: *The belief in the inherent superiority of one race over all others and there by the right to dominance.*

Sexism: *The belief in the inherent superiority of one sex and thereby the right to dominance.*

Heterosexism: *The belief in the inherent superiority of one pattern of loving and thereby its right to dominance.*

Homophobia: *The fear of feelings of love for members of one's own sex and therefore the hatred of those feelings in others*

The above forms of human blindness stem from the same root—the inability to recognize or tolerate the notion of difference as a beneficial and dynamic human force, and one which is enriching rather than threatening to the defined self.

To a large degree, at least verbally, the black community has moved beyond the "two steps behind her man" mode of sexual relations sometimes mouthed as desirable during the sixties. This was a time when the myth of the black matriarchy as a social disease was being presented by racist forces for an excuse or diversion, to redirect our attentions away from the real sources of black oppression. For black women as well as black men, it is axiomatic that if we do not define ourselves for ourselves, we will be defined by others—for their use and to our detriment. The development of self-defined black women, ready to explore and pursue our power and interests within our communities, is a vital component in the war for black liberation. The image of the Angolan woman with a baby on one arm and a gun

WSQ: Women's Studies Quarterly 50: 1 & 2 (Spring/Summer 2022). Originally published in *The Black Scholar*, April 1978, vol. 9, no. 7, Blacks & the Sexual Revolution: 31–35. Copyright © The Black World Foundation, reprinted by permissions of Taylor & Francis Ltd, http://tandfonline.com on behalf of The Black World Foundation.

in the other is neither romantic nor fanciful. Black women in this country coming together to examine our sources of strength and support, and to recognize our common social, cultural, emotional, and political interests, is a development which can only contribute to the power of the black community as a whole. For it is only through the coming together of self-actualized individuals, female and male, that any real advances can be made. The old sexual power-relationships based on a dominant/subordinate model between unequals have not served us as a people, nor as individuals.

Black women who define ourselves and our goals beyond the sphere of a sexual relationship can bring to any endeavor the realized focus of a completed and therefore empowered individual. Black women and black men who recognize that the development of their particular strengths and interests does not diminish the other, do not diffuse their energies fighting for control over each other. We focus our attentions against the real economic, political, and social forces at the heart of this society which are ripping ourselves and our children and our worlds apart.

Increasingly, despite opposition, black women are coming together to explore and to alter those manifestations of our society which oppress us in ways different from the oppression of black men. This is no threat to black men, and is only seen as one by those black men who choose to embody within themselves those same manifestations of female oppression. For instance, enforced sterilization and unavailable abortions are tools of oppression against black women, as is rape. Only to those black men who are unclear as to the paths of their own self-definition can the self-actualization and self-protective bonding of black women be seen as a threatening development.

Today, the red herring of homophobia and lesbian-baiting is being used in the black community to obscure the true double face of racism/sexism. Black women sharing close ties with each other, politically or emotionally, are not the enemies of black men. Too frequently, however, an attempt to rule by fear tactics is practiced by some black men against those black women who are more ally than enemy. These tactics are sometimes expressed as threats of emotional rejection: "Their poetry wasn't too bad but I couldn't take all those lezzies (lesbians)." The man who says this is warning every black woman present who is interested in a relationship with men—and most black women are—that (1) if she wishes to have her work considered she must eschew any other allegiance except to him and (2) any woman who wishes his friendship and/or support had better not be "tainted" by woman-identified interests.

If such threats of labelling, vilification, and/or emotional isolation are not enough to bring black women docilely into camp as followers, or persuade them to avoid each other as political or emotional support for each other, then the rule by terror can be expressed physically, as on the campus of a New York college recently, where black women sought to come together around feminist concerns. Violently threatening phone calls were made to those black women who dared to explore the possibilities of a feminist connection with non-black women. Some of these women, intimidated by these threats and the withdrawal of male approval, did turn against their sisters. When threats did not prevent the attempted coalition of black feminists, the resulting hysteria left some black women beaten and raped. Whether the threats by black men actually led to these assaults, or merely encouraged the climate of hostility within which they could occur, the results upon the women attacked were the same.

Wars and jails have decimated the ranks of black males of marriageable age. The fury of many black heterosexual women against white women who date black men is rooted in this unequal sexual equation, since whatever threatens to widen that equation is deeply and articulately resented. But this is essentially unconstructive resentment because it extends sideways, and can never result in true progress on the issue, because it does not question the vertical lines of power or authority, nor the sexist assumptions which dictate the terms of the competition. And the racism of white women can be better addressed where it is less complicated by their own sexual oppression. In this situation it is not the non-black woman who calls the tune, but rather the black man who turns away from himself in his sisters, or who, through a fear borrowed from white men, reads her strength not as a resource but as challenge.

All too often the message comes loud and clear to black women from black men: "I am the prize and there are not too many of me and remember I can always go elsewhere. So if you want me you'd better stay in your place which is away from each other, or I will call you lesbian and wipe you away." Black women are programmed to define themselves within this male attention and to compete with each other for it, rather than to recognize their common interests. The tactic of encouraging horizontal or lateral hostility to becloud the real and more pressing issues of oppression is by no means new, nor limited to relations between women. The same tactic is used to continue or exacerbate the separation between black women and black men. In discussions around the hiring and firing of black faculty at universities, the charge is frequently heard that black women are more easily hired than are black men. For this reason, black women's problems of promotion and tenure are not to be considered as important, since they are only "taking jobs away from black men." Here again, energy is being wasted on battles which extend horizontally, over the pitifully few crumbs allowed us, rather than being used in a joining of forces to fight for a more realistic representation of black faculty. This would be a vertical battle against the racist policies of the academic structure itself, one which could result in real power and change. And of course, it is the structure at the top which desires changelessness, and so profits from these apparently endless kitchen wars.

Instead of keeping our attentions focused upon the real enemies, enormous energy is being wasted in the black community today by both black men and heterosexual black women, in anti-lesbian hysteria. Yet women-identified women—those who sought their own destinies and attempted to execute them in the absence of male support—have been around in all of our communities for a long time. As Yvonne Flowers of York College pointed out in a recent discussion, the unmarried aunt, childless or otherwise, whose home and resources were often a welcome haven for different members of the family, was a familiar figure in many of our childhoods. And within the homes of our black communities today, it is not the black lesbian who is battering and raping our under-age girl-children, out of displaced and sickening frustration.

The black lesbian has come under increasing attack from both black men and heterosexual black women. In the same way that the existence of the self-defined black woman is no threat to the self defined black man, the black lesbian is an emotional threat only to those black women who are unsure of, or unable to, express their feelings of kinship and love for other black women, in any meaningful way. For so long, we have been encouraged to view each other with suspicion, as eternal competitors, or as the visible face of our own self-rejection.

But traditionally, black women have always bonded together in support of each other, however uneasily and in the face of whatever other allegiances which militated against that bonding. We have banded together with each other for wisdom and strength and support, even when it was only in relationship to one man. We need only look at the close—although highly complex and involved—relationship between African co-wives; or at the Amazon warriors of ancient Dahomey, who fought together as the Kings' main and most ferocious bodyguard. We need only look at the more promising power wielded by the West African Market Women Associations of today, and those governments which have risen and fallen at their pleasure.

In a verbatim retelling of her life, a 92-year-old Efik-Ibibio woman of Nigeria recalls her love for another woman:

> I had a woman friend to whom I revealed my secrets. She was very fond of keeping secrets to herself. We acted as husband and wife. We always moved hand in glove and my husband and hers knew about our relationship. The villagers nicknamed us twin sisters. When I was out of gear with my husband, she would be the one to restore peace. I often sent my children to go and work for her in return for her kindnesses to me. My husband being more fortunate to get more pieces of land than her husband, allowed some to her, even though she was not my co-wife.[1]

The Fon of Dahomey still have 12 different kinds of marriage, one of which is known as "giving the goat to the buck," where a woman of independent means marries another woman who then may or may not bear children, all of whom will belong to the blood line of the other woman.[2] Some marriages of this kind are arranged to provide heirs for women of means who wish to remain "free," and some are homosexual relationships. Marriages of this kind occur throughout Africa, in several different places among different peoples.[3]

In all of these cases, the women involved are recognized parts of their communities, evaluated not by their sexuality but by their respective places within the community.

While a piece of each black woman remembers the old ways of another place and time, when we enjoyed each other in a sisterhood of work and play and power, other pieces of us, less functional, eye each other with suspicion as we have been programmed to do. In the interests of separation, and to keep us out of touch with our own power, black women have been taught to view each other as always suspect, heartless competitors for the scarce male, the all-important prize that will legitimize our existence. This becomes an ultimate and dehumanizing denial of self, no less lethal than that dehumanization of racism which is so closely allied to it.

If the recent hysterical rejection of lesbians in the black community is based solely upon an aversion to the idea of sexual contact between members of the same sex (a contact existing for ages in most of the female compounds across the African continent, from reports) why then is the idea of sexual contact between black men so much more easily accepted, or unremarked? Is the reality of the imagined threat the existence of a selfmotivated, self-defined black woman who will not fear nor suffer some terrible retribution from the gods because she does not necessarily seek her face in a man's eyes, even if he has fathered her children? Female-headed households in the black community are not always situations by default.

The distortion of relationship which says "I disagree with you, or I do not share your lifestyle, so I must destroy you" leaves black people with basically uncreative victories, defeated in any common struggle. That is jugular vein psychology, based on a fallacy which holds that your assertion or affirmation of yourself must mean an attack upon myself—or that my defining myself—will somehow prevent or retard your self-definition. The supposition that one sex needs the other's acquiescence in order to exist prevents both from moving together as self-defined persons toward a common goal.

This is a prevalent mistake among oppressed peoples, and is based upon the false notion that there is only a limited and particular amount of freedom that must be divided up between us, with the largest and juiciest pieces going as spoils to the victor or the stronger. So instead of joining together to fight for more, we quarrel between ourselves for a larger slice of the one pie. Black women fight between ourselves over men instead of pursuing and using who we are and our strengths; black women and men fight between ourselves over who has more of a right to freedom, instead of seeing each other's struggles as part of our own; black and white women fight between ourselves over who is the more oppressed, instead of seeing those areas in which our causes are the same. (Of course, this last separation is worsened— by the intransigent racism that white women too often fail to, or cannot, address in themselves.)

As black women we have the right and responsibility to define ourselves, and to seek our allies in common cause with black men against racism, and with white women against sexism. But most of all as black women we have a right to recognize each other without fear and to love where we choose, for both homosexual and heterosexual black women today share a history of bonding and strength that our particular sexual preferences should not blind us too.

Notes

1. Andreski, Iris. *Old Wives Tales: Life Stories of African Women.* Schocken Books. New York. 1970. p. 131.
2. Herskovits, Melville. *Dahomey.* Northwestern Univ. Press. Evanston. 1967. 2 volumes. I, pp. 320–321.
3. Ibid., i, p. 322.

There are parts in me without place

Arisa White

There are parts in me without place,
accessories for womanhood hang on the doorknob.

She slips from a layer of defenses, freshly showered, licks
water from her wrists, wants to know, *Do you love me, do you?*

I have learned to keep my erections from getting in the way
of his—but it's odd to be idle on the body's welcome mats.

I hold my breath to put kisses where speech happens,
stroke her arms as if they will lead to someplace new.

I run my tongue along the circumference of another day,
because in the end, the black body is never believed.

To my regret, I'm fixed to her want suckling.
I sepal and stem and river and do best what I know to do.

Our propensity for traumas and trips makes me electric,
wet and wasted, capable of standing for so little.

And when the math of her is gone from my sheets,
and I feel a crow and spike in my mouth—

It is now I understand the lure I am
and why I never take the hook out.

Arisa White is an assistant professor of English and creative writing at Colby College. She is the author of *Who's Your Daddy*, coeditor of *Home Is Where You Queer Your Heart*, and coauthor of *Biddy Mason Speaks Up*, the second book in the Fighting for Justice Series for young readers. As the creator of the Beautiful Things Project, Arisa curates poetic collaborations that center queer BIPOC narratives. She is a Cave Canem fellow and serves on the board of directors for Foglifter and Nomadic Press. To learn more about her other publications and projects, visit arisawhite.com. She can be reached at arisawhite@gmail.com.

WSQ: Women's Studies Quarterly **50**: 1 & 2 (Spring/Summer 2022) © 2022 by Arisa White. All rights reserved.

PART VIII. **BOOK REVIEWS**

Black Queer Love in an Empty Place

Terrance Wooten

Robert Jones, Jr.'s *The Prophets*, New York: G. P. Putnam's Sons, 2021

The Prophets tells a gripping narrative about the struggle to find love in an Empty place. Centered around the queer intimacy and lifeworlds of two enslaved Black teens, Isaiah and Samuel, the novel attempts to reimagine plantation life in the Deep South by reading slavery through the analytics of gender and sexuality. Moving beyond gendered and sexual acts of violence, which is most often how we come to know the sexual lives of those who were enslaved—indeed, the necessity of gendered sexual violence to the making of modernity, the colonial landscape, the plantation, and what Cedric Robinson (1983) describes as the system of racial capitalism is taken seriously in this novel—Robert Jones, Jr. also asks us to consider how love and intimacy figure into the lives of enslaved Black people.

The novel does not concern itself with historical accuracy but rather endeavors to help readers see and know Black queerness in those spaces and times constructed as otherwise incompatible: the plantation, precolonial Africa, early America, and the South. Jones Jr. makes Black queerness legible without reducing it down to a set of sexual acts or identities only knowable, searchable, or indexed and archived through what Michel Foucault describes as the psychoanalytic processes of confession as a form of truth sharing (Foucault 1990). Or, as historian John Howard puts it, the novel allows us to "read the silence" by not "privileg[ing] the spoken (or written) over the unspoken (or unwritten)" in the way that queer history has often been called to do (Howard 2001, 28). That is, it takes as historical fact the presumption that Black queer love has a history before the archive, rooted in the flesh, that does not always pronounce itself; the word "gay" or "queer" does not appear in the novel. Instead of trying to "prove" through archival records that Black queers are historical subjects and their

WSQ: Women's Studies Quarterly 50: 1 & 2 (Spring/Summer 2022) © 2022 by Terrance Wooten. All rights reserved.

love is a historical object that can be analyzed, Jones Jr. uses the novel as a way to imagine how Black queer love might take shape in the scant presence of "official" documentation.

What the novel brilliantly reveals is the value of fiction in recovering that which has been erased, that which seems to remain ineffable, and that which is often named as undiscoverable in the historical record: Black queerness. Indeed, even within the deeply attentive and much-needed edited collection by historians Daina Ramey Berry and Leslie M. Harris, *Slavery and Sexuality: Reclaiming Intimate Histories in the Americas* (2018), men like Isaiah and Samuel remain apparitions. At the same time, there has been a growing body of scholarship that has documented "same-sex" intimacies during enslavement. Increasingly, Black scholars have pointed out how elements of same-sex desire played out on slave ships and plantations, sometimes through rape and other times as consensual practices used for survival (Nero 1996; Tinsley 2008, 2010; Abdur-Rahman 2006; Foster 2001, 2019; Woodard 2014). Rarely, however, is slavery taken as a central site of knowledge production within studies of and literature about Black queerness (Sears 2018). Robert Jones, Jr. seems to be responding to that void, a void that perhaps only a novelist can fill.

The Prophets settles on Samuel and Isaiah, two Black teen boys (sixteen and seventeen) who fall in love in the red-and-white barn under the heat and humidity of the Delta sun in Mississippi, in the place the enslaved call "empty," and among the mundane violence that structures the everyday life of enslavement. They are opposites, Samuel and Isaiah—"one black, the other purple; one smiling, the other brooding" (75). Samuel is often characterized as the more militant partner, plotting to escape the plantation and find a life outside of enslavement, whereas Isaiah wants to make the most out of what is given to him despite being enslaved. The boys share a love that is no secret to other Black people; though it is never attached to an identity category. These are not gay-identified men; they are Black boys who love each other, the living embodiment of the revolutionary act Joseph Beam articulated thirty-five years ago (Beam 1986). And they are loved on and cared for by others, a point that later causes contention in the novel.

Without romanticizing agency, Jones, Jr. offers their love as an act of resistance. I do not mean it is an act of resistance simply by the fact that it is deviant, a framework that continues to dominate our understandings of racialized deviance—the fact of *being* is resistance. I return to Cathy Cohen's insistence that we must consider how intent works and how or if acts, decisions, or behaviors are attempts to change distributions of power. She urges: "We must begin to delineate the conditions under which transgressive behavior becomes transformative and deviant practice is transformed into politicized resistance" (Cohen 2004, 38). Isaiah and Samuel's love is a form of politicized defiance because it operates as an explicit refusal both to rape the Black women who love them and to reproduce the future of the plantation. They love on one another as a way to also love the Black women in their lives and disrupt the logics of their propertiedness. Through this shared love, readers learn about the interior lives of the Black women who have lost parts of themselves while being turned into white sexual property and who put themselves back together by loving others. For instance, the Black women—Be Auntie, Maggie, Essie, Puah, and Sarah—come together to love Isaiah and Samuel back to health after they both receive a brutal lashing following the plantation owner's wife's failed attempt to rape Samuel. Drawing on their knowledge and ancestral memory of the earth, as caretakers of the soil, the Black women concoct a balm that heals the boys in the dead of the night. It is an act of love that serves as a refusal to let their queer children die.

Love can also be cruel, evidenced by the titular struggle in the novel wherein Amos, also enslaved, attempts to save his wife, Essie, from the ravenous grips of the plantation owner, Paul. To curry favor with Paul, Amos feigns interest in Christianity and with his master's permission, uses it to turn the planation against Isaiah and Samuel, which he also sees as necessary to protect those enslaved on the plantation. Isaiah and Samuel's refusal to allow themselves to be forced onto the bodies of those they love puts the whole plantation at risk, in Amos's calculation. In using Christianity as a tool to dominate, Jones Jr. offers an alternative to popular critiques that either name Black communities as inherently exceptionally homophobic or articulate homosexuality as a form of secondary "effeminacy" orchestrated by white supremacy to undermine Black masculinity and the Black family as Frances Cress Welsing so infamously wrote (Welsing 1991, 86). Jones, Jr. instead shows how white supremacy functions as the driving motivator behind homophobia—but for the conditions of captivity, Amos would have never had to act in the way he did—and the destruction of the Black family.

The novel's conclusion attests to a collective love among enslaved Black people, bound together by the queerness of the central characters. After Samuel is lynched and burned for killing the white plantation owner's son,

Timothy (a progressive Southerner educated in the North who decides he, too, wants Isaiah for his own), the enslaved revolt. Black women and men take up arms to defend the dead, to protect the living, and to fill the Empty with their joy, rage, pain, sorrow, grief, and determination. There is no happy ending, because this is a novel about possibilities not closure(s). Readers are left with uncertainties: what happened to those who revolted, those who got away, and ultimately to Isaiah, whose fate remains unclear? If the historical record serves as evidence, it is likely that all the enslaved Black people were killed. But, Jones, Jr. refuses that ending. In this refusal, he allows his readers to imagine an otherwise possibility for them, just the same as he allows them to read queerness in the places where it has otherwise been deemed unimaginable.

The Prophets is not for everyone. Praised for its stylistic choices and themes, readers might find themselves overwhelmed by the lyricism, metaphors, and aphorisms throughout the text. It does not follow a linear narrative structure or plotline, which is intentional but can also be distracting. Most characters in the text get their own separate, unevenly distributed, chapters in the novel. This sometimes moves the story of Isaiah and Samuel to the background, even as it also allows a richer character development of the Black women. Jones, Jr., in this way, is clear to not construct Black women as incidental objects in the narrative. For all its strengths, though, the novel suffers from attempting to make too many connections in such short space. What felt particularly underwhelming was all of the clear Biblical references that did not always clearly work. These small shortcomings aside, the novel draws readers in and charges them with doing the work it cannot do, evidenced by its last lines: "The then is arriving now. And nothing in creation able to stop the coming. *Nothing.* except You" (378). I hope readers accept this calling.

Terrance Wooten is an assistant professor in the Department of Black Studies at the University of California, Santa Barbara. His scholarly interests are located at the intersections of Black studies, gender and sexuality studies, studies of poverty and homelessness, and carceral studies. He can be reached at terrancewooten@ucsb.edu.

Works Cited

Abdur-Rahman, Aliyyah I. 2006. "'The Strangest Freaks of Despotism': Queer Sexuality in Antebellum African American Slave Narratives." *African American Review* 40, no. 2: 223–37.

Beam, Joseph. 1986. *In the Life: A Black Gay Anthology*. Washington, DC: RedBone Press.

Berry, Daina Ramey, and Leslie M. Harris. 2018. *Sexuality and Slavery: Reclaiming Intimate Histories in the Americas*. Athens, GA: University of Georgia Press.

Cohen, Cathy J. 2004. "Deviance as Resistance: A New Research Agenda for the Study of Black Politics." *Du Bois Review: Social Science Research on Race* 1, no.1: 27–45.

Foster, Thomas A. 2011. "The Sexual Abuse of Black Men under American Slavery." *Journal of the History of Sexuality* 20, no. 3: 445–64.

———. 2019. *Rethinking Rufus: Sexual Violations of Enslaved Men*. Athens: University of Georgia Press.

Foucault, Michel. 1990. *The History of Sexuality, Volume 1: An Introduction*. New York: Vintage Books.

Howard, John. 2001. *Men Like That: A Southern Queer History*. Chicago: University of Chicago Press.

Nero, Charles I. 1996. "Toward a Black Gay Aesthetic: Signifying in Contemporary Black Gay Literature." In *Cornerstones: An Anthology of African American Literature*, edited by Melvin Donalson, 229–51. New York: St. Martin's Press.

Robinson, Cedric. 1983. *Black Marxism*. Chapel Hill: University of North Carolina Press.

Sears, Clare. 2018. "Centering Slavery in Nineteenth-Century Queer History (1800s–1890s)." In *The Routledge History of Queer America*, edited by Don Romesburg, 39–51. Abingdon: Routledge.

Tinsley, Omise'eke Natasha. 2008. "Black Atlantic, Queer Atlantic: Queer Imaginings of The Middle Passage." *GLQ* 14, no. 2–3: 191–215.

———. 2010. *Theifing Sugar: Eroticism between Women in Caribbean Literature*. Durham, NC: Duke University Press.

Welsing, Frances Cress. 1991. *The Isis (Yssis) Papers: The Keys to the Colors*. Chicago: Third World Press.

Woodard, Vincent. 2014. *The Delectable Negro: Human Consumption and Homoeroticism within U.S. Slave Culture*. New York: NYU Press.

Love as an Act of Recovery: Alicia Garza's *The Purpose of Power* and the Black Lives Matter (BLM) Global Network

Mélena Laudig

Alicia Garza's *The Purpose of Power: How We Come Together When We Fall Apart*, New York: Penguin Random House, 2020

In her 1993 *Sisters of the Yam: Black Women and Self-Recovery*, Black feminist activist-scholar bell hooks asserts that radical futures will only be possible when Black women live in a world where they experience love. "For such a world to exist," she writes, "racism and all other forms of domination would need to change" (1993, 158). Because love enables us to "transform the present and dream the future," both "the act and art of loving" make possible the obliteration of the patriarchy, homophobia, and other forms of domination (141, 159). Published almost thirty years later, the story of Black queer organizer Alicia Garza summons bell hooks's insights about love. After the 2013 acquittal of Trayvon Martin's murderer, Garza penned a "love letter to Black people" on social media that included the phrase "our lives matter," a refrain that propelled her, Patrisse Cullors, and Ayọ (formerly Opal) Tometi to cofound the Black Lives Matter (BLM) Global Network. While *The Purpose of Power: How We Come Together When We Fall Apart* does narrate the story of BLM, it is far more than an organizational history. The book is a memoir, a guide to imagining, starting, and sustaining social movements, and a vision for systems of care that facilitate the livelihood of all, even as they aim for the liberation of Black folx.

In an era when digital activism thrives, Garza challenges the notion that movements must start on social media. For Garza, her lived experiences— *not* her coinage of #BlackLivesMatter—spurred the development of the movement. She begins the book by highlighting her Reagan-era childhood with her mom in California, as well as the decades she has spent organizing for women's protection against sexual violence, workers' rights, and a gamut of other social causes. "Hashtags don't build movements," she asserts, but "people do" (137). Garza's argument that her late mother, who didn't

WSQ: Women's Studies Quarterly 50: 1 & 2 (Spring/Summer 2022) © 2022 by Mélena Laudig. All rights reserved.

identify as a feminist, catalyzed her own radical politics raises questions about who holds the keys to feminist epistemologies and knowledge. For Garza, feminism isn't a lofty ideal theorized in an ivory tower but a practice of fighting "to survive by any means necessary" (7). Her mother's lesson to "always know your exits" to protect yourself against rape, for instance, activated Garza's intersectional feminist consciousness and informed the platform of BLM.

Throughout the text, Garza recenters Black women's leadership in the BLM movement, particularly by setting the historical record straight about Black male activist DeRay Mckesson. Mckesson is neither the founder nor the cofounder of BLM, she tells us, though he has often been complicit in media attempts to paint him as such. Narratives that center Mckesson in the history of an organization founded by three Black women are not only "ahistorical," she writes, but they also contribute to "the erasure of Black women's labor, strategy, and existence" (267). Garza encapsulates her distaste with the mainstream media's affirmation of Mckesson and other "palatable" Black male figureheads in a question: "Why do we continue to search for the second coming of the Reverend Dr. Martin Luther King, Jr.?" (264–5). Despite the fact that Mckesson exemplifies the trope of not "crediting the work of Black women" and "handing that credit to Black men," she does view his work generously to the extent that it offers an easy entry point into activism for individuals just starting to gain awareness about the primary issues for which she fights (267).

Mckesson represents a larger phenomenon of intra- and interracial organizations marginalizing Black women, who often carry "the lion's share of the work" but go unrecognized as formal leaders (201). At times, Black women themselves can prop up the multidirectional racialized patriarchy, as Garza's experiences of some Black women's ambivalence or hostility toward her leadership exhibit. When it comes to interracial movement-building, Garza claims that women's movements have often understood "gender oppression only through the lens of white women," a deficit that Kimberlé W. Crenshaw sought to correct through her framework of intersectionality (189). In the vein of Jennifer C. Nash's recent *Black Feminism Reimagined: After Intersectionality*, Garza debunks common misreadings of intersectionality, which isn't "a synonym for diversity or representation" but a conceptual tool that maps power distribution across racial lines, gender spectrums, and more (146).

Some of Garza's most compelling insights arrive in the memoir's moving epilogue, which draws on her experience coping with her mother's sudden death to explore the types of care that movement-building requires. First, systemic forms of oppression necessitate practices modeled after hospice care, care that treats "the cancer [that] has localized itself in particular communities [such as racism, poverty, etc.] but also spreads across all of our communities in unique ways" (288). Yet *The Purpose of Power* also advocates for prenatal care, "the work of dreaming and acting to create the world we deserve" (289). Thus, the Black Lives Matter Global Network is both *reactive* as it confronts police violence and *creative* as it reinvents society to promote human flourishing. Though Garza's new political organization Black Futures Lab embodies the concept of prenatal care, so do practices of resting and dreaming. Remarkably, she co-established BLM a few months after taking a six-week hiatus from community organizing in the solace of the Washington state mountains. In a generation where prepackaged forms of "self-care" keep the machine of capitalism running, Garza contends that care for oneself facilitates care for community, conjuring bell hooks's poetic line that "we recover ourselves in the act and art of loving" (141). While the text is sure to appeal to a diverse array of readers, Garza's memoir would be especially useful in undergraduate courses focused on women, gender and sexuality, social activism, and race in modern America.

Mélena Laudig is a PhD student in religion and African American studies at Princeton University. She received her BA in religious studies from Yale University and primarily works on the intersection of Black girlhood and religion in the nineteenth century. She can be reached at melenas@princeton.edu.

Black Women and Historical Wellness

Kimberly Akano

Stephanie Evans's *Black Women's Yoga History: Memoirs of Inner Peace*, Albany: SUNY Press, 2021

Amid individual, interpersonal, and sociopolitical stressors, what resources have Black women leveraged to care for themselves and their communities? For some like Harriet Jacobs or Angela Davis, stretching served as a lifeline for dealing with physical confinement during periods of enslavement or imprisonment. For Black women like Anna Julia Cooper, writing and mindfulness nurtured their intellectual health while navigating challenging academic institutions. Still, others such as Eartha Kitt and Tina Turner found comfort while moving their bodies to accomplish daily household chores—out of view from the public eye that typically followed them. For all of these women, such strategies formed the building blocks of robust practices that aligned the mind, body, and spirit. These women and many others are part of a larger tradition of Black women's embodied efforts to pursue health and healing.

In *Black Women's Yoga History: Memoirs of Inner Peace*, historian Stephanie Evans traces an expansive history of Black women's ideas surrounding mental health and physical well-being as they navigate stress and trauma in their everyday lives. This history decenters an emphasis on South Asian and white American iterations of yoga to shed light on African and African American contributions to yoga history—what she ultimately calls "Africana yoga" (365). By adopting a capacious understanding of yoga to include prayer, exercise, and meditation practices, Evans argues that African American women's pursuit of wellness is anything but new. Instead, Black women's healing traditions reflect an enduring legacy of "historical wellness," the sustained ways of being and knowing that Black women apply to prioritize individual and communal health (364). For Evans, a

WSQ: Women's Studies Quarterly **50**: 1 & 2 (Spring/Summer 2022)

historical wellness approach to Black women's understandings of wellness requires situating their healing traditions within the larger context of Black women's struggles against racism, sexual violence, and the many other challenges that threaten African American women's flourishing. In doing so, she reorients readers toward a critical examination of the role that both gender and race play in histories of mental and physical health—an aspect that is sorely understudied within most scholarship on yoga. This approach also seeks to consider how the experiences and epistemological contributions of Black women "show us inner peace is possible, historical, practical, and teachable" (136).

As a work of intellectual history, Evans attends to a selection of Black women's memoirs and autobiographies to analyze how African American women have narrated their stress management strategies over time. In particular, she focuses on the writings of Black women senior elders (those age seventy and above) and Black women midlife elders (those age fifty and above). Evans situates these writings before and after 1975 when the first issue of *Yoga Journal,* a national publication, gained national attention. Using her method of "narrative portraiture," Evans artfully weaves biographical data with historical analysis to provide robust depictions of African American women's lives (43). These portraits offer an intimate look at subjective experiences of loss, trauma, and healing. They also suggest that past and present socio-political developments such as enslavement, the Great Migration, and the #MeToo movement required African American women to assess and refashion their varied approaches to health over time. For example, Evans gestures toward an increasing need for Black women to reconsider how nuanced understandings of wellness may positively contribute to more contemporary conversations about social media usage, classroom pedagogy, and public health policy. Indeed, rather than settling for one-dimensional portrayals of Black women that overemphasize life's trials or triumphs, Evans considers the "beautiful, ugly, and healing" moments that inform the dynamism of African American women's wellness writings (36).

Perhaps one of the most striking examples of what Evans ultimately calls "Africana yoga" involves Rosa Parks's dedicated yoga practice, which, in part, sustained her lifelong commitment to activism. Evans's keen analysis of Rosa Parks's engagement with yoga stands as an apt illustration of one of her primary assertions that "it is political for Black women to claim ownership or possession, of their own bodies" (47). In other words, Black women's wellness practices serve the individual and have larger consequences for how Black women embody their dedication to the well-being of larger communities. Such dedication is a political act insofar as it rejects acts of oppression and dehumanization. In addition, Rosa Parks's reliance upon both yoga and her religious faith troubles assumptions that religious activity is necessarily in conflict with practicing yoga. Readers may be pleasantly surprised to find that the narratives Evans analyzes are penned by Black women from a range of religious traditions, such as Buddhism, Christianity, and Rastafarianism. Moreover, as with the other Black women she examines, Evans succeeds in rejecting images of historical figures that leave them frozen in time and fail to account for how their seemingly private embodied practices have consequences for their more public contributions to social and cultural life.

By examining African American women's wellness from historical, feminist, and womanist perspectives, *Black Women's Yoga History* insists on an interdisciplinary approach to studying Black women's health. As a result, the implications of Evans's work resonate with other studies of African American women's wellness. For example, Evans's work joins Michele Tracy Berger's text *Black Women's Health: Paths to Wellness for Mothers and Daughters* (2021) in exploring intergenerational approaches to Black women's well-being. In addition, texts such as Deirdre Cooper Owens's *Medical Bondage: Race, Gender, and the Origins of American Gynecology* (2017) pair well with Evans's aim to shed light on systemic public health practices and policies that constrain Black women's access to proper care. Moreover, more could be said in Evans's work about her effort to "connect and recognize yoga as a potential force for the global decolonizing project" (53). Despite her use of seemingly inclusive terms such as "Africana yoga" and "Africana mindfulness," the most sustained narrative portraits are reserved for African American women in the United States. As Evans notes, this raises questions about the role of "Africa in Africana wellness" (352). In Evans's attempt to highlight the "ancient" origins of Africana wellness, ultimately there remained little room for delving into the ways that African understandings of wellness continue to be revised in the narrations of African women themselves.

Nevertheless, Evans's work is poised to animate a wellspring of further studies at the nexus of race, gender, and mental health. As an accessible text for general readers, students, and scholars of Black women's studies alike, *Black Women's Yoga History* opens new avenues for examining how self-care practices are intimately bound with communal efforts toward social change. Many will also find Evans's final reflection on the fiftieth anniversary of Black women's studies and a wellness-centered approach theory and praxis especially insightful. Taken together, Evans's text invites readers to dive into an intellectual treasure trove of Black women's collective wisdom regarding health and wholeness.

Kimberly Akano is a PhD student in the Department of Religion at Princeton University. She is also pursuing a certificate in African American studies. Her work focuses on American religious history with an emphasis on race, gender, and migration among African immigrants living in the U.S. She can be reached at kakano@princeton.edu.

Love Reimagined: On Nash, Black Feminism, and Possibility

Leigh-Anne K. Goins

Jennifer Nash's *Black Feminism Reimagined: After Intersectionality,* Durham, NC: Duke University Press, 2019

Jennifer Nash's newest text *Black Feminism Reimagined: After Intersectionality,* continues the work of disentangling Black feminism from itself and intersectionality. Building on the work developed in *The Black Body in Ecstasy* (2016), this text works to transform how we think about Black feminism and intersectionality through love, care work, and surrender. Nash introduces the book by positioning her central concern regarding the intrinsic connection between intersectionality and Black feminism—that Black feminists have conjoined the two through their stewardship, thus limiting the radical imaginings and potential of both Black feminism and intersectionality. For Nash, Black feminists' stewardship has placed Black feminism on its deathbed, stifled, lacking radical potential. Through the text, she analyzes how and why this happened and how we can move forward. For instance, she critiques how we, as Black feminists, respond to critics based upon body politics. She then outlines the varying ways we read critics and their critiques (as in reading sideways), delineating how requirements for intersectional genealogy and citational lineage can act as stagnating metrics. From this, she turns to intersectionality's history and polemic or juxtaposed relationship with transnationalism and positions the current space—with potential promiscuous intimacies between the two—as a way forward. As Nash begins to conclude, she situates love and care work as radical praxis that can bring Black feminism from its deathbed—resultant from stifling stewardship—into a space of radical imagination and theorizing. In the Coda, Nash returns to intersectionality's history, proposing we (re)root ourselves in law, Crenshaw's original space of theorizing, surrendering stewardship to gain freedom. *Black Feminism Reimagined: After Intersectionality*

WSQ: Women's Studies Quarterly 50: 1 & 2 (Spring/Summer 2022) © 2022 by Leigh-Anne K. Goins. All rights reserved.

is a complicated and loving text that pushes some Black feminist engagements toward radical imaginings.

To be defensive is to take a stance in preparation for an attack. It relies upon the presumption that something *will* happen, that something *has* happened, or that it *is* happening. Though some may argue Black feminism and intersectionality require consistent vigilance and prepared defense, Nash argues this stewardship requirement has stifled and limited their growth, theorization, and field. Further, using intersectionality as an originating and required central principle of Black feminism transitions both to immutable property, or a "terrain that has been gentrified, colonized, and appropriated, and as territory that must be guarded and protected through the requisite black feminist vigilance, care and stewardship" (3).

Black feminists' responses to appropriation, traveling, and the intentional removal of Black women and their lived experiences from intersectionality—anti-identity politics—impacted stewardship. It led to demands for proper citational lineage and genealogy. For Nash, this requirement further ties intersectionality to Black feminism as exclusionary and positions non-Black folx as outsiders.

Nash analyzes how Black feminists take up critique and respond to critics differently. Through relational opposition between herself and Jasbir Puar, another critic of intersectionality, she questions if care is bound by body and the critic's proximity to being an insider—being Black and a woman. Puar has been treated with less care and concern, Nash argues, largely because Puar is not Black, while Nash is. As a Black feminist, I admit that I see the ontological construction of Black womanhood and Black femininity as central components for engagement with Black feminism. I see those who experience or have experienced the systemic effects of white supremacy and its erotic ties to racism as sharing in the lineage of Black feminist and intersectional theorizing. This, for me, is expansive; trans, cis, queer, femme, and other folx grappling with "femininity" and "womanhood" *and* who are Black share an ontologically similar and unique space, one that their critique arises from. I, like those Nash critiques, may be less inclined to engage in the same level of love or generosity when reading intersectional or Black feminist critique from non-Black folx, which stems from anti-Black discourse and reframed lineages woven within non-Black retellings of intersectionality. Thus, requiring citational lineage, while also moving sideways or reserving my generosity is a move filled with care and love, simply love and care *for* Black women. It is in moments of critique like mine that Nash pushes her reader (for example, me) to consider if their active stewardship works in service of expanding and radically imagining intersectionality and Black feminisms or stifles and maintains inextricable links between intersectionality and Black feminism. To be clear, Nash argues that it is not that links between intersectionality and Black feminism should not exist. For her, while intersectionality helps us understand Black feminism, it should not be a sole determinant or monolithic originating principle. Further, that intersectionality has its own life within theory and scholarship and should have the ability to travel outside Black feminism and Black women's bodies. However, due to stewardship bound within a defensive position, Black feminists have disallowed intersectionality from traveling and, in turn, have stifled both Black feminisms radical imaginings and intersectionality's radical potential.

Nash outlines one way we can reframe (controlling) stewardship through two paths: intersectional originalism—the need for faithfulness and historically contingent readings shown through correct citational lineage and genealogy and judicial activism moving toward contemporary and situationally bound readings that expand intersectionality (62–64). The former, which requires one to remain bound within historical definitions of intersectionality that center Blackness, does not, Nash argues, allow for traveling or expansion (including to women of color). The latter opens the space for multiple forms and types of engagement, including sideways engagement (as in queer critique). Scholars who write about and employ intersectionality while removing Black women from its history, its lineage (for example, scholarship cited, avoidance in argument construction/narrative) are attempting to relocate intersectionality outside of Blackness. These attempts are uncritical and done in the service of appropriation (73). When this occurs, Nash argues it requires more than stewardship bound in defensiveness; it requires an attempt to understand the "institutional rationales" that remake intersectionality and frame the machinations at work, which would actively resist anti-Black and sexist violence and create expansive and radical spaces for both Black feminism and intersectionality (76). This is the type of stewardship Nash envisions; stewardship through an ethic of care rereads *and* reimagines intersectionality and Black feminism while situating Black women as knowledge producers, as subjects, and safeguarding their intellectual production (80). Though this is, in fact, stewardship, the ethic of care and love Nash outlines shifts the burden from defending intersectionality and stifling its theoretically radical potential to protecting and unleashing Black women's radical productive labors and pulling Black feminism from its deathbed.

Continuing her discussion of productive labors and the need to reimagine engagement, Nash outlines what she terms the "intersectionality wars." Within this, she asks the reader to interrogate history, to answer known questions with new answers. She entices the reader to reconsider the reasons feminist and critical scholars ignored and neglected transnationalism (for example, the NWSA) (93), and pushes them to consider why it existed in relational opposition to intersectionality. For Nash, the ability to retell and reimagine breathes life into Black feminism. In giving up defensive stewardship, surrender, we can embrace a vision so "capacious" that it can center women of color while bringing the juxtaposed and willfully neglected (as in transnationalism) into intimate conversation (84). This intimate surrender requires we move from coalitional spaces built from identity politics toward feminist promiscuity, and it is in this space, where Black feminism is on its deathbed, that Nash illuminates the path toward rebirth (113).

Nash concludes with a rumination on Black death, love, and the law. For Nash, the law may be the place we need to move forward; it may, in fact, be home. Within this newly rooted and returned to home, intersectionality travels and transforms again as a loving practice; as a way Black feminists articulate their love-politic and center an ethics of vulnerability. It seems that as Black feminists find home and space to theorize in the law, returning anew to Crenshaw with a juridically activist frame transforms and opens coalitional possibilities within a radically reimagined space. Through the ethics of vulnerability and surrender, in opening ourselves to rooting and new homes, we find new sites of resistance and begin to locate "radical black feminist politics in a myriad of sites" (130).

As a Black feminist and steward, I grappled with this text. While I see intersectionality as part of Black feminism, it is not a sole determinant, nor is it something that lacks the ability to travel and assist other critical scholars in articulating their lived experiences. Though I agree that stifling stewardship leads to stagnation, or for Nash death, Black feminism to me feels vibrant and alive, filled with promise and radical imaginings. And so, I wonder who some of the Black feminists Nash calls in, questions, and attempts to lead toward rebirth are. Black feminists push the boundaries of Blackness, of gender, sexuality, and ability. They create intimacies between Afro-pessimism and Black feminism and draw upon a strong lineage that is both historically situated and expansive. Perhaps my closeness and deep love for this field, the scholars I am in community with, and those intersectional scholars I share intimacies with impact my vision. As I conclude this review, I can say this text pushed me to rethink Black feminism, within, through, and outside of intersectionality. Whether or not my vision was clear, *Black Feminism Reimagined: After Intersectionality* helped me better situate my lineage and genealogy and pushed me to be a better steward of Black feminism.

Leigh-Anne K. Goins is an interdisciplinary Black feminist scholar and associate professor in the Women's, Gender, and Sexuality Studies Program at DePauw University. Her research focuses on mediated representations of Black, Indigenous, and Peoples of Color, and outlines the ways Black folx—specifically, femmes, cis and transwomen—negotiate, challenge, and create spaces of resistance and belonging in the digital sphere. She can be reached at leigh-annegoins@depauw.edu.

The Historicity of a Cultural Narrative

Brianna Eaton

Tyler D. Parry's *Jumping the Broom: The Surprising Multicultural Origins of a Black Wedding Ritual*, Chapel Hill: University of North Carolina Press, 2020

Jumping the Broom begins as a matter-of-fact account documenting the origins of the "jumping the broom" marriage tradition, where a couple walks forward and backward over a broomstick to signify their union. Historian Tyler D. Parry focuses on its historical foundations in Europe and the United States before delving into the potential reasons behind its cultural manifestations. Not content with simple explanations about the custom, Parry is concerned with the central question of why, why did some ethnic groups engage in this ritual, and why did it persist? What are the origins of the tradition, and what rich symbolism is contained within the ritual? (2). Moreover, Parry challenges the popularly held notion that jumping the broom is an exclusively Black American practice, exploring its European origins and gesturing to the broader multicultural roots of traditions throughout the African Diaspora (4).

Though insistent on the varied ethnic origins of the custom, Parry cautions that the enslavement of Black people in the U.S. was unique, and therefore requires careful attention concerning the broomstick ceremony. In his introduction, he asserts that the ethnic groups explored, including Romani, Celts, and rural Euro-Americans, have similar "degrees of marginalization," but in the proceeding chapters notes the distinct experiences of Black people who were forced into enslavement (13). While the text comments on the connection between marginalization and jumping the broom, the importance of relating the traditions of varying ethnic groups to one another is not pursued in great detail, other than to clarify historical genesis.

The elements I found most compelling in the text dealt with the tradition's appearance in Black American history. In chapter 2, Parry contends

WSQ: Women's Studies Quarterly 50: 1 & 2 (Spring/Summer 2022)

with the experiences of enslaved Black people, parsing their agency in relation to the nearly complete power enslavers had over their lives. Differentiating degrees of autonomy in the midst of marriage ceremonies is an act made virtually impossible due to the relative lack of firsthand accounts from the enslaved and the dearth of specifics within the accounts available (47). The search for an expression of personal power leads Parry to speculate over the broom itself as an object of agency: a tool that allowed enslaved people to assert some control over their own domestic space and establish their own marriage rituals with meaning particular to their communities (55). Despite the chapter's sojourn into this history, how much control enslaved people had over their marriage rituals remains a matter of debate. Ultimately, Parry is forced to accept a sense of mystery that haunts so much of the work around the intimate lives of enslaved people.

Determining the meaning of the broomstick custom becomes a much more attainable goal in chapter 6, where Parry explores the modern incarnation of the ritual as one steeped in symbolism, resurrected into the mainstream by the descendants of enslaved people who want to honor and connect to their ancestors (121). He pays particular attention to the impact of Alex Haley's book and consequent television series *Roots* and the contributions of authors Margaret Walker and Ernest J. Gaines (137). As scholars and storytellers, they brought jumping the broom into the popular imagination of Black Americans, distinguishing the ritual as uniquely Black. During this era, the effort to establish the history of Black culture as one separate from white Americans obscured the multicultural roots of the broomstick ritual. What impact this obfuscation ultimately had on the broader culture is difficult to discern. How does unveiling the multicultural nature of the ritual change its symbolic importance to Black Americans? Whether or not Celts or rural white Americans performed it, it was also practiced by some enslaved Black people, which is the only origin story relevant to most of the descendants of the enslaved who wish to engage with the practice.

Continuing his analysis of the muddled origin story of the custom, in chapter 7, Parry discusses the shaky attempts by some historians and intellectuals to connect the broomstick ritual to the African continent throughout the 1990s in popular Black publications. However, he is careful not to allow the inaccuracy of these claims to displace the importance of the ritual to Black Americans who sought a deeper connection to their heritage. Parry's discussion of the myth of African beginnings suggests that the tradition does not need an African foundation to be valuable. The fact that enslaved people learned the tradition from British or other European migrants and their descendants does not diminish the importance of the ritual in the lives of those who practiced the custom. Moreover, it does not challenge the custom's significance to the descendants of the enslaved who choose to jump the broom to connect to their ancestors (166). Like the ancestors who made use of the broom, the descendants are reinterpreting the tradition to suit their own needs, infusing it with symbolism that is relevant to their own communities (142).

This point is emphasized in chapter 9, where Parry engages the spread of the tradition into African Diasporic communities with Caribbean origins, whose ancestors largely have no recorded connection to the custom. He gestures to the potential for diasporic solidarities born not only from increased migration to the U.S. from other African and African Diasporic communities, but also from cultural and political affinities between Black people. Within Parry's carefully researched account, there is a coherent throughline emphasizing the cultural innovations of marginalized groups and their capacity to subvert dominant traditions. A possibly generative parallel to Parry's research in this book is an analysis of the custom's role in reinscribing, or contradicting, traditional Anglo-Christian ideals of marriage in the U.S. Parry writes of the potential for undermining normative ideas about marriage in reference to a singular modern woman in chapter 9, but not in reference to its function for enslaved people or those, heterosexual or homosexual, who jump the broom while also adhering to broadly traditional conventions about marriage ceremonies.

If, under enslavement, the act of marriage was often one of defiance, signaling the communal recognition of relationships that were not sanctioned by the state, what do marriage ceremonies mean now? Is the broomstick ritual still an act of resistance, even in the popularized form Parry describes? As Black feminist scholar Patricia Hill Collins explains in her landmark book *Black Feminist Thought*, Black families, including those formed through marriage, exist outside the imagined, traditional family ideal in the American context (Collins 2000). Perhaps, then, Parry's book provides the historical backing to suggest that jumping the broom still serves to recognize Black relationships that are marginalized within hegemonically white American society. This may be why, as Parry makes note, it is Black Americans and not white Americans who have revived the broomstick ritual in such high numbers. Generations later, conceivably, the ritual is still a communal recognition of relationships that remain forcibly on the outside of traditional ideals.

Jumping the Broom serves as a reminder that the foundations of Black American traditions cannot be simplified into singular narratives and that popular ideas about these traditions often inaccurately turn enslaved people and their descendants into monoliths. Acknowledging the multicultural historical records behind cultural rituals need not diminish their importance but potentially illuminates the complex cultural worlds of ancestral communities.

Brianna Eaton is a PhD student in the Africana Studies Department at Brown University. She earned a BA in film and media studies and Black studies from the University of California, Santa Barbara, and an MA in cinema studies from New York University. Her research focuses on Black media creators throughout the African Diaspora. She can be reached at brianna_eaton@brown.edu.

Works Cited

Collins, Patricia Hill. 2000. *Black Feminist Thought*. New York: Routledge Classics.

Parry, Tyler D. 2020. *Jumping the Broom: The Surprising Multicultural Origins of a Black Wedding Ritual*. Chapel Hill: University of North Carolina Press.

"Nobody Defines Us, We Define Ourselves"

Eziaku A. Nwokocha

E. Patrick Johnson's *Black. Queer. Southern. Women. An Oral History*, Chapel Hill: University of North Carolina Press, 2018

If you want to laugh, cry, be angry, get up from your seat to walk away, or grab your imaginary fan because the tea is too hot, then E. Patrick Johnson's *Black. Queer. Southern. Women. An Oral History* deserves your complete attention. The book offers an oral history of southern Black lesbians and their understanding of their own selfhood. Focusing on the interior lives of Black queer women, Johnson illustrates how the featured narrators embody and relay historical material about race, region, class, sexuality, and gender while showcasing the vital role of storytelling as a form of communication that illuminates same-sex desires, identity formation, and community building (5). This book stands firmly alongside its queer brethren, *Sweat Tea: Black Gay Men of the South* (Johnson 2008), emphatically asserting that Black queer women are not simply the mirror image of Black queer men but contain their own distinct and complex narratives. Their lived experiences are uniquely shaped by patriarchy, sexism, and misogyny. By centering Black queer women, Johnson has masterfully chronicled another exceptional set of oral histories, capturing the complexity of southern Black queer folks without falling into prevalent tropes that place singular focus on Black men and turn Black queer women into an afterthought.

Black. Queer. Southern. Women draws on Black women fiction and nonfiction writers, both heterosexual and queer, as a framework to consider the lived experiences of southern Black lesbians (7). Through contemporary oral history, readers grapple with the multiplicity of southern queer women and understand their realities through their self-depictions, contending with their worldviews in all their contradictions and complexities. What is most evident in Johnson's methodology is his attention to intimacy and care in his interviews. He applies a Black feminist approach that is self-reflexive

WSQ: Women's Studies Quarterly 50: 1 & 2 (Spring/Summer 2022) © 2022 by Eziaku A. Nwokocha. All rights reserved.

of his own privileges as a cisgender, effeminate Black gay man, recognizing that despite his personal politics, he still benefits from patriarchy and must reckon with how that impacts his communication with his interlocuters (9–10). Johnson applies a "male feminist praxis." This requires him to consider the sense of ethics and moral obligation he owes the Black queer women he interviews by asking them to describe their feelings and attitudes rather than viewing them as objects with information one can extract and disseminate (11); he is deferential to their interpretations of their lives and feelings, wary of imposing his own biases onto their words. While interviewing and assembling the stories of over seventy Black queer women, Johnson draws from Black feminist scholar Patricia Hill Collins, calling himself an "insider/outsider" who recognizes that although he shares both queerness and southerness with his interviewees, their gender and possible class differences produce a unique point of view in relation to power and patriarchy.

Throughout the book, Johnson uses italicized comments to contextualize the narrators, relating their desires with all the complexities, ambivalences, and raunchiness they might entail. For example, he describes a woman named Priscilla who grew up in East Austin, Texas, in 1967, as having an "infectious laugh," and explains that "underneath [her] gregarious personality is a fierce activist who is quite serious about the freedom of queer people of color," (55). Guided by Priscilla's story, he details the landscape of her hometown and relays the history of its Black population, once clustered in East Austin due to segregation but now withered as a result of ongoing gentrification (55). Johnson beautifully segues from the personal stories of individual interviewees into the histories of southern cities like Austin and New Orleans, and states such as Alabama, Mississippi, and Georgia, effortlessly articulating the importance of region in shaping the contours of Black women's particular experiences. Johnson carefully lays out these stories, never allowing them to be easily pinned down as narratives of only pain or trauma, joy or laughter. The women he interviewed are too fascinating to be summed up simply. Their ages ranged from eighteen to seventy-nine and, over the course of over five hundred pages, Johnson captures a change over time in the ways Black women identified themselves, from "butch," "dyke," or "bulldagger," to "femme," "no-labels," "studs," and "androgynous." He was clearly conscious of engaging a broad cross section of Black queer women, with interlocutors ranging in occupation: academics, athletes, bus and truck drivers, artists, scientists, entrepreneurs, and professionals provide a range of distinct personalities, hopes, dreams, and loves that are captivating and sincere. Johnson incorporates discussions about health as well, such as the impact of the HIV and AIDS epidemic in the Black community or the health issues related to mothering (441). Moreover, it is refreshing that Johnson writes about the mental and emotional exhaustion of undertaking these interviews for himself and the women he spoke with. Even as a reader, *Black. Queer. Southern. Women* can be an emotionally taxing endeavor, though well worth the effort.

Black. Queer. Southern. Women is divided into two parts containing thirteen chapters. Part one consisted of stories thematically centered on budding girlhood to adulthood, showcasing conversations about intimacy that focused on themes like segregation, gender nonconformity, sexual desires, religion, spirituality, motherhood, and activism. Part two features one woman per chapter, allowing a single narrative to unfold with great detail and complexity, encompassing many of the themes of the text in an individual tale. Within the first half of the book, one of the most notable chapters is five, where women candidly express their first sexual desires, exploring the ability to communicate their joy and pain in the midst of self-discovery. Johnson portrays the nostalgia wrapped up in memories of burgeoning queer desires, deftly navigating stories about first kisses and self-pleasure (216–23). Interestingly, in comparison to the men, Johnson interviewed in his previous book *Sweet Tea*, many of the women he interviewed did not "always know" they were attracted to women and at times spoke about queer sexual awakenings later in their lives, even after being intimate with and married to men (213). By engaging many different ages, the array of stories of self-discovery were compelling and diverse.

Johnson's book does oral history the right way, addressing potentially sensitive subjects with respect and generosity. Because of this, he makes another commendable contribution to Black feminist studies, oral history, performance studies, queer studies, and Africana studies. Johnson ends by imploring readers to reflect on what Black feminist scholar Evelyn Hammonds wrote about the void at the center of scholarship about Black lesbians, an absence that could only be filled once their experiences were placed at the heart of discourses of race, sexuality, and gender (561). *Black. Queer. Southern. Women* addresses that void, employing oral history as a source of knowledge to combat the persistent erasure of Black, queer women's histories and lived realities from academia and beyond.

Eziaku A. Nwokocha is a Presidential Postdoctoral Research Fellow in the Department of Religion at Princeton University. In fall 2022, she will be an assistant professor in the Department of Religion at the University of Miami. Nwokocha is a scholar of Africana religions with expertise in the ethnographic study of Vodou in Haiti and the Haitian diaspora, with research grounded in thorough understanding of religions in West and Central Africa, the Caribbean, and the United States, in gender and sexuality studies, visual and material culture, and Africana Studies generally. Her book manuscript, *Vodou en Vogue: Fashioning Black Divinities in Haiti and the U.S.* is under an advance contract with UNC Press. She can be reached at nwokocha@princeton.edu.

PART IX. **THE MOMENT LOVE MOVES:
FROM THEORY TO [ART] PRACTICE**

Is she as pretty as a picture
Or clear as crystal
Or pure as a lily
Or black as coal
Or sharp as a razor?
        —Lorna Simpson,
          Twenty Questions
          (A Sampler) 1986

All the Gifts You Gave Us
Ink, Pencil and Gouache on Stonehenge paper, 8" × 10", 2021
OZ Sanders

WSQ: Women's Studies Quarterly **50: 1 & 2 (Spring/Summer 2022)** © 2022 by OZ Sanders. All rights reserved.

LOVE
Ink, Pencil and Gouache on Stonehenge paper, 8" × 10", 2021
OZ Sanders

WSQ: Women's Studies Quarterly **50: 1 & 2 (Spring/Summer 2022)** © 2022 by OZ Sanders. All rights reserved.

Crabbing Bayou Como, Royal Oaks Plantation
Photography (Black + White), 2014
Mel Michelle Lewis

WSQ: Women's Studies Quarterly **50: 1 & 2 (Spring/Summer 2022)** © 2022 by Mel Michelle Lewis. All rights reserved.

Yellow Mary Artist Self Portrait, Daughters of the Oaks
Bayou Como, Royal Oaks Plantation
Photography (Black + White), 2014
Mel Michelle Lewis

WSQ: Women's Studies Quarterly 50: 1 & 2 (Spring/Summer 2022) © 2022 by Mel Michelle Lewis. All rights reserved.

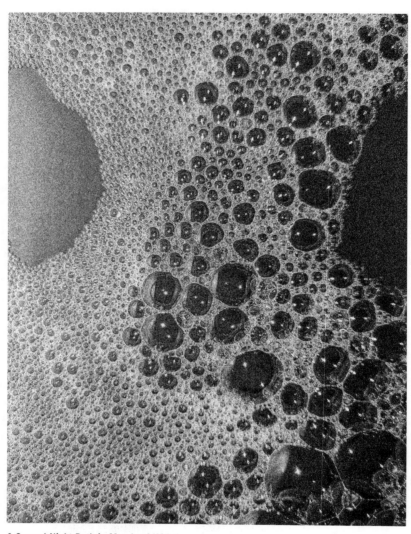

A Sacred Night Bath in Maryland USA 1.
Photography (Black + White Version), 2021
Nina Q. Allen

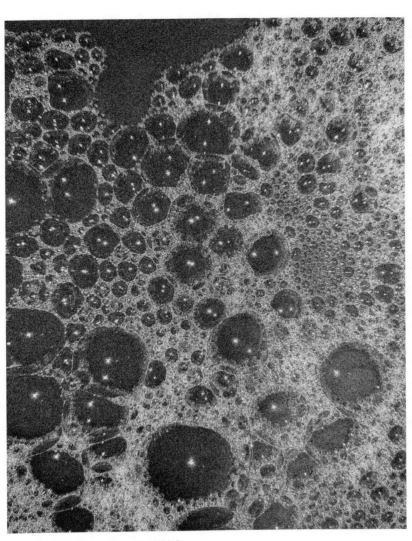

A Sacred Night Bath in Maryland USA 2.
Photography (Black + White Version), 2021
Nina Q. Allen

WSQ: Women's Studies Quarterly 50: 1 & 2 (Spring/Summer 2022) © 2022 by Nina Q. Allen. All rights reserved.

OZ Sanders is a mixed Black visual storyteller from the East Coast in the U.S. Her imaginative illustrations provide episodic glimpses into the worlds of complex and determined protagonists as they navigate their journeys.

Originally from Bayou la Batre, on the Alabama Gulf Coast, **Dr. Mel Michelle Lewis**'s creative writing and multimedia projects feature their ancestral lands, lineages, and queer longings. They explore queer-of-color themes rooted in rural coastal settings and southern port cities; specifically, Bayou la Batre, Coden, Mobile, New Orleans, Biloxi, and Baltimore. These projects present local and regional Black and Indigenous southern folklore, dialect, foodways, religious and spiritual practices, music, and cultural events. Dr. Mel is the Inaugural Visual Arts Editor for *WSQ*.

NINA Q. ALLEN IS AN ARTIST (INDIGO EMPATH + STARSEED) WHO USES THE LANGUAGE OF THE OCEAN TO SYMBOLIZE MATRILINEAL HEALING (DIVINATION) &&& AFROFUTURISM. THE INTERIOR/EXTERIOR OF A WOMXN'S ANATOMY REQUIRES DEEP CLEANSING OF AURAS ONTO PAST, PRESENT, &&& FUTURE. *ALL-CAPS USED INTENTIONALLY TO BRING THE ENERGY OF EPITAPH STYLES AT CEMETERY/MEMORIAL SITES . . . PRECISELY OF OWN BLOODLINE. TO MOTHER MOON/ MOTHER OCEAN . . . REST IN PEACE.

PART X. **ALERTS AND PROVOCATIONS**

a bell tolls for bell hooks (1952–2021)

Namulundah Florence

I was surprised to recently receive compliments from family members for having completed my doctorate well over twenty years ago. The three email messages followed a picture I sent home of a recent college graduation ceremony. I was in cap and gown. On the other hand, I have sat at academic meetings trying to focus on discussions as I wondered if the people with me ever had to worry about the price of a gallon of milk. Village life is rooted in interdependency. The obligations of older or financially able family members can be overwhelming and endless. My other world poses its own unique challenges. The focus of academic journals and language can appear far removed from everyday struggles to make ends meet by peoples to whom I owe my good fortune. The growing individualism and consumerism across the globe are unnerving, although extremely seductive. Self-sufficiency is reassuring, promising, as it does, independence and control. Accolades and possessions offer a tangible measure of success. However, this is a partial picture. I hear and watch colleagues' and neighbors' concerns of despair, depressions, divorce, family betrayals, and losses of jobs, houses, or deaths of loved ones that comprise our collective pain and grief. We all share in moments of joy, hope, intimacy, solidarity, often beyond social groups. bell hooks's corpus of work bridges these two "world" experiences that have shaped me and which I continually navigate. hooks speaks to our cultural enclaves and reminds us of the greater call to our common humanity, beyond family, beyond community and country to the entire planet. In these spaces, we engage in critical and loving discourses on how to transform society. This is the face of loving practice. Many credit bell hooks with affirming their lives on the margins and giving voice to their pain, as well as possibilities for healing.

WSQ: Women's Studies Quarterly **50**: 1 & 2 (Spring/Summer 2022) © 2022 by Namulundah Florence.

Only bell hooks can get away with saying, "Do as I say," in promoting a lifestyle. The seeker of love admits, it was "a longing so intense it could not only be spoken but was deliberately searched for" (2001, xvii). The physical, psychological, and spiritual journey involved years of disengaging from "learned patterns of behavior that negated my capacity to give and receive love" (10). Self-reflection and acceptance helped hooks commit to life affirming and nurturing choices in her quest, often unsuccessful, for love and its transformative power. The love ethic of "care, commitment, trust, responsibility, respect, and knowledge in our everyday lives" provides inner resources to address the pain of lovelessness (94). Like the tradition of religious evangelization, "we want to know how to seduce those among us who remain wedded to lovelessness and open the door to their hearts to let love enter" (xxvii). It is possible. It takes time. There is a price, and yet, "love is the only force that allows us to hold one another close beyond the grave" (202).

hooks's analysis of lovelessness and proposed ethic of love also draws on multiple professors, psychiatrists, authors, motivational speakers, feminists, activists, poets, philosophers, psychotherapists, theologians, attorneys, journalists, Catholic saints, Buddhists, Christian ministers, and educators who link unethical behaviors to a false self that diminishes the spirit and dehumanizes others. A common instinct in times of trial and threat, is to blame, attack, break up, and disperse. In writings and lecture circuits, all call for a commitment to personal and collective well-being.

Emotional instability and anxiety are symptomatic of lovelessness: "In a world anguished by rampart destruction, fear prevails. . . . Power gives us the illusion of having triumphed over fear, over our need for love" (221). A collective fear of love suppresses this naturally deep-seated emptiness. Futile attempts at love reflect a gnawing longing for love in the face of previous failures. In these emotional replays, partners are objectified as individuals to "pick, use, and then discard and dispose of at will" (115). Admissions of love are in hushed, sometimes rushed confessions. Love like the spiritual is dismissed, commercialized, sentimentalized, and considered naive. False notions of love promise "a state of constant bliss." To sustain the fantasy of a prince charming or the girl of one's dreams, partners "substitute romance for love." Public discourse on lovelessness and accompanying grief would establish its significance to happiness, physical well-being, and national survival. The growing industry of self-help books on love and esteem illustrate the mystery and need for explicit interventions. Paradoxically, while men write and sell more romantic and self-help books, women are the primary consumers: "Male fantasy is seen as something that can create reality, whereas female fantasy is regarded as pure escape" (xxii).

hooks's attempts at finding love are typical. Memories of love or its lack shape subsequent choices. Suffering is a reminder of the loss of that childhood sense of belonging, a source of pleasure. hooks views her search for love as retracing her way to the first home, the space of love's first rapture. In love, experience precedes understanding. hooks recalls being cherished at birth, valued with the sense of belonging but also moments of reproach and dismissal. In youth, good friends offer some emotional stability laced with secrets, laughter, and tears: conditional experiences of love. By adulthood, many take refuge in instant gratification and transient affairs to avoid the pains and frustrations of negotiating maturity. Like hooks, we are "not really ready to love or be loved in the present" (x).

Genetic, familial, and cultural inheritance and historical movements influence personal attributes and self-esteem. In the past, religious and cultural traditions provided moral guidance and helped cement relations of interbeing and interconnectedness, although religious fundamentalism sanctions dominations. Replacing the alienation of the '60s, many sought the good life in "the fulfillment of hedonistic, materialistic desire . . . making corruption acceptable and the ostentatious parading of material luxury the norm" (108–9). The materialistic focus on acquisition, exploitation, and narcissistic greed normalized an ethic of domination. Some selectively oppose dominations like sexism, racism, or capitalism. hooks also laments the obsession with immediate success and lotteries evident in the ruthless, media- and money-driven culture that exacerbate the spiritual void many dismiss. Although spirituality fosters loving practice, hooks only exposed her spirituality after confronting disruptions, rejections, and suffering in others. Despite a shared humanity and surrounding communities, many feel alienated, alone, and lost. The other is enemy or means to another's end. Rich people remain insatiable and discontent in a land of thirty-five million starving people.

Mass media compounds the crises of individualism, materialism, and addictions that offer an illusory sense of relief from the pain and negation of everyday life. The mystification of love gives it an "erotic and transgressive edge." Action-packed image depictions draw crowds and command big budgets. Love practices in simple living or solitude that capture cultural imagination, yet again, take backstage. The chosen few fall in love and winning has a price: "To maintain and satisfy greed, one must support domination. And the world of domination is always a world without love" (123).

hooks roots domination in the interlocking system of imperialistic-capitalist, white-supremacist patriarchy. Patriarchy pervades socialization patterns, social interactions, and perceptions of adulthood. The traditional focus on the nuclear family fosters dependency and abuses of power, although enlightened witnesses like caregivers can compensate for nuclear family excesses. In general, individuals experience some level of acceptance, even though few families offer the foundation of healthy narcissism (self-love). Children are either cherished or not cherished enough. Reflecting familiar insecurities and ignorance, parents also give too much or too little. In some small communities, the level of scrutiny borders on intrusion, while urban centers starve the marginalized of loving attention.

Even without language, children respond to gestures of affection and its absence, meted out as rewards and punishments. Family shame and abuse add to the burden of an incomprehensive insatiable longing for love. Regardless of severity, individuals mature by working through unfinished childhood grievances within families or social relationships. Many arrive at adulthood emotionally frayed and invested in a false, insecure self. Youth are cynical about love, to mask the "stress, strife, and personal discontent" of relationships (147). They seek "intimacy without risk, for pleasure without significant emotional investment" (xviii). Adults are no different.

Women raised to be empathetic, nurturing, and mostly listeners assume subordinate roles, although hooks dismisses the apparent "selfless adoration and care" in women as "a covert way to hold power" (152). Perfecting the art of pretense, women feign "emotional vulnerability and neediness." By contrast, men avoid admission of vulnerability or longing for love. In an era of social equality, insecure men, "deploy subtle strategies to colonize and disempower" confident and assertive women by giving and withholding love (41). To avoid a macho masculinity, some remain boys who seek mothers in partners. Materialism and accompanying individualism, dominations and lies offer ephemeral reprieve.

Love Ethic: A Path

The mainstream silence on love defies reality. Despite the collective need for a sense of love, what hooks links to knowing one belongs, and the grief of failed attempts at its achievement, communities downplay its significance to unity and national survival. As interdependent beings, one's healing and growth are inseparable from the collective malaise. Similarly, since community was the first encounter at birth and departure to the next phase of life, communal solidarity is the core of social relations. Extreme anxiety and dread will persist despite high military budgets and billion-dollar security systems in homes.

Three stages emerge in hooks's transformation process—transparency to self and others, communal solidarity, and re-creation/self-assertiveness. Self-reflection exposes the mystifying assumptions about love and lingering fear and shame underlying a false self. Individuals construct a façade against a dehumanizing, dominating, attention-substituting world to ease the pain of lovelessness. By contrast, loving practice releases inner energy to weather transitions: "No matter what happened in our past, when we open our hearts to love we can live as if born again, not forgetting the past but seeing it in a new way, letting it live inside us in a new way. . . . Or if our past was one in which we were loved, we know that no matter the occasional presence of suffering in our lives we will return always to remembered calm and bliss" (209). The energy invested in upholding old wounds and a false self goes to compassion toward others. Unrelenting grief reflects a denial of loss. Wallowing in guilt and shame depresses, demoralizes, and drags one down in lovelessness.

Self-acceptance leads to acknowledgment of what is and letting go of what one thinks one should be to grow into the next phase of life. It prepares us for taking "responsibility in all areas of our lives . . . (and choosing) how to respond to acts of injustice" (57). The process encompasses an assessment of choices and insightful dialogue among fellow seekers of love. hooks also utilized therapy. Regardless of our past indiscretions, insincerity in relationships, shame and anger at others' infractions and betrayals, it is possible to stop condemning ourselves and harboring guilt. The greater challenge is to recognize others share one's struggles and foibles as well as reluctance to forgive. Self-love gives one the confidence to recognize imperfections as a shared humanity. The grounding in truth of one's life and choices allows one to reach out to similarly situated human beings. Love engages the other in mutual recognition of actual and potential attributes. Healing and forgiveness sustain our spirits on the journey back to wholeness. Freed from unethical and defensive behaviors, individuals actively participate in community to enhance the collective good. hooks confronted her childhood fears and negations, consciously made nurturing choices, and settled in a small town away from the whirlwind of power, prestige, and pleasure.

Self-assertiveness eliminates the gap between a false and real self, genuine from insecure conditional relationships that reflect misperceptions of self and others. Individuals tend to put up a front at first encounters particularly with those whose attentions they court. Unfortunately, the fear of exposure fills one with lingering dread. When it ends badly, the rejection reinforces familiar self-consciousness of distrust and dejection. Starting over, time and again, hinges on the awareness and acceptance of human frailties. Things come into being and stop existing at some point. Love, hooks insists, is a verb not a noun. There is always room for improvement; someone out there who needs loving. Self-actualization, in the face of recurring transgressions, calls for endless start overs among community members and for mutual benefit. The loving practice of solidarity and self-giving "militate against the proliferation of greed" and strengthens community (117). Communion, affirmation, and forgiveness transform society in ways that foster the collective good. Fellow beings are sojourners on our spiritual journey. They witness our pain, affirm, and critique our integrity, and advocate for our growth, cheering our victories.

hooks speaks to a world that is skeptical and dismissive of love and vulnerability. Poor self-esteem drags us into an abyss of lovelessness that many experience and few acknowledge. Self-awareness and acceptance make of seekers wounded healers of self and others. One way to reject consumerism, model sustainability, and inspire countercultural ways of life is to love and live simply. Loyalty and commitment undergird relationships that transcend death: "Love empowers us to live fully and die well. Death becomes, then, not an end to life but a part of living" (197). I matter. You matter. They matter. What we do here and now matters.

hooks joins a tradition of truthsayers who call out to a lost herd. The pervasive partisanship sweeping across the globe is a phenomenon of misplaced priorities. In a language for the masses, hooks writes extensively on ignorance about and barriers to love, the shame and abuse within families, lies and objectification in relationships, glamorization of dominations and violence by media, obsession with instant gratification, in short, anything to fill the spiritual void and ease the pain of lovelessness. hooks honors our collective pain and shame. She challenges us to go beyond instinctive insecurities rooted in dualisms and hierarchical ordering of society that pits one person, group, religion, and country against the other.

hooks decries the pathological narcissism that privileges a few at the expense of the majority. Fear, shame, and self-serving dominations and violence separate us, although we all have felt unloved, unwelcomed, afraid, shameful, desperate, or physically and emotionally bereft. Loving practice embraces this lovelessness and isolation to energize us toward the pursuit of a collective good. Acceptance and forgiveness unite us in communal solidarity. This is our destiny. Herein lies our survival as a race.

If someone on earth recalls bell hooks, she lives on.

Namulundah Florence's research and teaching interests explore the impact of formal and informal structures on self-image and cultural identity. She is author of *bell hooks' Engaged Pedagogy: A Transgressive Education for Critical Consciousness* (1998); *From Our Mothers' Hearths: Bukusu Folktales and Proverbs* (2005); *Multiculturalism 101: The Practical Guide Series* (2009); *Immigrant Teachers, American Students: Cultural Differences, Cultural Disconnections* (2011); *The Bukusu of Kenya: Folktales, Culture and Social Identities* (2011); and "Bukusu (Kenya) Folktales: How Women Perpetuate Patriarchy" in *The International Feminist Journal of Politics* (2013), as well as *Wangari Maathai: Visionary, Environmental Leader, Political Activist* (2014); *Adapting to Cultural Pluralism in Urban Classrooms* (2021); book review of Besi Brillian Muhonja's *Womanhood and Girlhood in Twenty-First Century Middle Class Kenya, Hypatia 2021).* She can be reached at NFlorence@brooklyn.cuny.edu.

Works Cited

hooks, bell. 2001. *All About Love: New Visions.* New York: HarperCollins.